WARS OF LAW

Wars of Law

Unintended Consequences in the Regulation of Armed Conflict

Tanisha M. Fazal

Cornell University Press

Ithaca and London

First published 2018 by Cornell University Press

Printed in the United States of America

Library of Congress Cataloging-in-Publication Data

Names: Fazal, Tanisha M., author.
Title: Wars of law : unintended consequences in the regulation of armed conflict / Tanisha M. Fazal.
Description: Ithaca : Cornell University Press, 2018. | Includes bibliographical references and index.
Identifiers: LCCN 2017054550 (print) | LCCN 2017057125 (ebook) | ISBN 9781501719806 (epub/mobi) | ISBN 9781501719790 (pdf) | ISBN 9781501719813 | ISBN 9781501719813 (cloth ; alk. paper)
Subjects: LCSH: War (International law)—History. | Humanitarian law—History. | Conflict of laws—History.
Classification: LCC KZ6385 (ebook) | LCC KZ6385 .F39 2018 (print) | DDC 341.6—dc23
LC record available at https://lccn.loc.gov/2017054550

For my parents, Maydene and Abul

CONTENTS

ACKNOWLEDGMENTS

I began this project over a decade ago, in the shadow of September 11, 2001. As a newly minted postdoctoral scholar, I observed from afar as US troops deployed to Afghanistan and wondered: why did the United States not declare war? If there was ever a clear-cut case to do so, this seemed to be it. As events unfolded and, in particular, as the infamous "torture memos" came to light, along with then-attorney general Alberto Gonzales's dismissive tone regarding the 1949 Geneva Conventions, I was even more puzzled. But as I expanded my scope temporally and geographically, I realized that these kinds of decisions were not limited to the United States. As the standards set by the laws of war rose, states were increasingly engaged in legal gymnastics to limit their obligation to comply.

At the same time, as a scholar of sovereignty, I observed secessionist groups in Mexico, Indonesia, and Western Sahara plead with the international community for recognition. They pointed to their capacity to govern, the grievances they had endured, and, increasingly, their own compliance with international law as signs of the merits of their cases.

I was (and remain) sufficiently skeptical of the motives and power of the international community to expect that these groups would be successful in their aims. But their invocation of the laws of war impressed me as both strategic and a signal of the power of this body of international law. Indeed, as this book goes to press, recent events in Catalonia and Iraqi Kurdistan underline the importance of understanding phenomena such as why and when secessionists issue unilateral declarations of independence. I am extremely curious to see how these groups navigate the "secessionists' dilemma" outlined in these pages.

This book has been a long time coming. Since beginning work on this book, I have gotten married, had two children, been denied tenure, received tenure, moved twice, and lost my father. I would not have been able to manage all these life-changing events, and, certainly, this book would not have been completed, without the support of family, friends, and colleagues who have made critical contributions along the way. The hardest part about writing acknowledgments is knowing how many people one will forget to thank. I therefore begin with an apology, and my gratitude, to those who lent a hand to this project but whose names I neglect to mention below.

I began serious work on this book at Columbia University, where I was exceptionally lucky to have generous colleagues in Dick Betts, Michael Doyle, Robert Jervis, Erik Gartzke, Melissa Schwartzberg, and Pablo Pinto, all of whom read and commented on various parts of the book, while Ingrid Gertsmann at the Saltzman Institute of War and Peace Studies made sure all the necessary trains were running on time. I am also grateful to my colleagues at Columbia Law School—especially Sam Moyn, Anthea Roberts, and John Fabian Witt—who allowed me to sit in on their classes and ask many annoying questions. My students at Columbia—many of whom are now colleagues—also contributed greatly to this project, especially Ryan Griffiths, Reyko Huang, Jessica Stanton, Alex Weisiger, and Marko Djuranovic. Page Fortna deserves more credit than I can give her here for reading innumerable drafts of papers and chapters, slogging through data with me, and providing steadfast friendship and support. There simply aren't enough cookies in the world.

At the University of Notre Dame, I was lucky to find generous colleagues in Sue Collins, Michael Desch, Gary Goertz, Madhav Joshi, Mary Ellen O'Connell, Emilia Powell, Jason Quinn, and, especially, Pat Regan, all of whom patiently answered many questions and gave excellent feedback. I was also fortunate to find two second intellectual homes at the Kroc Institute for International Peace Studies and the Political Science Department. I am grateful to both for institutional support.

I also thank David Armitage, Charli Carpenter, Bridget Coggins, Kathleen Cunningham, Mike Horowitz, Hyeran Jo, Helen Kinsella, Aila Matanock, Courtenay Monroe, Barry O'Neill, Sandesh Sivakumaran, and Michael Schmitt for their feedback on various parts of the project. Page Fortna, Pat Regan, Beth Simmons, and Peter Wallensteen attended a book workshop for this project in October 2014, and it is much improved as a result of their comments. I thank Ben Denison and Rita Konaev for serving as rapporteurs during the book workshop. David Ratzan and Svetlana Tsalik assisted with translation from Latin and Russian respectively. Several practitioners also generously lent their time and words to this project, especially Pascal Bongard, Bonnie Docherty, Andrew Lewis, and Willem Sopacua. Various sections of the project were presented at Columbia University, the University of Wisconsin at Madison, the University of Washington at Seattle, the University of Texas at Austin, MIT, the University of Connecticut, the School of Oriental and African Studies, Stanford University, Princeton University, the University of Pennsylvania, George Mason University, the University of Notre Dame, Cornell University and the University of Minnesota. I thank participants at all these seminars for their thoughtful comments and suggestions.

Two datasets, created by two armies of research assistants, provide the foundation for the empirical portion of this book. I thank all the research assistants involved in both the I-WIT and C-WIT projects, especially Marko Djuranovic, Jessica Stanton, Alex Weisiger, Shelley Liu, Leslie Huang, Gabriella Ann Levy, and Sarah Faith Thompson. The statistical appendix, replication data, and other supplementary materials can be found at http://www.tanishafazal.com/publications/. I also thank Allison Hostetler, Nora Keller, Simone Oberschmied, and Ilana Rothkopf, all of whom provided additional and extremely valuable research assistance. Theresa Lawson's careful edit of an earlier version of the manuscript tightened and improved it substantially.

At Cornell University Press, I thank Roger Haydon for his continued interest in and adoption of this project. It has been an honor to have the opportunity to work with Roger, whose outstanding taste has made an indelible mark on the field. I also thank the press's excellent staff, including

Susan Specter, Julia Cook, Martyn Beeny, and Meagan Dermody, for their help in transforming my manuscript into a proper book.

For financial support, I thank the Institute for Social and Economic Research and Policy at Columbia University, the Kroc Institute for International Studies at the University of Notre Dame, and the Institute for the Study of the Liberal Arts at the University of Notre Dame. The research in this book was also generously funded by the Ford Foundation, the Carnegie Corporation of New York, and the National Science Foundation (Grant #0904791).

Portions of this book are derived in part from: "Why States No Longer Declare War," *Security Studies* 21 no. 4 (November 2012), copyright Taylor & Francis, available at http://dx.doi.org/10.1080/09636412.2012 .734227; "The Demise of Peace Treaties in Interstate War," *International Organization* 67 no. 4 (Fall 2013); and "Rebellion, War Aims, and the Laws of War," *Daedalus* (Winter 2017).

My family has provided unending support and generous understanding of all the times work took me from home so that I could write this book. My husband Lou has patiently tended the home front without complaint and been my smartest and most effective editor. He challenges me to be better every day. Our children, Tag and Vi, have kept me grounded with their laughter, questions about the world, and discussions of the international humanitarian law of the Star Wars galaxy. My sister Shaena is always able to remind me that she thinks I know more than she does, but in fact she probably knows more than I do.

Finally, I thank my parents, Maydene and Abul, for forcing me out of my comfort zone and filling my earliest years with views of the world that most US-born children never get to see. Those formative experiences, along with their persistent and quiet belief that I could accomplish any goal, are more than anything else what have made me the scholar and person I am today. This book—which, as my father would have said, was written "slowly and slowly"—is dedicated to them.

WARS OF LAW

Declaring War and Peace

The United States has neither declared war nor concluded a formal peace treaty since it ended its post–World War II occupation of Japan in 1952. In this, the United States is part of a global trend. Since ancient times, instruments such as declarations of war and peace treaties have been commonly used to begin and end wars and to acknowledge that belligerents were in a state of war to which the laws of war applied. From the end of the Napoleonic Wars in 1815 to 1948, half of interstate wars were formally declared, and 70 percent concluded with a formal peace treaty. But since the conclusion of the 1949 Geneva Conventions, only two of thirty-six interstate wars begun have been accompanied by declarations of war; and only six of thirty-eight wars that have ended since 1949 were concluded with a formal peace treaty.

The formalities of war have seen equally puzzling trends in the civil war context. Immediately after the founding of the United Nations, about 48 percent of secessionists fighting civil wars issued formal declarations of independence; by 2007, the percent of secessionists in civil wars declaring independence had nearly halved. But in contrast to interstate war, civil wars are increasingly likely to conclude with formal peace treaties today. In 1946, none of the civil wars that concluded were accompanied by a formal peace agreement. Ten years after the end of the Cold War, this number had climbed from zero to over 40 percent.

Declarations of war and peace treaties are more than mere formalities; they tell us when wars begin and end. They activate and deactivate certain legal rules—the laws of war—that are meant to apply during wartime. In a perverse unintended consequence, it is the proliferation of these laws of war that has altered the incentives of states and rebel groups to adopt war formalities. As the laws of war have grown in strength and number since the mid-twentieth century, states have ceased engaging in formal interstate war; they have all but stopped issuing declarations of war and concluding peace treaties. This is because states increasingly seek to create ambiguity as to the applicability of these new laws of war—in particular, international humanitarian law (IHL),[1] the body of international law meant to regulate belligerent conduct during armed conflict—to their wars. In contrast, rebel groups fighting civil wars have been more responsive to the proliferating laws of war. This is particularly true for secessionist rebels—those that seek their own independent state—who require the support of the international community that has authored the laws of war to achieve their political aims.

Consider the interstate war fought between Armenia and Azerbaijan over the separatist region of Nagorno-Karabakh in the early 1990s. The war began without a formal declaration of war by either side. Had either Armenia or Azerbaijan declared war, the declaring state would have been unequivocally obliged to comply with any IHL treaties activated by a declaration of war. In fact, both states signed the 1949 Geneva Conventions during this conflict, which bound them to comply with the laws of war. But there were several plausible accusations of noncompliance with IHL during that war. For example, Azerbaijan is said to have engaged in indiscriminate bombing of civilian areas in Armenia.[2] Armenian ground troops reportedly targeted Azerbaijan's civilians indiscriminately, and forcibly displaced civilians.[3] Both sides appear to have violated the laws of war regarding prisoners of war by engaging in summary execution of POWs.[4] This war "ended" in 1994, but without a formal peace treaty. In the absence of a peace treaty, hundreds of thousands of Azeri refugees remain homeless.[5] A critical railroad cannot progress.[6] Sour trade relations between Armenia and Azerbaijan have weakened both economies, but especially that of Armenia.[7]

The conflict over Nagorno-Karabakh is one of an increasing number of "frozen conflicts" whose resolution remains undetermined. As these two countries new to the club of states have sought to integrate themselves into the trappings of the international community by signing various IHL treaties, they have simultaneously fought a ground war that appears divorced from these legal obligations. This discrepancy is due in part to the fact that the Nagorno-Karabakh war had no official ending or beginning, which is typical of interstate wars today.

States no longer refer to their interstate wars as wars. Perhaps the clearest recent example of this type of pretense is Russia's role in the invasion of Crimea. On February 28, 2014, hundreds of Russian soldiers took over airports and military bases in Ukraine's Autonomous Republic of Crimea.[8] Russia had taken pains to create deniability by stripping the insignia off its troops while arguing that any intervention was meant to prevent spillover of radicalism and civil conflict.[9] By investing in an international legal fiction, Russia gained at least a fig leaf to cover its lack of compliance with the laws of war regarding the resort to force—*jus ad bellum*—as well as with those governing belligerent conduct in time of war, or *jus in bello*. The United States, likewise, today refers to its conflicts as "police actions," "counterinsurgencies," or "counterterrorism"—but not war. Interstate war, increasingly, is conducted under the legal radar.

Now consider another enduring separatist conflict, this one from the perspective of the separatists. The Kurds have fought a series of civil wars over the past five decades, particularly against the Iraqi government. Iraq's Kurds are engaged in complex and careful diplomacy that they hope will gain them a state. While they are among the world's most viable separatists, they have refrained from issuing a formal declaration of independence because they seek to avoid violating the international community's stated aversion to unilateral declarations of independence. At this writing, Iraqi Kurdistan has recently completed an independence referendum, despite strong opposition from the international community; even so, Iraqi Kurds recognize that a vote in favor of independence cannot on its own get them they state they seek. As a leader of the referendum movement in Iraqi Kurdistan put it, "Statehood takes time."[10] To this end, the Iraqi Kurds have publicly rejected a strategy of targeting civilians, in contrast to Iraqi government forces in the past and those of the Islamic State more recently. The evidence suggests that they have kept this promise. Despite their lack of international recognition as an independent state, they have signaled their intention to abide by the constraints of the 1949 Geneva Conventions.[11] Erbil, the capital of Iraqi Kurdistan, hosts a regional office of the International Committee of the Red Cross, the group self-designated as a monitor of international humanitarian law (IHL).[12] The Kurds have signed a public "deed of commitment" pledging not to use land mines.[13] The official program of the Kurdish Democratic Party commits the Kurds to achieving their regional and international goals "by way of general international law and peace" and in accordance with the principles laid out in the UN Charter.[14]

The Kurdish example is similar to the efforts of many rebel groups in civil war, who are increasingly engaging with the laws of war. In 1960, the Provisional Government of Algeria attempted to accede to the 1949 Geneva Conventions, although it did not yet represent a recognized state.[15] The Polisario Front of the Western Sahara has established diplomatic missions in several African states.[16] The Eritrean independence movement created a relief organization that gained international legitimacy among nongovernmental organizations (NGOs) during the Eritrean war of independence.[17] These groups—particularly, among the set of rebel groups in civil war, secessionist rebel groups—must gain the support of the international community, defined here as the group of actors (states and NGOs) committed to the principles enshrined in the UN Charter, to achieve their political goals; this aim gives them incentives to send strong signals of their willingness and capacity to be good citizens of the international community.

Argument of the Book

The argument and evidence of this book are presented in three parts. In the first part, which is both historical and theoretical, I review the development of the laws of war. I show that as the number of codified international humanitarian laws has increased dramatically, their character has changed. In 1856, there was one codified law of armed conflict. In 2015, there were seventy-two. The earliest laws of war emphasized the rights of belligerents, as in the generous definition of contraband allowed by the 1856 Declaration of Paris. Over the course of the twentieth century, and in particular since the 1949 Geneva Conventions, IHL became much more focused on ensuring protection for civilians.

Today, the standards for compliance have risen so high that, some argue, full compliance is impossible even for the best-resourced militaries. This shift has been driven by an increasing split between the "law-makers" and the "law-takers": the percent of military attendees at the major IHL conferences where these laws are debated and drafted has decreased significantly since the turn of the twentieth century and, particularly, since the passage of the 1949 Geneva Conventions. New proposals for IHL are today made principally by well-intended humanitarians from NGOs and members of the international legal academy, so it is perhaps not surprising that IHL has evolved such high standards for compliance.

I also examine whether and why the framers of IHL considered how the laws they drafted would be perceived by rebel groups fighting civil wars. Here I find that, to the extent that the framers of IHL thought about rebel groups, they focused almost exclusively on ensuring that any mention of rebel groups in the laws of war did not accord legitimacy to these groups. This inattention to the behavior of rebel groups reflects the very state-centric nature of IHL, and the fact that states tend not to want to legitimize challengers. It also suggests one lesson for any rebel groups that wish to engage with IHL: it pays to be a state. For the most part, it is the soldiers, civilians, and property of state parties to international treaties that enjoy the protection of IHL.

The second part of the argument examines the consequences of the development of IHL for the commencement, conduct, and conclusion of interstate wars. I argue that the proliferation of IHL has created perverse incentives for states engaged in interstate war. The rising costs of compliance with ever-higher standards create incentives for states to avoid stepping over any bright lines that would unequivocally oblige them to comply with the laws of war. I focus on the conditions under which states issue formal declarations of war and conclude formal peace treaties in interstate war, and find that the use of such formalities has declined as IHL has proliferated.

The third and final part of the argument focuses on civil wars, and specifically on how secessionist rebel groups—those that seek a new, independent state—have engaged with the laws of war. I argue that secessionists are broadly responsive to signals sent by the international community. Compared to other types of rebel groups, secessionists have incentives to be responsive to such signals because approval from the international community is necessary for the realization of their political aims. When the international community objects to unilateral declarations of independence, the proportion of secessionists declaring independence declines. Secessionists are also less likely to target civilians than are nonsecessionist rebels, and this behavior is at least partially driven by their desire to be seen to comply with IHL and thus to please the international community. Finally, and in direct contrast to the declining rate of peace treaty usage in interstate wars, the percentage of civil wars concluded with peace treaties has increased over time; I show that this is in response to the modern international community's expressed preference for negotiated settlements.

The particular history of the laws of war has shaped compliance in both interstate and civil wars. It has also led to divergences in belligerents' relationship to the laws of war in interstate versus civil wars. If they persist, these patterns may also affect the trajectory of future laws of war. Failure to include the military in future lawmaking efforts could undermine compliance with new laws. And while certain rebel groups have thus far been eager to comply with these laws, if this compliance is not rewarded (and it has not been, to date), then the distance that the framers of IHL deliberately created between the law and non-state actors may backfire.

Why the Laws of War Matter

Skeptics argue that any international law, let alone law regulating war, is simply ineffective.[18] But states devote enormous resources to creating and upholding international law in general, and international humanitarian law in particular. And the most recent scholarship on the subject suggests that war is, indeed, often conducted within highly regulated constraints.[19]

Political scientists have sought to understand the conditions under which belligerents comply with IHL. A growing literature on civilian targeting in interstate war has found a strong relationship between certain types of war aims and military strategies, on the one hand, and civilian targeting, on the other.[20] Territorially ambitious states fighting interstate wars are especially likely to target civilians, as are states whose opponents use guerrilla warfare. Other research has applied these insights to treatment of prisoners of war, with similar findings.[21] A recent book on IHL compliance points to the importance of reciprocity, particularly in combination with democracy and joint ratification of major international humanitarian laws, in predicting compliance in the context of interstate war.[22] All of this research builds on a foundation laid by scholars of international law more generally, and human rights law in particular, who have examined the relationships between ratification, regime type, and compliance with international law.[23] These studies have applied sophisticated methods that allow their authors to account for the possibility that only the most law-abiding states will sign these international agreements, and have still found an important independent effect of signing on to international law on compliance.

The extensive political science literature on rebel group behavior such as civilian targeting has focused on the funding structure and disciplinary capacity of rebel groups, their recruitment procedures, their cohesiveness, their degree of territorial control, and their ties to local networks.[24] More recent work has begun to probe the effects of the political aims of rebels, as well as their internal governance structures, on behavior that is subject to IHL.[25] But few scholars have examined direct links between rebel group behavior and IHL.[26]

International legal scholars have also weighed in on the debate over the efficacy of international law in general, and the laws governing wartime conduct in particular. Eric Posner argues that international law has become so complex and constraining as to make itself irrelevant. Posner decries the hypertrophy of what he views as toothless human rights treaties, arguing that "human rights law has failed to improve respect for human rights [because] the law is weak—the treaties are vague and inconsistent, and the institutions are balkanized, starved of resources, and unequipped with legal authority."[27] Jens David Ohlin responds by positing that states nonetheless ought to comply because they value the long-term constraining power of international law.[28]

I build on this previous scholarship and enter these debates by taking the long view of the laws of war, a perspective that has been lacking in the literature. Another innovation of this book is that it analyzes trends in the laws of war and war formalities in interstate and civil war side by side. While this strategy is unusual, it is an important angle of approach for three reasons. First, our understanding of the relationship between interstate and civil wars has always been wrapped up in the making of the laws of war. Consider the fact that the Lieber Code, which was drafted to serve as a field manual for the Union Army during the US Civil War, is widely considered to be the foundation of much of today's codified laws of war. There is a striking disconnect here, in that most modern laws of war were designed with the principal aim of governing belligerent conduct during interstate, and not intrastate, conflict. Second, in a book that engages directly with the history of the laws of war, it is important to follow the historical arc of war itself. Over the time period I cover, war has shifted from occurring primarily between states to within them. To look only at the laws of war as they pertain to interstate wars would be to curtail this project's relevance to many of today's conflicts. Conversely, to restrict the analysis to civil wars would leave the work without important historical context, and more generally would undermine the historical perspective that the book offers. Third, I submit that the admittedly unusual decision to include an analysis of interstate and civil wars in the same book is a strength of the project. While scholars of interstate and civil wars may travel in different circles, these disciplinary divisions are often driven more by practical than intellectual reasons and, in fact, may not always make sense to maintain.[29] Stepping back and looking at how different forms of war and law have developed over time forces us to bridge those divides, and also affords much-needed perspective on future lawmaking efforts.

Plan of the Book

The remainder of this book is organized around the three parts of the argument laid out above. Chapter 1 presents an analytical history of international humanitarian law, drawing on original data on attendees at the major IHL conferences since 1899 as well as a text analysis of the commentaries to these conventions.[30] In chapter 2, I develop a theoretical argument based on the evidence presented in chapter 1 by analyzing the costs and benefits of compliance with IHL as it has developed over time. I present specific hypotheses on the use of war formalities, as well as compliance with IHL, in both interstate war and civil war. Chapters 3 through 5 cover the empirical ground of interstate war over the past 200 years. I use both quantitative analysis based on original data and a series of case studies based on primary and secondary sources to explain why states have all but stopped declaring war (chapter 3) and to examine levels of compliance with IHL (chapter 4) and the decline of peace treaties in interstate war (chapter 5). The interstate war cases are the 1898 Spanish-American War, the Boxer Rebellion of 1900, the 1971 Bangladesh War, and the 1982 Falklands/Malvinas War.

Chapters 6 through 8 mirror the previous set of chapters but with a focus on secessionist rebel groups that are fighting civil wars. As with the analysis of interstate war, I combine quantitative analysis based on original data with case studies that use primary sources, such as archives and interviews, to explain changing rates in secessionists' use of declarations of independence (chapter 6) and civilian targeting (chapter 7), and changes over time in the use of peace treaties to conclude civil war (chapter 8). Qualitative evidence from civil wars is based on the cases of nineteenth-century Texas, the 1950 South Moluccan separatist war, and South Sudan's secessionist conflict from the 1970s to its independence in 2011.[31]

In the concluding chapter, I address policy implications and unanswered questions. I examine two ongoing lawmaking projects to assess whether historical patterns of IHL lawmaking are evident in today's efforts to govern cyber armed conflict and lethal autonomous weapons systems ("killer robots"). I also consider the ongoing dilemma that proponents of international law face when dealing with secessionist rebel groups; secessionists seek to please the international community, but this trend is unlikely to last indefinitely if good behavior is not rewarded. Finally, I discuss two sets of contrasts in peace treaty use in interstate and civil war. Peace treaties are less used today in interstate war compared to the past, and more used in civil war. But the evidence suggests that peace treaties are more helpful to an enduring peace in interstate as opposed to civil wars. How ought these trends be reconciled with the international community's current preference for negotiated settlements in civil wars?

The project of modern international humanitarian law is founded on a desire to limit war's worst effects. But its own effects have been mixed, blurring the lines between war and peace and states and secessionists. If we are both never and always at war, then the scope and applicability of the laws meant to govern wartime conduct ought to be revised. If the carrot of statehood is always out of reach for well-behaved secessionists, they will eventually catch on and revert to bad behavior. And if peace treaties in civil wars are considered to be ends in themselves, then there is a real danger that these wars will, in fact, not end. My aim in this book is to expose these questions with the broader goal of uncovering patterns in the development of past and present laws of war that can inform and improve future international humanitarian lawmaking efforts.

1

THE PROLIFERATION AND
CODIFICATION OF THE LAWS OF WAR

In this chapter, I trace the development of international humanitarian law since its initial codification in the mid-nineteenth century. This body of law has changed dramatically in both quantity and quality. At the close of the Napoleonic Wars in the early nineteenth century there were no multilateral treaties on the law of war. The customary law of the day was such that prisoners taken in war were routinely shot, and brutality against civilian populations was common both inside and outside western Europe.[1] That the laws of war were tacit, not codified, made sense in a world where state boundaries and sovereignty were often unsettled. Indeed, the law was used in part to distinguish bandits and warlords from legitimate rulers.[2] Today, by contrast, over seventy law of war treaties and conventions are listed in the treaty database of the International Committee of the Red Cross (ICRC).[3] Most of these conform with the ICRC's mission of protecting victims of war. All these laws are state-centric, with a primary focus on the regulation of interstate rather than civil war; parties to the treaties are exclusively states.

In this historical overview of the laws of war, I focus on the process of the making of international humanitarian law. After laying out the basic history of the laws of war, I analyze the changing composition of the lawmakers present at the creation of modern international humanitarian law. I show that representation of the military in these lawmaking efforts has declined over time. I then approach the history of international humanitarian law from the angle of armed non-state actors. Via a content analysis of major international humanitarian law documents, I show that the framers of international humanitarian law were more concerned with avoiding conferring legitimacy on rebel groups than they were with trying to bind the *in bello* behavior of these groups. Combined, the changing composition of lawmakers and the consistent inattention to rebel group behavior explain how the changing nature of IHL bears directly on how—and which—actors opt to try to evade or instead to engage positively with this body of international law.

A Brief History of the Laws of War

For most of human history, the laws of war were informal or agreed to on an ad hoc basis. The ancient Greeks, for example, had an informal understanding amongst themselves that "[h]ostilities are sometimes inappropriate: sacred truces, especially those declared for the celebration of the Olympic games, should be observed," and, moreover, that prisoners of war should be ransomed rather than executed.[4] Cicero was famously skeptical of the power of law in the context of war, but even he recognized the need for some regulation of warfare. He exhorted the ancient Romans to treat prisoners of war well, and to offer some mercy to civilian populations.[5] Sun Tzu likewise urged kind treatment of captured soldiers, and argued that a skillful leader "captures cities without laying siege to them," to avoid causing undue suffering of the civilian population.[6] The ancient Greeks and Romans limited the application of these restrictions to their cultural cousins; pagans and barbarians did not receive the same consideration.[7]

The first western efforts at codification of the laws of war were made in the Middle Ages, by writers such as Aquinas and by representatives of the Christian Church. The Church had manifold, and sometimes conflicting, interests in regulating war. One was to apply Christian values of fairness and humanitarianism to the realm of warfare. Another was to limit where these values applied. The laws of war were clearly meant to apply to conflicts between and among Christians. Just as clearly, however, they were often *not* applied to non-Christian peoples, whose "barbarism" arguably justified the infliction of atrocities upon them, often in the name of civilizing native peoples and lands.[8] A third, extremely pragmatic reason for the Church's support of a system of laws to regulate war was that such a system protected the Church itself.[9] Its priests were among the earliest classes of protected peoples. Moreover, as the largest landowner in Europe, the Church was deeply interested in propagating and disseminating a set of rules that would protect its wealth in land, art, and sacred buildings.

Church doctrine regarding *jus in bello*—laws regulating conduct during war—was folded into the medieval chivalric code. Although the code of knights was a precursor to modern international humanitarian law and the word "chivalry" today has positive connotations, it did not approach current standards of humanitarianism.[10] As argued by scholars such as Helen Kinsella, the chivalric code perpetuated and sometimes exacerbated existing inequalities of race, class, and gender. It was meant to preserve a very specific system of social order. The code principally governed behavior among the knightly class. Rules regarding gentle treatment of prisoners of war, for example, did not apply to the foot soldiers who often bore the brunt of fighting.

Jurists such as Francisco de Vitoria, Emmerich de Vattel, and Hugo Grotius brought the laws of war from an ad hoc series of rules developed on the battlefield into a more theoretical and systematized realm. In the sixteenth century, Vitoria, a Spanish philosopher, took the position that militaries could target civilians only if it served military purposes, such as deterring other towns or boosting soldiers' morale. This position was moderated in the seventeenth century by Grotius, a Dutch jurist, and in the eighteenth century by Vattel, a Swiss jurist, both of whom argued for additional restrictions on military treatment of civilian populations.

While the writings of these legal scholars constitute, in a sense, the initial codification of the laws of war, the application of these rules on the battlefield remained generally informal, with the occasional exception of bilateral arrangements between belligerents.[11] The laws of war were largely customary, identified by state practice and the norms of the day, rather than by positive law embedded in international agreements.[12] By the mid-nineteenth century, however, the landscape of international law had altered dramatically. Martti Koskenniemi argues that it was the rise of international law as a recognized profession that led to a proliferation of international laws. Increasingly, such laws began to be codified in multilateral treaties.[13]

The first law of war codified in a multilateral agreement was the 1856 Declaration of Paris Respecting Maritime Law. The 1856 declaration is short, comprising just four main parts:

1. Privateering is, and remains, abolished;
2. The neutral flag covers enemy's goods, with the exception of contraband of war;
3. Neutral goods, with the exception of contraband of war, are not liable to capture under enemy's flag;
4. Blockades, in order to be binding, must be effective, that is to say, maintained by a force sufficient really to prevent access to the coast of the enemy.[14]

The minimalism of the declaration favored belligerent rights, in that belligerents could board and inspect neutral ships to look for contraband. The rights of neutral states were protected only to the extent that contraband was not found upon their ships. Notably, the declaration did not define contraband, effectively leaving the definition to the belligerents themselves, who, not surprisingly, took a very broad view of the question.[15] According to Stephen Neff, the premier modern scholar of neutrality rights:

> [A] belligerent right [of blockade] which had once been very tightly constricted had now become, in the eyes of some, breathtakingly broad. Where the law of blockade had once entitled belligerents to do nothing more—or less—than capture neutral ships which penetrated the physical line formed by a blockading squadron, it was now being invoked to allow belligerents to capture cargoes being carried on neutral ships between neutral ports, at indefinitely large distances away from the line of the blockade—even if the ship carrying the cargo never at any time encountered the blockading squadron.[16]

The next multilateral treaty in the realm of the law of war similarly benefited belligerents. The 1864 Geneva Convention on the Amelioration of the Condition of the Wounded on the Field of Battle was the brainchild of Henri Dunant, the founder of the International Committee of the Red Cross. In 1859, Dunant had been in pursuit of a business concession when he followed Napoleon III to the battlefield at Solferino during the Austro-Sardinian War. Dunant's desire for profit appears to have been quickly supplanted by the desire to ameliorate the suffering he observed on the battlefield. What most struck Dunant was not the brutality of fighting itself, but the lack of medical evacuation and care for the fallen:

> If there had been enough assistance to collect the wounded in the plains of Medola and from the bottom of the ravines of San Martino, on the sharp slopes of Mount Fontana, or on the low hills above Solferino, how different things would have been! There would have been none of those long hours of waiting on June 24, hours of poignant anguish and bitter helplessness, during which those poor men of the Bersagliere, Uhlans and Zouaves struggled to rise, despite their fearful pain . . . ; and there would never have been the terrible possibility of what only too probably happened the next day—living men being buried among the dead![17]

From Solferino, Dunant traveled back to his native Switzerland to raise funds for an organization that would "protect the lives and dignity of victims of armed conflict."[18] Thus was born the International Committee of the Red Cross, which has since been at the forefront of the development of modern international humanitarian law.

The 1864 Red Cross Convention was the ICRC's first effort to bring the nations of the world to agreement on a basic law of war.[19] The convention focused on an issue that was principally a coordination problem for belligerents: creating space and time for the war wounded to be evacuated from a battlefield. The founders of the ICRC knew that theirs was a steep hill to climb, but they also knew that it was a win-win proposition for all involved. Although state militaries had previously made efforts to improve their medical evacuation practices,[20] many of these services had atrophied over time and were no longer functional.[21] It would be a net improvement for all parties if their wounded could be removed from the battlefield and receive prompt medical attention. The wounded could no longer contribute to the battle, and thus returning them to their forces for medical treatment was a tactically neutral move. At the same time, each party to conflict greatly preferred for its own wounded to receive treatment. Knowing that they could receive medical care if wounded would boost soldiers' morale as well as the support for war on the home front.[22]

The ICRC solved the problem caused by states' lack of organizational capacity by proposing to do the work of evacuation and medical treatment itself. States, however, were opposed to the notion of having a third-party presence on the battlefield.[23] The problem was solved by identifying ambulances, military hospitals, medical personnel treating the wounded, and local civilians treating the wounded as neutral parties to the conflict. The famous "red cross" designation had been born.[24]

Thus the first two codified laws of war were written in ways that favored belligerent rights. But the tenor of the laws of war was about to change. Whereas previously written laws facilitated war, the Hague Conventions of 1899 began to constrain belligerents in their warfighting, a historical turning point in the codification of the laws of war.

Originally conceived by Russia's Tsar Nicholas II as a conference on disarmament—which would have been to Russia's advantage, but benefited few other states at the time—the convening of powers in 1899 at The Hague instead took a curious detour.[25] Three of the 1899 Hague Conventions—the first codified rules for land warfare—cover (1) conflict resolution, (2) land warfare generally, and (3) maritime warfare; a fourth—including three declarations—restricts the use of specific weapons such as expanding bullets.

Convention II, "with respect to the Laws and Customs of War on Land," restricts how civilian populations may be treated in times of war. The convention stipulates that "the right of belligerents to adopt means of injuring the enemy is not unlimited" (Article 22), and declares that "it is especially prohibited. . . . [t]o employ arms, projectiles, or material of a nature to cause superfluous injury" (Article 23). Further, "The attack or bombardment of towns, villages, habitations or buildings which are not defended, is prohibited" (Article 25). The convention also formally prohibits pillage (Section 2, Article 47) and, more generally, imposes a series of limitations on the rights of military occupiers (Section 3).

Although the customary laws of war as outlined by jurists such as Grotius and Vattel made important distinctions between combatants and civilians in specifying standards of fair treatment, the Second 1899 Hague Convention was the first positive law to do so. Notably, beyond the proscription against bombing undefended towns, the convention does not define "civilians." The drafters of the 1899 Hague Conventions likely did not view themselves as revolutionaries. However, these incremental changes were expanded in 1907 and, even more dramatically, in 1949, with the Fourth 1949 Geneva Convention, "Relative to the Protection of Civilian Persons in Time of War." The latter imposed clearly delineated obligations on militaries to avoid targeting civilian populations. The concept of "protected persons," which included all civilians but especially the sick, wounded, women, and children, would come to dominate what was now referred to as international humanitarian law. The Fourth 1949 Geneva Convention prohibited rape (Article 27), torture (Article 31), and the use of human shields (Article 28). With the Second World War fresh in lawmakers' memories, significant restrictions were placed on the behavior of occupying powers (Section 3). Such restrictions remain relevant today as parties to the Geneva Conventions, such as Palestine, argue that they have suffered from violations of the law of occupation.[26]

Although the definition of "civilian" continues to be a negative one in international humanitarian law—in that civilians are defined as "not combatants"[27]—the protections afforded civilians have increased in subsequent agreements. For example, the first 1977 Additional Protocol to the 1949 Geneva Conventions clearly outlines the principle of distinction in its Basic Rule (Article 48): "In order to ensure respect for and protection of the civilian population and civilian objects, the Parties to the conflict shall at all times distinguish between the civilian population and combatants and between civilian objects and military objectives and accordingly shall direct their operations only against military objectives." The focus on protected persons has become the centerpiece of the codified, multilateral treaties at the heart of modern international humanitarian law. This focus is also reflected in other sources of international law, such as legal writings and judicial opinions. Since the 1990s, the rise of international war crimes tribunals such as the International Criminal Tribunal for Rwanda (ICTR), the International Criminal Tribunal for Yugoslavia (ICTY), and the International Criminal Court (ICC) has increased the odds of punishment of war crimes, particularly those committed against civilians. Rulings from these tribunals have also clarified and even, at times, expanded international humanitarian law. For example, the ICTY prosecuted several Serbian and Croat military officers for violations of the laws of war regarding the treatment of cultural property, such as bombing and plundering the Old Town of Dubrovnik.[28] The notion of "civilian objects" has been expanded to include cultural property as well as critical infrastructure.

Another shift in the nature of international humanitarian law refers to the type of conflict this body of law is meant to govern. The earliest codified laws of war were clearly focused on state behavior and obligations in the context of interstate war. Beginning with the 1899 Hague Conventions, however, delegates reluctantly acceded to arguments that this body of law could also govern civil war. The famous "Martens Clause" of the 1899 and 1907 Hague Conventions is the first formal attempt to cover this gap in law: "Until a more complete code of the laws of war is issued, the High Contracting Parties think it right to declare that in cases not included in the Regulations adopted by them, populations and belligerents remain under the protection and empire of the principles of international law, as they result from the usages established between civilized nations, from the laws of humanity and the requirements of the public conscience."[29] The brevity and vagueness of the Martens clause limited its applicability. It was effectively replaced by Article 3, common to all the 1949 Geneva Conventions (hereafter "Common Article 3"), which in theory extends the reach of the conventions to civil wars:

> In the case of armed conflict not of an international character occurring in the territory of one of the High Contracting Parties, each Party to the conflict shall be bound to apply, as a minimum, the following provisions:
>
>> Persons taking no active part in the hostilities, including members of armed forces who have laid down their arms and those placed *hors de combat* by sickness, wounds, detention, or any other cause, shall in all circumstances be treated humanely, without any adverse distinction founded on race, colour, religion or faith, sex, birth or wealth, or any other similar criteria.
>
> To this end, the following acts are and shall remain prohibited at any time and in any place whatsoever with respect to the above-mentioned persons:
>
>> violence to life and person, in particular murder of all kinds, mutilation, cruel treatment and torture;
>> taking of hostages;
>> outrages upon personal dignity, in particular humiliating and degrading treatment;

the passing of sentences and the carrying out of executions without previous judgment pronounced by a regularly constituted court, affording all the judicial guarantees which are recognized as indispensable by civilized peoples.

The wounded and sick shall be collected and cared for.

An impartial humanitarian body, such as the International Committee of the Red Cross, may offer its services to the Parties to the conflict.

The Parties to the conflict should further endeavor to bring into force, by means of special agreements, all or part of the other provisions of the present Convention.

The application of the preceding provisions shall not affect the legal status of the Parties to the conflict.

Common Article 3 is often discussed as a "convention in miniature"; that is to say, it contains many of the elements of the 1949 Geneva Conventions but not all of them, at least not explicitly.

Although an improvement on the Martens clause, Common Article 3 left many gaps in coverage of non-international armed conflicts. The concept of the "civilian" remained undefined, and the notion of a "conflict not of an international character" was so broad as to impair its utility. In theory, it could be applied to events ranging from riots to coups to major civil wars; this unworkable potential scope made it easier for governments not to apply it to internal conflict at all. The 1977 Protocols Additional to the 1949 Geneva Conventions were meant to fill these holes, first by outlining the laws of war that would apply to "wars of national liberation" or decolonization and, second, by outlining the laws of war for all other internal conflicts, aside from wars of national liberation, that were more than "riots and isolated or sporadic acts of violence."[30] Protocol I also offers the first definition (albeit a negative definition) of "civilian" in codified IHL. A controversy that has endured from the conference report on the protocols until the present day is whether granting the protection of law to non-state actors effectively confers recognition upon them, with other legal implications. This tension is evident wherever IHL is sought to apply to civil wars: states seek to maintain the protection of the law for themselves and to deny it to non-state actors.

The development of international humanitarian law has thus been characterized by an increase in the number of codified laws of war (see fig. 1.1) and also by a change in the character of these laws.[31] Table 1.1 lists all

TABLE 1.1 Codified international humanitarian law

Treaty title	Year
Declaration Respecting Maritime Law	1856
Red Cross Convention	1864
St. Petersburg Declaration	1868
Hague Convention I, for the Pacific Settlement of International Disputes	1899
Hague Convention II, with Respect to the Laws and Customs of War on Land	1899
Hague Convention III, Adaptation to Maritime Warfare of Principles of the Geneva Convention of 1864	1899
Hague Convention IV, 1: Declaration to Prohibit, for the term of Five Years, the Launching of Projectiles and Explosives from Balloons, and Other Methods of a Similar Nature	1899
Hague Convention IV, 2: Declaration on the Use of Projectiles the Object of Which is the Diffusion of Asphyxiating Gases	1899
Hague Convention IV, 3: Concerning Expanding Bullets	1899
Hague Convention I, Pacific Settlement of International Disputes	1907
Hague Convention II, Limitation of Employment of Force for Recovery of Contract Debts	1907
Hague Convention III, Opening of Hostilities	1907
Hague Convention IV, Laws and Customs of War on Land	1907
Hague Convention V, Rights and Duties of Neutral Powers and Persons in Case of War on Land	1907
Hague Convention VI, Status of Enemy Merchant Ships at the Outbreak of Hostilities	1907
Hague Convention VII, Conversion of Merchant Ships into War Ships	1907
Hague Convention VIII, Laying of Automatic Submarine Contact Mines	1907
Hague Convention IX, Bombardment by Naval Forces in Time of War	1907
Hague Convention X, Adaptation to Maritime War of the Principles of the Geneva Convention	1907
Hague Convention XI, Relative to Certain Restrictions with Regard to the Exercise of the Right of Capture in Naval Wara	1907
Hague Convention XIII, Concerning the Rights and Duties of Neutral Powers in Naval War	1907
Hague Convention XIV, Prohibiting the Discharge of Projectiles and Explosives from Balloons	1907
Geneva Protocol for the Prohibition of the Use of Asphyxiating, Poisonous or Other Gases, and of Bacteriological Methods of Warfare	1925
Geneva Convention Relative to the Treatment of Prisoners of War	1929
Convention on the Prevention and Punishment of the Crime of Genocide	1948
Geneva Convention I, for the Amelioration of the Condition of the Wounded and Sick in Armed Forces in the Field	1949
Geneva Convention II, for the Amelioration of the Condition of the Wounded, Sick and Shipwrecked Members of Armed Forces at Sea	1949

Treaty title	Year
Geneva Convention III, Relative to the Treatment of Prisoners of War	1949
Geneva Convention IV, Relative to the Protection of Civilian Persons in Time of War	1949
Hague Convention for the Protection of Cultural Property in the Event of Armed Conflict	1954
Convention on the Prohibition of the Development, Production and Stockpiling of Bacteriological (Biological) and Toxin Weapons and on their Destruction	1972
Additional Protocol I to the 1949 Geneva Conventions, Relating to the Protection of Victims of International Armed Conflicts	1977
Additional Protocol II to the 1949 Geneva Conventions, Relating to the Protection of Victims of Non-International Armed Conflicts	1977
Convention on Prohibitions or Restrictions on the Use of Certain Conventional Weapons Which May be Deemed to be Excessively Injurious or to Have Indiscriminate Effects—Protocol I, on Non-Detectable Fragments	1980
Convention on Prohibitions or Restrictions on the Use of Certain Conventional Weapons Which May be Deemed to be Excessively Injurious or to Have Indiscriminate Effects—Protocol II, on Prohibitions or Restrictions on the Use of Mines, Booby-Traps and Other Devices	1980
Convention on Prohibitions or Restrictions on the Use of Certain Conventional Weapons Which May be Deemed to be Excessively Injurious or to Have Indiscriminate Effects—Protocol III, on Prohibitions or Restrictions on the Use of Incendiary Weapons	1980
Convention against Torture and Other Cruel, Inhuman, or Degrading Treatment or Punishment	1984
Convention on the Rights of the Child	1989
Convention on the Prohibition of the Development, Production, Stockpiling and Use of Chemical Weapons and on Their Destruction	1993
Convention on Prohibitions or Restrictions on the Use of Certain Conventional Weapons Which May be Deemed to be Excessively Injurious or to Have Indiscriminate Effects—Protocol IV, on Blinding Laser Weapons	1995
Convention on the Prohibition of the Use, Stockpiling, Production and Transfer of Anti-Personnel Mines and on their Destruction	1997
Rome Statute of the International Criminal Court	1998
Convention on Prohibitions or Restrictions on the Use of Certain Conventional Weapons Which May be Deemed to be Excessively Injurious or to Have Indiscriminate Effects—Protocol V, on Explosive Remnants of War	2003
Additional Protocol III to the 1949 Geneva Conventions, Relating to the Adoption of an Additional Distinctive Emblem	2005

Source: Data retrieved from the ICRC data base of International Humanitarian Law, accessed January 13, 2010, http://www.icrc.org/ihl.nsf/INTRO?OpenView.

[a] Convention XII, Relative to the Creation of an International Prize Court, is excluded because only one state—Nicaragua—ratified it.

the conventions and treaties since 1816. The titles of these laws reveal a change in focus over time; for example, the Second Hague Convention of 1899 refers to the "Laws and Customs of War on Land," while the first 1977 Additional Protocol to the 1949 Geneva Conventions relates to "the Protection of Victims of International Armed Conflicts." The laws of war, which had formerly enabled belligerents to prosecute wars more easily, now sought to constrain their prosecution of war.

Another critical feature of the history of the laws of war is that, as shown in table 1.1, major additions to the laws of war tend to occur after major wars. The 1899 Hague Conventions followed the Spanish-American War of 1898. The Russo-Japanese War (1905) was followed by the 1907 Hague Conventions. And the 1949 Geneva Conventions were concluded on the heels of World War II.[32] This "call and response" suggests that law and war react to each other. The laws often "fight the last war" by, for example, banning weapons or practices recently experienced and deplored. But, as I will argue, law also constrains the prosecution of war, albeit not necessarily in the manner intended by the framers of the law. A spiral or spring is a useful metaphor in considering the perennial question of which comes first—behavior or law. Behavior leads to revisions in the law, which then shapes future behavior. The changing nature of who is in the room when the law is revised means that this rotation is likely to repeat indefinitely.

Figure 1.1 raises two additional legal questions. First, does a simple count of laws on the books reflect legal realities, or do new laws replace or subsume old ones? Overwhelmingly, new laws appear to supplement, but not subsume, previous ones. For example, the Fourth 1949 Geneva Convention explicitly states that it is supplemental to previous laws such as the 1899 and 1907 Hague Conventions (see Article 154).

Second, what is the relationship between international humanitarian law and human rights law? International humanitarian law evolved hand in hand with human rights law, which applied more broadly to state conduct toward citizens in peacetime, and both took expansive aim at human suffering.[33] Because many of the treaties listed in table 1.1, such as the Convention on the Rights of the Child, are often considered to be human rights agreements, rather than international humanitarian laws, it is worthwhile to consider the boundary between these two bodies of

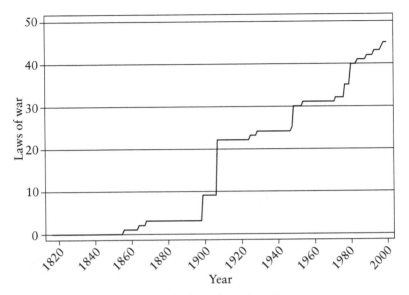

Figure 1.1 The laws of war since 1816

law. In a strict definition, international humanitarian law applies in times of war and governs the conduct of belligerents toward each other and toward neutrals. Human rights law is not so bounded in its scope and applicability; it applies in times of war and in times of not-war. Certain human rights treaties, such as the Convention against Torture and the Convention on the Rights of the Child, contain provisions that apply specifically to times of war.[34] These laws are included in table 1.1 both because of these provisions and because the ICRC—the world's most prominent international humanitarian law NGO—has identified them as part of international humanitarian law.

"Law-Makers" and "Law-Takers"

At least two questions emerge from the above history of positive international humanitarian law. First, how can we explain both the shift in IHL from belligerent rights to protected persons and the proliferation of new laws? And second, to what extent can and do these laws apply to civil wars, the most common form of warfare today?

To answer the first question, I examine who attended the major IHL conferences. I find that the earliest conferences included a fair number of representatives from the military; over time, however, this balance has shifted away from the military—those who must comply with the law, or the "law-takers"—and toward lawyers and representatives of NGOs. The growing distance between the "law-makers" and the "law-takers" may account in part for the rising standards for compliance, a rise that, I will argue later in this book, has led states to manage their legal risk by avoiding admitting they are in a state of war.

To approach the second question, I examine the transcripts of key moments in the codification of IHL to try to understand whether these same lawmakers viewed non-state actors as an audience for their laws. In a very broad sense, states have been the authors and intended audience of these laws. But the reality of civil war has always been present at these lawmaking conferences. Even when international humanitarian lawmakers gave time and thought to the regime that ought to govern intrastate conflict, they did not involve rebel groups in their discussions.[35] To what extent did the lawmakers anticipate how their output would be received by rebel groups in civil war?

Who Is in the Room?

The pivot from soldier to civilian as the principal object of protection in the laws of war defies simple explanation. Certainly, the World Wars were horribly destructive and disastrous for noncombatants, but previous wars had been at least as devastating. What distinguished wars of the twentieth century from those of past eras was a combination of literacy, mass (versus mercenary) armies, communications technology, and a ready base of NGOs interested in advancing an increasingly broad view of humanitarianism.[36]

I argue that those who are making the laws of war have become increasingly distant from those who are meant to comply with them. This logic fits with the narrative that the making of international humanitarian law is increasingly within the purview of activists and international lawyers who, although sincerely committed to mitigating the human costs of war, pay insufficient attention to the practicalities of some of their proposals.[37] My argument borrows from Martti Koskenniemi's claim that a growing international legal profession sought to perpetuate itself through creation of more international law.[38]

The earliest codified laws of war were written by those serving in the military or with a military background. For example, Francis Lieber had fought in the Prussian army prior to emigrating to the United States and, in 1862, had searched Civil War battlefields in Missouri for his missing soldier son. He was later the author of General Orders 100, generally thought to be the first codification of the laws of war as a military manual, for the Union Army during the US Civil War.[39] The Lieber Code is famous for its doctrine of "military necessity," and is more humane in its requirements for the treatment of the wounded than it is, for example, in its requirements for the treatment of civilian populations during wartime.[40] During the 1874 Brussels Conference, which met to begin to codify the laws of land warfare, most delegations were headed by uniformed military. According to historian Peter Holquist, "This preference for military men reflected the nature of the Russian proposal [for the conference]—to codify existing laws and customs of warfare (on which military men were the greatest experts), and to do so in a way that would not extend the code beyond actual military usages."[41] Similarly, the military dominated the negotiations over the 1868 St. Petersburg Declaration, which banned the use of exploding bullets.[42] Fedor Martens, author of the "Martens Clause" in the Hague Conventions of 1899 and 1907, credited the "great captains," more than the philanthropists and the publicists, as the originators of the earliest laws of war during the deliberations over the 1899 Hague Conventions.[43] Geoffrey Best writes of the nineteenth century, "The [early] law of war could not be developed at all without the assent of the generals and admirals, and these were years when their power and influence were very great."[44] Isabel Hull similarly notes that "military influence was strong, even predominant according to some interpreters" in this early period of the codification of IHL. She also indicates that, while military participants favored precision in the law, their political counterparts preferred vagueness.[45]

Data from the past century of international humanitarian lawmaking are consistent with the notion of a growing divide between the "lawmakers" and the "law-takers." The lists of delegates to the 1899 and 1907

Hague Conventions, the 1949 Geneva Conventions, the 1977 Additional Protocols, and the 1998 Rome Statute reveal a sizable proportion of military delegates through the 1949 Geneva Conventions. As figure 1.2[46] shows, delegates with military rank accounted for 20 to 30 percent of the delegates at these conferences through the turn of the twentieth century. Since 1900, however, military participation has declined significantly, down to the single digits.

Another approach to the issue of civilian versus military roles in the making of the laws of war is to examine how many national delegations were headed by persons holding military rank. As figure 1.3 shows, the numbers here are smaller; delegations headed by military personnel never exceeded 5 percent, and the number declined dramatically after the 1949 Geneva Conventions. Thus, not only were military delegates fewer in number over time, they also became less powerful within their delegations, increasingly relegated to the role of "technical advisor." As such, military delegates might be called upon to render an opinion on a specific technical matter, but would not have been as involved in the decision-making as those in the role of delegation head, or even as a regular delegate.

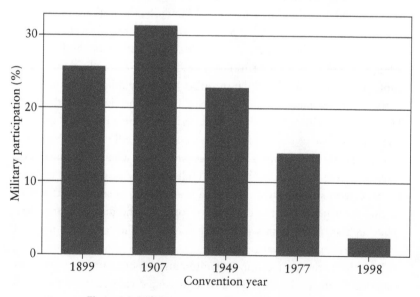

Figure 1.2 Military representation at IHL conventions

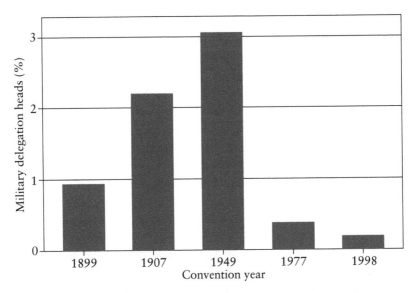

Figure 1.3 Military delegation heads at IHL conventions

Lack of data precludes a more refined coding of who the nonmilitary participants were at these conferences. What data we do have suggest a shift toward humanitarian organizations. The historian Calvin Davis briefly noted the presence of "peace people"—activists and journalists, few of whom were affiliated with organizations, and none of whom were granted official status—at the 1899 and 1907 Hague Conferences.[47] In 1949, 59 states and 9 NGOs and international governmental organizations (IGOs) were represented at the 1949 Geneva Conventions. In 1977, there were 134 states and 50 organizations—NGOs, IGOs (including UN agencies), and private organizations—in official attendance at the meetings that produced the Additional Protocols. In 1998, 163 states but just 31 NGOs, IGOs, and private organizations were present for the discussions around the Rome Statute. The historical record suggests that these non-state organizations were not silent observers, but rather active participants who engaged in persistent lobbying of state parties. In 1998, NGOs had "unprecedented access" to the delegates and negotiations.[48] Similarly, scholars of the international law of armed conflict as it pertains to cultural property note the critical role of experts—by which they mean experts in cultural property—as well as organizations such as UNESCO in pushing forward the 1954 Hague Convention for the Protection of Cultural Property.[49] A key debate during the 1954 Hague Conference hinged on whether there should be a "military necessity" exception to laws and norms for the protection of cultural property.[50] Although those in favor of military necessity won the day, the long duration of the discussion is revealing, and illustrates how distant mid-twentieth century international humanitarian lawmakers were from their predecessors one hundred years earlier.[51]

We do not know to what extent the delegates listed on the final act of each of these conferences are representative of the true drafters of these laws. Treaties such as the 1949 Geneva Conventions were preceded by years of preparatory meetings. Few of the ambassadors and foreign ministers listed as delegates to the final conventions were present at those preparatory meetings. Compiling a list of all the attendees at all the preparatory conferences might not be possible, given limited paper trails, particularly for the earlier conventions. But histories of these conferences, as well as the archives of the *travaux préparatoires* for the 1949 Geneva Conventions, suggest that the preparatory meetings were principally populated by members of the Red Cross (both members of the ICRC and national Red Cross organizations) and by representatives of foreign ministries.[52] The military may, in fact, be more represented in the final conferences than in the *travaux*.

If it is indeed the case that the military has become less represented in the lawmaking process, why is this so? Does the military opt out of such conferences? Or are they not invited? In her analysis of the effort to ban autonomous weapons systems, Charli Carpenter notes that the International Committee for Robot Arms Control, an NGO formed to limit the development and deployment of "killer robots," invited several military representatives to a 2010 meeting of experts, but most of these invitations were declined.[53] A US National Academy of Sciences group tasked with addressing the ethical and legal issues of emerging weapons technology conferred with more military personnel than did the Campaign to Stop Killer Robots, but still received only a handful of briefings from the military.[54] If, indeed, military personnel opt against participating in the early stages of meetings on norm and law creation, this supports the notion of a growing gap between the "law-makers" and the "law-takers."

Perhaps, though, it is not that military personnel opt out, but that they are not given the chance to opt in. Examining the appointment process to major IHL conventions could help shed light on this issue; unfortunately, original archival research suggests that the records for these particular meetings are not available, at least not for the United States.[55] Appointments records for other conferences that are more available suggest a political process whereby, for example, congressional representatives and senators write a letter to the relevant party in the State Department advocating that a certain constituent be invited to an upcoming meeting. Appointments themselves are made formally at the request of the State Department; for example, Theodore Roosevelt Jr.[56] was appointed to the US delegation to the 1922 Conference on the Limitation of Armament.[57] In the case of the 1899 Hague Convention, President McKinley and Secretary of State Hay chose delegates who would "give firm support to proposals to advance arbitration and international law."[58] The process of selecting delegates relied heavily on networking and political connections to McKinley, Hay, and their friends.[59]

The worldwide decline in numbers of military heads of delegation could be due in part to trends in global democratization. Military governments have become fewer in number over time, and so perhaps military representatives are less likely to be present at any international conferences, including those making international humanitarian law. Data from José Cheibub, Jennifer Gandhi, and James Vreeland, which cover the post–World War II period (from 1946 to 2008), suggest that the percent of states governed by military dictatorships takes an upside-down U-shape over this time period; what is more, the share of states governed by military dictators is nearly equal in 1946 and 2008.[60] This suggests that trends in the number or rate of military dictatorships are not driving these results.

The increased professionalization of international lawyers, combined with a dramatic proliferation of NGOs focused on humanitarian affairs, is a more likely explanation for the changing composition of international humanitarian lawmakers. One indicator of this shift comes from the list of humanitarian affairs NGOs registered with the United Nations Economic and Social Council (ECOSOC). In 1947, only a handful of such NGOs were on the roster. Today, the number of humanitarian affairs NGOs registered with ECOSOC exceeds 750. Humanitarian NGOs leading the charge to develop new laws of war may appear, or even be, less welcoming to military participation than past conveners.

The gap between the "law-makers" and the "law-takers" appears to be widening. It may be because members of the military are not represented at the *travaux préparatoires* preceding final IHL conventions, are unwilling to attend law of war meetings, are less likely to be appointed to attend such meetings because of increased politicization of the process, or because they are less likely to rule today compared to the past. As I will discuss in the following section, a similar gap is evident in international humanitarian lawmaking processes as they apply to rebel groups in civil wars.

Armed Non-state Actors as Audience

Another question pertinent to the development of the laws of war refers to how much attention is paid by the crafters of IHL to rebel groups as "consumers" of IHL. The laws of war were first designed by states to regulate state militaries even if, as discussed above, military representation at IHL conventions has diminished over time. To a large extent, these laws are meant to govern state-versus-state conflict. How international humanitarian law would and could treat civil wars has always been a concern, but one that was never fully addressed. Most armed conflict today occurs within state boundaries. At issue is not only the scope and applicability of IHL as it pertains to states engaged in civil war, but also the reach of IHL as it pertains to rebel groups.

I conducted a content analysis of the official, original ICRC commentaries to each of the 1949 Geneva Conventions and the two Protocols Additional to the 1949 Geneva Conventions in an effort to understand how and whether international humanitarian lawmakers understood their project's application to rebel group behavior.[61] These commentaries explain and discuss the law and the original lawmaking process behind the conventions and protocols. For example, Article 1 of the first 1949 Geneva Convention states, "The High Contracting Parties undertake to respect and to ensure respect for the present Convention in all circumstances." The commentary focused on Article 1 notes the novelty of this language, and interprets it as strengthening prior laws. Each clause in the Article is analyzed. The authors of the commentary point out that the phrase requiring states "to ensure respect" for the convention was inserted deliberately, and they explain that it means that "it would not, for example, be enough for a State to give orders or directives to a few civilian or military authorities, leaving it to them to arrange as they pleased for the details of their execution. It is for the State to supervise their execution."[62]

Similarly, the interpretation of the phrase "in all circumstances" is discussed as not extending to cases of civil war. Part of the reasoning is that Article 3, common to all of the 1949 Geneva Conventions, includes non-international conflicts under the ambit of the conventions.[63] There is little evidence to suggest that lawmakers considered how non-state actors might respond to the treaties they created.

I conducted two types of content analysis on the commentaries.[64] I searched for the term "non-international" in each commentary in order to produce a frequency count. I selected the term "non-international" because it is the term most frequently used to describe civil wars in the international legal world: civil wars are called "non-international armed conflicts" (NIACs) by most international lawyers. (An analysis using synonyms, such as "civil war," "insurgent," and "rebel," yielded nearly identical results.)

Figure 1.4 is a word cloud from the commentary to the Fourth 1949 Geneva Convention. It gives a sense of which words (apart from stop words such as "a" and "the") appeared most frequently in the commentary: greater frequency results in a larger font. The phrase "non-international" is not in the cloud, which is dominated by legal terms such as "article," "convention" and "paragraph," followed closely by "power," "war," and "international." Word clouds for the commentaries to the other three 1949 Geneva Conventions produce similar results.

Figure 1.5 shows a frequency count (how many mentions per number of pages in each document) of the phrase "non-international" across the commentaries to the four 1949 Geneva Conventions and the two 1977 Additional Protocols. Prior to the second Additional Protocol (also known as "Protocol II"), the mean frequency per page was .01—in other words, "non-international" appeared approximately once per 100 pages. Additional Protocol II is an outlier with a frequency of .43, unsurprisingly, given that its purpose is to extend the 1949 Geneva Conventions to the realm of civil wars.

The frequency counts suggests that, relative to other subjects, little attention was paid in IHL to the context of civil wars until Additional Protocol II. A more fine-grained content analysis lends further support to this claim. In searching for the term "non-international," I counted the number of mentions, and also analyzed the text around the term. My goal was to determine whether the commentators or lawmakers viewed non-state actors as

Figure 1.4 Word cloud for commentary to fourth 1949 Geneva Convention showing the most frequently appearing words. Produced using Voyant.

an audience for the laws under discussion. The clear finding emerging from this analysis is that they did not. Throughout, the commentaries focus on the obligations incumbent on states rather than rebel groups.

The analysis of the commentaries on the first three 1949 Geneva Conventions can be presented simultaneously, as there is a great deal of duplication among these commentaries, particularly surrounding the term "non-international." Discussions involving the term "non-international"

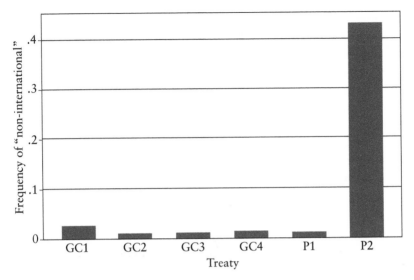

Figure 1.5 Frequency count of "non-international." "GC" refers to 1949 Geneva Conventions; "P" refers to 1977 Additional Protocols.

center on the obligations attendant upon states that were party to the conventions. The one exception, worth quoting at length, describes the obligations attendant upon rebel groups fighting civil wars, but it is confusing, even contradictory:

> The legality of a Government involved in an internal conflict suffices to bind that Government as a Contracting Party to the Convention. On the other hand, what justification is there for the obligation on the adverse Party in revolt against the established authority? At the Diplomatic Conference doubt was expressed as to whether insurgents could be legally bound by a convention which they had not themselves signed. But if the responsible authority at their head exercises effective sovereignty, it is bound by the very fact that it claims to represent the country, or part of the country. The "authority" in question can only free itself from its obligations under the Convention by following the procedure for denunciation laid down in Article 63. But the denunciation would not be valid, and could not in point of fact be effected, unless the denouncing authority was recognized internationally as a competent Government.[65]

The paradox of this paragraph is that it claims that Article 3 makes the Geneva Conventions binding on any rebel groups that seek to represent a state, while at the same time stating that these groups cannot be accorded the rights and privileges of statehood (here, the right of denunciation of the Conventions). Convoluted and dismissive thinking about the roles of rebel groups—key parties to the type of conflict under discussion—is also evident elsewhere in the Commentaries: "If an insurgent party applies Article 3, so much the better for the victims of the conflict. No one will complain. If it does not apply it, it will prove that those who regard its actions as mere acts of anarchy or brigandage are right."[66]

The discussion of civil wars in the commentary to Convention IV differs slightly in substance, but not with respect to whether rebel groups are considered as a potential audience. Approximately one-third of the mentions of "non-international" overlap with those in the commentaries to the first three conventions. More interesting are mentions of "non-international" focused on whether making agreements with rebel groups regarding wartime conduct could have the effect of causing governments to recognize their rebel group opponents. The commentary notes that "each [party to the conflict] is completely free—and should be encouraged—to declare its intention of applying all or part of the remaining provisions [of the Convention]," but then notes that the government of a state party to the convention is "free to make the express stipulation that its adherence to [any bilateral agreement with a rebel group] in no way implies recognition of the legality of the [rebel group] opposing party."[67] This discussion would have been the likeliest location for an analysis of how non-state actors might receive or be bound by the convention, but such a discussion is missing—adherence by non-state actors appears to be entirely optional in the eyes of the commentators.[68]

Additional Protocol I to the 1949 Geneva Conventions expands Convention IV, and the 1949 Conventions more generally, in at least two respects. First, it provides broader and clearer protections to civilians in time of war and, in fact, offers the first definition of a civilian in the context of positive international humanitarian law. Second, Additional Protocol I expands its scope of application to "armed conflicts in which peoples are fighting against colonial domination and alien occupation and against racist regimes in the exercise of their right of self-determination" (Article 4). This second expansion was primarily meant to cover national liberation movements such as those emerging during the post–World War II decolonization period. Additional Protocol I's field of application, while broader than preceding treaties, is not as broad as Additional Protocol II, which is meant to apply to non-international armed conflicts more generally.[69] As such, the majority of the mentions of "non-international" in the commentary to Additional Protocol I are focused on distinguishing the two additional protocols and their fields of application.

The commentary to Additional Protocol I thus fits the pattern of not considering how non-state actors might perceive their obligation to comply with international humanitarian law. One slight exception is in Article 96, which outlines procedures for "the authority representing a people engaged against a High Contracting Party in an armed conflict" to deposit a unilateral declaration to adhere to the additional protocol. The commentary, however, then goes on to clarify that the status of liberation movements as covered by Protocol I is very different from those of other groups participating in non-international armed conflict, as covered by Additional Protocol II. Even these national liberation movements, however, could not become High Contracting Parties to the additional protocol.[70]

As figure 1.5 shows, the commentary to Additional Protocol II yielded the highest frequency (and also the highest absolute number) of mentions of the term "non-international." This result is not surprising given that the focus of Additional Protocol II is non-international armed conflict. For the purpose of determining whether the drafters of the additional protocol viewed rebel groups as audiences, however, it is not only the quantity of mentions but also their context that matters.

Even though the term "non-international" is mentioned with much greater frequency in the commentary to Additional Protocol II than in other commentaries, the answer to the question of whether lawmakers anticipated that rebel groups would be attentive to these laws is the same. Most mentions of "non-international" speak to the definition of the term, the history of the additional protocol, its relation to existing laws, or the application of the additional protocol to specific issue areas, such as the treatment of prisoners of war. Both the commentary and the additional protocol are overlaid by states' concern that rebel groups should not be accorded any type of international recognition as a result of application of the conventions. Indeed, some states were deeply concerned that their own internal conflicts not rise to a legal level such that they would be covered by these new legal instruments. As Giovanni Mantilla writes of the British, "Preventing the application of any new instruments of humanitarian law

to Northern Ireland was, in fact, the Brits' most important goal throughout the revisions process in the 1970s."[71] This concern set up a balancing
act for the drafters of the additional protocol, if they were to get any
states to sign the instrument. The resolution of the balancing act was that
rebel groups may be considered parties (note the lowercase "p") to a conflict, but are not official Parties to the additional protocol. "Only the legal
government, or the government in power, of the State Party to common
Article 3, or to Protocol II, is a 'High Contracting Party'; in fact, even if
the *de facto* authority leading the struggle against the government exer-
cises the same rights and undertakes the same humanitarian obligations in
the context of those instruments, it is not a High Contracting Party in the
eyes of the law."[72] The conclusion of the commentary appears to be that,
because rebel groups are not Parties to the protocol, there is no point in
explicating their rights and obligations under the law.[73]

Concern over the possibility that the content of Additional Protocol II
might lead to recognition of rebel groups ultimately quashed any efforts
to include explicit obligations for non-state actors in the additional protocol, which was designed to cover the kinds of conflicts in which they were
involved. This lack of recognition notwithstanding, international law does
consider armed non-state actors operating in states party to the additional
protocols to be bound by the protocols, by virtue of the law regarding
state responsibility.[74] But this route to obligation of armed groups is atten-
uated at best. Even with this imbalance built into the additional protocol
and reinforced by the commentary, Additional Protocol II has one of the
lowest ratification levels of all the major IHL treaties.

At this writing, the ICRC has issued updated commentaries to the
first and second 1949 Geneva Conventions. Content analysis of these
new commentaries reflects the ICRC's recognition of today's realities of
war; non-international armed conflicts receive significantly more attention from the new commentaries than the old. In this new version of the
commentaries (particularly the section pertaining to Common Article 3,
S529), the ICRC presents several legal theories that would oblige rebel
groups to comply with IHL. Among these legal theories is the notion that
a state's obligations transfer to all residents and armed groups within
the territory of that state. This is so even though, as the commentaries
acknowledge, non-state actors cannot sign the Geneva Conventions. This
notion of obligation without consent or participation is consistent with,

albeit a slight departure from, past inattention to the reception of the laws of war by armed groups.

Content analysis of the commentaries to the 1949 Geneva Conventions and 1977 Additional Protocols demonstrates a consistent lack of attention to how rebel groups might receive these laws. The lack of participation by rebel groups in lawmaking is reflected in these results. The final act of the 1949 Geneva Conventions does not list any rebel groups as having participated in the conference. Eleven such groups attended the meetings for the 1977 Additional Protocols. Palestine and the Sovereign Military Order of Malta were the only two non-state groups with sovereignty claims present at the 1998 negotiations for the Rome Statute. Given their lack of representation, it is perhaps not surprising that the laws that emerged did not explicitly bind non-state actors. But non-state actors paying attention would notice the law's bottom line: to enjoy the benefits of law, statehood was necessary. Statehood is conferred by the international community—the same group that authored the laws of war. Insofar as the international community valued the laws it created, a reasonable inference could then be that following the laws of war (or, at least, appearing to do so) could help a group gain recognition as a state.

This history of the codified laws of war reveals their increase in number, their change in character, a shift in lawmakers, and a consistently deliberate bracketing of how rebel groups might receive the laws of war. The changing landscape of the laws of war is strongly correlated with who was in the room. As military personnel have been replaced by international lawyers and NGO representatives, the constraints imposed by the laws of war have grown. But one aspect of international humanitarian law has remained relatively constant; armed non-state actors are typically only discussed in the context of denying them legitimacy and recognition. In the next chapter, I use this history to develop an argument for how states and rebel groups have responded to the laws of war over time, focusing particularly on attempts to evade the law, or to engage with it.

2

INTERNATIONAL RECOGNITION, COMPLIANCE COSTS, AND THE FORMALITIES OF WAR

How have potential belligerents reacted to the development of international humanitarian law presented in chapter 1? As the laws of war have proliferated in number and changed in character, belligerents' incentives to abide by this body of international law have also changed. But this change has not been uniform; even though the legal landscape has shifted at the systemic level, belligerents hold different political aims and confront varying circumstances, and these differences condition their reactions to the laws of war.

A potential belligerent's reaction to the evolution of the laws of war will depend in large part on the extent to which it requires aid from the international community in achieving its political war aims. I conceive of aid from the international community (as opposed to aid from specific patrons) primarily in terms of international recognition, defined here as the widespread international acknowledgement of a potential belligerent's right to rule the territory it claims.[1] Focusing on international recognition makes sense because subsequent aid—such as loans from the International Monetary Fund (IMF)—is contingent on such recognition. Warring parties vary in the degree of international recognition they hold, and those that lack recognition may wish to seek it from the international community. Because the international community has propagated the laws of war and values them, belligerents with less (or no) recognition will be more likely to engage with these laws than recognized belligerents, who will tend to seek ways to evade their application. More generally, belligerents seeking international recognition will also be more likely to try to abide by the expressed preferences of the international community, even beyond the laws of war. As an example, states like Germany already possess a great deal of international recognition. Presently, Germany is at no risk of losing its membership in key international institutions such as the United Nations and the IMF. While its policies may be challenged on normative or practical grounds, execution of these policies generally does not require additional support from the international community. For instance, when German Chancellor Angela Merkel decided that Germany would welcome thousands of refugees in August 2015, this created problems for many neighboring European Union states; but Germany's membership in the EU was not challenged. By contrast, secessionist Somaliland cannot engage in international trade because it lacks the international recognition that would permit membership in major international financial institutions, foreign aid, and even such mundane logistics as insurance for freight shipped abroad. Importantly, certain rebel groups, such as the Islamic State, do not seek formal international recognition.

In the next section of this chapter, I further discuss the relationship between international recognition and the laws of war. I then introduce three international legal instruments: declarations of war, declarations of independence, and peace treaties. These formalities of war are used throughout the remainder of the book as critical indicators of a belligerent's stance of evasion or engagement with the laws of war. The balance of this chapter is then devoted to laying out the costs and benefits of evasion versus engagement with the laws of war for states involved in interstate war and for rebels—particularly, secessionist rebels—fighting civil wars.

International Recognition and the Laws of War

International recognition is a key background variable in understanding belligerents' stance toward the laws of war. By "international recognition," I mean the recognition of an entity as a member state by the international community of states. This conception of international recognition is similar to Stephen Krasner's notion of international legal sovereignty, which "has been concerned with establishing the status of a political entity in the international system."[2] By "international community," I mean the collectivity of actors—primarily states, but also intergovernmental organizations (IGOs) and NGOs—whose aims transcend national interests and are grounded in the Charter of the United Nations. Part of the power of this community lies in its ability to propagate and support standards of appropriate behavior for international actors[3]—the norms of international politics. This community also has the power to admit—or not—petitioners to the "club" of states, membership in which offers many desired perquisites such as formal diplomatic representation, the protection of international law, and access to financial assistance offered by international organizations such as the United Nations and International Monetary Fund.[4]

My definition of international recognition stipulates its possession by all United Nations member states today. Pre-UN-era measures of international recognition are less universal, and rely on instruments such as the placement of embassies, statements of recognition by political leaders, membership in institutions such as the League of Nations, and the conclusion of international treaties.[5] To be clear, to say that a state is internationally recognized is not to endorse its rule as legitimate. Certainly, the actions of recognized states including the United States, the People's Republic of China, Russia, North Korea, and Syria have been deeply contested in the international and domestic arenas. But it is to say that the needs of internationally recognized states with respect to the international community differ significantly from the needs of polities that receive no, or even less than full, international recognition. Take the right to travel as an example. Citizens of polities such as Kosovo and Taiwan that have received some international recognition—but not UN membership—cannot get visas to travel to countries such as Brazil. Instead, they may apply for a *laissez-passez*, which restricts travel more than a visa. By contrast, citizens of Serbia or the People's Republic of China may either travel to

Brazil without a visa or obtain a visa with fewer restrictions on travel than a *laissez-passer*.

The first major dividing line allowed by a focus on international recognition is therefore one between internationally recognized and internationally unrecognized actors. The second dividing line focuses on the set of actors who lack international recognition, and distinguishes those who value international recognition from those who do not. Rebel groups engaged in civil war display significant variation in this regard. Groups fighting wars for profit, such as the Revolutionary United Front (RUF) in 1990s Sierra Leone, lack international recognition but also require little or no support or recognition from the outside world, aside from access to markets in which to sell the resources they have obtained by illicit means (such as the "blood diamonds" from Angola, Ivory Coast, or Sierra Leone). For different reasons, groups such as the Islamic State and Boko Haram also do not seek international recognition; their vision of victory is one that appears to be detached from the world of modern statehood, and from the international community itself. Groups that seek to overthrow the central government, such as the Unified Communist Party in Nepal, might like to have international recognition, but do not require it for the realization of their political aims. These groups often focus on attracting aid from specific state patrons, rather than support from the international community as a whole. In Mozambique, the Resistencia Nacional Mocambicana (RENAMO) was beholden first to white-dominated Rhodesia, then the Afrikaner South African regime, as these countries provided RENAMO necessary material support against the Mozambican government.[6] Among rebel groups, it is secessionists for whom international recognition is essential to the achievement of their political aims. Secessionists like those in Aceh who fought (unsuccessfully) to separate from Indonesia recognize that "because membership in [the nation-state] system is conditional upon recognition by its other members, separatist movements are compelled to seek support from other nation-states."[7] Even if secessionists such as those governing Somaliland today successfully exercise control over the territory they claim, this control is limited in its effect without international recognition. Because Somaliland is not an internationally recognized state, it does not, for example, have the legal right to defend itself against incursions from its (also-secessionist) neighbor Puntland, nor can it negotiate directly with foreign banks; these limitations constrain Somaliland's sovereignty on several dimensions.[8]

In addition to the fact that secessionists require international recognition more than other types of rebel groups, the climb to recognition is much steeper for secessionists than for nonsecessionists.[9] It is much harder to achieve recognition for an entirely new state than it is to achieve recognition for a new government in an existing state. Secessionists are well aware of this fact.

The international community's criteria for new membership in the club of states have changed over time. In the distant past, would-be states had to fight for recognition, and territorial boundaries between states were, to at least some extent, a result of these fights.[10] The international community then laid out specific criteria for statehood in the 1934 Montevideo Convention on the Rights and Duties of States. Its criteria for statehood include: (a) a permanent population; (b) a defined territory; (c) a government; and (d) the capacity to enter into relations with other states.[11] More recently, groups such as the European Union have extended this list, requiring also proof of democracy and respect for human rights before admission to EU membership.[12]

While recognition policy is a complex mosaic whose pieces vary from country to country, a brief description of the United Kingdom's recognition policy helps illustrate the distinction between the recognition of new governments and the recognition of new states. Until 1980, the UK would recognize governments—that is to say, new regimes of existing states, including those that came to power via coups d'état or revolution—if they held effective control over the state's territory, and if this control was firmly established and expected to continue.[13] This policy, however, led to negative political ramifications for the British, such as when, in 1979, they recognized autocratic and unsavory regimes led by Pol Pot in Cambodia and Jerry Rawlings in Ghana, who came to power via coups d'état, both of which technically met the above criteria.[14] Thus, in 1980, the British changed their policy to recognize states, rather than governments.[15] The implication is that recognition of the state continues, and requires no further action on the part of the British government, when a new government—even an unpleasant one—is installed. This shift provided political cover lacking under the previous policy.

The UK's bar for recognizing a new state is considerably higher. In addition to meeting the Montevideo criteria for statehood described above, the British government requires that the would-be state not be in violation of any UN resolutions, respect the UN charter and basic principles of international law, guarantee the rights of minorities, accept commitments regarding disarmament and regional stability, and commit to a raft of other human rights obligations.[16] The British criteria appear to reflect a consensus within the international community: it is no longer sufficient to demonstrate effective territorial control; rather, to be recognized today, new states must also conform to standards set by the Western liberal order.[17] These standards are quite different from and more demanding than those laid out for even implicit recognition of new regimes of existing states. The international community in general appears more willing to accept political alterations than cartographic ones. Knowing that theirs is the more difficult path to follow, secessionists understand that courting the international community is critical to their chances of success.

Because membership and good standing in the international community are, at least ostensibly, linked to behavior that is acceptable to the international community, groups that seek international recognition are likely to try to be on their best behavior, at least until they achieve their goal of international recognition as a new state. Consistent with this claim, Hyeran Jo attributes the decision by the Sudan People's Liberation Movement (SPLM) to stop using child soldiers in 2010 to their secessionist aspirations: "The group wanted to shape their reputation and bolster their legitimacy."[18] And Bridget Coggins finds that secessionist groups in particular were decreasingly likely to employ terrorism in the wake of September 11, 2001, as the international community rallied around the United States and, concurrently, against terrorism.[19]

Precisely because they have strong incentives to send positive signals to the international community, secessionists pay attention to more than the laws of war when fighting their wars. In fact, it is probably easiest for secessionists to learn—and abide by—publicly stated preferences of the international community that are contemporaneous with their conflict, but not necessarily codified in international humanitarian law, especially when these statements are directed specifically at them. Two such kinds of statements from the international community are particularly common: those opposing unilateral declarations of independence as issued by secessionists, and those supporting the use of formal peace agreements to conclude civil wars. For example, the UN Security Council deplored the declaration of independence and attempted secession by the Turkish Republic of Northern Cyprus in 1983, "consider[ing] the declaration . . . as legally invalid and call[ing] for its withdrawal."[20] In an illustration of the second kind of statement, the international community strongly pushed the Sierra Leonean government to negotiate with the Revolutionary United Force (RUF) rebels, even though the government could have won militarily.[21] Thus, secessionists should be attentive not only to the body of formal international law governing wartime conduct, but also to these broader norms of war propagated by the international community.

As David Armitage shows, the designation of a conflict as an international versus civil war has serious implications for the application of the laws of war. The first codified law of land warfare—the 1864 Geneva Convention on the protection of the wounded—was assumed *not* to apply to civil wars.[22] The application of the laws of naval warfare was contested during the US Civil War, a key question being whether said laws could apply in a civil war context.[23] More recently, an International Criminal Tribunal for the former Yugoslavia (ICTY) ruling on whether and when "the Bosnian war had mutated from an international war to a civil war" was used by defendant Dusko Tadíc to argue that the court "had no jurisdiction over his actions because the statute creating the tribunal applied only to international armed conflicts."[24]

For much of the rest of this book, international recognition remains an important independent variable, but one that will often be in the background. The starkest line can be drawn between states—which already possess international recognition—and non-state actors. Because the empirical chapters treat interstate and civil wars separately, however, I do not discuss the role of recognition in my analyses of interstate war. But this issue resurfaces in the context of civil wars, where we observe variation both between rebel groups and the governments they fight, as well as amongst rebel groups, only some of which seek international recognition.

The Formalities of War

Belligerents that have and do not require additional international recognition can better afford to evade the laws of war than those that lack and seek international recognition. Belligerents that do not have, but require, international recognition should, by contrast, seek to engage with the laws of war because they reflect the preferences of the international community, which these rebels seek to please. Unrecognized rebels also should seek to abide by preferences expressed by the international community in war-related areas, even if these preferences are uncodified. In the context of armed conflict, belligerents can signal their intent to evade or engage the international laws and norms of war via their use of traditional war formalities. Use of these war formalities is equivalent to an acknowledgment that the belligerents are in a state of war, during which the laws of war clearly apply. In the following chapters, I focus on trends in the use of three such formalities: declarations of war, declarations of independence, and peace treaties.

I use signaling by means of war formalities as my key dependent variable in exploring the consequences of the proliferation of the laws of war, which is my primary independent variable. Although the proliferation of IHL documented in chapter 1 might suggest that this book focuses on compliance with the laws of war, this book is not, primarily, about compliance. Compliance with international law in general and international humanitarian law in specific is an extremely complicated subject, as previous scholars have demonstrated.[25] The evidence suggests variously that democracies are more, or less,[26] likely to comply with the laws of war than nondemocracies; that violations are likely to occur earlier, or later, in a war;[27] and that ratifying the laws of war increases, or decreases, compliance.[28] Battlefield imperatives compete with political ones and there exists considerable variation in compliance across issue areas within the laws of war. Some issue areas are more subject to centralized control, and therefore less prone to violation, than others.[29] I expect the proliferation of IHL to affect compliance, but I also expect that this effect will be an indirect one, as discussed below.

To drive home this point, consider the relationship between ratifying IHL treaties and complying with the laws of war. Unlike many other issue areas covered by international law, such as international trade or human rights, the obligation to comply with IHL is limited to wartime. States typically sign and ratify IHL treaties when they are not at war (in fact, many of these treaties are developed in response to, rather than in anticipation of, major wars). While states may have some sense of which future opponents they may face, and under what circumstances, those expectations are generally uncertain. Given that states ratify IHL treaties not knowing precisely what wars they will fight, it is not surprising that the effect of ratification is often overwhelmed by strategic imperatives when it comes to compliance with IHL.

States ratify IHL treaties not knowing what wars they will fight, but they go to war knowing what treaties they have ratified. As the number of treaties goes up, belligerents' willingness to put themselves in a situation where there is no ambiguity as to their obligation to comply should also vary, depending on the net benefit of compliance. The use of war formalities such as declarations of war eliminates any ambiguity as to the applicability of the laws of war. Notably, these same mechanisms operate differently in the context of civil war, where rebel groups do not ratify IHL treaties, and there is little to no time passed between acquiring knowledge of IHL requirements and application of those requirements.

The proliferation of the laws of war should therefore have a more direct effect on the use of the formalities of war than on compliance with these laws, particularly in interstate war. Compliance may be as difficult to predict for belligerents as it is for scholars. But by invoking the formalities of war, belligerents step over a bright line and thus trigger their obligation to comply and in so doing, send signals to the international community. States that declare war are unequivocally bound to comply with international humanitarian law. Rebel groups that declare independence do so with the purpose of sending an unambiguous message to the international community. Belligerents that sign a peace treaty often do so at the urging of the international community—especially today—and also do so knowing that a peace treaty may open a window to liability for any violations of IHL that they may have committed during the conflict. For example, the September 2015 peace agreement between the Fuerzas Armadas Revolucionarios Colombia (FARC) and the Colombian government was negotiated under the shadow of an ongoing investigation of the conflict by the International Criminal Court (ICC). The ICC prosecutor issued a statement after the agreement was announced, noting "with optimism that the agreement excludes the granting of any amnesty for war crimes and crimes against humanity, and is designed, amongst others, to end impunity for the most serious crimes."[30] The strategy involved in deciding whether to engage or evade the formalities of war is inherently political, while the strategy involved in deciding whether to comply with the laws of war is both political and military. Sometimes—as in cases where individual soldiers have discretion as to compliance or violation—compliance is a multi-layered process very challenging to analyze in the aggregate. I therefore expect that the effects of the proliferation of the laws of war will be most visible at the level of the formalities of war rather than compliance.

Trends in the use of war formalities over the past two centuries help introduce four puzzles that comprise the subjects of chapters 3 and 5 concerning interstate wars, and chapters 6 and 8 concerning civil wars:

1. State participants in interstate wars have stopped issuing formal declarations of war since the 1949 Geneva Conventions. Why? [Chapter 3]
2. Also since the Geneva era, interstate wars are decreasingly likely to conclude with formal peace treaties. Why? [Chapter 5]
3. Secessionist rebel groups are decreasingly likely to declare independence since the founding of the United Nations in 1945. Why? [Chapter 6]
4. Civil wars are increasingly likely to conclude with formal peace treaties in the UN era. Why? [Chapter 8]

I argue that the answers to these questions are found in the proliferation of the laws of war and, more generally, in changes in the attitude of the international community toward the regulation of armed conflict. As the laws of war have proliferated in number and changed in character, states—the actors that require and desire relatively little additional recognition from the international community—fighting interstate wars are decreasingly likely to use the formalities of war. Declaring war and concluding peace treaties puts states in a position without any legal wiggle room as to their obligations to comply with the laws of war. As there are more, and more restrictive, laws on the books, flexibility becomes increasingly valued.

At the same time, certain rebel groups are especially attuned to the preferences of the international community. As discussed above, this will be particularly true for secessionist rebels. The international community has signaled its increasing aversion to unilateral declarations of independence since the creation of the United Nations in 1945. The objection to declarations of independence is twofold. First, secessionism itself has historically been frowned upon. One of the founding principles of the United Nations is the preservation of territorial integrity. Territorial integrity can be challenged from within, via secessionism, and from without, via territorial conquest. The framers of the UN charter decided to privilege the stability of the international system over self-determination claims, and thus prohibited territorial aggression and strongly discouraged secessionism. Second, and related, one exception to this rule was for consensual secessionism, such as the nonviolent dissolution of Czechoslovakia in 1993. Unilateral declarations of independence challenge both these norms, as they represent the statements of secessionists engaged in movements disapproved of by their central governments.

Two early UN-era cases demonstrate this point. The Katangan secessionist movement begun in the 1960s was received uniformly negatively by the international community, which rallied around the newly independent Democratic Republic of Congo. UN Security Council Resolution 169 clearly stated the Security Council's grave concern regarding "the continuing deterioration of the situation in the Congo and at the prevalence of conditions which seriously imperil peace and order and the unity and *territorial integrity* of the Congo."[31] Similarly, the Biafran attempt to secede from Nigeria in 1967 was met with hostility from the international community; in a "Resolution on the Situation in Nigeria," the Organization of African Unity "reiterated their condemnation of Secession in any member states."[32] The international community's distaste for unilateral declarations of independence extended through the dissolution of Yugoslavia at the end of the Cold War, when clear signals opposing unilateral declarations of independence were sent to Croatia and Slovenia, among others. While not linked formally to international law (for reasons discussed in chapter 6) in the same way that declarations of war are linked formally to IHL in the interstate war context, declarations of independence can be considered part of an emerging customary *jus ad bellum* for civil wars.

Likewise, the international community has expressed, increasingly, a preference for negotiated settlements, rather than military stalemates or victories, as a means to conclude civil wars. For example, Myanmar has been on the receiving end of international pressure for democratization as well as peace negotiations with the various rebel groups challenging the Burmese government.[33] More generally, Jessica Stanton finds that "the United Nations Security Council issued resolutions calling for a halt to fighting in more than half the wars that took place from 1989–2010. In many of these resolutions, the Security Council also demanded an end to violations of humanitarian law."[34]

My argument suggests that the proliferation of the laws of war has indirect effects on compliance, and these are discussed in detail in chapters 4 and 7. If states are increasingly reluctant to issue formal declarations of war because they fear being held responsible for any violations of increasingly broad IHL, we should expect that when we do observe declarations of war, compliance will be high. Conversely, if states expect to violate the laws of war at the outset, their likelihood of declaring war will be lower. And insofar as rebel groups in general and secessionists in particular are eager to please the international community when it comes to declarations of independence and peace treaties in civil wars, they also should be more compliant—compared to other rebel groups whose political aims do not require the same extent of support from the international community—with international humanitarian laws such as those prohibiting the targeting of civilians.

Why, when, and how belligerents engage with the formalities of war is tied to the proliferation of the laws and norms of war. I outline the costs and benefits of complying with these changing laws of war in the next section of this chapter. My claim is that belligerents anticipate the costs and consequences of compliance and noncompliance with the laws of war when deciding whether to use war formalities. As the net benefit of complying with the laws of war and the preferences of the international community have changed, so has the likelihood that belligerents will use declarations of war, declarations of independence, and peace treaties. But we should expect variation in the nature of this change depending on the degree of international recognition belligerents hold, and seek. I next analyze states' response to the proliferation of IHL, and then turn to how rebel groups engaged in civil war have reacted to the altered landscape of international community preferences regarding both *jus ad bellum* and *jus in bello*.

State Response to the Proliferation of IHL

Notwithstanding today's growing legal restrictions on the conduct of war, the proliferation of codified international humanitarian law is not the main reason why states are less likely to engage in conflict.[35] But it does place constraints on the way states fight.

From an international legal perspective, international humanitarian law places considerable restrictions on how states may comport themselves in war. They may not, for example, target civilians. They must treat prisoners of war well. They may not loot. From the perspective of states using military means to pursue political aims, these restrictions can appear counterproductive—if, for example, civilians are located in a critical strategic area, or if a belligerent lacks the capacity to treat prisoners of war well. Given the lack of strong, centralized monitoring and enforcement, the consequences of violating IHL are uncertain. Thus, states find themselves in a strange space—international humanitarian laws, while increasingly numerous, operate under a weak legal regime, but a legal regime nonetheless.

As the costs of complying with the obligations of international humanitarian law have risen over time, states are increasingly likely to make legal arguments that rationalize circumventing these obligations. If states can argue that the law does not apply to them, they limit their material costs and potentially their legal risks. Below, I lay out the costs and benefits of compliance and noncompliance with today's international humanitarian law to make the point that the proliferation of IHL has led to higher standards for compliance that states may decide are impossible to meet.

The Calculus of Compliance

In considering whether to use war formalities, states weigh the benefits of compliance with the laws of war against costs because using war formalities is a much more immediate tie to the obligation to comply than the ratification of treaties. As opposed to the war-specific decision to use formalities of war, IHL treaties may have been ratified decades prior to any given war. The costs of compliance with these treaties reside in two dimensions. First, in order to comply with the laws governing belligerent conduct during war, states must pay the bureaucratic cost of training their military to observe the laws of war. Such training is costly even for the most advanced militaries. Second, by agreeing to eliminate or limit use of specific military tools or strategies, states may deprive themselves of battlefield advantage. Weapons in which states have already invested may lie unused, and certain strategies—such as targeting civilians—become unavailable. Additionally, there are also costs of noncompliance. That is to say, if states are clearly obliged to comply with IHL, they must consider what happens if they fail to meet those obligations. If the combined costs of compliance and noncompliance are sufficiently high, states may try to argue that their obligation to comply is, in fact, limited.

States must also consider the benefits of complying with international humanitarian law. This body of international law exists for many reasons, among them the protection it affords to civilians as well as combatants. States may prefer a world with international humanitarian law to one without it. But as IHL has changed over time, one must ask whether the compliance cost-benefit analysis is altered as well.

Bureaucratic Costs   When US infantry were deployed to Iraq in 2003, soldiers carried with them cards stating the rules of engagement: the conditions under which it was acceptable to engage Iraqi forces.[36] When US troops set up camps for enemy prisoners of war they were under instructions to provide laundry facilities and to provide for their prisoners' dietary needs, especially those based on religion, in accordance with the third 1949 Geneva Convention.[37] All aerial targeting decisions were vetted by a judge advocate-general for compliance with international humanitarian law, which meant avoiding targeting civilians, medical institutions, and cultural property; the list of targets not to be struck was "in the thousands."[38] The bureaucratic effort that went into compliance was enormous. Soldiers around the world spent weeks of training time on compliance with IHL.[39] The military contractor Halliburton alone received $28 million for the construction of prisoner-of-war camps in Iraq.[40]

According to one US brigadier general, the US military spends "at least hundreds of millions [of dollars on *jus in bello* compliance], regardless of how one counts."[41] I use the US case as an example because the US military is more able to bear these costs than most other militaries. Data from the Correlates of War (COW) project suggest that average annual

US military expenditures in the post-Geneva era are at least an order of magnitude greater than those of any of its nearest competitors, including Russia/USSR, China, the United Kingdom, Saudi Arabia, and India.[42] Thus we can imagine the relative cost to other militaries of attempting to comply with the laws that govern conduct during wartime.

Despite these efforts, US compliance with IHL during the 2003 invasion of Iraq was far from perfect. Even conservative estimates put civilian deaths through 2010 at over 110,000.[43] And while collateral damage in wartime is not illegal, it is incumbent upon belligerents to try to avoid causing collateral damage; it is not clear that the United States took sufficient measures to accomplish this goal.[44] The scandal of prisoner abuse at the infamous Abu Ghraib prison in April 2004 grabbed headlines for months and did enormous harm to US standing in the world.[45] Failing to prevent the looting of the Baghdad Museum constituted a clear violation of the laws of war regarding protection of cultural property.[46]

What more should or could the United States have done to comply with the laws of war? One could argue that the nature of the obligations attendant on belligerent states today is such that compliance is virtually impossible, and that the additional costs the United States would have had to bear to comply would hinder warfighting to the extent that war itself would be impossible. Regardless, this case illustrates that even imperfect compliance can be extremely costly in bureaucratic and financial terms.

Strategic Costs   The strategic costs of complying with *jus in bello* are also considerable. One primary strategic cost of compliance is that certain categories of weapons are no longer permitted on the battlefield. Beginning in 1868, international law has prohibited the use of certain explosive projectiles, asphyxiating and poisonous gases, expanding bullets, mines, incendiary weapons and, more recently, cluster munitions. The 1972 Biological Weapons Convention and 1993 Chemical Weapons Convention, respectively, prohibit the use of chemical and biological weapons (CBW) in armed conflict. While the military utility of such weapons is somewhat doubtful, these conventions as well as others limit state arsenals in ways that force reorientation of military operations and strategy.

Compliance with the laws of war regarding the protection of cultural property also can be challenging. During the 1991 Persian Gulf War, for example, the Iraqi Air Force used the temple of Ur as a shield for military aircraft parked nearby; the MiGs were safe from coalition targeting as a result of their proximity to a major cultural landmark.[47] Thirteen years later, Iraqi Ba'athists took cover near the Imam Ali Shrine in Najaf, confronting coalition forces with a trade-off between achieving a military objective and protecting cultural property.[48]

The laws regarding treatment of civilians present similar challenges. NATO's policy of telling its pilots to maintain high altitude during daytime missions in the Kosovo War of 1999—a policy geared toward force protection—undermined pilots' abilities to distinguish civilians from combatants and resulted in, among other errors, the unintentional killing of a convoy of Albanian refugees by a NATO pilot who was flying, per orders, at 15,000 feet.[49] A policy more focused on avoiding collateral damage would likely have recommended lower altitudes for NATO pilots. International humanitarian law appears to be moving in this direction; the International Criminal Tribunal for the former Yugoslavia (ICTY) ruled in 2011 that an error rate in artillery targeting in excess of 5 percent would make an attack illegal. Along these lines, Richard Betts criticizes what he viewed as an overabundance of legal advice in this war; "NATO's lawyers," he argues, "became its tactical commanders."[50]

Finally, the most important nonbureaucratic cost paid by militaries attempting to comply with *jus in bello* is that of lives lost. If soldiers are deployed in tactically suboptimal ways in order to comply with IHL, force protection becomes more challenging. Particularly in counterinsurgencies, it is almost inevitable that a state's compliance with IHL will lead to greater casualties and fatalities on its own side. As a captain in the Australian Army puts it:

> There is absolutely no doubt that LOAC [law of armed conflict] is to some extent inconvenient (in a realpolitik sense). But this is precisely the point— LOAC is meant to be both contextually sensible and inconvenient. This is how it achieves its aims. However, the flip side of this is that compliance with LOAC does cost own lives—no debate. And although this is simply accepted as one of the costs of fighting in accordance with the law, and is a cost which all law abiding military forces solemnly accept as inevitable and necessary, it is a compliance cost nonetheless.[51]

The Costs of Noncompliance

Unlike domestic and even some other international law, *jus in bello*—
the law that applies during wartime—has historically lacked enforcement
mechanisms. Given the apparent lack of legal sanction for violation, why
would states care about complying with *jus in bello*? Below, I identify
three costs of noncompliance with *jus in bello* that would be borne by
states that, having clearly put themselves in a realm where codified *jus in
bello* applied unambiguously, proceeded to violate the laws of war.

Liability Costs   Legal liability for violation of the laws of war could
be borne internationally or domestically. Internationally, Article 8 of the
1998 Rome Statute, which established the International Criminal Court
(ICC), details the lists of prohibited behaviors according to international
humanitarian law, distinguishing war crimes from other violations. The
list of war crimes includes willful killing, torture, unlawful confinement,
and extensive destruction of property. The ICC follows the principle of
complementarity, whereby national governments with the judicial capacity and willingness to investigate any possible war crimes committed by
their citizens have the right to try them domestically; but it retains jurisdiction to indict alleged war criminals itself if those conditions are not
satisfied. Placing soldiers and policymakers in the realm of the law of
war also subjects them to criminal prosecution. This concern has driven
the US decision not to become a party to the Rome Statute. Even without being a party to the statute, however, states may still be considered
subject to the court's jurisdiction, leaving those belligerents that are concerned about issues of culpability for war crimes with few options.[52]
Cases may be referred to the ICC prosecutor via three primary routes:
states party to the statues may request an investigation; the prosecutor
herself may initiate an investigation if she deems domestic judicial procedures insufficient; or the UN Security Council (UNSC) may refer a case
to the ICC. This last route all but guarantees that only two of the permanent five veto-wielding members of the UNSC could be referred for an
investigation, because the other three are not parties to the Rome Statute.[53] Although NGOs such as Human Rights Watch do not have the
power of referral, they may send information to the Office of the Prosecutor to inform her about possible war crimes. In fact, the international

nongovernment organization (INGO) community appears to be mobilizing to operate along these lines by creating a possible parallel fourth referral track.[54]

The ICC's relatively recent founding coupled with the decline in interstate war since 1945 means that the ICC would not have been able to hear
many cases related to interstate war. The International Court of Justice
(ICJ), on the other hand, was founded in 1945, just as the use of war
formalities in interstate war were declining. Since its founding, twenty-
three cases that invoke IHL have been brought before the court. Only
one—Pakistan v. India—pertained to a clear-cut interstate war. Of these
twenty-three cases, the court found it lacked jurisdiction in eleven cases,
and an additional five cases were discontinued by the applicant. The court
ruled in favor of the applicant in two cases, both of which involved a
violation of maritime mining law. In four cases, three of which pertained
to civil wars, the court ruled in favor of the respondent; two of these
cases were about genocide, and two about the disposition or extradition
of alleged war criminals. The final case is pending. As discussed below,
the only interstate war case in which states were at risk of bearing liability
costs for having violated the laws of war was one where the states in question had formally declared war against each other, making bringing the
case to the ICJ that much easier.

In the domestic realm, many national military codes contain provisions
for violation of *jus in bello*. The punishments meted out by militaries to
their own members can be more severe than sentences rendered by civilian courts. For example, the military codes of countries like the United
States and Nigeria can include the death penalty as a possible sentence,
while the International Criminal Court, International Criminal Tribunal
for the former Yugoslavia (ICTY) and International Criminal Tribunal
for Rwanda (ICTR) do not. In certain cases, the scope and applicability
of these codes are limited to times clearly identified as war. For example,
Section 802 Article 2(10) of the US Uniform Code of Military Justice
states that the code applies to "persons serving with or accompanying
an armed force in the field," but only "in time of war."[55] To the extent
that *jus in bello* as it is codified in multilateral treaties is incorporated
domestically into national military justice systems, states may have an
additional reason to avoid stepping over the bright line into an official
state of war.

Domestic Political Costs   Contrary to the conventional wisdom that voters—at least US voters—tend not to care about foreign policy,[56] recent and innovative scholarship on this issue suggests the opposite. Eyal Benvenisti and Amichai Cohen suggest that domestic support for IHL is likely driven by concerns over how one's own soldiers and citizens may be treated in war, and thus may rest in part on a logic of reciprocity.[57] What is more, voters and policymakers appear to value compliance with international law for its own sake. Using a mix of field and survey experiments, Michael Tomz and Geoffrey Wallace each find that respondents were less likely to support policies that violated international law compared to policies that were in compliance with, or had no apparent bearing on, international law.[58] Wallace also found that the preference to abide by laws relating to treatment of prisoners of war was directly related to the respondents' perceptions of the precision of the law; respondents told that the United States had signed an international agreement that "did not allow the use of torture under any circumstances against prisoners" were fifteen percent less likely to support torture than respondents told that the terms of the agreement "might, or might not, allow for the use of torture against prisoners."[59]

Even if voters prefer that their governments not violate international law, these preferences might be overridden by other concerns when it comes time to cast ballots. Tomz, however, found that the preference for compliance outweighed a preference to avoid negative material consequences that might ensue as a result of compliance.[60] This result conforms with a broader literature on (primarily US) public opinion and foreign policy that shows that public opinion regarding foreign policy can be identified, and that this opinion can influence votes and, in turn, policy.[61] As part of the same project, Tomz also found that British policymakers shared these preferences for complying with international law. Although such survey results have not been definitively linked to electoral consequences, they lend support to the notion that IHL violations may impose political costs electorally and reputationally.

Reputational Costs   Among states that value their reputations as law-abiding citizens of the international community, violations of *jus in bello* could carry severe reputational costs, either perceived or actual. One strategy to mitigate such costs might be to create ambiguity as to whether the

state's actions actually oblige compliance. In equilibrium, we should expect that states tend not to bear these reputational costs. They should look
down the game tree and do what they can to avoid culpability if they anticipate not being able or willing to comply with IHL. Or, if they have already put themselves in a position where they are unequivocally obliged to
comply, we should expect that they will avoid the most flagrant violations.

History provides at least one example of behavior that illustrates reputation costs via a state having left the equilibrium path. Following India's
intervention in then–East Pakistan, Pakistan issued a formal declaration
of war against India on November 22, 1971. India responded in kind
two weeks later.[62] Although both parties were mainly compliant with *jus
in bello* for the duration of the Bangladesh War, the Indians were clearly
noncompliant with rules relating to treatment of prisoners of war: they
refused to repatriate tens of thousands of Pakistani prisoners of war in a
timely manner, which was a violation of the 1949 Geneva Conventions.
Instead, they effectively held them hostage in order to gain leverage at the
peace table.

After fighting ceased and a year of fruitless talks led to a breakdown
in negotiations, Pakistan brought a case against India before the International Court of Justice (ICJ), charging violation of the Third 1949
Geneva Convention. Within three months, India and Pakistan had quickly
resolved all but a few hundred of the most egregious of the POW cases.[63]
India's quick concession in the face of a trial at the ICJ was exactly the
outcome Pakistan had hoped to achieve; Pakistan believed that "bringing
the dispute before the Court would focus attention on the Indian government in a way that it would find intolerable."[64] The potential cost to
India was reputational loss in the eyes of the international community.
The Bangladesh War had been an opportunity for the Indians to take
the moral high ground against a persistent foe; the Indians argued that
their intervention in Pakistan's civil war was justified in order to prevent
further atrocities against civilians in East Pakistan. Exposing India's noncompliance with *jus in bello* in a forum such as the ICJ would have eroded
this high ground, and the Indians knew it. As a self-proclaimed leader of
the nonaligned movement and champion of international law and equity,
India faced a real reputational cost were its noncompliance to be exposed
during an ICJ trial. Having issued a declaration of war against Pakistan
made India's situation all the more pressing. Without the declaration, the

Indians might have been able to argue nonapplicability of the Geneva Conventions, thus mitigating the reputational costs of the lawsuit; indeed, knowing this, the Pakistanis might not have filed the suit at all. In fact, however, India could in no way argue that the Geneva Conventions did not apply, because it had already declared war against Pakistan.

The Benefits of Compliance

Compliance with *jus in bello* generates benefits as well as costs. A lawless battlefield does not serve belligerents well; those fighting on both sides would prefer to have rules govern the treatment of prisoners of war, treatment of civilians, and conduct on the high seas. Moreover, a military that did not adhere to law could quickly become a domestic liability, even a domestic threat.[65] It is perhaps for these reasons that, even prior to today's plethora of codified laws of war, *jus in bello* existed as part of customary international law and was frequently agreed on an ad hoc basis through bilateral arrangements. One efficiency of today's body of codified IHL is that it does not require renegotiation prior to or during each war (although laws have often been revised postwar), and it is meant to allow belligerents to coordinate on acceptable comportment during war.[66]

Compliance as a Net Cost

For states fighting interstate wars, while the benefits of complying with international humanitarian law have remained relatively constant over time, the costs have risen dramatically. As monitoring of compliance has improved, the likelihood of bearing the costs of noncompliance has risen as well. For example, Seymour Hersh of the *New Yorker* broke the story of US abuse of Iraqi prisoners at Abu Ghraib.[67] As a result, support for President George W. Bush's prosecution of the war in Iraq declined to an all-time low in May 2004 after the scandal broke, congressional hearings were held, eleven US soldiers were sent to jail, and local Iraqi opposition to the US presence in their country increased dramatically.[68] A coalition of NGOs published a book that exposed abuses committed by the Hissène Habré regime in Chad in the 1980s. As a result, Habré not only was removed from power, but is currently standing trial for crimes against humanity, war crimes, and torture before the Extraordinary African Chambers in Senegal.[69] The increased scrutiny of soldiers and policymakers may give them greater incentives to avoid placing themselves in situations where they are unambiguously obliged to comply with IHL. When combined, the bureaucratic and strategic costs of war, the costs of noncompliance, and greater media attention to breaches of *jus in bello* place today's belligerents under intense examination. States will, as a result, seek ways to lessen the costs associated with any potential noncompliance and, thus, the consequences if their missteps were to be seen. With the increasing number—and changing character—of codified laws of war, the costs of admitting to being in a state of war that would unequivocally oblige a state to comply with the laws of war may today be perceived to outstrip the benefits.

Non-state Actors and the Laws of War

Like states involved in interstate wars, rebel groups in civil wars must also make a cost-benefit calculation regarding whether to comply with international humanitarian law. These same rebel groups also pay attention to norms of war supported by the international community that lie outside the set of codified laws of war discussed in chapter 1. Rebel group calculations will vary dramatically depending on the political aims and military capacity of the group in question. Secessionist rebel groups—those that seek an independent state as their ultimate political goal—will be most likely to pay heed to, and to comply with, the laws and norms of war. This is because, while these rebels face many of the same costs of compliance as states, the perceived potential benefits are greater; indeed, the benefits are increasing with the proliferation of the laws and norms of war. The number of secessionists engaged in civil war is also on the rise. These combined historical dynamics—an increase in codified IHL, a new set of norms of war in the UN era, and an increase in secessionism itself—produce a very different outcome in civil wars than in interstate wars. Whereas states in interstate wars, I have argued, react to the increase in codified IHL by trying to evade their formal obligations to comply, we may expect secessionists in civil wars to actively engage the laws of war as part of a strategy to gain international recognition.

Rebel Group War Aims and Compliance with the Laws of War

Civil wars are empirically and analytically messy. Considering them in terms of ideal types can offer initial purchase on understanding how they are begun, fought, and ended. I propose a fourfold—albeit admittedly incomplete—distinction among civil wars: revolutionary (or center-based) conflicts; resource wars; religionist wars; and ethnic or secessionist conflicts. These labels also correspond to types of rebel groups, and to some extent identify the aims of the various rebel groups.

Revolutionary rebels typically seek to overthrow the government. Examples include the Syrian National Council/Free Syrian Army in the current Syrian civil war, the Farabundo Martí para la Liberacíon Nacional (FMLN) in 1980s El Salvador, and the various perpetrators of coups in Cote d'Ivoire from the late 1990s to the mid-2000s. In resource wars, rebels seek to line their own pockets with the proceeds from selling commodities such as "blood diamonds" or illicit drugs on the black market. Although these wars are not necessarily precipitated by the presence of lootable resources, the war economies they produce tend to prolong conflict, as in the case of the National Union for the Total Independence of Angola (UNITA), which earned billions from illegal diamond sales during its war against the Angolan government in the 1990s. Indeed, the Angolan civil war lasted as long as it did in large part because both sides were funded through sales of oil as well as diamonds.[70]

Religionist rebel groups seek to remake the world—or at least one part of it—along theocratic lines. Examples include: the Lord's Resistance Army, which has been operating in northern Uganda since the late 1980s; Boko Haram, operating in Nigeria since 2002; and, the Islamic State, which declared a caliphate in parts of Syria and Iraq in 2014. While recent religionists have grabbed headlines, religionist rebel groups are not a new phenomenon. The Yellow Cliff Revolt of 1866 was fought to defend members of a group following the practices of an occultist and magician against the Chinese government.[71] Around the turn of the twentieth century, the Brazilian government fought to regain control over its Canudos region, parts of which had been taken over by a religious leader who sought to create a theocratic state founded on the belief that a Portuguese Crusader king would rise from the dead to vindicate his followers.[72] There are, of course, other recent examples alongside those of the

Lord's Resistance Army, Boko Haram, and the Islamic State. A religious cult launched a major rebellion in Kano, Nigeria, in 1980, hailing their leader as the latest prophet of Islam and believing that they were invincible against modern weaponry even though they were poorly armed.[73] These examples notwithstanding, it is important to distinguish between religious and religionist rebel groups. For example, the Front Islamique du Salut (FIS) was an Islamist rebel group that used brutal means to fight the Algerian government in the 1990s.[74] But FIS aims were to overthrow and replace the central government; they did not seek to replace the existing structure of sovereignty with a new one where sovereignty emerges from the divine.

Ethnic or secessionist rebel groups generally seek to redress local grievances against the central government. For example, in the early phase of the north-south civil war in Sudan, the Sudan People's Liberation Movement/Army (SPLM/A) sought, first, regional autonomy and the overthrow of the government, prior to adopting the aim of secession that eventually led to the independence of South Sudan. The Zapatistas have fought, on and off since 1994, for independence from Mexico; Chechnya seeks independence from Russia.

Some rebel groups fall into multiple categories. The secessionist Acehnese declared independence from Indonesia in part because they sought to control the lucrative natural gas industry located in Aceh.[75] The Free Syrian Army/Syrian National Council has stated the goal of overthrowing the Assad government, from which it is divided along sectarian lines. The Revolutionary United Front (RUF) in Sierra Leone sought to replace the central government, but also relied heavily on illegal trade in diamonds for its financing.

The differing political goals held by rebel groups are reflected in their military and diplomatic strategies. Revolutionary rebels must win on the battlefield—with or without help from outside—to succeed in their claim. Resource warriors may need only to perpetuate conflict. Religionist rebels often reject the international community, along with the normative restrictions on means and ends that it promotes. Secessionists must secure not only military victory, but also international recognition, in order to achieve their political goals. It is this distinction that sets secessionists apart from other types of rebel groups in their relationship with the laws of war.

Unlike other types of rebel groups, secessionists must care about their reputations with the international community. Even if they have acquired effective control over their territory and exercise de facto sovereignty, only the international community can give them what they seek: de jure recognition, statehood status, and attendant benefits.[76] Thus, it is critical that secessionists be able to signal both their willingness and their capacity to be good citizens of the international community.[77] Complying with the laws of war helps accomplish this aim.

A candidate for statehood ought, in the eyes of the international community, to be able to control its military and territory, as specified in the Montevideo Convention on the Rights and Duties of States. To be sure, these traditional requirements for statehood have been frequently violated in recent years, with the emergence and recognition of a number of very weak states.[78] But for states that would like to extend international recognition, secessionists with strong capacity are still preferred to weak ones.[79] Clearly stating and enforcing a policy of compliance with the laws of war helps rebel groups signal such capacity to the international community.[80] For instance, Idean Salehyan, David Siroky, and Reed Wood find that rebels who exercise restraint are more likely to be supported by "democratic countries with strong human rights lobbies."[81]

Importantly, the international community is not the only international audience to whom rebels are playing. All rebel groups—secessionist and not—might prefer to have support from individual states. For instance, the Syrian Free Army today benefits from a supply of arms from the United States, and has appealed for more robust outside aid and intervention. In the early stages of Hezbollah's organizational development, the preferences of its Iranian sponsor were critical to its planning: As Daniel Byman and Sarah Kreps note, "For many years Iranian officials played direct roles on different Hizbollah councils, and the terrorist group professed obeisance to Ayatollah Khomeini, the revolutionary leader of Iran, and incorporated his decisions into their formal decision-making process."[82] Great power patronage can have a significant effect on the success of a rebellion, including secessionism.[83]

There are thus two important distinctions to be made with respect to international audiences and rebel groups. First, potential great or regional power interveners may have different preferences from those of the international community. To the extent that rebels value external patronage over the support of the international community, we might therefore expect the former's preferences to take precedence.[84] This insight highlights a second point on this subject: the assent of the international community is a necessary condition for successful secessionism. In contrast to nonsecessionist rebels such as the Houthi in Yemen, who rely on Iran for support, but may be able to achieve their political aims without the support of the broader international community, secessionists must pay close attention to the preferences of the international community if they are to realize their political aims. Many of the observers of civil conflict empowered to recognize new states value greatly the international normative landscape in which any new state would be operating. Organizations—such as the European Union and the United Nations—that can grant not only recognition but also critical financial aid have clearly stated their commitment to modern humanitarianism on multiple occasions. The 1991 guidelines on the recognition of new states in Eastern Europe and in the Soviet Union, which were adopted at an extraordinary meeting of the Foreign Ministers of the European Community (today the European Union) required new members to respect "the rule of law, democracy, and human rights," as well as to concede that borders "can only be changed by peaceful means and by common agreement."[85] Key features of this landscape include major laws of war.

Secessionists are not the only rebel groups that care about the approval of the international community. Reyko Huang and Hyeran Jo have each argued that legitimacy-seeking groups (including, but not limited to, secessionists) will be most likely to behave in ways acceptable to the international community precisely because they seek support from that community.[86] They define legitimacy-seeking groups as having "future-oriented goals that define their motivations" and the organizational capacity to pursue those goals.[87] In this vein, the African National Congress deposited a declaration of its intention to comply with the Geneva Conventions with the Swiss government long before it gained victory over the Afrikaner regime in South Africa. I agree with Huang and Jo's basic logic, but choose to focus on secessionists as those rebels that, by definition, must seek support from the international community in order to achieve their political aims. But the arguments and evidence provided by Huang and Jo make the important point that the claim made here may extend beyond secessionist rebel groups to those who seek political support from broad domestic or international constituencies, such as the so-called "moderate" Syrian opposition—center-seeking rebels courting the public support of several of the permanent five members of the United Nations Security Council.

The Calculus of Compliance

Because I expect the calculus of compliance to be most salient for secessionists, I focus on this set of rebel groups in developing theoretically the relationship among the proliferation of the laws of war, the use of war formalities, and the costs and benefits of complying with IHL in civil war. I begin by asking: what is the cost-benefit analysis for secessionists in choosing (or attempting) to comply with the laws of war? A first point to be made is that secessionists may be more likely to comply with the laws of war simply because they are more aware of international law than are nonsecessionists, for reasons I explain below. Second, many of the costs that states must bear in order to comply with the laws of war must also be borne by rebel groups. Accomplishing these tasks, however, may be somewhat cheaper for rebel groups than for states; thus, the costs of compliance are perhaps declining, or at least not increasing at the same rate as they are for states. Third, however, the benefits of complying with IHL have been increasing over time for secessionists, while they have been stable for states.

Why Secessionists Know the Laws of War   While it could be the case that secessionists comply with international humanitarian law without being aware of the law itself, it would be difficult to argue in that case that their compliance was driven by a desire to please the international community. Secessionists clearly have incentives to learn international humanitarian law. They must do so both to please the international community, and to prepare for the tasks of statehood.

Secessionists appear to be disproportionately likely to reach out to consultants beyond their claimed territory whose job it is to train them in the trappings of statehood, including compliance with the laws of war. The use of (primarily) western consultants by polities trying to navigate the European-based system of international relations and law is not new. Nineteenth-century Polynesians, for example, hired Western consultants to help them negotiate with the states that would end up conquering them.[88] What is new is the greater availability and institutionalization of such consultants. For example, the Tuareg, seeking to secede from northern Mali, reached out for advice to separatist groups in Europe including the Britons, Catalans, and Corsicans.[89] The NGO Independent Diplomat (ID) has as its mission to "provide confidential advice and practical assistance in diplomatic strategy and technique to governments, political groups, international organizations and NGOs" and to "promote greater inclusiveness in diplomacy."[90] Independent Diplomat counts among its current and former clients Kosovo, South Sudan, Somaliland, and the Polisario Front, all secessionist groups. Other groups, such as the Unrecognized Nations and Peoples Organization (UNPO), have also historically represented secessionist groups. Neither ID nor UNPO will represent groups that are guilty of large-scale violations of international law.[91] In order to receive assistance from these NGOs, then, secessionists must have some awareness of which behaviors are acceptable and which are not in the eyes of the international community.

Regardless of whether they work with western consultants, secessionists have many other opportunities to learn about international humanitarian law. Some NGOs, such as Geneva Call, take as part of their mission the training of rebel groups in the intricacies of IHL. According to their mission statement, "Geneva Call responds to requests from [Armed Non-State Actors, or ANSAs] to help build their knowledge of, and capacities to implement, international humanitarian norms, such as through providing training and technical advice."[92] Geneva Call reaches out to rebel groups, and also responds to requests for information and training. Although requests initiated by rebel groups are rare, groups such as the Kurdish People's Protection Units (YPG) are increasingly approaching Geneva Call for assistance.[93] In some cases, rebel groups have promoted Geneva Call's Deeds of Commitment—which are public online platforms through which armed non-state actors can commit not to use land mines, child soldiers, or sexual violence—to other rebel groups (sometimes at the request of Geneva Call); for example, the Sudanese People's Liberation Army (SPLA) reached out to rebel groups in Darfur.[94] What is more, secessionists might be more likely than other types of rebel groups to sign onto Geneva Call's Deeds of Commitment, thereby publicly committing to abide by international humanitarian laws.[95] In addition to newer groups such as Geneva Call, long-established NGOs like the ICRC also train armed non-state actors in international humanitarian law. Part of the agreement with any state that gives the ICRC permission to work in the country is access to other conflict actors operating within state borders. The ICRC has recently expanded its efforts in this regard, for example by creating a "Unit for Relations with Arms Carriers" that is tasked specifically with interfacing with armed non-state actors on international humanitarian law issues.

Both secessionist and revolutionary rebel groups are likely to have greater knowledge of IHL than, for example, groups fighting resource or religionist wars, because some among their number are more likely to have defected from the state military.[96] While military defectors could be present in all types of rebel groups, there is good reason to expect that defectors to center-seeking and secessionist groups are likely to be of higher rank than defectors to, for example, resource rebel groups, because higher-ranking military personnel are typically sufficiently well-paid and therefore unlikely to be lured away from a stable job with the promise of tenuous riches, riskily obtained. Training in IHL is standard in most state militaries, and thus this knowledge will be conveyed to the rebel military command. "Their Words," a website hosted by Geneva Call that contains rebel groups' internal rules and regulations and stated commitments to abide by IHL, illustrates this point.[97] As an example, General Order No. 1 of the secessionist Moro Islamic Liberation Front (MILF) in the Philippines, "Promulgating a Code of Conduct Regulating the Affairs of the Bangsamoro Islamic Armed Forces, Prescribing its Powers, Duties and Functions, and Other Related Purposes," reads very much like a state military code of conduct and is authored by the group's General Staff.[98]

Secessionists may recognize that they are ill equipped to navigate the waters of the international community. They will therefore often hire western consultants. In doing so, secessionists become increasingly aware both of the scrutiny they will be under and of the rules they are expected to follow. Compared to past eras, the mechanisms—including social media, which is widely used in civil wars—to transmit this information to secessionists are generally available today. Secessionists are more likely to be informed about the requirements of IHL than are nonsecessionists, and today's secessionists are more likely to be informed of these requirements than were secessionists of the past.

The Costs of Compliance

Secessionist rebel groups must consider the same costs of compliance and noncompliance with IHL as states, as discussed above. But their assessment of these costs will differ. The tenuous nature of rebellion—which is typically shorter-lived than the average state—as well as the specific strategic imperatives faced by secessionists lower many of the costs of compliance for secessionists as compared to those faced by states.

Like states, rebel groups often—although not always—invest in training their forces as to proper behavior with respect to those domains covered by IHL, such as treatment of civilians, protection of cultural property, and treatment of medical personnel. Unlike states, however, rebel group militaries tend to be relatively short-lived. Even the longest civil wars tend not to last longer than the shortest-lived states. The shorter time horizon for rebel groups means that they are unlikely to need to revise their training standards in light of changes in IHL, which tend to occur slowly. Insofar as rebel groups intend to comply with IHL from the outset, those standards can be incorporated into their military training at the beginning of a conflict, and will likely carry them throughout the duration of a war. The bureaucratic adjustment costs to the proliferation of codified IHL are therefore much lower for secessionists in civil wars than they are for states engaged in interstate war simply because the time periods are shorter.

Particularly for secessionists, the strategic costs of complying with IHL are also much lower than for states. As I explain in chapter 7, secessionist rebels have fewer incentives to violate IHL than do other kinds of rebels. Whereas states may believe that targeting civilians will serve their political aims, the civilians to which secessionists have the greatest access are those meant to populate their new state. Secessionists also will not have made the same investments in advanced military technology that states often make, and thus will not face a strategic loss if use of some technologies is deemed noncompliant with IHL. Like states, however, the costs of noncompliance for secessionist rebels can be quite high. Members risk being tried for war crimes and jeopardizing their own political aims by alienating both the local population as well as the international community.

Secessionism Rising

Since the turn of the twentieth century and continuing through today, the percentage of civil wars that are secessionist has been increasing (see figure 2.2). This trend reflects a broader rise in secessionism, both violent and nonviolent. Ryan Griffiths and I have demonstrated that secessionism is on the rise in both an absolute and relative sense since 1900, as shown in figure 2.1.[99] We attribute this rise to the increased benefits of statehood, including current norms against violent territorial conquest, globalization, and a modern international aid regime that delivers significant benefits to those who can claim leadership of a state.

Because of the rise in secessionism, the claim that secessionists will respond positively to the proliferation of codified IHL becomes salient in at least two respects. First, the sheer number of secessionists today demands attention to any particularities of their behavior. And second, the increasing numbers of secessionists mean that they must compete more for the attention of the international community, which may increase each group's incentives to comply with IHL.

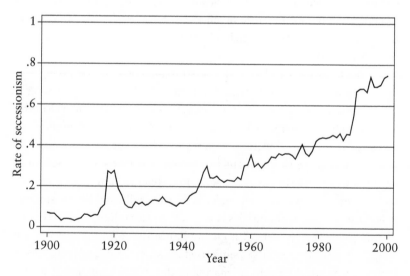

Figure 2.1 The rate of secessionism. From Fazal and Griffiths 2014.

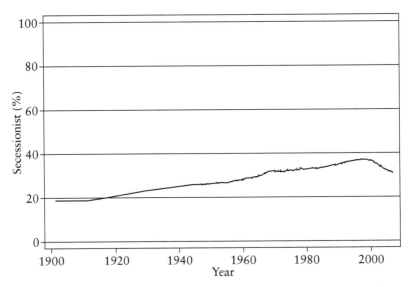

Figure 2.2 Secessionism in civil war, 1900–2007

Compliance as a Net Benefit

The comparatively low costs of compliance, the high costs of noncompliance, and the benefits of compliance mean that the net calculus will favor compliance more for secessionists than for states. Where the proliferation of codified international humanitarian law has given states incentives to create ambiguity regarding their obligation to comply, secessionists have positive incentives to engage with this body of international law. Secessionists view public and visible compliance with IHL as a means to advance their political aims.

We also see important combinations in more general trends regarding secessionism. Secessionism has been on the rise over the past century. The number of civil wars that have secession as their goal is increasing over the same time period. The twentieth century has also been a period of proliferation of codified IHL (as shown in fig. 1.1). Secessionist rebels—belligerents already prone to comply with IHL—thus appeared in greater numbers at the same time that codified IHL proliferated. Taken together, these trends suggest that secessionists will be increasingly likely to engage with the laws of war, while states try to avoid their obligations to abide by this same body of international law.

Theoretical Expectations

The proliferation of codified international humanitarian law holds significant consequences for the conduct of war. How these consequences are manifested is governed by the interaction of the laws of war with belligerents' political and military aims. The argument made in this chapter generates several broad hypotheses, which are explored in greater theoretical and empirical depth in the following chapters.

I propose four main hypotheses regarding the use of war formalities in interstate war. As the laws of war proliferate over time, states will seek to avoid their obligations to comply with this body of international law in their wars with each other. This effect should be most observable with respect to the formalities of war. Thus, my first hypothesis is that states' likelihood of issuing formal declarations of war should decrease as we see more laws of war on the books. Second and related, we should also expect to observe a relationship between declarations of war and compliance with IHL. If states are reluctant to declare war because they want to maintain ambiguity as to their obligation to comply with IHL, then those states that are fairly certain they will comply should be the most likely to issue formal declarations of war. Third, compliance during the conflict should affect the likelihood that states are willing to conclude formal peace treaties at war's end. Like declaring war, signing a peace treaty signals unequivocally the prior existence of a state of war and, by extension, the existence of obligations under IHL. Thus, states that violated IHL during a conflict ought to be especially unlikely to conclude peace treaties. And fourth, as with declarations of war, states in general should be less likely to conclude peace treaties as their obligations under IHL increase.

The civil war context—particularly, the secessionist civil war context—yields a different set of predictions. First, because they are sensitive to the preferences of the international community, and because the international community has expressed a clear aversion to unilateral declarations of independence in the UN era, we should expect a decline in the use of this instrument after 1945. Second, secessionists' sensitivity to the preferences of the international community should spill over into their conduct during their wars. Secessionists, unlike other rebel groups, should thus be especially likely to comply with the laws of war. And third, as the international community has also signaled its preferences for negotiated settlements over military victories at the same time that civil war has become the dominant mode of warfare, we should observe an increasing use of peace treaties in civil war, particularly in the latter half of the twentieth century and into the twenty-first century as this preference has become internalized in key international institutions.

Insofar as the quest for international recognition conditions belligerents' responses to the proliferation of the laws of war, it makes sense to compare the behavior of these different types of belligerents within the pages of one book, but in separate chapters. The remainder of this book is therefore divided into two main empirical sections. In chapters 3 through 5, I consider declarations of war, compliance with the laws of war, and the conclusion of peace treaties, all in the context of interstate war. In chapters 6 through 8, I examine declarations of independence, compliance with the laws of war (specifically, civilian targeting), and the conclusion of peace treaties in the civil war context, and with a focus on secessionist civil war. The book's conclusion recombines the two types of belligerents—and wars—in an assessment of the past trends and future opportunities for the laws of war.

3

Declarations of War
in Interstate War

One of the most famous sentences in Thucydides's *History of the Peloponnesian War* speaks of the practice of declaring war. After reporting debates on the justness of a war against Athens, Thucydides writes, "The Spartans voted that the treaty had been broken and that war should be declared not so much because they were influenced by the speeches of their allies as because they were afraid of the further growth of Athenian power."[1] While most international relations scholars have focused on the logic of preventive war embedded in Thucydides's description of the causes of the Peloponnesian War, the fact that this description refers to a declaration of war is instructive.

For millennia, war was truly war only when it was declared. Declarations of war were required by both the ancient Romans and ancient Greeks for wars to be considered just.[2] The power to declare war was a signal of sovereignty.[3] As I show in this chapter, however, by the twentieth century declarations of war were in decline, and today they are virtually defunct in the realm of interstate war.

By way of illustration, consider the controversy over President Barack Obama's February 2015 request for a congressional Authorization for the Use of Military Force (AUMF) against the Islamic State.[4] One of the issues at stake was whether the president required a new AUMF to engage in military action against the Islamic State.[5] Another issue was whether a declaration of war was possible against a non-state actor. While Congress is constitutionally empowered to declare war, it no longer tries to do so. The AUMF is the new default, but it is significantly weaker than a declaration of war. What is more, Congress ultimately failed to vote on—let alone pass—a new AUMF.[6]

The shift away from the use of declarations of war to begin wars is a dramatic one in international history. In this chapter, I argue that states' incentives to create legal ambiguity regarding their obligation to comply with international humanitarian law as that body of law has proliferated over time best explain the declining use of declarations of war. States that declare war are acknowledging, explicitly, that they are in a state of war. In a state of war, there is no ambiguity as to the applicability of IHL. Declarations of war clearly activate states' obligations to comply with IHL. As the burdens of compliance have become increasingly heavy, the incentives to step over those bright lines have declined.

In the next section of this chapter, I provide an overview of the history and legal function of declarations of war along with a definition of a declaration of war. I then lay out my explanation for the decline of declarations of war in greater detail, and present the conditions under which we might be more or less likely to observe states in interstate war issuing formal declarations of war. Following that, I present my empirical analysis, beginning with the quantitative analysis, which is based on an original dataset—the Interstate War Initiation and Termination (I-WIT) dataset—that is also used in chapters 4 and 5. The results of the quantitative analysis suggest a strong inverse relationship between the proliferation of codified laws of war and the use of declarations of war. I explore this relationship further by delving into four case studies: the 1898 Spanish-American War; the Boxer Rebellion of 1900; the 1971 Bangladesh War between India and Pakistan; and the 1982 Falklands/Malvinas War. Using both primary and secondary sources, I find specific evidence of states trying to sidestep the laws of war by deciding not to declare war formally.

Declarations of War: An Overview

Declaring war is a long-standing custom of international relations. The ancient Romans declared war in the following way: an envoy would be sent to the border of the enemy state with "a cornetwood spear, iron-pointed or hardened in the fire." Once three adult men appeared on the other side of the border, the envoy would recite the declaration of war and then hurl the javelin into enemy territory.[7] Ritualized declarations of war through the use of heralds continued through the chivalric Middle Ages, after which publicly printed proclamations became the standard for declarations of war.

Declarations of war were a subject of study for the earliest international legal scholars. In the 17th century, Hugo Grotius argued that wars that were unaccompanied by the typical formalities—specifically, declarations of war and peace treaties—were "imperfect," or not "solemn."[8] Citing Cicero and Livy, Grotius argued that wars—particularly offensive wars—required declarations: "That a war may be lawful in the sense indicated, it is not enough that it be waged by sovereign powers on each side. It is also necessary, as we have said, that it should be publicly declared, and in fact, proclaimed so publicly that the notification of this declaration be made by one of the parties to the other."[9] A century later, Vattel made a similar argument as to the necessity of a declaration of war, and noted two additional reasons for declaring war: that it be known who one's enemies are, and that grievances causing the war be stated at the start of the war so as to avoid extraneous claims at the peace table.[10]

One of the major reasons for the custom of declarations of war, according to both Grotius and Vattel, was that they helped distinguish banditry or piracy from wars prosecuted by sovereign powers.[11] These analyses of declarations of war—like the rise of international legal scholarship itself—emerged along with the development of the modern system of sovereign states. To declare war was a means for a state to distinguish itself from what today are called non-state actors; the importance of this distinction resurfaces in chapter 6, when we consider the role of and reasons for similar declarations by rebel groups in civil wars.

Today, declaring war (or not) has policy implications in at least three categories: (1) the implications under domestic law, (2) the governance of behavior between belligerents, and (3) rules pertaining to nonbelligerents. In each domain, declarations of war trigger important rules of behavior.

The domestic legal implications of declaring war vary by country. The Iranian constitution, for example, delays elections during a time of war. Israel's Basic Law requires full governmental participation in a declaration of war and allows for the suspension or alteration of laws and taxes when a state of emergency is declared. India's constitution empowers the federal government to, in effect, take over state governments following a proclamation of a state of emergency, which is India's equivalent of a declaration of war. Following India's 1962 proclamation of a state of emergency prompted by war with China, the Defense of India Act expanded the government's detention authority and placed restrictions on citizen appeals to the Supreme Court for protection of certain basic rights.[12]

Less variance exists with respect to the rights and obligations of belligerents engaged in a declared war. Fundamentally, a declaration of war can give warning of the commencement of hostilities: it tells states when they are at war. Historically, declarations of war also present the justifications for the war and statements of war aims; these roles are important for international as well as domestic publics. Typically, a declaration of war is also accompanied by a break in diplomatic relations (although diplomats and diplomatic missions must continue to be protected); termination of commerce; suspension of treaties; and the applicability of international law governing the conduct of war, such as the 1949 Geneva Conventions.[13] In the case of the United States, a declaration of war activates wartime (as distinct from peacetime) rules of engagement: how US soldiers may treat foreign military forces changes dramatically once war is declared.[14]

Nonbelligerent states also assume rights and obligations with respect to parties to a declared war. For example, alliance obligations may be invoked. Neutral states who do not act with complete impartiality and nondiscrimination toward belligerents by respecting the belligerents' contraband lists and shipping routes risk having their vessels and cargo seized, and risk attacks on citizens on these vessels.[15]

Defining Declarations of War

I define a declaration of war as a public proclamation of a state's intention to engage in hostilities with another state, issued according to the laws of the declaring state. This definition is based on international legal scholarship, which states that a declaration of war must be public, must state an intent to engage in hostilities with another party, and must be issued according to the laws of the declaring state.[16]

The requirements for declaring war can vary widely by country. Thus it is essential to understand a state's mechanism for issuing declarations of war in order to identify any such declarations made by that state. In the United States, only Congress has the power to declare war. In many autocracies, by contrast, the head of state can declare war without legislative consultation or approval. For example, North Korea's National Defence Commission (which is headed by North Korea's head of state, Kim Jong Un) holds the power to declare war, according to the 1998 constitution.

Because existing datasets do not include a variable for declarations of war as defined here, I use the Interstate War Initiation and Termination (I-WIT) dataset as the foundation for the quantitative analysis in this chapter and in chapters 4 and 5. I-WIT is an original dataset, which I collected with my colleague Page Fortna. We use the most recent version of the Correlates of War list of interstate wars—which covers wars between states that produce at least 1,000 battle deaths, from 1816–2007—to establish our universe of cases.[17] I-WIT thus covers all major interstate wars since the Napoleonic Wars. It codes for seventy variables—including declarations of war—missing from previous datasets. Each war was coded by at least two researchers; when the initial two coders disagreed, a third coder acted as a tiebreaker. If disagreement remained amongst the three coders, we analyzed the case ourselves to determine the coding. Detailed descriptions of each case, including coder reports on each war and documentation of how any discrepancies were resolved, are available via the Qualitative Data Repository.[18]

In coding declarations of war, I-WIT requires, first, a description of the belligerent state's procedures for declaring war and, second, a description (and, if possible, documentation) of the actual declaration.[19] The Russian declaration of war against Turkey in 1828 is a typical declaration of war. Following a detailed description of Ottoman infractions, the declaration states: "Russia, now placed in a situation in which her honour and her interests will not suffer her any longer to remain, declares war against the Ottoman Porte, not without regret, after having, however, for 16 years together neglected nothing to spare it the evils which will accompany it. The causes of this war sufficiently indicate the objects of it. Brought on by Turkey, it will impose upon it the burden of making good all the expenses caused by it, and the losses sustained by the subjects of his Imperial Majesty."[20] The Ottomans did not respond, having issued a *Hatti-Sherif*—an official note from the Sultan—four months prior to the Russian declaration of war and nearly five months before hostilities erupted. But the *Hatti-Sherif* was meant for domestic consumption, and thus did not serve as a declaration of war against Russia.[21] By contrast, at the start of the Crimean War, the Ottoman Empire declared war against Russia via a note sent to Russian Prince Gorchakov, but Russia's response was in the form of "a private dispatch stating that when the Czar read the said Declaration he fell into a fury, and declared that he retracted every concession he had made, and that nothing now remains for him but a war of extermination against the Turks."[22] This note did not rise to the level of a formal declaration of war, because it was meant for a very limited domestic audience. Indeed, Russia appears to have carefully avoided responding, not only to the Ottoman declaration of war, but also to similar notes from the British and French.

Two special types of cases are jihad and states of emergency. For Islamic states, a call to jihad, or Holy War, is considered a declaration of war if it is issued by the requisite domestic authority and publicized both domestically and internationally. In the Second Russo-Turkish War of 1877, for example, the Ottoman Empire declared jihad domestically and also sent notice to various European capitals detailing the Sultan's complaints against Russian aggression and the Ottomans' right to defend themselves: "It is to defend these sacred principles, and to beat back the most hateful and the most criminal of aggressions, that the Ottoman Army is about to march to meet its assailant, with the whole nation marshalled round its august head, confident in the triumph of the justest of causes, prepared for any sacrifice, resigned to all kinds of suffering, and ready to fight and die for its independence—may the Most High protect the right."[23] The form of the Ottoman statement is virtually identical to European declarations of war.

Like calls to jihad, states of emergency can, under certain conditions, be considered declarations of war. In some countries, such as the United States, states of emergency and declarations of war are distinct instruments. While there is significant overlap in the statutory authorities triggered by a declaration of war versus a state of emergency, in the United States the presidential authority triggered by a declaration of war is much more extensive and includes such powers as the quarantining of individuals diagnosed with infectious diseases, the elimination of the statute of limitations for prosecution of certain crimes against the United States, and expansive powers over the armed forces, such as the elimination of limits on tours and retirement age; in the United States, none of these powers is activated by a national state of emergency.[24] In other countries, such as India and Pakistan, declaring a state of emergency is the only route to declaring war.[25] It is therefore important to investigate each belligerent's domestic procedures for declaring war before making a determination as to whether the belligerent did declare war.

Two prior codings of declarations of war exist. First, the Militarized Interstate Dispute (MID) dataset includes "declaration of war" as a level of hostility between states, but coding at the highest level of hostility does not necessarily indicate whether, for example, a war (which is ranked higher than other hostile acts such as blockade or occupation) was preceded by a declaration of war.[26] Thus, it is possible that information regarding declarations is simply lost in the MID dataset.

More recently, James Morrow codes for "War Declarations" in his dataset on twentieth century compliance with the laws of war, but does not necessarily code for formal declarations of war. His concern with compliance with the laws of war appears to lead him to code cases of attack without warning or declared ultimatum as a violation of the requirement that war be declared.[27] Thus, Morrow is not technically coding for declarations of war but, rather, for failure to notify of an impending attack.[28] He codes Germany as committing gross violations of the obligation to declare war in its war with the Soviet Union, for example, despite the fact that von Ribbentrop issued a declaration of war on June 22, 1941, the date of Operation Barbarossa.[29] Similarly, he codes Japan as not declaring war against Russia in the 1905 Russo-Japanese War (the Japanese declaration of war was issued two days after the attack on Port Arthur) and Pakistan as not declaring war against India in the 1971 Bangladesh War, although the Pakistanis declared war against the Indians on November 23, 1971, two weeks prior to the start of hostilities.[30]

Historically, it has not been required that declarations of war be issued prior to the commencement of war. Grotius writes, "By the law of nations, in fact, no interval of time is required after the declaration [for war to be waged]."[31] Vattel disagrees somewhat, arguing that war can be declared at the enemy's borders, but that it "must precede the commission of any act of hostility."[32] In a nineteenth-century treatise on declarations of war, John Frederick Maurice found that a surprisingly small percentage of eighteenth and nineteenth century wars had been *preceded* by a declaration of war warning of the commencement of hostilities.[33] In the relatively recent history of declarations, the most infamous is the Japanese declaration of war against the United States, which was delivered two-and-a-half hours after the attack on Pearl Harbor.[34] Earlier examples of declarations issued well after the commencement of hostilities include the declarations accompanying the War of the Spanish Succession of 1701, the War of the Quadruple Alliance of 1718, the Spanish War of 1727, and the War of Austrian Succession of 1740.[35]

The recent notion that a declaration of war must precede hostilities is codified in the Third 1907 Hague Convention on the Opening of Hostilities: "The contracting Powers recognize that hostilities between themselves must not commence without previous and explicit warning, in the form either of a reasoned declaration of war or of an ultimatum with conditional declaration of war" (Article 1). In the wake of the 1905 Russo-Japanese War, the Russians in particular were sensitive to the fact that the Japanese declaration had been issued after Japan's attack on Port Arthur. But none of the international legal scholars present at the 1907 Hague Convention—including T. J. Lawrence, John Bassett Moore, and Frederick Maurice—believed that declarations of war must precede hostilities. The nub of the disagreement here appears to have been the precise meaning of a declaration of war. Relying on custom, those scholars pointed out that declarations of war need not precede hostilities. But the French and Russians, the main proponents of Article 1, wanted notification of attack (the Belgians requested, in addition, notification to neutral parties). The final language of Article 1 of the convention appears to have been more a product of not wanting to offend the Russians and French, as well as semantics, than a true argument about the role of declarations of war.[36]

It is also not technically necessary that declarations of war be accompanied by hostilities. At the close of the Second World War, for example, numerous Latin American states, without committing troops, issued formal declarations of war against the Axis powers for the express purpose of being invited to the United Nations organizing conference in San Francisco. Although I do not include instances of declarations unaccompanied by hostilities in my analysis, highlighting the existence of these types of cases helps clarify my definition of a declaration of war.

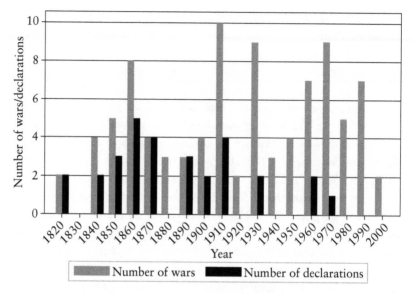

Figure 3.1 Declarations of war, 1820–2007

Figure 3.1 illustrates the decline in declarations of war over the past two centuries, showing both the total number of wars by decade and how many of those wars were declared. Among eighty-one states involved in ninety-three interstate wars between 1820 and 2007, there were 142 declarations of war. Sixty-five percent of wars were accompanied by a declaration of war in the nineteenth century; this number drops to 17 percent in the twentieth century. In the post-1945 era, the number of declarations of war drops precipitously to just three (of thirty-four belligerents participating in interstate war), and there have been none since 1972.[37]

Theoretical Expectations

The arguments presented in chapters 1 and 2 suggest that states should be less likely to take actions that would clearly oblige them to comply with the laws of war as these laws have proliferated over time. Declaring war unequivocally binds states to comply with the laws governing wartime conduct of belligerents. If a state has declared war, it has admitted to being in a state of war. And international humanitarian law clearly applies when a belligerent has admitted to being in a state of war.

One of the criticisms that can be leveled against this argument is that, according to international humanitarian law, *jus in bello* applies in undeclared as well as declared wars. This is stated most clearly in Common Article 2 of the 1949 Geneva Conventions: "The present Convention shall apply to all cases of declared war or of any other armed conflict which may arise between two or more of the High Contracting Parties, even if the state of war is not recognized by one of them." I am not arguing that the laws of war do not apply unless war is declared. My claim is that by engaging the formalities of war, belligerents cross a bright line that leaves them unable to equivocate about the applicability of the laws of war. Remaining silent on whether one is in a state of war maintains a certain amount of ambiguity and, more specifically, exploits ambiguity inherent in codified *jus in bello*, including Common Article 2. Thus, not declaring war is a legal strategy that may allow states to reduce the costs of compliance and of noncompliance with *jus in bello*.

Common Article 2 claims applicability of the Geneva Conventions in declared wars, undeclared wars, and armed conflicts. There is no room for ambiguity as to the applicability of the laws of war in declared wars. Declared wars are clearly identifiable, precisely because states must take the step of issuing a declaration of war. "Undeclared wars" and "armed conflicts," by contrast, are murky categories, undefined in international law. The proceedings of the 1907 Hague Convention highlight this fact. Calvin Davis recounts the following: "Colonel Ting of China asked if a state upon which war had been declared could regard the declaration null and void, and suggested that the conference should determine the meaning of the word *war*. He observed that war had often been made under the word 'expedition,' as anyone could learn by studying the history of China. All the delegates recognized the resentment against Western violations of Chinese sovereignty which Ting was voicing. A few individuals felt embarrassment: no one had anything to say in response."[38] As Isabel Hull writes in her history of international humanitarian law during World War I, "Fundamental disagreements among the European states meant that the codified laws of war (the Hague Rules) were silent on important issues."[39] Similarly, during a preparatory conference to the 1949 conventions, when pressed regarding a clearer delineation of the applicability of the conventions, the International Committee of the Red Cross (ICRC) representative stated that the ICRC "was not in favour of too much precision."[40]

The absence of a clear definition of undeclared war or armed conflict persists. The most recent word on the subject is contained in the Final Report on the Meaning of Armed Conflict in International Law, produced by the International Law Association in 2010. Although the conference preceding the report was convened in part to address the lack of any definition of armed conflict in treaty law, the definition it produced is extremely broad and nonspecific. The report "confirmed that at least two characteristics are found with respect to all armed conflict: (a) The existence of organized armed groups, (b) Engaged in fighting of some intensity."[41]

From a purely legal perspective, the obligation to comply with *jus in bello* ought not to hinge on whether war is declared. But political actors can and do act as if it does, by avoiding stepping over the bright line of declaring war that would unequivocally bind them to comply.[42] Even though they are engaged in conflicts that meet most ordinary-language (and even social-scientific) definitions of "war," ordinary language and legal strategy frequently diverge. Thus very large conflicts are often labeled "police actions," "counterterrorism," or "incidents" precisely because the actors want to avoid the legal ramifications of calling their conflicts "war."

We should therefore expect the declining use of declarations of war to be correlated with the proliferation of codified IHL. There are at least two ways to gauge this relationship. First, it could simply be that the decline in the use of declarations of war reflects the rise in codified IHL. This is a system-level version of the hypothesis. Here, the expectation would be that, as codified international humanitarian law proliferates over time, belligerents should be less likely to declare war.

Second, a belligerent-level version of the hypothesis would focus on the number of IHL treaties ratified by a given warring party at the time of the conflict. Here, the expectation is that the more IHL treaties a state has ratified, the less likely that state should be to declare war.

Empirical Analysis of Declarations of War

I draw on both qualitative and quantitative evidence to analyze when, and which, states issue formal declarations of war. I present the quantitative analysis first, to give the reader a global perspective on declarations of war. This chapter includes descriptions of key variables used in quantitative analyses of declarations of war, compliance with IHL in interstate war, and peace treaties in interstate war, laying the groundwork for the following two chapters. This chapter also includes background information for several case studies used in my analysis of war formalities and compliance with IHL in interstate war throughout the portions of this book dealing with interstate war: the 1898 Spanish-American War; the Boxer Rebellion of 1900; the 1971 Bangladesh War; and the Falklands/Malvinas War of 1982.

Quantitative Analysis

The quantitative analysis for this chapter, as well as for chapters 4 and 5, is based on data from the Interstate War Initiation and Termination (I-WIT) dataset. As described above and also in the statistical appendix, I-WIT is an original dataset that covers all interstate wars, as identified by the Correlates of War list of interstate wars, from 1816 to 2007. Below, I describe coding of key independent and control variables included in the quantitative analysis of declarations of war before proceeding to a discussion of the results of the quantitative analysis.

Description of Variables Because many of the variables described below are also used in chapters 4 and 5, I offer considerable detail on their coding here. Unless otherwise noted, all variables are drawn from I-WIT. Note also that many of the control variables described below are included to test alternative explanations for the decline in declarations of war, and are discussed in greater detail below.

THE PROLIFERATION OF CODIFIED INTERNATIONAL HUMANITARIAN LAW

I employ two measures of my key independent variable of the proliferation of codified IHL. Both are based on the list of seventy-two codified international humanitarian laws, beginning with the 1856 Declaration of Paris and ending with the 2005 Third Additional Protocol to the 1949 Geneva Conventions, as presented in table 1.1. Because the unit of analysis differs for analyses of declarations of war versus peace treaties, the measure of the key independent variable also will vary. First, I count how many IHL treaties and conventions a particular state has ratified during the year in which a conflict begins, to examine the relationship between the codification of IHL and a state's decision whether to declare war.[43] I obtained information regarding ratifications from the International Committee of the Red Cross's "War and Law" treaty database.[44] This is my preferred measure of the key independent variable of codified IHL because it gets directly at the number of obligations particular states have taken on at the moment they must decide whether to engage the formalities of war. States do not automatically ratify laws of war; indeed, they often wait a great deal of time to do so. For example, the United States did not ratify the 1980 Conventional Weapons Convention until 1995, the UK did not ratify the 1856 Declaration of Paris until a century later, in 1956, and China did not ratify the 1954 Hague Convention for the Protection of Cultural Property until 2000.[45]

Second, I code for an annual, systemic version of codified IHL, which is a simple count variable of how many such treaties are in existence in any given year. The belligerent-specific version of this variable—how many treaties a particular state has ratified—shows much more cross-case variation. It is also much less correlated with the year in which a war begins than the systemic version of the variable.[46]

MEMBERSHIP IN INTERNATIONAL ORGANIZATIONS

International lawyers explain the declining use of declarations of war with reference to the United Nations.[47] Their claim is that, because the UN system makes war nearly illegal, member states will be reluctant to declare war either because resort to war is illegal or because declaring war would broadcast the illegal act of resorting to war.[48]

If this argument is correct, members of international institutions that prohibit, or highly circumscribe, the conditions under which states may go to war should be especially unlikely to declare war. To test this hypothesis, I code signatories to the Kellogg-Briand Pact, the Covenant of the League of Nations, and the United Nations Charter ($UN + LN + KB$). I vary both the mix of institutions and whether both parties in a warring dyad are members of the institution in the statistical models whose results are reported below.

CONTROL VARIABLES AND ALTERNATIVE EXPLANATIONS

Democracy. Democracies may be more likely than nondemocracies to engage in the formalities of war. Declarations of war are consistent with the principles of transparency that underlie democratic theory.[49] Reasoned argument, another bedrock of democratic theory, also matches nicely with declarations of war, which typically contain within them the justification for war.[50] Indeed, scholars such as Brien Hallett have warned that the decline in use of formalities is a harbinger of the erosion of democracy in the United States and elsewhere.[51]

Polity represents the standard Polity IV measure of democracy here. A country's polity score in any given year is based on six variables that fall into three categories: the means of executive recruitment, constraints on executive authority, and political competition. It is meant to capture the "authority characteristics of states," and is the most widely used measure of democracy in political science today. *Polity* ranges on a twenty-one-point scale from –10 (least democratic) to +10 (most democratic).[52] Alternative measures of democracy, such as Freedom House, the Democracy-Dictatorship dataset, and the V-Dem dataset, lack the temporal or geographic coverage needed to test this set of hypotheses.[53]

Veto players. A related argument suggests examining the balance of power between the executive and legislature within belligerent states. Particularly if the formalities of war require legislative assent, divided government can make it harder for leaders to go to war, and also harder to deploy the formalities of war.[54] The potential—and potentially lost—role of veto players is often invoked in discussions of why the United States no longer declares war. Here, one argument is that Congress, which holds the constitutional power to declare war, has ceded foreign policy to the "imperial presidency," perhaps to limit its own political liability for international misadventures.[55] But even if there are effectively declining veto players in the US foreign-policymaking landscape, this would not be the case globally given the rising number of democracies in the world over the past 200 years.

Three measures of the degree to which an executive's power might be constrained are available. First, Witold Heinisz's measure of political constraint (*POLCON_III*) is based on the number of veto players in any given political system. A veto player is an "individual or collective actor whose agreement (by majority rule for collective actors) is required for a change of the status quo."[56] The more veto players in the political system, the greater the degree of political constraint on the executive.[57] Second, the Varieties of Democracy dataset also includes a measure of executive constraint, but it is not used here because it begins at the year 1900.[58] And third, the *xconst* variable from Polity IV measures the independence of the executive by identifying "the extent of institutionalized constraints on the decision making powers of chief executives, whether individuals or collectivities."[59] Because *xconst* is very highly correlated with *polity* (indeed, it is one of the constitutive elements of *polity*), I adopt Heinisz's measure in the regressions below.

The decline of major power war. Major powers have not made war on one another since World War II.[60] A decline in war declarations might follow from this fact, if major powers are especially likely to engage the formalities of war when fighting each other. Insofar as declaring war signals respect, great powers might be less likely to participate in these formalities when fighting nongreat powers. If so, because great powers have tended not to fight each other over the past sixty years, this may serve as another explanation for the declining use of war formalities. However, although this logic speaks to great-power behavior, it does not shed much light on the decisions of nongreat powers to engage (or not) the formalities of war.

I use the Correlates of War list of great powers over the past two centuries to identify great powers singly and in dyads. They are: the United States (1898–2011); the United Kingdom (1816–2011); France (1816–1940, 1945–2011); Germany (1816–1918; 1925–45; 1991–2011); Austria-Hungary (1816–1918); Italy (1860–1943); Russia/USSR (1816–1917; 1922–2011); China (1950–2011); and, Japan (1895–1945, 1991–2011).[61] This variable takes a value of "1" if both members of the dyad are great powers at the time of war.

Counterinsurgency. States planning to fight wars using guerrilla warfare may anticipate that they will be especially unlikely to be able to comply with the laws of war and, therefore, may be less likely to issue formal declarations of war. I use David Cunningham and Douglas Lemke's coding of (counter)insurgency in interstate wars as a foundation for *COIN*.[62] Cunningham and Lemke identified fifteen interstate wars where guerrilla warfare was used by one or both sides. I refined their variable by identifying which side(s) employed guerrilla warfare, as well as when this strategy was employed. I also updated their coding to reflect additions to the list of interstate wars from the Correlates of War project (version 4). Eleven wars were coded as counterinsurgencies from their start; four occur prior to 1949, and seven after.

Identity. Invoking a logic similar to that used to predict great powers' relationship with the formalities of war, European states might view the formalities of war as a sign of respect they choose not to accord to their non-European enemies because they do not consider them legitimate or civilized foes. European states might thus be unwilling to declare war upon non-European states. Recent scholarship has shown that European states were historically less likely to comply with international humanitarian law when fighting non-European states.[63] Italy, for example, targeted hospitals, civilians, and used poison gas against Ethiopia in 1935; the Ethiopians did not respond in kind (at least in part because they could not).[64] If European states anticipate violating or wish to be free to violate IHL in their wars with non-European states, they may be less likely to declare war against them.

In previous work, Brooke Greene and I developed a coding scheme to distinguish European from non-European states; I use our coding to test this hypothesis. For the purposes of testing how the historical development of the laws of war affected compliance, Greene and I code European states as those that "(1) participated in the initial codification of the law of war in the late nineteenth century and (2) were generally perceived by European states as members of the European community at the time of codification."[65] This variable takes a value of 1 if State A in the dyad is European, and State B is not.

Reciprocity. There might be a stigma to issuing a declaration of war in that states may prefer not to admit to being in a state of war for fear of sanction by the UN. That stigma could, however, be obviated if one's opponent also issues a declaration of war. By this logic, we might expect the likelihood of a declaration of war to increase when the other side in a war dyad has declared war.

War start years. I include the start years of a war to account for a possible secular time trend driving the declining use of declarations of war. Start years are based on the Correlates of War start dates.

Regression Analysis and Discussion   My unit of analysis for declarations of war is the directed war-dyad. War dyads were identified using version 4 of the Correlates of War list of interstate wars, which covers the period 1816–2007. For each dyad, I-WIT coded for whether one, both, or neither state declared war on the other. A "case" here is State A's decision to declare war (or not) on State B. Thus, the United States and Germany in World War II are represented twice in the analysis—one of these observations focuses on the United States' declaration of war on Germany and the other focuses on Germany's declaration of war on the United States. Because the decision to declare is state-specific, this unit of analysis is appropriate in that it allows us to focus on other state-specific variables, such as the level of democracy and the number of law of war treaties ratified by the state that is considering whether to declare war.

Because the dependent variable is binary—did the state declare war or not?—I use simple logistic regressions for the quantitative analysis. I find strong support for the argument advanced here. The results are presented in table 3.1. Models 1 and 2 cover the nineteenth and twentieth centuries and control for membership in the United Nations, the League of Nations, and/or the Kellogg-Briand Pact; model 2 also controls for the year the war

TABLE 3.1 Logistic regressions on declarations of war

	1	2	3	4	5	6 (pre-1899)
Ratifications	−.08 (.02) $p=.00$	−.04 (.02) $p=.08$	−.05 (.02) $p=.01$	−.04 (.02) $p=.03$		−.29 (.42) $p=.49$
Laws of war					−.05 (.03) $p=.05$	
UN			−3.38 (1.00) $p=.00$	−3.06 (1.19) $p=.01$	−3.04 (1.17) $p=.01$	
UN+ LN + KN	−.14 (.54) $p=.79$	1.06 (.64) $p=.10$				
Initiator	−1.40 (.39) $p=.00$	−1.57 (.44) $p=.00$	−1.25 (.42) $p=.00$	−1.33 (.41) $p=.00$	−1.38 (.43) $p=.00$	
Polity	.06 (.03) $p=.04$	.07 (.04) $p=.09$	.08 (.03) $p=.00$	.08 (.03) $p=.00$	.09 (.03) $p=.00$	.07 (.08) $p=.38$
Polcon_III	−.12 (1.29) $p=.93$	.26 (1.10) $p=.81$	−.15 (1.45) $p=.92$	−.02 (1.32) $p=.99$	−.21 (1.21) $p=.86$	
COIN	−1.78 (1.13) $p=.12$	−1.38 (1.09) $p=.21$	−1.36 (1.08) $p=.21$	−1.20 (1.06) $p=.26$	−1.29 (.97) $p=.19$	

Identity	.76	.48	.80	.72	.61	−.17
	(.35)	(.37)	(.32)	(.33)	(.35)	(1.03)
	p=.03	p=.19	p=.01	p=.03	p=.08	p=.87
Reciprocity	.56	.18	.03	−.03	−.12	
	(.57)	(.56)	(.58)	(.51)	(.52)	
	p=.33	p=.75	p=.95	p=.95	p=.81	
Great power	**1.61**	**1.19**	**1.27**	**1.16**	.97	.94
	(.52)	(.57)	(.41)	(.52)	(.49)	(.45)
	p=.00	p=.04	p=.00	p=.03	p=.05	p=.04
War start year		−.03		−.01		
		(.01)		(.01)		
		p=.00		p=.35		
Constant	−.33	**54.22**	−.06	15.31	.61	−.15
	(.49)	**(11.99)**	(.47)	(16.08)	(.54)	(.66)
	p=.50	p=.00	p=.90	p=.34	p=.26	p=.82
Pseudo R-squared	0.1893	0.2447	0.2757	0.2812	0.2828	0.0402
Chi2	0.0000	0.0000	0.0000	0.0000	0.0000	0.2291
% Correctly predicted	77.91	78.86	81.71	78.86	77.91	67.95
N	421	421	421	421	421	78

Note: Robust standard errors in parentheses.

started. Models 3 and 4 also cover the entire time period, but control for UN membership only; model 4 controls for the year the war started.

As shown in figure 3.2, the substantive effect of having ratified more IHL treaties on the probability of a state declaring war is robustly significant, and also substantively large.[66] The states that have ratified the most *jus in bello* treaties are 68 percent less likely to issue formal declarations of war than states that have ratified no, or very few, such treaties. Even more dramatically, we are over 90 percent less likely to observe declarations of war today, when there are many laws of war on the books, compared to the pre-1856 period, when there were no codified laws of war.[67] Consistent with my argument, the results are weaker when the analysis is restricted to nineteenth-century wars. During the nineteenth century, not only were there fewer laws of war, but they were written in a way that favored belligerent rights; thus, belligerents should not be deterred from declaring war due to the existence of these laws.

Several of the control variables are significantly correlated with declarations of war. I discuss the role of the United Nations and related variables in greater detail below. Democracies appear to be about 50 percent more likely to declare war formally compared to nondemocracies. Also,

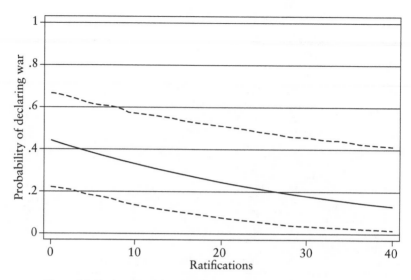

Figure 3.2 Declarations of war and law of war ratifications. Confidence intervals are represented by dashed lines.

great powers dyads are much more likely—in fact, almost 90 percent more likely—to feature declarations of war compared to dyads where neither belligerent is a great power. And, contrary to expectations, dyads where one state is a European state while the other is not are almost 150 percent more likely to include declarations of war than are other types of dyads.

Jus ad bellum, Jus in bello, and Declarations of War   The most important alternative explanation as to why declarations of war have declined refers to the development of the body of international law that governs belligerents' resort to force—*jus ad bellum.* This argument looks to institutions such as the Kellogg-Briand Pact, the League of Nations, and the United Nations, which severely circumscribed the conditions under which states party could legally go to war.[68] The logic of the argument is that state signatories will be less likely to declare war because doing so would be to admit violating the founding principles of these organizations.

There are weak and strong versions of this argument. The weak version supposes that states will be limited in their warmaking by these institutions, and thus they will be less likely to declare war. Elihu Lauterpacht, for example, argued that the prohibition on war in the UN Charter meant that aggressors in particular were not entitled to any rights that might otherwise be activated by declarations of war.[69] Lauterpacht is less clear on whether victims of aggression—or even those states who might come to their aid in compliance with collective security provisions of the charter—are entitled to declare war.[70] This type of case is particularly interesting in light of the UN-sanctioned response to Iraq's invasion of Kuwait in 1990. While, according to Lauterpacht, Iraq did not have the right to declare war, Kuwait and members of the US-led coalition may have had the right to declare war. But the question remains: why was war undeclared?

Lauterpacht's argument suffers from a critical flaw: he assumes that, once states recognize that they *should not* declare war, they *will not* declare war. Were this the case, the more important aim of eliminating war (with or without a declaration) would have been realized decades, if not centuries, ago.

Nicholas Katzenbach, a State Department legal advisor during the Johnson administration, was a vocal advocate of the related position that Article 51 of the UN Charter makes declarations of war—especially in wars of self-defense—obsolete. In his testimony before the Senate Foreign Relations Committee at the start of the Vietnam War, he dismissed declarations of war as "something of an anachronism."[71] But he did not explain why a state should not declare war, even a defensive war; he dismisses international legal concepts such as neutrality, although many of these issues remain relevant beyond the Vietnam War;[72] and he justified US participation in the Vietnam War as a war of self-defense with arguments that are, to say the least, unpersuasive. The history of interstate war over the twentieth century, in other words, does not allow a *prima facie* case for the weak version of the argument.

The strong version of this argument is that states will continue to engage in war, but will try to minimize the appearance of wrongdoing by not labeling their actions as war.[73] In many ways, the logic of this argument resembles my own claim that states have stopped using the formalities of war in a strategic move to limit their obligations to comply with IHL. The distinction between the two arguments lies in the body of law in question—*jus ad bellum* versus *jus in bello*. If the evidence were to support the strong version of this argument, it would therefore complement rather than contradict my own logic.

Membership in the broader class of international organizations that circumscribe the resort to war does not yield statistically significant coefficients in the analysis of declarations of war. But the results on UN membership only are stronger. The results suggested by the statistical analysis therefore do not help in assessing whether there is a stronger effect from *jus ad bellum* or from *jus in bello* on the use of declarations of war. A closer look at the relationship between declarations of war and UN membership is therefore in order.

The first two columns of table 3.2 clearly indicate that the use of war formalities has declined in the UN era. Can we attribute this change to the institution of the United Nations? If so, any declarations of war in the UN era would be issued by nonmembers of the United Nations. The third and fourth columns of table 3.2, however, show something close to the opposite: not only do nonmembers never issue declarations of war, but the only UN-era declarations of war were issued by member states of the United Nations.

It is possible that the causal mechanism linking declarations of war and UN membership is about engaging in aggressive war; thus, we should expect initiators to behave differently from noninitiators. Columns 5 and 6 of table 3.2 examine the relationship between war initiation and declarations of war among UN members. Among UN members, about one in every forty initiators declared war, while one in every thirty noninitiators declared war; although there is a difference, it is not significant. It must be acknowledged, however, that the numbers here are extremely small, highlighting the need to examine specific cases in greater depth. It could be that UN members see no need to declare war in cases where they can argue self-defense, but are reluctant to declare war in other instances that might be in violation of the UN Charter.

TABLE 3.2 Declarations of war and United Nations membership

	1816–2007		UN Era		UN Members	
	Pre-UN era	UN era	UN member	Non-UN member	Initiator	Noninitiator
Declaration	37%	2%	3%	0%	2%	3%
	(138)	(4)	(4)	(0)	(1)	(3)
No declaration	63%	98%	97%	100%	98%	97%
	(237)	(204)	(149)	(55)	(56)	(93)
Column total	100%	100%	100%	100%	100%	100%
	(375)	(208)	(153)	(55)	(57)	(96)

Note: Percent of belligerents in each cell is listed above the absolute number of belligerents in that cell.

The 1962 Sino-Indian War is an interesting case in this regard. India was a member of the UN in 1962; China was not. Contrary to expectations of international legal scholars, such as Lauterpacht and Katzenbach, who argue that UN membership should create hesitation to declare war, here we have a case where the UN member—India—declared war, but the nonmember—China—did not. Although the Indians certainly cared about world opinion on the war, debates in the Lok Sabha (the Indian parliament) suggest that they preferred not to bring the case to the UN, not because they feared being branded aggressors, but because they were skeptical of the organization's efficacy, given its previous rulings regarding Kashmir.[74]

A related argument sometimes made by those who claim that the rise of the UN accounts for the decline of declarations of war suggests that UNSC authorizations substitute for declarations of war. In other words, the argument goes, wars are no longer declared because they are instead authorized by the UN Security Council. While this argument is plausible, it is not borne out by the facts. There have been thirty-eight interstate wars since the birth of the UN, but only two—Korea and Gulf I—were accompanied by UNSC authorizations.[75] Adding UNSC-authorized wars to the coding of declarations of war does not change the results regarding the relationships between either international organizations or the proliferation of the laws of war and declarations of war.

Qualitative Analysis

The case studies that follow serve several purposes. First, they allow for more careful comparison and controlling of cases, helping to isolate the effect of a country having ratified more or fewer *jus in bello* treaties. Second, they allow for process tracing; I use the cases to see whether the belligerents appear to have been concerned with the laws of war. And third, the post-1945 cases also allow for deeper evaluation of the causal role of UN membership.

I examine two pairs of cases to explore the causes of declaring war. These four cases are also used in chapters 4 and 5 in analyses of compliance with IHL and the conclusion of peace treaties after interstate war. Because the key independent and dependent variables both exhibit important trends over time, I divide these pairs of cases by era. The first pair, the Spanish-American War and the Boxer Rebellion, occurs in an era of relatively low levels of codified *jus in bello* but high levels of declaring war. The second pair of cases, the 1971 Bangladesh War and the 1982 Falklands/Malvinas War, by contrast, occurs in an era of high codification of *jus in bello* and low rates of declaring war. For reasons of feasibility as well as methodology, I focus on the United States in the first pair of cases, and on India and Britain in the second pair, but I also discuss the decisions made by the other belligerents in each war.

Each pair of cases controls for a series of variables that might affect a belligerent's propensity to declare war, such as UN membership, legislative-executive balance, level of democracy, surprise, and counterinsurgency (see table 3.3). The cases were selected to maximize variation

TABLE 3.3 Congruence testing of selected cases

	Spanish-American War	Boxer Rebellion	Bangladesh War	Falklands War
Jus in Bello treaties in effect	2	12	27	30
Compliance with *jus in bello*	US and Spain very compliant toward each other	Noncompliance on all sides	India and Pakistan compliant toward each other	British noncompliance
Military victory	US wins decisively	Relief Expedition wins decisively	India wins decisively	British win decisively
Territorial change	US receives Puerto Rico, Philippines, Guam	None	None	None
UN membership	No	No	Both	Both
Joint polity score	4	–6	5[a]	–8
Great power	US	US	Neither	UK
State death	No	No	No	No
Multilateral war	No	Yes	No	No
Duration	114 days	59 days	15 days	88 days
Declaration of war	Yes	No	Yes	No
Peace treaty?	Yes	No	Yes	No

[a] Polity values for Pakistan are missing for 1970–71. Pakistan's 1972 Polity2 score is 4. Constitutional reforms in 1973 led to an increase in Pakistan's polity score to 8. I use the 1972 Polity2 score here, as it is a more accurate reflection of Pakistan's domestic political situation in 1971, when the war occurred, as compared to Pakistan's polity score after the 1973 constitutional reforms.

on both the key independent and dependent variables. Although such a strategy would not be preferred if my empirical strategy were purely qualitative,[76] the reporting of the quantitative analysis above should dispel concerns over selection bias or representativeness of cases.

A simple congruence analysis of table 3.3 supports the notion that belligerents that have ratified more *jus in bello* treaties are less likely to declare war or conclude peace treaties compared to belligerents in similar positions that have ratified fewer *jus in bello* treaties. But how would increasing ratification of *jus in bello* treaties affect belligerents' decision to use war formalities? This particular series of cases makes it possible to trace various relationships between the proliferation of IHL and use of the formalities of war.

The Spanish-American War The Spanish-American War serves as a representative case for this analysis: a pre-Geneva-era war with both mutual declarations of war and a formal peace treaty.[77] Anti-Spanish hawks in the United States pointed incessantly to Spain's brutal treatment of insurgents in its Cuban colony and, more proximately, the sinking of the USS *Maine* in the Havana harbor.[78] The Spanish preferred to avoid war given their comparative military weakness. Although they had a larger standing army—and certainly a larger contingent in Cuba—than the United States, historians agree that the Spanish army was "poorly led, poorly trained and, for the most part, poorly equipped."[79] Despite its glorious naval tradition, Spain's navy was outdated and outgunned. Moreover, Spain lacked resources, which the United States had in abundance; when Congress authorized $50 million for military expenditure in anticipation of the conflict, the Spanish knew their fate was sealed. But honor ruled the decision: the Spanish could no more accept the insult to their reputation by admitting to blowing up the *Maine* (which, in fact, they had not done) than they could concede to the "ungrateful" and "bad lot"[80] of Cuban insurgents. They preferred to lose to a more prestigious foe. The Americans would do.

CUSTOM, *JUS IN BELLO*, AND DECLARATIONS OF WAR

While both sides sought to delay the onset of war, neither appears to have considered conducting the war without an accompanying declaration. A declaration of war was assumed to be an inevitability, so much so that both the United States and Spain had already written instructions to their diplomats and military officers to be executed when war was officially declared. Assistant Secretary of the Navy Theodore Roosevelt telegraphed Commodore George Dewey in the Pacific with the following instructions: "In the event of a declaration of war Spain, your duty will be to see that the Spanish squadron does not leave the Asiatic coast, and then offensive operations in the Philippine islands."[81] A special series of bells and whistles was set to go off in Chicago in the event of a Spanish or US declaration of war.[82]

The specific timing of the US and Spanish declarations of war was more complicated. In the United States, Congress was so far ahead of President McKinley in the press for war that Secretary of War Russell Alger remarked, of McKinley, "Congress will declare war in spite of him."[83] To stall the hawks, McKinley asked Congress for an authorization for the use of force, which it approved on April 19. The authorization fell short of a declaration of war, a deliberate decision by McKinley.[84]

As the United States and Spain were gearing up for war, the rest of the world also prepared. On April 20, 1898, the president of Switzerland sent letters to both Spain and the United States requesting that the two warring states commit to adhering to the 1868 addendum to the 1864 Geneva Convention on treatment of the wounded.[85] Anticipating war, his goal was to broker an understanding, before hostilities commenced, of each side's intent to comply with these laws.

Two days later, the United States blockaded Havana Harbor. According to the 1856 Declaration of Paris, one of the few codified laws of war of the day, blockades had to be effective and erected during a state of war in order to be legal. This blockade was certainly effective, but McKinley had not yet declared war on Spain.

Spain, however, argued that the congressional authorization was "equivalent to a declaration of war" and responded by issuing a formal declaration of war, by royal decree, on April 23.[86] McKinley was left with no choice but to ask Congress for a declaration of war. The debate in both houses was swift and the decision unanimous.[87] The final declaration of war against Spain was approved and signed on April 25—the same day it was requested—and made retroactive to April 21.[88]

To declare war was customary in the late nineteenth century, but to backdate a declaration of war was not.[89] Because the debate on the declaration of war resolution occurred behind closed doors, the official record offers little explicit explanation for the discrepancy in dates. But in his message to Congress requesting the declaration of war, the usually circumspect McKinley notes explicitly that the United States had declared a blockade as of April 22. When one representative raised the dating issue, it was made clear that the backdating request came from the attorney general.[90] Concern over the legality of the preexisting blockade appears to have governed the decision to backdate the declaration of war.

Even in an era when declaring war was customary and there were few codified laws of war, states like the United States quickly responded strategically to the recent laws of war, in this case to take advantage of the laws in their favor. The Spanish objected to this legal sleight of hand. In a memorandum to Spanish ambassadors abroad, the Spanish minister of state Pio Gullón argued that the capture of Spanish ships prior to April 25 was illegal given that the US declaration of war was issued on the 25th, because of the "strange and unlawful particularity" of the retroactive declaration.[91]

The Boxer Rebellion   China in 1900 was, in many ways, a failed state. The empress's reach was short, and popular disaffection with the perceived encroachment of Westerners was strong. Many Chinese found the inroads of Western missionary societies particularly offensive. Resentment grew into rebellion in the spring of 1900, as the "Boxers," a group of antimissionary zealots, began attacking Westerners—missionaries and others—as well as Chinese who had converted to Christianity.

Boxer attacks on Christians and Western missionaries evoked a response from the West, but the real offense occurred when attacks began on Western legations in Beijing. A "Relief Expedition" was formed, comprising troops from Japan, the UK, the United States, France, Germany, and Russia. After landing at the forts of Taku, south of Beijing, the foreign troops made their way north through heavy resistance at Tientsin. They took Beijing on August 14, 1900.

The Boxer Rebellion contrasts starkly with the Spanish-American War on the dimensions of formality and compliance with *jus in bello*. Although the Chinese issued a declaration of war, the Relief Expedition members certainly did not, and the "Final Protocol" concluding the war was explicitly *not* a peace treaty. Moreover, while the Spanish-American War was characterized by nearly ideal comportment by both state belligerents toward each other, both the Chinese and their Western opponents violated both customary and positive *jus in bello* with great frequency (compliance with the laws of war is discussed in detail in chapter 4). These violations are all the more surprising given that the Boxer Rebellion occurred so soon after the 1899 Hague Conventions—the first broad-ranging set of multilateral treaties to codify *jus in bello*—to which all the members of the Relief Expedition were signatories (the Chinese were not). Thus, at the same time obligations to comply with *jus in bello* increased, use of the formalities that would clearly trigger *jus in bello* decreased.

SOVEREIGNTY, THE LAWS OF WAR, AND DECLARATIONS OF WAR

Decisions to declare war during the Boxer Rebellion were conditioned by questions about sovereignty, *jus ad bellum*, and *jus in bello*. It is important to note, first, that the fragmented nature of the Chinese state raises questions over whether there really was a Chinese declaration of war.[92] The most recent literature suggests that China's internal contests over sovereignty provided a reason to declare war. As Ward suggests, the ability to issue a declaration of war was a clear signal of sovereignty.[93] At a time when the empire was under siege from within and without, issuing a decree that supported the Boxers may have been a means to assert control over Chinese domestic politics.

Anticipated links between *jus ad bellum* and *jus in bello*, on the one hand, and declarations of war, on the other, help explain why the members of the Relief Expedition did not declare war. The United States, riding high upon its recent victory against Spain, was rightly concerned about its partners' motives toward China. Protection of missionaries and diplomats provided the perfect excuse to capture markets and secure railroad concessions. But the United States was opposed to such schemes. Various contemporary reports indicate that the United States was able to persuade its alliance partners not to issue formal declarations of war on the grounds that doing so would raise the status of the conflict to "war," legitimizing the right of conquest at the war's conclusion.[94] According to the *New York Times,* "The United States . . . clearly indicated its purpose to accept nothing as an act of war unless that could not be avoided. . . . The object of this policy is to avert the partition of China."[95] The argument against declaring war on China was couched in terms of concern over China's domestic sovereignty: against whom could war be declared if China had no effective government?

The Boxer Rebellion occurred a mere year after the conclusion of the 1899 Hague Conventions. All the members of the Relief Expedition—that is, those that did not declare war—were signatories, while China—which did declare war—was not. Not surprisingly, the historical record does not reveal evidence of high-level policymakers arguing against declaring war so as to avoid having to comply with the Hague Conventions. But, as discussed in the next chapter, many violations of IHL were committed by the Relief Expedition.

Bangladesh War   The 1971 Bangladesh War is atypical in at least two respects. First, and most important for this study, it is one of the few formal wars of the post-Geneva era. Both India and Pakistan declared war on each other, and the war was concluded with a formal peace treaty, the 1972 Simla Agreement.

Second, it was both a civil war and an interstate war. Post-colonial partition had created a two-part Pakistan, its eastern and western provinces separated by Indian territory. Such geography would be challenging to the preservation of any state, and the process of partition created a host of grievances between India and Pakistan. The bloody transfer of Hindus and Muslims east and west had been followed by two wars—both over Kashmir—prior to 1971.

Thus, the Indo-Pakistani rivalry was firmly entrenched by the time the East Pakistan–based Awami League won national elections in Pakistan. Sheikh Mujibur Rahman had been pressing for East Pakistani autonomy for months. His possible ascendance to the Pakistani premiership was unacceptable to Islamabad's elite. Pakistan's Bengalis braced for a fight as its prime minister Yahya Khan flew to the eastern capital to negotiate the formation of a national government and possible greater autonomy for the east with Rahman.[96] Negotiations failed, and the West Pakistanis cracked down brutally on their secessionist eastern compatriots.

The Pakistani military action led to a rush of refugees over the western border of East Pakistan and into India.[97] The Indians were reluctant to house and feed approximately 10 million extra people, and also feared that the refugees would create political instability in other provinces that Delhi was watching warily.[98]

The refugee problem was the ostensible reason for India's protestations against Pakistan's behavior in its eastern province.[99] But even those authors who speak from the Indian perspective in this conflict acknowledge that India's intervention in East Pakistan served several additional strategic goals for Delhi.[100] A dismembered Pakistan would be a weaker rival, and an independent Bangladesh would provide greater security to India's east, all helpful to India's ongoing war for Jammu-Kashmir.

Thus, India supported the Mukti Bahini—the East Pakistani secessionist rebels—with shelter and training.[101] Then India itself intervened, citing humanitarian reasons for doing so. India's desire for a quick war was realized; its army reached Dacca in two weeks. A decisive military victory over Pakistan led, ultimately, to the realization of India's goal of a greatly weakened neighbor and a more secure eastern border.

AN UNUSUALLY FORMAL WAR

Sequencing and context are critical to understanding why India and Pakistan declared war on each other in 1971. Disputed sovereignty over Jammu and Kashmir has colored the relationship of India and Pakistan since partition and independence. Even though the main issue at stake in 1971 was not Kashmir, that concern hung over the Bangladesh War. Pakistan in particular had good cause to be wary of India, knowing that its much larger neighbor would not hesitate to take advantage of any perceived weakness.

Indian army troops entered East Pakistan on November 21, ostensibly to help manage the refugee flow but, in reality, to set the groundwork for the larger invasion to follow.[102] Pakistan accused India of violating its sovereignty. This state of affairs was insupportable to the Pakistani elite.[103] West Pakistani public opinion regarding India became so negative that declaring war seemed to be Prime Minister Khan's only option. Khan responded to the situation by declaring a state of emergency— the Pakistani equivalent of a declaration of war—in a radio address on November 22, 1971.

While domestic politics were the critical driving force behind the Pakistani declaration of war, the Indian declaration was caused as much by international as domestic factors. Chief among these was the Pakistani declaration itself. The Indian prime minister Indira Gandhi took two weeks to respond in kind, declaring a state of emergency for India on December 3. The historical record suggests a reluctance to declare war; it is not clear that Gandhi would have done so had the Pakistanis not forced the issue.

Somewhat unusually, there were few reasons for the Indians and Pakistanis to expect to engage in major violations of *jus in bello* during the war, and thus few reasons to be concerned about the legal implications of declaring war. India's plans called for a blockade of East Pakistani ports; the Pakistani navy was no match for its Indian counterpart. Moreover, because the Indians were crossing the border to defend the East Pakistanis from the west, there was no reason to anticipate Indian attacks on West Pakistani civilians or cultural property. For their part, the Pakistanis were fighting a defensive war; they did not expect to fight on Indian soil, thus eliminating the possibility that they might violate civilian targeting or cultural property laws with respect to Indians. Operational plans did not call for the use of chemical or biological weapons by either side.[104] Thus, the main issue areas where violations were possible were armistice observation, treatment of the wounded, and treatment of prisoners of war. The shared history of the Indian and Pakistani militaries—their common training under the British and the experience of the senior officer corps of having fought side by side during World War II—made maltreatment of each other's soldiers less likely. In fact, compliance with virtually every aspect of *jus in bello* was quite high during the interstate portion of this war.[105]

DID UN MEMBERSHIP MATTER?

The argument that states no longer declare war because they fear being found in violation of the UN Charter is not supported in this case. If states refrain from declaring war in order to avoid having to justify their behavior before the UN, we should see nondeclaring states avoid the UN, while declaring states issue declarations after they have received a stamp of approval from the UN. In 1971, while neither the Indians nor the Pakistanis shied away from the UN, they also did not actively seek its approval. If anything, India in particular sought to delay UN participation in the war until after it had altered the military balance on the ground.

Both the Indians and Pakistanis felt they had right on their side. Both states appealed to *jus ad bellum* in their pleas to the international community, Pakistan by complaining of India's violation of its sovereignty, and India by justifying its action on humanitarian grounds.[106] Indeed, India lodged a UN complaint against Pakistan on December 3, the day India declared war.

At the same time, the Indians in particular were distrustful of the UN. The institution's previous inefficacy in dealing with the Kashmir question in a manner satisfactory to the Indians did not bode well for its ability to settle the issue of East Pakistani sovereignty. Moreover, the Indians were rightly suspicious that the UN would call for an immediate ceasefire, an outcome Delhi wanted to avoid until it could attain a decisive military victory. Having sufficient time to take Dacca was key; once that goal was accomplished, the Indians could negotiate from a position of strength.

Pakistan's prime minister Yahya Khan was also reluctant to approach the Security Council, but for different reasons. Khan knew that Pakistan would lose the war in the east, but he hoped to use India's focus there to make gains in the west. As a matter of principle, Khan also found the notion of the UN becoming involved in what Pakistan viewed as an internal matter distasteful.[107] In particular, he opposed the notion that representatives of secessionist Bangladesh would be permitted to address the United Nations in the organization's consideration of the war.[108] The aversion of both India and Pakistan to going to the UN was driven by the UN's history regarding Kashmir and by Pakistani reluctance to recognize Bangladesh, not by any concerns over the legality of their war.

The Falklands/Malvinas: An Almost-Formal War   The Falklands/Malvinas War is a typical post-Geneva case with respect to failure to use declarations of war and peace treaties. Neither the British nor the Argentines issued a formal declaration of war and, while the war was concluded with a formal surrender, that surrender was never extended into a peace treaty.

The history of the Falkland Islands (also called the Islas Malvinas) is a fraught one. Since their discovery by Europeans in the seventeenth century, the islands were traded several times between the British and Spanish and, after independence, by the Argentines. Prior to the 1982 war, the last change of hands occurred in 1833, when a British warship expelled the small Argentine population from the islands.[109] By 1982, the Falklands/Malvinas were populated by nearly 1,800 people who thought of themselves as British (although they were 8000 miles away from the British isles), who clearly did not want to become Argentine, and whose influence in Britain's House of Commons was disproportionately "formidable," having successfully tapped into British nostalgia for its imperial past and determination to maintain its current sovereignty claims.[110]

Argentine domestic politics were contentious in the late 1970s and early 1980s. During the *guerra sucia* (dirty war) that followed the overthrow of Isabel Perón, Argentina's military rulers held a tight grip on power that was nevertheless brittle. In late 1981, General Roberto Viola, the head of state, was overthrown by a three-man junta led by General

Leopoldo Galtieri. One of the conditions of Galtieri's ascension to the presidency was his commitment to a demand by Admiral Jorge Anaya—the head of the navy and a critical member of the junta—to retake the Malvinas from the British.

WHY NO DECLARATION OF WAR?

The Argentines attacked the Falklands on April 2, 1982. The initial British reaction was disbelief.[111] But once the Argentines landed on the Falklands, the British were determined to evict them using whatever means necessary, including military force.

Negotiations in the UN had been underway for weeks prior to the Argentine invasion. Immediately following the invasion, several rounds of shuttle diplomacy involving the mediation of the US secretary of state Alexander Haig began.[112] Although the negotiations between the British and Argentines preceding the British counteroffensive were lengthy, the decision to send the British fleet was made quickly, on the very day that Margaret Thatcher's government learned of the invasion.[113] All hoped that fighting could be avoided, but war plans were drawn up in London as well as in Buenos Aires. British frigates, cruisers, and two aircraft carriers headed toward the Falkland Islands. The decision to go to war was not a particularly difficult one for the British; although they were willing to see where the negotiations took them, they largely expected to be fighting the Argentines as soon as the fleet arrived in the South Atlantic.

The decision to declare war, on the other hand, was not so clear-cut. The question of declaring war came up at least twice during the course of the conflict. First, following the Argentine occupation of the Falklands, several primary accounts by key players on the British side mention a reporter asking, "Are we going to declare war on Argentina?"[114] It is not clear whether this question referred to the general plan to go to war, or to the specific act of declaring war. Second, Thatcher's War Cabinet did seriously consider issuing a declaration of war against Argentina. Sir Ian Sinclair, the legal advisor to the Foreign and Commonwealth Office, played a critical role in this decision. In Sinclair's own words:

> Michael Palliser (who took the chair) began by saying that we had all no doubt heard the news and then continued: "By the way, Ian, the Prime Minister would like legal advice within the next half-hour as to whether we should

declare war on Argentina." I simply said: "Well, I had better go and dictate a note for her on that point." Which I duly did. It was perhaps the most momentous piece of legal advice which I ever had to give during 34 years of service in the Legal Branch of the Diplomatic Service, but it was also one of the easiest. I pointed out that, under Article 51 of the United Nations Charter, the United Kingdom had the inherent right of individual self-defence in the case of an armed attack against United Kingdom territory; and as the Falkland Islands were under the sovereignty of the United Kingdom, it was entitled, by virtue of that inherent right, to take whatever action was necessary to restore the situation, including the use of force, provided that any forcible action was consistent with the principle of proportionality. I also advised that action by the United Kingdom in reliance upon the right of individual self-defence (including the despatch of a Task Force to the South Atlantic) did not require a declaration of war and that, indeed, a declaration of war could have far-reaching side effects, including, among other things, the activation of the Trading with the Enemy legislation, which would have serious economic consequences.

I also recall the intense discussions that were subsequently undertaken between Ministry of Defence, FCO [Foreign and Commonwealth Office] and Cabinet Office officials about the declaration of a 200-mile exclusion zone around the Falkland Islands during the period when the British Task Force was steaming towards the Islands. The wording of the declaration contained a saving clause designed to ensure that action by British Naval vessels to protect the advancing British Task Force could still be taken in exercise of the inherent right of self-defence of the Task Force itself, even if the action were taken beyond the limits of the exclusion zone.[115]

Three of Sinclair's points are of particular note. First, it is clear that the British were not trying for an end-run around the United Nations. Contrary to the conventional wisdom of international legal scholarship described above, the UK was not at all made uncomfortable about the notion of declaring war by its membership in the UN. Indeed, Sinclair argued that any UK action could be justified specifically under the UN charter. Sinclair also argued that this position made a declaration of war unnecessary under the UN Charter. John Nott, the secretary of state for defence during the conflict, confirms this view: "One of the most vexing questions, extraordinary as it seems, was whether we could say that we were at war. Evidently not; we were strongly advised by the excellent Foreign Office lawyers not to declare war but to act entirely under Article 51 of the United Nations Charter, which gave the right to countries to act in their own self-defence. This legal distinction caused no end of puzzlement in the Ministry of Defence—and when asked the question in the Commons, I said, 'No, we are not at war,' which caused some mirth."[116] Second, and more important, Sinclair also notes the downside of declaring war. He mentions the activation of the Trading with the Enemy legislation, which would have exposed any British citizen engaged in financial dealings with an Argentine counterpart to criminal conviction.[117] And although he clearly believed that *jus ad bellum* was not at issue, complying with international laws governing wartime conduct may not have been so straightforward. Britain's Official History of the war states that declaring war "would attract considerable baggage in international law."[118]

Third, and related, Sinclair mentions the Exclusion Zone implemented by the British around the Falklands. Although never referred to as such, this zone was meant to be a kind of blockade. According to the 1856 Declaration of Paris, in order to be legal, and thus to give belligerents the right to board and search neutral ships for contraband, a blockade must be effective. But an effective blockade in 1856, when ships had to prevent other ships from crossing the line, was a simpler matter than in 1982, when a blockade had to cover from the sea floor to the atmosphere.[119] The British knew that they would never be able to mount an effective blockade in these terms. The Exclusion Zone was a critical element of the British war effort; the law of the high seas ought to have dominated in this maritime war. But without a declaration of war, the applicability of this law was uncertain. The Royal Navy understood this position completely. Admiral Sir Terence Lewin, the chief of the Defence Staff during the Falklands War, seems to have been in the distinct minority regarding the efficacy of the exclusion zone (perhaps because of his focus on the naval aspect of the conflict), but he expressed no doubts about its label: "The Total Exclusion Zone was a complete blockade by another name aimed at stopping reinforcement by whatever means. What a pity we couldn't call it a blockade, but the lawyers told us we couldn't do that unless we were in a state of declared war, which no one wanted for all sorts of reasons—Art. 51 was our guiding light."[120] Declaring war would have compromised the UK's ability to conduct the war as it planned, in particular the quasi-blockade of the Falklands that was necessary to prevent the Argentines from resupplying and reinforcing their forces on the islands. Without the exclusion zone, it is not clear that the British would have been able to retake the Falklands. Not declaring war may thus have been necessary to winning the war.

That Argentina did not declare war may have been overdetermined. Argentina's attacks on South Georgia and on the Falklands were surprise attacks.[121] Certainly, a declaration of war preceding hostilities would have been counterproductive for the Argentines. Perhaps more important, the junta did not, in the end, expect a war. They modeled their invasion after the 1961 Indian attack on Goa, which drew only a limited military response from Portugal and the broader international community. Argentina had previously set up a base on Southern Thule without provoking a military response from Britain, so they believed that they could similarly move on to the Falklands without a stronger response than new and more serious negotiations.[122] Argentina's expectation of war was so low that "neither Lombardo's command in Puerto Belgrano nor Mendendez in Stanley [the military governor installed in the Falklands by the Argentine junta] acted as if they expected anything other than a diplomatic resolution of the conflict. Little military planning was done."[123] Indeed, the official Argentine post-mortem on the war views this misperception as the junta's most egregious error in its conduct of the war: "It is evident that the Military Junta operated under the false assumption that Great Britain would not respond militarily and that the US would not permit military escalation."[124]

Argentina's failure to expect war with Britain is especially surprising when examining the records of Alexander Haig's negotiations with the junta just prior to the conflict. In nearly one thousand pages of documents on this conflict, the phrase "declaration of war" is mentioned exactly once. On the evening of April 16, 1982, the Argentines indicated to Secretary Haig that one of their conditions for withdrawing from the Falklands included full freedom of travel—including movement of persons—between the Argentine mainland and the Malvinas islands. Given the interim governing structure proposed in the provisional agreement under negotiation at the time, such freedom of movement would lead to an effective loss of sovereignty over the islands for the British. Haig responded that the British would never accept such a condition, and that the Argentine position was, in the end, quite bellicose. "The Secretary [Haig] then said, 'This means war.' Ambassador Enders [Thomas Enders, US ambassador to Argentina] added that this is tantamount to a declaration of war."[125] The Argentine foreign minister Costa Mendez "was surprised that the United

Kingdom would go to the edge of war for such a small problem as these few rocky islands."[126]

Like the British, the Argentines felt they had the right to go to war. In fact, the Argentine approach to the UN and the Security Council seeking a resolution of support slightly preceded the British; the Argentines were trying to get a jump on the situation prior to the British fleet's arrival in the South Atlantic.[127] Argentine diplomats lobbied very hard against what eventually became UN Resolution 502, which demanded Argentina's withdrawal from the Falklands. But once again, poor planning impeded the process; the key players in the Argentine diplomatic corps in New York were all new to their jobs, and lacked the knowledge or contacts that might have helped them to execute their agenda successfully at the United Nations.

The proliferation of codified international humanitarian law explains a puzzle in international relations: why states no longer declare war. To declare war is to step over a bright line. On one side of the line, the obligation to comply with the laws of war is clear. If a state declares war, it is unequivocally obligated to comply. On the other side of the line, a state leaves room for arguments justifying any failures to comply. Maintaining this wiggle room is important as the costs of compliance with the laws of war have risen dramatically.

In the early days of the codification of the laws of war, stepping over that bright line could benefit belligerents, as the earliest laws of war favored belligerent rights. This is why, for example, the US Congress backdated its declaration of war against Spain in 1898. But as the laws of war proliferated over time, the incentives to engage the formalities of war declined. The few states that declared war—such as India and Pakistan in 1971—did so in the knowledge that it would be very unlikely they would violate international law governing wartime conduct.

My explanation for the decline of declarations of war contrasts with the standard explanation given by international legal scholarship. International lawyers point to the UN system as eliminating the need, and decreasing the incentive for, declarations of war. While it is true that UN members are significantly less likely to declare war compared to non-UN members, this is because the decline in declarations of war occurs during the UN era. But a closer examination of the aggregate data as well as specific cases does not support the claim that the decline of declarations of war is driven by UN membership. If this were the case, UN members would be the most circumspect when it comes to declaring war. But in fact, only UN members have issued declarations of war during the UN era; no non-UN members (few though they are) have done so. UN members that declared war—as in the case of India and Pakistan during the Bangladesh War—did not do so under UN auspices. UN Security Council resolutions authorizing the use of force have been so few in interstate conflicts that they could not have replaced declarations of war. And UN members that engaged in undeclared wars did not refrain from declaring war because they wanted to avoid the UN; instead, they often appear to engage the UN actively, as in the Falklands/Malvinas War.

That states no longer declare war might at first appear trivial. But the longstanding custom of declaring war serves important functions, and declarations of war have not been replaced by alternative institutions. Perhaps the most important function of a declaration of war is in official notification to all interested parties—belligerents, neutrals, citizens, and soldiers—of the activation of a state of war. In the absence of such an instrument today, war has been renamed as "counterterrorism," "police actions," and "counterinsurgency." We are both never and always in a state that approximates war, but without a clear demarcation of this status.[128]

4

Compliance with the Laws of War in Interstate War

International law typically lacks strong enforcement mechanisms. International humanitarian law lacks even an official monitor. In the absence of both enforcement and centralized monitoring, conventional wisdom regarding compliance with *jus in bello* tends to follow Cicero's famous dictum: "In times of war, law falls silent." But the reality is that compliance is often observed, and therefore deserves attention and explanation.

A growing literature on compliance with IHL in interstate war has focused on the roles of regime type, reciprocity, war aims, and military strategy as predictors of compliance. My interest lies in exploring the consequences of the proliferation of codified IHL for compliance. The logic and evidence presented in the previous chapter suggest that states that issue formal declarations of war may also be particularly likely to comply with IHL. By declaring war, these states have intentionally stepped over a bright line that unequivocally obliges them to comply with the laws of war.

Compliance with international law, and international humanitarian law in particular, however, occurs at various stages and levels of war. Decisions to comply taken at the top might be difficult to enforce at the individual level. Decisions to comply—or not—also might change over the course of a conflict. While declarations of war might be part of this mix, the fact that such declarations tend to be issued at the start of a conflict and far from the battlefield must temper any expected relationship between declarations of war on the one hand and compliance with IHL on the other.

As discussed in chapter 2, the proliferation of codified IHL is likely to have a greater effect on the use of the formalities of war than on overall compliance. Expectations of compliance, rather, should affect states' likelihood of declaring war: if a state believes it has little risk of violating IHL during the course of a conflict then, all else equal, it should be more likely to declare war than if it anticipates a high risk of violation.

In the remainder of this chapter, I explore the link between the proliferation of codified IHL, declarations of war, and compliance with the laws of war. I begin with an overview of the existing literature on compliance with IHL to highlight the complexity of this issue. I then discuss my main theoretical expectation for this chapter: that this complexity will obscure a possible relationship between declarations of war and compliance with IHL. While this expectation is borne out by the regression analysis below, digging deeper into the data suggests that states do in fact refrain from declaring war when they anticipate many opportunities to violate the laws of war. The causal arrow thus begins with expectations of compliance and stops at declaring war, rather than the reverse.

Compliance with the Laws of War: What We Know

A growing literature on compliance with the laws of war speaks directly to when, where, and why states and soldiers adhere to, or violate, IHL. This literature points to four main types of variables. First, as several scholars have argued in explaining targeting of civilians as well as treatment of prisoners of war, wars of attrition and counterinsurgency may be especially likely to be accompanied by violations of the laws of war, as belligerents become desperate to end, and win, their conflicts.[1] Second, these same scholars have also argued that maximalist war aims—including territorial war aims and the aim of regime change—often lead to violations of IHL. For example, belligerents seeking to annex a territory may have few scruples in targeting civilians residing on that territory so that it may be "cleansed."[2] Third, a logic of reciprocity may govern compliance: if a state complies, its opponent may be more likely to comply.[3] And fourth, democratic institutions combined with international legal commitment may create a structural framework favorable to compliance.[4] Because declarations of war are typically much more distant in time from these more pressing concerns that impact compliance, my expectation is that declarations of war will, on average, exert a weak or nonexistent effect on compliance with the laws of war.

Theoretical Expectations

If states avoid war formalities in order to limit their obligation to comply with IHL, their nonuse of formalities might be tied to levels of compliance. States that declare war may be less likely to violate IHL. The infamous "Rape of Nanking" that occurred during the 1937 Sino-Japanese War is one case consistent with this hypothesis. The Japanese had not declared war on China in 1937, and thus might argue that they had little obligation to comply with IHL. US treatment of detainees in Afghanistan also illustrates how this argument may work in practice. The "torture memos" that came out of the office of Alberto Gonzales, the attorney general, argued that the Third Geneva Convention regarding the treatment of prisoners of war did not necessarily apply to the detainees because al Qaeda is not a state and the Taliban was not recognized by the United States as the government of Afghanistan. Had the United States declared war on Afghanistan, however, there would have been no ambiguity as to the applicability of the convention. Insofar as there was an expectation of using "enhanced interrogation techniques," declaring war was certainly not in the interest of the United States.

These two examples—where states may have decided not to declare war in part because they sought to avoid the obligations of compliance with IHL—suggest that we might be more likely to observe nondeclaring states violating IHL than we are to observe declaring states complying with IHL. It is likely easier for a state to anticipate noncompliance—particularly if such behavior is part of a state's war strategy—than it is to be certain of compliance beforehand. In other words, states might begin a war expecting to comply with IHL, but these expectations may change over the course of a conflict. The knowledge of previous violations is more likely to influence the decision to conclude a formal peace treaty (as discussed in the next chapter) than the knowledge of a past declaration is likely to influence compliance.

The sequencing of the decision to declare and any subsequent compliance or noncompliance also suggests a selection effect in the relationship between declarations of war and compliance with IHL. If states decline to declare war because they do not want to be held responsible for violations of IHL, then they might be most likely to declare war when they do not fear being held responsible for violations of IHL. States are least likely to fear being held responsible for violations when they anticipate few opportunities for violation. For example, states fighting a land war would not be concerned about violating the laws of war regarding conduct on the high seas. Belligerents that do not expect to violate IHL, then, might be especially likely to engage the formalities of war, particularly at the start of a conflict when formal declarations of war are typically issued.

The claims made above are of the "all else equal" variety. When it comes to predicting compliance with IHL, however, all else is typically not equal. The exigencies of the battlefield often supersede commitments to comply with IHL. Thus, while these logics are important to outline because they follow from the argument, the skepticism presented in chapter 2—that the proliferation of IHL should not have such a direct effect on compliance—is also justified here.

Assessing Compliance

In analyzing compliance with IHL in interstate wars, I draw on existing theoretical and empirical work. The analysis below combines two sets of arguments that have not previously been analyzed together.[5] The quantitative analysis suggests, as expected, that on-the-ground issues (such as whether the conflict is a war of attrition) bear much more on the probability of compliance with IHL than whether a state issues a formal declaration of war. The case studies discussed below allow a more refined analysis of the relationship between declarations of war and compliance with IHL, and provide more support for the claim that states that declare war might be particularly likely to comply with IHL.

Quantitative Analysis

I base my quantitative analyses of compliance with IHL in interstate war on James Morrow's 2007 analysis. Morrow uses an ordered probit model to predict noncompliance. I make several amendments to this model. First, I do not use all of Morrow's independent variables.[6] I dropped many of the interactions from the analysis, as these seemed theoretically untenable and some were not significant in Morrow's own analyses. Second, I add two versions of the two strategic variables—military strategy and war aims—from the literature on IHL compliance. Third, I include a measure of whether State A in the dyad is a European state, while State B is not, for reasons I explain below. Fourth and finally, I include a variable for whether State A declared war on State B (where declaration of war is taken from I-WIT, as described in chapter 3) to determine whether states that declare war are more likely to comply with IHL.

Description of Variables   Variables used in this analysis are described below, with a particular focus on variables not used in chapter 3.

Dependent variable: Noncompliance with the laws of war. I use James Morrow and Hyeran Jo's data on compliance with the laws of war in all interstate wars in the twentieth century to measure compliance with IHL.[7] The analysis presented below employs Morrow's *ordinal compliance index*, a composite compliance score based on the magnitude, frequency, degree of centralization, and clarity of violations.[8]

The Morrow and Jo data cover nine issue areas: aerial bombardment; armistice/ceasefire; chemical and biological weapons; treatment of civilians; protection of cultural property; conduct on the high seas; prisoners of war; declarations of war; and treatment of the wounded. I exclude aerial bombardment from the analysis because this area of IHL remains uncodified. I also substitute my measure of declarations of war for the Morrow and Jo measure, as their measure identifies cases of surprise attacks, rather than formal declarations of war. Note that I do not include compliance with the laws of war regarding surprise attacks in the dependent variable, as I am interested in the possible effect of my coding of declarations of war on compliance. An important feature of the Morrow and Jo dataset is that, for most of the other issue areas they consider, some proportion of the documents used to generate their coding rules are not actual treaties, but rather declarations or draft conventions. Given that my key causal mechanism rests precisely on the proliferation of codified *jus in bello* treaties, incorporating the additional element of uncodified laws of war into a measure of compliance could potentially add a great deal of error to the analysis. Combined with the fact that the Morrow and Jo data also do not include wars added to the latest COW list of interstate wars, nor do they include nineteenth-century wars, this dataset is not ideally suited to the task of assessing the relationship between declarations of war and compliance with IHL suggested by my argument.[9] Nonetheless, Morrow and Jo deserve credit for creating the best available dataset on compliance with the laws of war in interstate conflicts. In interpreting the results reported below, note that the dependent variable is noncompliance with the laws of war; thus, a positive coefficient means a greater observed degree of violation.

War aims and military strategy. Additional variables are taken from the scholarship of Benjamin Valentino, Paul Huth, and Sarah Croco, and that of Alexander Downes. Downes uses a binary variable to code for wars of attrition when "the defense has the advantage" and the wars "thus tend to be enormously costly and protracted."[10] He also codes for annexationist war aims "when a state aims to conquer and permanently annex land from a neighboring state."[11] Valentino, Huth, and Croco generate a continuous measure of military strategy that captures "the percentage of the conflict that the combatant devoted to attrition and/or counterinsurgency strategies."[12] Like Downes, they rely on a binary coding of maximalist war aims, which takes a value of one when the combatant seeks regime change and/or territorial conquest.[13]

Identity. The *European v. non-European* variable is taken from Fazal and Greene, who show that European states are particularly likely to violate IHL when fighting non-European states. This measure is based primarily on the geographic location of states as well as their role in the history of the development of IHL.[14]

Additional control variables. The remainder of the variables comes from Morrow, who is particularly interested in whether belligerents ratified the relevant laws of war, how democratic each belligerent was (this measure is based on *polity* scores), the possible logic of reciprocal violations, and the specific relationship between democracy and joint ratification. Indicator variables for each issue area included in the analysis are also in the model; treatment of the wounded is the reference category.

TABLE 4.1 Ordered probit analysis of noncompliance with the laws of war (1900–2000)

	Downes strategy variables	Valentino strategy variables
Declaration of war	.13 (.09) p=.16	.14 (.10) p=.13
European v. non-European	.18 (.12) p=.12	.19 (.12) p=.11
Attrition warfare	.25 (.09) p=.01	
Annexationist war aims	.41 (.12) p=.00	
Counterinsurgency		.24 (.09) p=.01
Maximalist war aims		.51 (.10) p=.00
Victim's noncompliance	.64 (.05) p=.00	.63 (.06) p=.00
Joint ratification	.05 (.15) p=.71	.03 (.15) p=.86
Violator ratified	−.10 (.15) p=.51	−.12 (.15) p=.41
Violator democracy	.10 (.16) p=.51	.23 (.15) p=.14
Violator democracy x joint ratification	−.29 (.19) p=.13	−.35 (.19) p=.07
Power ratio	.17 (.22) p=.46	−.14 (.22) p=.54
Armistice	−.51 (.18) p=.01	−.45 (.18) p=.01
CBW	−1.34 (.16) p=.00	−1.34 (.16) p=.00
High seas	−.44 (.16) p=.01	−.48 (.16) p=.00

(Continued)

TABLE 4.1 *(Continued)*

	Downes strategy variables	Valentino strategy variables
Civilians	.45 (.13) p=.00	.48 (.14) p=.00
Cultural	−.01 (.17) p=.96	.04 (.17) p=.82
POWs	.20 (.13) p=.14	.20 (.13) p=.14
Violator initiator	.20 (.09) p=.02	.25 (.09) p=.00
Violator battle deaths per 1,000 of population	.02 (.00) p=.00	.02 (.00) p=.00
Violator lost	.72 (.18) p=.00	.80 (.18) p=.00
Violator lost x power ratio	−.80 (.30) p=.01	−.98 (.30) p=.00
1st cutpoint	1.10	1.00
2nd cutpoint	2.77	2.69
3rd cutpoint	3.96	3.91
N	906	906
Log-likelihood	−792.11	−784.33
Significance probability of model	639 w/20 d.f.	655 w/20 d.f.
Pseudo-R^2	.29	.30

Note: Standard errors in parentheses.

The results reported in table 4.1 do not suggest a relationship between declarations of war and compliance with international laws governing wartime conduct. As a reminder, the dependent variable is noncompliance; thus, negative coefficients indicate greater compliance. As discussed above, more proximate concerns than declarations of war—such as reciprocity, military strategy, and war aims—affect compliance. The military-strategic variables argued for by Valentino, Huth, and Croco; Downes; and Wallace appear to exert a stronger effect on compliance than do the reciprocal and institutional variables suggested by Morrow.

It is not surprising that states generally have difficulty predicting their levels of compliance with IHL and that compliance therefore will not correlate closely to declarations of war. This is particularly true when we contrast who makes the decisions to comply with who makes the decisions to declare. As Morrow shows, compliance and violation are often decided in the field. Declarations of war are issued from the halls of power. Too many factors intervene between declaring war and complying with IHL to expect to see a tight relationship between the two. In addition, as stated above, the Morrow and Jo dataset includes so many uncodified laws of war that it cannot on its own serve as the only test of this claim.

Does the Opportunity to Violate IHL Inform the Decision to Declare War? Another lens that can be used to examine the possible relationship between declarations of war and compliance with the laws of war reverses the sequence. The logic of my argument suggests that states that anticipate violating the laws of war will be especially unlikely to issue a formal declaration of war. This type of anticipation would be extremely difficult to identify in the historical record because policymakers are unlikely to admit to intending to violate the laws of war, and certainly unlikely to commit any such intentions to paper.

In lieu of identifying intentions to violate the laws of war, I examine opportunities to violate the laws of war. I focus particularly on decisions that could be taken at a high level of government, and also issues that could be apparent before, or at the start of, a war.[15] I identify opportunities to violate the laws of war in three realms: maritime warfare, chemical and biological weapons, and treatment of civilians. I assume that policymakers can accurately assess whether a war would be fought at sea, whether their country possesses chemical and/or biological weapons, and whether at least part of any anticipated fighting is likely to occur in a populated area where civilians could be placed at risk. Following Morrow, I focus on twentieth and twenty-first century wars, where the laws of war have been more fully codified. For each of these sixty-four wars, I coded whether the war was expected to be maritime, whether it was fought in a populated area, and whether any of the belligerents possessed chemical or biological weapons. If any of these conditions were met, I assumed that there would be significant opportunities to violate the laws of war, and predicted that the belligerents would not issue a declaration of war.

Table 4.2 summarizes the findings of this analysis. Two points are of note. First, this very simple model was highly accurate, predicting the correct outcome 80 percent of the time. And second, it is much easier to predict the absence of a declaration of war, based on opportunities to violate the laws of war, than the presence of a declaration of war.

To investigate this relationship further, it is worth looking at the mispredicted cases—those where I would have expected a declaration of war, but none was forthcoming (bottom left cell of table 4.2), or those where I would not have expected a declaration of war, but one was issued (top right cell of table 4.2). Table 4.3 lists these cases; "overpredicted declarations" refers to cases where I would have expected a declaration but there was none, and "unpredicted declarations" refers to cases where I would not have expected a declaration, but there was one.

Most of the cases where I predicted a declaration of war but none was forthcoming can be accounted for quickly. The Fourth Central American War of 1907 escalated as a result of Nicaraguan support for Honduran rebels seeking to overthrow Honduran President Manuel Banilla. The

TABLE 4.2 Declarations of war predictions based on opportunities to violate the laws of war (1900–2003)

	Predicted declaration	Predicted no declaration
Actual declaration	2	9
No actual declaration	4	49

TABLE 4.3 Mispredicted cases

Overpredicted declarations	Unpredicted declarations
Fourth Central American War (1907)	Russo-Japanese War (1904)
Lithuanian-Polish War (1920)	Italo-Turkish War (1911)
First Kashmir War (1947)	First Balkan War (1912)
Cenepa Valley War (1995)	Second Balkan War (1913)
	World War I (1914)
	Chaco War (1932)
	World War II (1939)
	Bangladesh War (1971)

indirect, and, initially, covert, nature of this conflict likely accounts for the absence of a declaration of war.

Both the Lithuanian-Polish and First Kashmir War were fought by brand-new states, newly recognized by the international system. The mechanisms for declaring war were not necessarily clear as constitutions were being drafted.[16] In the case of the First Kashmir War, conflict technically erupted prior to independence; had there been a declaration of war, one part of the United Kingdom would have been declaring war against the other. As both India and Pakistan were being counseled by British advisors, such declarations were unlikely to be forthcoming.[17]

The absence of a declaration of war in the case of the Cenepa Valley War is more difficult to explain. A long-standing territorial conflict between Ecuador and Peru escalated in January 1995, as Ecuador attempted to evict Peruvian troops from the disputed territory. Given that this war occurred almost fifty years after the previous mispredicted case (the First Kashmir War), it is possible that the number of codified laws of war was so high at this point that they served as a deterrent to any declarations of war; it is also possible that declarations of war had fallen into desuetude by 1995. A third possibility is that neither the Ecuadorians nor the Peruvians expected the conflict to escalate; indeed, amongst the wars included in the Correlates of War list of interstate wars, this one produced relatively few casualties, and in fact may not even meet the threshold of 1,000 battle deaths.[18]

I turn now to the cases where I did not predict a declaration of war, but at least one declaration was issued formally. It should be noted that the data presented in tables 4.2 and 4.3 are presented in the aggregate—they do not distinguish, for example, whether some or all belligerents declared war. It should also be noted that, with one exception, all the cases of unpredicted declarations of war occurred prior to the creation of the 1949 Geneva Conventions. The one exception is the 1971 Bangladesh War. In this case, there was no expectation that the war would be fought at sea, and neither India nor Pakistan possessed chemical or biological weapons. The war was, however, fought in an area heavily populated by civilians. But as discussed below, neither India nor Pakistan expected to target each other's civilians—it was principally the Bengali East Pakistani population that was at risk of attack from their West Pakistani brethren—and thus India and Pakistan were relatively safe in issuing declarations of war.

The remaining eight mispredicted cases all occurred during the pre-Geneva era. Not only were there fewer—and fewer humanitarian-focused—laws of war on the books in the first half of the 20th century, but declaring war was considered to be part of the tradition of warfare at that time. A significant portion of the 1904–5 Russo-Japanese War, for example, was fought at sea, and at a time when the laws of war regarding the high seas favored belligerents. While there was also a substantial land warfare component of this war, it was fought in Korea and Manchuria, not Russia or Japan—thus, neither belligerent was in a position to target the other's civilians. The World Wars, on the other hand, were expected to be fought on land and at sea. The web of alliances preceding both World Wars suggests that the belligerents would have had a sense of the scope of participation. It was perhaps the sheer size of these wars, combined with the fact that they were fought in an era with relatively few truly humanitarian (and, thus, constraining) laws on the books, that led belligerents to declare war in those cases.

Qualitative Analysis

Analysis of the four cases introduced in chapter 3 provides another opportunity to evaluate the relationship between declarations of war and compliance with IHL. Rather than revising an entire dataset to focus exclusively on compliance with codified IHL, investigating these four cases allows closer inspection of whether the belligerents had ratified any laws of war and, if so, which ones, as well as discussion of the possible connections between declarations of war and compliance with the laws of war then in effect. Looking at a smaller number of cases also allows me to bring in one out-of-sample (nineteenth-century) case and two nineteenth-century laws of war not included in the Morrow and Jo dataset.

Spanish-American War   When the Spanish-American War began in 1898, two laws of war had been codified. The 1856 Declaration of Paris governed maritime warfare, with a particular focus on the criteria for a legal blockade. The 1864 Geneva Convention on the protection of the wounded allowed for evacuation and treatment of the battle wounded. While neither the United States nor Spain was a party to the 1856 Declaration of Paris in 1898,[19] both states had formally accepted the declaration as binding international law.[20] Both states were party to the 1864 Geneva Convention at the time of the war. My expectation in this case is of high compliance with few laws of war in existence, particularly because both sides had issued formal declarations of war.

With the possible exception of having backdated its declaration of war, US compliance with both the 1856 Declaration of Paris and the 1864 Geneva Convention (and subsequent additional articles) appears to have been quite high. According to David Trask, a historian of the Spanish-American War, "during the first few weeks of the campaign [Admiral] Sampson and his subordinate commanders labored unceasingly to improve the blockade."[21] The historical record does not yield much information regarding any neutral ships that may have been unlawfully detained or improperly treated by US marine forces.

Both sides also appear to have complied with the 1864 Geneva Convention (and additional articles, from 1868), although there is more information available concerning US treatment of Spanish wounded than there is about Spanish treatment of US wounded. General William Shafter, commander of US ground forces in Cuba, noted several times in his dispatches to Washington that he was caring for Spanish wounded with great attention.[22]

Spain's Admiral Cervera, commander of the Spanish squadron at Santiago de Cuba, wrote to General Ramón Blanco upon the capture and sinking of his fleet, "The commander of the *Viscaya* surrendered his vessel. His crew are very grateful for the noble generosity with which they are treated by U.S. forces."[23] Spanish soldiers and sailors were similarly cared for by US military personnel in the Philippines.[24]

The United States also complied with customary international law regarding treatment of civilians. Shafter delayed the bombardment of the city of Santiago de Cuba so that noncombatants could depart before the shelling; he also agreed to share field rations with these same noncombatants.[25] He wrote to the War Department on July 5, 1898: "Large number of women and children coming out of Santiago this morning. With assistance of Miss [Clara] Barton will try and feed them. Do not believe there will be any firing to-day on account of all the people not being able to get out. Have also the enemy receiving some of his wounded which I am sending him."[26] US forces in the Philippines similarly committed to protect noncombatants, places of worship, and cultural institutions following their capture of Manila.[27] In the Puerto Rican campaign, the US military's emphasis on respect for noncombatants was so high that one US soldier was court-martialed and sentenced to thirteen months of hard labor in federal prison for paying a local restaurant owner with Confederate dollars.[28]

Reports on Spanish compliance with codified *jus in bello* are harder to come by. Blockade maintenance was not an issue, as the Spanish did not declare any blockades. But the Spanish had opportunities to treat wounded US soldiers fairly or poorly. The captain and crew of the *Merrimac*, the US collier sunk by its own crew in an attempt to blockade the harbor of Santiago de Cuba, reported careful treatment of their wounded.[29] Other—perhaps less accurate—reports, however, had the Spanish firing on US field hospitals marked by a Red Cross.[30]

The burdens of compliance in the portion of the war fought between the United States and Spain were not very heavy. Indeed, as discussed in chapter 3, the United States sought to take advantage of blockade law by backdating its declaration of war. The laws of war at this time favored belligerent rights (as described in chapter 1). It is therefore not surprising that Spain and United States declared war, complied with the laws of war, and, in the US case, manipulated the declaration of war with the express purpose of activating blockade law that favored it.

Even though the United States and Spain were largely compliant with the laws of war in their formal war with each other, their treatment of local populations in Cuba, Puerto Rico, and the Philippines fell far from today's standards of humanitarianism. Spanish General Valeriano Weyler's infamous policy of *reconcentración* in Cuba demanded that all civilians completely evacuate districts where insurgents were active; according to historian David Trask, "no one was supposed to travel without permission; military commanders were empowered to act summarily against insurgents; and those aiding or abetting the insurrection became subject to military law, a much more drastic code than the civilian alternative."[31] As a result of Weyler's policies, approximately 100,000 *reconcentrados*—displaced Cuban civilians—died in Weyler's camps.[32] Even though the war was prompted in part by Spain's maltreatment of the Cuban people, US troops viewed their Cuban insurgent allies with disdain that was likely based in racial prejudice.[33] Similarly, when making plans to fight alongside Puerto Rican and Filipino insurgents, the assumption was that these local allies were incapable of conducting "civilized warfare," and thus undeserving of respect.[34] The expected relationship between war formalities and good behavior therefore did not extend beyond the relationship between the United States and Spain and, if anything, compliance with the laws of war may have eroded dramatically once non-European armies were included as both allies and adversaries.[35]

The Boxer Rebellion   In 1900, as the Relief Expedition set off to fight the Boxers in China, the international legal landscape had recently seen a major shift with the conclusion of the 1899 Hague Conventions. Although they were a far cry from current IHL protections for civilians, they were much stronger than prior restrictions on belligerents. The second convention in particular noted for the first time that "the right of belligerents to adopt means of injuring the enemy is not unlimited" (Article 22). It prohibited "attack or bombardment of towns, villages, habitations or buildings which are not defended" (Article 25). In the year before the start of the Boxer Rebellion, all the members of the Relief Expedition had agreed to abide by these constraints.[36] China was not a party in 1900. My expectation is that the members of the Relief Expedition—having just signed the 1899 Hague Conventions, and (as discussed in chapter 3) having carefully avoided declaring war on China—would have violated the laws of war during this conflict.

Indeed, with one exception, all of the members of the Relief Expedition committed serious violations of both the 1899 Hague Conventions and the 1864 Geneva Convention.[37] As William Duiker writes, "At the time it was common in the West to cite the unspeakable atrocities committed by the Boxers, often with official support, against innocent missionaries in the provinces of China. That such evils did occur is undeniable. Yet the allied advance to Peking provided little in the way of contrast. In the end, neither side had much to be proud of."[38] The Chinese were the first to violate customary *jus in bello*, with attacks on and murders of foreign diplomats. Besieging the foreign legations where diplomats and their families resided certainly amounted to targeting civilians. Even Chinese provincial governors argued that attacking foreign envoys was "beyond the pale of international law."[39] Article 25 of the Second Hague Convention of 1899—to which all of the belligerents except the Chinese were a party at the time—prohibits targeting undefended buildings and compounds.[40] Although the legations were lightly defended at the time of the first attack, it seems sophistry at best to argue that they were legitimate targets. As few European soldiers were captured by the Boxers, it is difficult to know whether prisoners of war were treated well by the Chinese; sources suggest they were probably murdered.[41] All that said, as the side that declared war, the Chinese may have been more compliant with those positive *jus in bello* codes to which they were a party than the Relief Expedition was.

For its part, the Relief Expedition—which consisted of the UK, France, Russia, Germany, the United States, and Japan—was about equally culpable under the international law of war. The Russians and Germans appear to have been especially brutal and rapacious in their pillaging and other post-victory activities.[42] All parties looted.[43] Duiker notes that US troops routinely "bayoneted Chinese troops taken in battle, then threw them over the wall."[44] Beijing's famous White Pagoda was destroyed by British troops who believed that its survival might make the Chinese believe that their deities were more powerful than the Christian God.[45] The 1899 Hague Conventions did accord protection to cultural and religious property; the White Pagoda likely would have come within this category. Keown-Boyd wrote of the Battle of Tientsin, "There seems to be little doubt that the behaviour of the Allied troops in the immediate aftermath of the battle was atrocious."[46]

The one exception to widespread violations of *jus in bello* was the Japanese force. They maintained strict discipline at almost all times, refraining from rape and from targeting civilians. "At Tientsin and elsewhere the Japanese won universal praise for their fighting performance, but, much more surprisingly, their behavior towards the civilian population seems to have been superior to that of their allies. Certainly the battle for Tientsin and its aftermath reflected little credit on either Western arms or chivalry."[47] Prisoners of war who fell into Japanese hands were neither tortured nor murdered. The only offense that the Japanese appear to have committed was to engage in some looting in Beijing following the relief of the embassies. One reason for Japanese restraint was its desire to join the club of great-power states.[48] And indeed, Japan sufficiently impressed its allies that it entered that group within the next ten years.[49]

Bangladesh War   The 1971 Bangladesh War occurred in the post-Geneva era. IHL had firmly shifted to a focus on protected persons—that is, civilians. Restrictions on belligerents engaged in interstate war were high.

In this context, it is perhaps surprising that Pakistan and India—both of which had ratified the 1949 Geneva Conventions—issued formal declarations of war against each other. My expectation is that neither party anticipated violating the laws of war as they pertained to *interstate* war in this conflict, and that this anticipation was justified.

Compliance with *jus in bello* during the Bangladesh War was high, as long as we restrict our analysis of compliance to Indian-Pakistani relations. Pakistan was not in a position to target Indian civilians or cultural property in the east, and India had no incentive to abuse the citizens or culture of East Pakistan. The Indian blockade of Chittagong in the east and Karachi in the west was effective, as the Pakistani navy was not strong enough to challenge it.[50] Moreover, it covered both sea and air.[51] By and large, wounded and prisoners on each side were treated well; here, the Indians shouldered most of the compliance burden, as the Pakistanis captured few Indian soldiers.

That said, there are four dimensions in which compliance with *jus in bello* could be questioned. First, both the Indian and Pakistani air forces attacked in the west. These attacks, however, appear to have been limited to air bases.[52] Any civilian casualties would clearly be in the category of collateral damage, and not intended.

Second, although the Indian blockade was effective, questions about its legality were raised because of initial uncertainty about whether India and Pakistan were in a state of war.[53] These doubts, however, were quickly cleared up by the Indian declaration of war.

Third, India likely was in violation of the third 1949 Geneva Convention when it extensively delayed the repatriation of Pakistani prisoners of war. This delay, discussed in chapter 5, was part of India's negotiating tactics at the peace table; this likely violation did hold important implications for the negotiation of the Simla Agreement that ended the war. However, it was not part of the conduct of the war itself.

Finally, the Pakistanis were certainly guilty of war crimes in their treatment of Pakistani Bengalis. "Operation Searchlight," begun on March 25, 1971, to capture Awami League separatists, was carried out ruthlessly. Bengali soldiers serving in the Pakistan army were killed. Students at Dacca University were gunned down almost indiscriminately on suspicion of organizing resistance.[54] Civilians were shot at directly and also caught in the crossfire, in part because the West Pakistanis were unable to distinguish among Bengalis and thus could not identify the faces of the

Awami League members they were ordered to capture (most of whom had already fled to India in any case).[55] But these violations pertain to a civil war within Pakistan, and not the interstate war between India and Pakistan. Thus, on the whole, the statement that India and Pakistan were both highly compliant with *jus in bello* in their 1971 formally declared war with each other stands.

The Falklands/Malvinas War   Like the Bangladesh War, the 1982 Falklands/Malvinas War occurred in the post-Geneva era. Unlike the Bangladesh War, however, this war was fought primarily at sea. Thus, most of what we think of as modern IHL does not apply or is applicable to a limited portion of the conflict, as modern IHL speaks primarily to land warfare. Instead, the laws of war that were key to earlier maritime conflicts, such as the Spanish-American War, were salient. But law is not static. Although a statute—in this case, the 1856 Declaration of Paris—may not have been revised, its meaning was affected by decades of interpretation and case law. The critical update in this case reflected changes in military technology. With the availability of submarines and airplanes, effective blockades had to cover a much larger vertical extent in 1982 than in 1898.

As argued in chapter 3, knowing that they would be unlikely to erect an effective blockade contributed to British hesitation to declare war against Argentina. The Argentines also refrained from declaring war, but for different reasons, namely, that they did not expect a war. My expectation is that British compliance with maritime law in particular would be low in this war.

In all but this one key area, both Argentine and British compliance with *jus in bello* was quite strong.[56] Many areas covered by international humanitarian law were not relevant to the conflict. Protection of cultural property was not at issue, for example, because the Falklands are lacking in cultural landmarks. Neither side contemplated using chemical or biological weapons,[57] although the British Task Force set out for the South Atlantic in such haste that nuclear-armed depth charges were not offloaded until later.[58]

Each side was faced with a different set of opportunities to violate or comply with *jus in bello*. Treatment of civilians was not at issue for the British, who aimed to relieve the 1,800 Falklanders who viewed themselves as British. Although British forces may have employed an unnecessary degree of force in retaking key parts of the Falklands,[59] there is no evidence that they maltreated the wounded.[60] The almost 12,000 Argentine prisoners of war generally received treatment consistent with the Geneva Conventions,[61] although there were a few instances of possible violations.[62] There appears to have been some discussion of holding onto Argentine prisoners of war to pressure the Argentines to surrender, which would have been an ambiguous strategy in international legal terms, not to mention generally unpalatable in the eyes of the international community.[63]

The major violation of *jus in bello* in this case lay with Britain's creation of the Maritime Exclusion Zone (MEZ) on April 12 and the Total Exclusion Zone (TEZ) on April 30. The MEZ was meant to prevent any Argentine naval vessels from entering a 200-mile zone around the Falklands, while the TEZ extended this mission to exclude all Argentine sea and air vessels that might be engaged in activities in support of Argentina's war effort, such as surveillance.[64] Two British aircraft carriers, six submarines, eight destroyers, and 15 frigates were the main patrolling force, supported by amphibious warfare vessels, support ships, and merchant vessels. Eleven squadrons of armed aircraft also were sent to patrol the zone.[65]

Both the MEZ and TEZ were meant to blockade the Falklands. According to the 1856 Declaration of Paris, blockades are only legal (giving belligerents rights against neutral ships) when they are effective. Mounting an effective blockade of the Falklands presented an enormous challenge for the British. The distance between the UK and the Falklands is approximately 8,000 miles. Dispatching and supplying an effective blockading fleet without considerable assistance from nearby allies would be nearly impossible. The task was made even more difficult with the addition of an air blockade.[66] The Royal Navy and Air Force were expected to cover a 200-mile perimeter from the sea floor to the atmosphere, 8,000 miles from home.

The British leadership understood the difficulty, even the infeasibility, of this task. Margaret Thatcher writes of a potential blockade, "Due to the terrible weather conditions and the problems of keeping the task force supplied and maintained so far from home, there was no way this could have been done."[67] Admiral Sir Terence Lewin, the chief of the Defence Staff, also recognized the incompleteness of the blockade, especially with regard to air support: "We had only 22 Harriers. They could not maintain a continuous air patrol over Stanley airfield. They were needed for the air defence of the Task Force at a later stage (if, indeed, it had reached that stage), and they might later be needed for the ground support of forces who landed."[68] Lewin also noted, pointedly, that he had not come up with the label "total" exclusion zone; this term he attributed to the War Cabinet.[69]

And indeed, the MEZ and TEZ were not completely effective. At least one enemy ship and several enemy aircraft entered the zone.[70] Had the South Atlantic been populated by more than Argentine and British ships at the time, the likelihood is that the zone would have been further breached. Moreover, the apparent efficacy of the zone may have been due to the timidity of the Argentine navy (ironically so, given that its commander, Admiral Anaya, had conditioned his support of Galtieri's presidency on a demand for repossession of the Malvinas). The *Rattenbach Report*, commissioned by the Argentine government as a postmortem on the war, condemned Anaya for "approving the suspension of maritime traffic to Puerto Argentino [also called Port Stanley], which made it impossible to supply adequately the forces on the Islands";[71] "approving the decision to limit the fleet to shallow waters, for security reasons, due to the enemy submarine threat, in hopes of an opportunity [to attack], and not demanding their use—which would have been limited but possible—in intercepting surface vessels from the British Task Force for the purpose of dispersion or harassment, given that they [the British] acted with total impunity in the sea";[72] and generally "ceding to the enemy, without a fight, absolute dominion of the sea."[73] The implication here is that the decision to keep the Argentine fleet in port following the sinking of an Argentine cruiser on May 2 was not necessary; if the fleet had been at sea, it would have limited the efficacy of the British zones.

Additional problems undermined both the efficacy and legality of the exclusion zones as blockades. Because there was some ambiguity regarding the central point of the zone, its perimeter was vague.[74] It is difficult to enforce a blockade whose boundaries are unclear. More important, the British appear to have violated their own perimeter by authorizing an attack on an Argentine cruiser, the *General Belgrano*, which was operating outside of the exclusion zone.[75] Legal consensus is that "blockades do not allow for attack without warning on vessels not otherwise subject to such attack."[76] The British appear to have been aware of this view; they justified orders to attack vessels outside the exclusion zone by reference to Article 51 of the UN Charter, rather than the declaration of the exclusion zones.[77]

The British were well aware of the legal tightrope they were walking. The desire to remain in a realm of legal ambiguity was behind the decision to call the MEZ and TEZ "exclusion zones" rather than "blockades." According to Britain's Official History of the war, the "Legal Advisor [of the Foreign and Commonwealth Office, FCO] strongly advised against describing this as a 'blockade' in any public statements, as in international law this term was closely connected with a declared or acknowledged war."[78] Similarly, according to historians and coauthors Lawrence Freedman (author of the UK's official history of the conflict) and Virginia Gamba-Stonehouse (an Argentine historian who helped the Argentine foreign minister Costa Mendez organize his archives from the war), "the military would have been content to call it a blockade, but this created problems in international law."[79]

The British thus had two reasons not to invoke the terminology of "blockade." First, doing so would lead them dangerously close to the realm of declared war. And second, calling the exclusion zone a blockade would have placed a burden on British military forces that they could not meet, especially in an era when blockades were expected to cover the air as well as the sea. Refraining from a declaration of war allowed the British to retain ambiguity necessary to prosecute the war according to their capabilities and limitations.

While it would be consistent with my argument to claim that states that declare war will be especially likely to comply with the laws of war, prudence demands skepticism of this claim. On-the-ground compliance is a function of a multitude of factors, many of which cannot be anticipated by the political decision-makers who determine whether to make a declaration of war. The political and temporal—and, often, geographic—distance between declarations of war and compliance with IHL is sufficiently great that the link between the two is likely to be fragile.

The quantitative analysis reported in this chapter confirms the tenuousness of this link. Battlefield imperatives associated with reciprocity, attrition warfare, and annexationism overwhelm any effect of declaring war. This relationship between declarations of war and compliance with the laws of war is more visible in the case studies, where earlier belligerents declared war for the express purpose of taking advantage of the laws of war of the day, and later belligerents avoided doing so because they expected, correctly, that they would later be violating the laws of war. Even so, the evidence presented in this chapter confirms the view that the effects of the proliferation of IHL will be much more visible in belligerents' decision to employ the formalities of war—declarations of war and peace treaties—than in their compliance with IHL. As discussed in the next chapter, however, it may well be that compliance conditions the conclusion of peace treaties in interstate war.

5

PEACE TREATIES IN INTERSTATE WAR

Peace treaties have been used to conclude war formally at least as long as—and perhaps even longer than—declarations of war have been used to begin wars. Like declarations of war, however, the use of peace treaties to end interstate war has been in decline since the end of World War II. The rate of peace treaty use to conclude interstate wars today is less than a quarter of what it was during the nineteenth and early twentieth centuries.

Peace treaties punctuate the end of wars. In the absence of peace treaties, relations between states that have been at war may remain unsettled. The United States did not conclude peace treaties with Iraq following Operation Iraqi Freedom or with Afghanistan after Operation Enduring Freedom. Instead, a bilateral security agreement was concluded in 2014 that allowed thousands of US and NATO troops to continue to conduct operations in Afghanistan.[1] Similarly, a series of agreements—none amounting to a peace treaty—provided a framework for the withdrawal of most US forces from Iraq and specified the status of remaining forces.[2] In Central Asia, the lack of a peace treaty between Armenia and Azerbaijan following their three-year (1991–94) war over Nagorno-Karabakh has impeded trade and cooperation between the two countries, resulting in serious damage to Armenia's economy.[3]

I argue that the proliferation of codified international humanitarian law has created incentives for states to refrain from signing peace treaties to end their wars with each other. Belligerents that conclude peace treaties acknowledge that they were in a state of war. In a state of war, the applicability of the laws of war is indisputable. Peace treaty negotiations can be forums for accountability: they are often where war crimes are tallied and punishments determined. As there are more laws of war on the books, there is more exposure to potential punishment, and therefore greater incentives for states to avoid making peace treaties. The disincentive to conclude peace treaties should be particularly great for states aware of their own noncompliance with the laws of war.

Peace Treaties: An Overview

The origin of the Latin *pax* is *pangere*, which means "to make a pact or contract wherein the rights and duties of both parties were specified."[4] Historically, such contracts in the context of war have been made in the form of peace treaties. The earliest known peace treaty is the Treaty of Qadesh, concluded in 1269 BCE between the Hittite Emperor Hattusilis and Ramses II of Egypt. Historian Trevor Bryce argues that Hattusilis's main motivation for concluding the peace treaty with Ramses II "was the legitimacy which the agreement conferred upon Hattusilis's occupancy of the Hittite throne."[5] Bryce suggests that Hattusilis's usurpation of his nephew's throne had placed him in an awkward position with respect to domestic and international legitimacy. Because vassals swore allegiance to specific kings and lineages and because the "Great Kings" of the Bronze Age treated with each other on a personal basis, Hattusilis could not be secure in his reign until he received recognition from key external actors. Among the four kings, Ramses was first among equals. Ramses was also sheltering Hattusilis's displaced nephew. By recognizing Hattusilis as a brother king in the Qadesh Treaty, Ramses acknowledged Hattusilis as an equal. Like declarations of war, the earliest peace treaties may therefore have been used as a means of signaling and solidifying sovereignty.

Although the form of peace treaties has changed over time, they have always been characterized by highly ritualized and formal behaviors. The Ancient Greeks erected pillars to mark the conclusion of peace treaties.[6] In the Middle Ages, these agreements were often concluded through highly symbolic acts such as the "kiss of peace," or *osculum pacis*; the kiss of peace was similar to today's handshake between heads of state upon the conclusion of a peace agreement. But the kiss of peace was even more meaningful in an era when such agreements were not likely to be written down. It was considered to confirm a solemn oath. England's King Henry II refused to give Thomas à Becket the kiss of peace upon the conclusion of a twelfth-century peace treaty between France and England, part of which revoked Becket's exile; Becket returned to England and was murdered shortly thereafter.[7] Even before peace treaties began to be written, concluding such treaties was a public act surrounded by great formality. Moreover, to refuse to engage in these formalities, as Henry II did, was frowned upon; and to disobey the dictates of a peace agreement risked punishment from the heavens.

Whether and when a war ends with a peace treaty has practical as well as theoretical implications. Peace treaties are primarily meant to terminate wars and restore friendly relations among belligerents, including the resumption of diplomatic relations and trade.[8] Furthermore, recent scholarship has illustrated that formal peace treaties may do more than informal (or no) peace treaties to cement peace.[9] While it is possible that the known correlation between peace agreements and subsequent duration of peace might be attributable to peace agreements being concluded in easier cases, scholars have anticipated this criticism and found that peace agreements—perhaps especially so in interstate war—in fact tend to be concluded in the harder cases.[10] Based on the I-WIT data, I find that, of interstate wars that stop and resume at a later date, those ending in peace treaties see on average four more years of peace compared to wars ending without peace treaties. Similarly, among the set of war-dyads that see a resumption of war at a later date, the average duration of peace for wars ending without peace treaties is 11 years, while the average duration of peace for those ending with peace treaties is 20 years. What is more, according to the 2012 Human Security Report, wars that resume despite the conclusion of peace agreements may also be less lethal compared to wars that resume without having been first ended via a peace agreement.[11]

Concluding peace treaties serves as an implicit acknowledgement that a state of war existed previously; at least as important, peace treaties eliminate ambiguity as to whether two countries are still at war.[12] By contrast, the absence of a peace treaty can create difficulties for belligerents seeking to normalize relations, resolve disputes, or remove troops from disputed areas, even when the original conflict appears to have ended. The absence of a Russo-Japanese peace treaty following World War II, for example, prevented the normalization of relations between these two countries for decades.[13]

Defining Peace Treaties

I define a peace treaty as a written document that describes a contract between belligerents to cease hostilities and resolve issues under dispute. It must be signed and ratified by parties to a conflict. *Black's Law Dictionary* similarly defines a peace treaty as "a treaty signed by heads of state to end a war."[14] Typically, peace treaties include several articles meant to specify the terms of settlement of disputes, especially: a preamble; political and territorial clauses; financial, economic, and juridical clauses; and safeguards and guarantees.[15] Although wars can end—even formally—via unilateral declarations, such declarations do not constitute peace treaties precisely because they are unilateral. Ceasefires, armistices, and truces also do not in themselves constitute peace treaties because they are meant to create temporary cessations of hostilities; they do not necessarily resolve issues in dispute.

The Treaty of Paris that concluded the Spanish-American War is a good baseline example of a peace treaty. Subsequent to the cessation of hostilities in early August 1898, the US and Spanish representatives negotiated a temporary peace protocol, signed on August 12. The protocol left several key issues unresolved, notably the future status of the Philippines; these issues were deferred to the official peace conference, which opened in Paris on October 1, 1898. The final treaty included provisions regarding the US occupation of Cuba, transfer of Puerto Rico and the Philippines to the United States, repatriation of prisoners of war, and relinquished indemnities on both sides.

It is worthwhile to consider some more ambiguous cases, most of which I do not code as peace treaties. Several of these cases refer to instances of wars that preceded and then became part of World War II, making it difficult to distinguish the conclusion of these wars from the conclusion of World War II. These cases include the Sino-Soviet War of 1929, where a planned peace conference was preempted by Japan's invasion of Manchuria; the 1937 Sino-Japanese War, whose conclusion was complicated by the subsequent civil war in China; and the 1939 Nomonhan War between the USSR and Japan, whose conclusion seems to have been determined as much by a border commission as by a formal peace agreement.[16] None of these wars is coded as being concluded via a peace treaty.

Some formal agreements do not resolve all of the political issues under dispute. The 1966 Tashkent Declaration that concluded the Second Kashmir War between India and Pakistan, for example, provided for the withdrawal of both militaries and resumption of diplomatic relations, but deferred resolution of political issues to another series of talks (which remained unsuccessful). Thus, while the Tashkent Declaration includes some political content, it did not really address the issues at stake in the war and is therefore not coded as a peace treaty here. This agreement contrasts with the Simla Agreement that concluded the 1971 Bangladesh War. The Simla Agreement and the Tashkent Declaration read very similarly, but the main issue under dispute in the Bangladesh War—the independence of East Pakistan/Bangladesh—was resolved via the Simla Agreement, which is therefore coded as a peace treaty here.[17] Similar to the Tashkent Agreement is a 1991 agreement associated with the 1977 Vietnamese-Cambodian war, which set the stage for a UN peacekeeping mission to prepare for free elections in Cambodia, but did not resolve the main issues at stake.

The UN's role in peace negotiations complicates our understanding of post-1945 peace treaties. Both the Iran-Iraq War and the 1990 Persian Gulf War were followed by UN Security Council resolutions that laid out the terms of peace, and to which the relevant parties agreed. Some scholars argue that such resolutions substitute for peace treaties today.[18] Although these resolutions serve similar purposes to peace treaties, their *form* diverges so dramatically from that of a traditional peace treaty that I do not code them as such. Rather than two sides negotiating terms across a conference table, these resolutions were more like mandates imposed by a third party, especially in the case of the Iran-Iraq War.

The main distinctions between peace treaties and non–peace treaties arise from both form and substance. On substance, agreements that address procedural but not substantive issues are not appropriately coded as peace treaties; for example, a ceasefire agreement that demarcates a buffer zone and establishes a timeline for future talks would not constitute a peace treaty, but an agreement that specified a border and resolved other outstanding issues could. On procedure, a peace treaty must be written, must be negotiated by the belligerents, and must be considered a peace treaty by the belligerents. Thus, an oral agreement, unilateral withdrawal, UNSC resolution, or written agreement that expressly states that it is not a peace treaty would not be considered or coded as one.

The decline in peace treaty use has gone mostly unnoticed in the scholarly literature, partly because previous scholarship on peace agreements has not focused on peace treaties *per se*, or has covered a much more limited time period than I do here. For example, Fortna's analysis of the durability of peace in interstate war takes as its unit of observation the years after ceasefires—not peace treaties—between 1946 and 1998.[19] The Uppsala Conflict Data Program's Peace Agreement Dataset, which covers all armed conflicts that produce at least twenty-five battle deaths, does include what I would code as peace treaties, but only since 1975.[20]

Looking at a broader span of history, of the fifty-six wars that ended after 1820 and before 1950, forty (over 70 percent) were accompanied by peace treaties. By contrast, only six of thirty-eight (approximately 15 percent) of wars ending after 1950 were concluded with peace treaties.

As figure 5.1 shows, the drop in peace treaty use is especially visible after World War II. The Korean War ended with an armistice, but no peace treaty. The Paris Peace Accords that terminated US military involvement in Vietnam served as a formal ceasefire document between the US and North Vietnamese without resolving any of the political issues motivating the war. The 1991 Persian Gulf war ended with a series of resolutions handed down from the UN Security Council, not negotiated between belligerent factions; although the United States certainly had a say in this document, the Iraqis played no role in determining the content of the resolutions.[21] Iran and Iraq agreed to a ceasefire and the promise of future peace treaty negotiations in 1988, but those negotiations never materialized.

On the other hand, some of the bitterest rivals of the late twentieth century have concluded peace treaties, but inconsistently so. For example, India and Pakistan signed a peace treaty after the 1971 Bangladesh War, but not after their prior (or subsequent) wars over Kashmir. Israel and

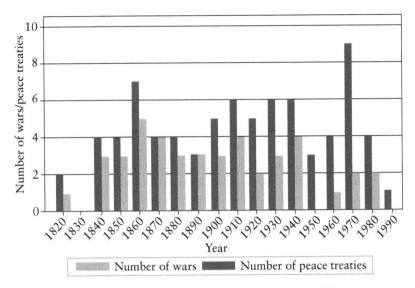

Figure 5.1 Interstate wars and peace treaties, 1820–2000

Egypt signed the Camp David Accords in 1978 and, decades later, Jordan also concluded a peace treaty with Israel. The "Football War" between El Salvador and Honduras was punctuated by the Treaty of Lima.[22] These few exceptions notwithstanding, the clear trend in the post–World War II era has been away from the use of formal peace treaties to conclude interstate war.

Theoretical Expectations

The same logic that links the proliferation of IHL to a decrease in declarations of war can be applied to the parallel decrease in peace treaties in interstate war. Like declarations of war, concluding a peace treaty constitutes a clear admission of having been in a state of war. In a state of war, there is no ambiguity as to the applicability of IHL. As IHL has increased in number and changed in character over time, states engaged in interstate wars are increasingly reluctant to admit to being or having been in a state of war, or to take any step that clearly indicates a state of war. Concluding peace treaties constitutes one of these unambiguous steps.

There are at least two additional implications of the argument that the proliferation of codified IHL has produced a decline in the use of peace treaties to end interstate wars. Generally speaking, states that violate *jus in bello* ought to be particularly averse to concluding peace treaties that would leave their leaders and soldiers vulnerable to demands for restitution or punishment. Peace treaties can serve as forums for accountability that these belligerents would prefer to avoid. Here, the war formality of peace treaties follows compliance or noncompliance (as opposed to compliance following a declaration of war, as discussed in chapter 4). The Allied Powers certainly viewed the Treaty of Versailles in this way, and used it as a vehicle to punish Germany for starting World War I, and for "the savage and inhuman manner in which it was conducted."[23]

More precisely, the first corollary of this argument is that violations of those laws of war that are most specific regarding consequences for violation may be especially likely to dissuade parties from the conclusion of a peace treaty. An example is the 1954 Geneva Convention on the Protection of Cultural Property. Although appropriating cultural treasures as spoils of war was a norm of international politics at least as far back as the Roman Empire, this norm changed dramatically beginning in the nineteenth century. Following the Napoleonic Wars, both art appreciation and international lawyers gained greater prominence.[24] This combination led to growing norms in favor of protecting cultural property during warfare; these norms were written down in a series of draft treaties and, most important, in the 1954 Geneva Convention.[25] In the 1954 Convention, "The High Contracting Parties undertake to take, within the framework of their ordinary criminal jurisdiction, all necessary steps to prosecute and impose penal or disciplinary sanctions upon those persons, of whatever nationality, who commit or order to be committed a breach of the present Convention" (Article 28). Many postwar trials have included charges of plundering based on that Convention. Several high-level Nazis were convicted of looting and plunder of cultural property as a result of the Nuremberg trials.[26] The International Criminal Tribunal for the former Yugoslavia (ICTY) prosecuted several Serbian and Croat military officers for such actions as bombing and plundering the Old Town of Dubrovnik and bombing the ancient Stari Most bridge in Mostar.[27]

Even when criminal charges are not on the table, the practice of requiring restitution and return of plundered cultural treasures has become accepted and common after war. Restitution is often required as part of peace terms, especially for the losing party. For example, the Allies' peace treaty with Austria after World War II contains extensive provisions for the return and restitution of various types of property, including cultural property. By contrast, Germany and Russia—two countries that did not conclude a peace treaty with each other—continue to debate the fate of thousands of cultural objects taken from Germany by Russian soldiers during World War II. In the absence of a peace treaty, the Russians are unable to make legal arguments about compensatory restitution that could allow them to keep these objects.[28] Thus, we should expect that belligerents that violate the laws of war regarding protection of cultural property should be less likely to conclude formal peace treaties than belligerents that comply with such laws.

One route around this kind of liability could be to include amnesty for an opponent's war crimes in a formal peace treaty. While it would be theoretically possible to use peace treaties to exonerate war criminality, a survey of the interstate war peace treaties analyzed in this chapter did not reveal a single instance of peace treaties being used in this way. Occasionally, such as in the 1920 Treaty of Tartu that ended Estonia's war with the USSR, provisions that grant amnesty to returning prisoners of war may be included, but states do not appear to build in amnesty for crimes committed by their former foes.

Second, we should also expect to see that the use of the two formalities of war are related. Wars that begin with declarations of war should be especially likely to conclude with formal peace treaties because the declaration would have already placed belligerents over the bright line of having to comply with *jus in bello*. There may be some exceptions to this rule: states that are eliminated by war from the international system would not be able to conclude a peace treaty. It is also possible that belligerents begin a war expecting to be compliant with *jus in bello*, but then are not compliant; thus, their incentive to conclude a formal peace treaty is diminished.

It is entirely possible, maybe even likely, that states and their militaries generally enter armed conflicts with intentions to comply with *jus in bello*, even without a formal declaration of war. But declaring war and concluding peace treaties erase all ambiguity with respect to legal liability for violations. In the cases where we see declarations of war and peace treaties in eras of high levels of codification of *jus in bello*, we should expect that the states engaging these formalities are those that have reason to believe in their ability to comply with international humanitarian law.

Empirical Analysis of Peace Treaties

I draw on qualitative and quantitative evidence to examine the conditions under which peace treaties are concluded after interstate war. The quantitative analysis is presented first, to illustrate general correlations and also to rule out some alternative explanations. The qualitative analysis is drawn from the same four cases used in chapters 3 and 4, in which declarations of war and compliance with the laws of war were discussed.

Quantitative Analysis

As with the analyses of declarations of war and compliance with the laws of war, the quantitative analysis presented below is based on the original I-WIT dataset. The quantitative analysis serves to test my hypotheses as well as to rule out others, and also points to new avenues of inquiry when considering trends in the use of peace treaties in interstate war.

Description of Variables   Below, I describe codings of key independent variables. Variables described previously in chapters 3 and 4 are discussed only briefly; others introduced for the first time in this chapter receive a fuller treatment. Many of these new variables are included to test alternative explanations that pertain to when and why peace treaties might be concluded, as opposed to when and why states might declare war or comply with the laws of war. As with the analysis from chapters 3 and 4, many of these variables are drawn from the I-WIT dataset. Following this description, I present and then discuss results from a series of logistic regressions on the conclusion of peace treaties in interstate war.

THE PROLIFERATION OF CODIFIED INTERNATIONAL HUMANITARIAN LAW

The main independent variable capturing the proliferation of IHL comes in two versions. The first version, *laws of war*, is simply a count of how many laws of war are codified at the time of the start of the war.[29] Wars examined that began prior to the first codification of IHL in 1856 include the Anglo-Persian War, the Italian Wars of Unification, and the Franco-Mexican War. Wars begun with the most laws of war on the books are, not surprisingly, the world's most recent wars, including the Kosovo, Kargil, Iraq, and Afghanistan wars. I find this version of the measure of the proliferation of IHL particularly useful for analyzing peace treaties, as belligerents considering concluding a peace treaty may have ratified different—and different numbers of—IHL treaties. Theoretically, it is difficult to know which belligerent's level of ratification should be most predictive of the conclusion of a peace treaty. This issue becomes especially complicated in multilateral wars. The second version, *mean ratifications*, takes the average number of *jus in bello* treaties ratified between the two dyad members. My hypothesis is that the higher the number of laws of war or mean ratifications, the lower the likelihood of the conclusion of a peace treaty.

NONCOMPLIANCE WITH CULTURAL PROPERTY LAWS

To test the claim that states that violate those laws of war specifying punishments are especially unlikely to conclude peace treaties, I use data from James Morrow and Hyeran Jo on compliance with the laws of war regarding protection of cultural property in all interstate wars in the twentieth century.[30] As in chapter 4, my analysis employs Morrow's "ordinal compliance index," which is a composite compliance score based on the magnitude, frequency, degree of centralization, and clarity of violations.[31] I focus on noncompliance with cultural property protection laws for two reasons. First, it is one of the issue areas among the laws of war that contains specific provisions for punishment. Second, unlike for most of the other issue areas considered by Morrow and Jo, all the documents used to generate their coding rules for protection of cultural property are actual treaties, rather than declarations or draft conventions. Given that my key causal mechanism rests precisely on the effect of proliferation of *jus in bello* as codified in international treaties, incorporating the additional element of uncodified laws of war into a measure of noncompliance might add a great deal of error to the analysis.

DECLARATION OF WAR

The analysis presented below also begins to assess the relationship between declarations of war and peace treaties. One corollary hypothesis of my argument is that the formalities of war go together: states that declare war also tend to sign peace treaties; conversely, wars begun informally are also more likely to end informally. The data on declarations of war are taken from I-WIT. This variable is binary, capturing whether at least one member of the war-dyad has declared war upon the other.

Military victory. Military victory is often accompanied by spoils, the ability to rewrite history, and an increased likelihood of durable peace. When one side has clearly won a military conflict, conference tables may become more efficient than battlefields as locations for resolving political issues. This is not to say that the winning side necessarily dictates the terms of peace unilaterally. While there are certainly cases where this has occurred (the Treaty of Versailles is an obvious example), as long as the losing side has not been eliminated completely, negotiations can be prolonged even in the wake of a decisive military defeat.[32] Nonetheless, military victory may be more likely to produce a peace treaty than would a war that ends in a draw, because the alternative—a return to the battlefield—would not be a very credible threat by the losing side. This logic suggests that wars ending in military victory will be more likely to be accompanied by peace treaties than will wars that end in draws.

Separately, Page Fortna and Monica Toft have noted a decline of outright victories in wars.[33] Both interstate and civil wars are much more likely to end in draws today. If one of the key purposes of a peace treaty is to codify a settlement of the issues over which war is fought,[34] we should expect that peace treaties will decline as draws increase. I-WIT includes a variable for military outcome as a tie or draw, a slight victory for one side, a clear victory for one side, or an extreme victory. I transform this variable into a binary variable, where *military victory*=1 if the war ended in a clear or extreme victory.[35]

Territorial change. Another circumstance that could increase the probability of a peace treaty being concluded is territorial exchange as a result of the war. Territorial disagreements are a major cause of war.[36] If territory is ceded or taken in war, a peace treaty provides an opportunity to codify that change. In effect, the peace treaty can serve as a type of deed: a public document certifying ownership of a particular piece of territory. Indeed, this may be one of the most important purposes of peace treaties. This suggests that more wars in which one side receives territory from another are accompanied by peace treaties than are wars in which territory does not change hands.

Recent scholarship on territorial conflict and, in particular, on the emergence of a norm against territorial conquest in the mid-to-late twentieth century, suggests that territorial exchange as a result of warfare is likely to be less acceptable today.[37] This does not seem to prevent the emergence of territorial wars in the same era; territory remains an extremely salient cause of war. Two of the most important post-1945 clusters of wars—those between India and Pakistan over Kashmir and those in the Middle East over Israel's borders—are indisputably territorial conflicts. Nonetheless, if a war is being fought over territory, but a strong international norm exists against territorial aggression, the public transfer of territory as a result of interstate war may become unacceptable to the international community.

Territorial change simply describes whether territory changed hands as a result of the war. Taken from the I-WIT dataset, it is coded relative to the territorial status quo ante bellum, on a 5-point scale: no territory changing hands; colonial possessions or protectorates that change hands or become independent; ownership changes over small or unimportant bits of territory; large or important changes in territorial control of sovereign territory; or entire states being taken over. As with the military victory variable, I transform this variable into a binary variable, where *territorial change*=1 if any territory exchanged hands during the war.

Foreign-imposed regime change (FIRC). Many recent wars suggest another, related, change in war: today, wars are more likely to end in regime change than in territorial conquest or more traditional limited military victories. Insofar as regime change is an increasingly common mode of war termination, this may have rendered peace treaties unnecessary. Instead of forging an agreement between foes, what may be more useful in these types of cases is a treaty of alliance or friendship. This observation suggests that wars concluding with foreign-imposed regime changes (FIRCs) will be less likely to be accompanied by a peace treaty compared to wars that do not conclude with FIRCs. *FIRC* codes for whether a foreign-imposed regime change has occurred as a result of the war, and includes cases such as the occupations of Japan and Germany after World War II as regime changes. The coding for this variable is taken from the list by Alexander Downes and Jonathan Monten of such regime changes.[38] The Downes and Monten list was then cross-referenced with the Correlates of War list of interstate wars to determine which regime changes were associated with specific wars.

State death. A related possibility refers to wars that conclude with the destruction of a state, in which case there is no one on the other side of the table with whom a peace treaty could be signed. This logic suggests that wars ending in state deaths will be less likely to be accompanied by peace treaties than will wars ending with the retention of sovereignty for the belligerents.[39] For example, the wars that pitted Sardinia/Piedmont against the Two Sicilies and the Papal States in 1860, leading to the unification of Italy, as well as the 1866 Seven Weeks War that led to the unification of Germany, were not accompanied by peace treaties between Italy and Germany on the one hand and the countries they absorbed on the other. I use my own 2007 definition of state death as "the formal loss of control over foreign policy to another state" to code whether any dyad member was eliminated at the conclusion (or during the course) of hostilities.[40] The 2007 list of state deaths, however, is amended here to exclude cases of foreign-imposed regime change, so that *state death* and *FIRC* can be included in the same model. For example, while the original list of state deaths includes the post-World War II occupations of Germany and Japan, this amended list excludes those cases because they are already coded as foreign-imposed regime changes.

Duration and war end year. Both of these variables are taken from the Correlates of War. *Duration* is included as a proxy for wars where bargaining problems are particularly acute. Here, the expectation would be that longer wars are less likely to conclude in peace treaties precisely because their issues are so difficult to resolve. *War end year* controls for the possibility of a secular time trend.

UN membership. In the same way that international lawyers argue that the UN has made declarations of war obsolete, they could claim a similar effect of the UN on the conclusion of interstate peace treaties.[41] I therefore include a categorical variable for UN membership in the analysis of peace treaties. This variable ranges from 0 to 2, where 0 indicates that neither member of the war-dyad is a UN member, 1 indicates that one of the two belligerents is a UN member, and 2 indicates that both are UN members. The logic behind the claim that UN membership should decrease the use of peace treaties suggests that this variable should generate a negative coefficient.

Joint polity. As suggested in chapter 3, democracies may be particularly likely to employ the formalities of war. Peace treaties can be viewed as contracts and, as such, may be consistent with principles of transparency and reasoned argument underlying democracy. *Joint polity* is based on the Polity IV measure of democracy. I use the lower of the two polity scores to produce *joint polity*. The expectation here is that dyads with higher joint democratic scores will be more likely to conclude peace treaties compared to dyads with lower joint democratic scores.

Great powers. The variables *neither great power* and *one great power* capture whether neither or one of the two belligerents in the war-dyad holds great power status, according to the Correlates of War list of great powers. Great powers may see no need to deign to engage in the formalities of war with non–great powers. Thus, we should expect that the coefficient on *one great power* is negative. The sign of the coefficient on *neither great power* is more difficult to predict. *Both great powers* is the reference category.

Veto players. The more veto players in a state, the more difficult it may be to conclude a peace treaty. This logic mirrors the claim that civil wars with more veto players on either side will last longer than civil wars with fewer veto players.[42] As with the analysis of declarations of war, I used Witold Heinisz's measure of political constraint to identify the number of veto players in each dyad. Unfortunately, however, too much data is missing for the years in which wars end to include this variable in the analysis.[43]

European versus non-European. Just as European states might be less willing to declare war upon non-European states, because declarations of war constitute a sign of respect, European states might also have been reluctant to conclude peace treaties with non-European states. I therefore include an indicator variable, based on Fazal and Greene's coding of European and non-European states, for dyads that include one European and one non-European member.[44]

Counterinsurgency. Finally, it is possible that wars where at least one side employs guerrilla warfare will be less likely to conclude in peace treaties because both insurgency and counterinsurgency may be associated with higher rates of noncompliance with the laws of war—as the results from chapter 4 suggest—or because the counterinsurgent views the insurgent as an illegitimate opponent, unworthy of use of war formalities. As in chapter 3, I include a COIN variable that captures whether the war had a counterinsurgency element.

Regression Analysis and Discussion   The universe of cases for quantitative analysis of peace treaties is interstate war-dyads from 1816 to 2007. Here I use nondirected war-dyads as my unit of analysis; thus the United States versus Germany during World War II generates one observation (not two) in the dataset. Because the dependent variable—whether a peace treaty is concluded—is binary, I run a series of logistic regressions on peace treaties in interstate war. Robust standard errors are used, clustered on war.

The results reported in table 5.1 indicate that the number of IHL treaties in effect at the close of a war is significantly, and negatively, correlated

TABLE 5.1 Logistic regressions on peace treaties, by war-dyad

	1	2	3	4	5	6 (UNSC)	7
Laws of war	−.34 (.10) p=.00		−.25 (.11) p=.02	−1.34 (.38) p=.00	−1.14 (.71) p=.11	−.26 (.08) p=.00	−.33 (.10) p=.00
Mean ratifications		−.32 (.12) p=.01					
Noncompliance with Cultural Property Laws				−1.88 (1.00) p=.06			
Declaration of war	1.38 (.71) p=.05						1.47 (.72) p=.04
Military victory	.62 (.65) p=.34	1.20 (.76) p=.11	.91 (.67) p=.18			.84 (.69) p=.23	.47 (.61) p=.44
Territorial change	1.20 (.52) p=.02	1.21 (.41) p=.00	.91 (.50) p=.07	.98 (.58) p=.09	.74 (.49) p=.13	1.54 (.44) p=.00	1.22 (.52) p=.02
FIRC	−1.10 (.79) p=.17	−.48 (.59) p=.42	−1.21 (.66) p=.07	−.15 (.59) p=.80		−.72 (.61) p=.24	−1.15 (.81) p=.16
UN membership			−1.07 (.55) p=.05	1.01 (.93) p=.28			
Joint polity score	.11 (.07) p=.14	.12 (.08) p=.13	.15 (.08) p=.07			.05 (.07) p=.46	.11 (.08) p=.14

	1	2	3	4	5	6 (UNSC)	7
Neither great power	−1.35 (.69) p=.05	−2.87 (.85) p=.00	−1.51 (.82) p=.07	−1.24 (1.05) p=.24	−1.18 (.75) p=.12	−1.22 (.78) p=.12	−1.52 (.69) p=.03
One great power	−1.95 (.57) p=.00	−2.41 (.72) p=.00	−2.20 (.75) p=.00	−1.89 (1.28) p=.14	−2.03 (.67) p=.00	−1.86 (.67) p=.01	−1.87 (.50) p=.00
State death	−1.40 (.81) p=.09	−1.19 (.53) p=.03	−1.50 (.77) p=.05	.72 (.98) p=.47	−1.04 (.47) p=.03	.85 (1.44) p=.56	−1.45 (.78) p=.07
European v. non-European	.58 (.40) p=.15	.66 (.37) p=.08	.71 (.43) p=.10	.36 (.63) p=.57	.82 (.41) p=.04	.90 (.35) p=.01	
Duration	.00 (.00) p=.25	.00 (.00) p=.40	.00 (.00) p=.32	.00 (.00) p=.21		.00 (.00) p=.56	.00 (.00) p=.26
War end year					.07 (.05) p=.20		
Counterinsurgency							−.03 (1.05) p=.98
Constant	2.82 (1.01) p=.01	2.50 (1.33) p=.06	3.54 (1.12) p=.00	13.33 (3.70) p=.00	−122.00 (97.88) p=.21	1.94 (1.06) p=.07	3.12 (1.00) p=.00
Number of subjects	224	228	228	101	253	228	224
Pseudo R-squared	.4536	.2747	.4530	.5305	.3601	.3201	.4482
Chi2	0.0000	0.0000	0.0000	0.0001	0.0000	0.0000	0.0000
% correctly predicted	83.48	75.44	82.46	86.14	81.82	73.68	83.48

Note: Robust standard errors in parentheses.

with the frequency of use of peace treaties. Based on the analysis in model 1, wars that ended in 2000 when there were eighteen codified laws of war were 90 percent less likely to conclude with peace treaties, compared with wars ended in 1900, when there were four laws of war on the books.[45] Figure 5.2 illustrates this relationship. Put slightly differently, Russia and Britain, which fought on opposite sides of the Crimean War at a time prior to the codification of the laws of war, were 60 percent more likely to end their war with a peace treaty compared to Afghanistan and Britain after the 2001 Afghanistan War, when Afghanistan had ratified eight and the UK twenty-five laws of war (for an average of 16.5). The Crimean War

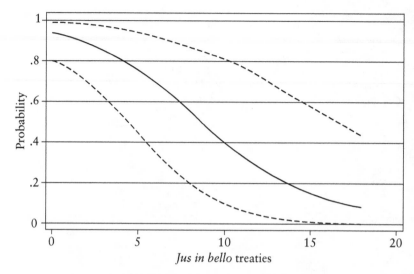

Figure 5.2 Probability of peace treaty as codified IHL increases. Data includes confidence intervals.

was in fact concluded with a peace treaty—the 1856 Peace of Paris—while the 2001 Afghanistan War was not.

The results are also consistent with two corollary hypotheses derived from the broader claim that the proliferation of codified IHL leads to a decreasing use of the formalities of war. Model 4 tests the claim that states that violate laws of war regarding protection of cultural property (which are unusually specific about consequences of violation) will be especially unlikely to conclude peace treaties. The logic behind this claim is that these states will want to avoid the forum of accountability established by peace treaty negotiations. The coefficient on noncompliance with laws of war protecting cultural property is negative and statistically significant: it appears that the states that most violate these laws of war are over 80 percent less likely to conclude peace treaties compared with states that are most compliant. Additionally, as predicted, wars that begin formally are approximately 40 percent more likely to conclude formally than wars where neither side has issued a declaration of war.[46]

Two sets of control variables are also correlated with the conclusion of peace treaties. The first set refers to the role of territory, or territorial control, in concluding peace treaties. Not surprisingly, belligerents that experience state death—that is, they are eliminated from the international system—are half as likely to conclude peace treaties compared to states that survive their wars. This result is interesting when compared with the lack of a statistical relationship between the conclusion of peace treaties on the one hand and foreign-imposed regime change on the other. In these latter cases, the state survives as an international legal entity able to enter into agreements such as peace treaties, but its regime or its leaders are replaced by the victorious powers as a result of the war.

Whether territory is exchanged as a result of the war is also significantly related to the conclusion of peace treaties. Wars ending with territorial exchange are nearly 40 percent more likely to be concluded with a formal peace treaty than wars not ending with a territorial exchange. Here, the peace treaty may serve as a type of contract that codifies the territorial exchange. But territorial exchange cannot explain the *decline* in peace treaties; fewer wars end with territorial exchange today than in the past, while wars ending in territorial exchange are significantly more likely to be codified via peace treaties.

The other set of significant control variables refers to the relative status of the belligerents. Dyads where neither state is a great power and those where only one state is a great power are significantly less likely to conclude their wars with formal peace treaties than the reference category of dyads where both states are great powers. Surprisingly, however, dyads where one state is European while the other is not tend to conclude their wars with peace treaties more so than dyads with zero or two European members. The unexpected result here could stem from the fact that the dyads outside the *European v. non-European* category are a particularly mixed lot (in other words, the reference category is very heterogeneous), or from the possibility that European states have been especially likely to win against and then impose peace treaties—on their preferred terms—on non-European states.

Additional alternative explanations do not fare as well. The relationship between military victory and peace treaties is not statistically significant, even when the *European v. non-European* variable is excluded from the model. Four other variables—*joint polity, duration, war end year,* and *counterinsurgency*—also fail to attain statistical significance. The result on *joint polity* contrasts with the analysis of the relationship between democracies and declarations of war presented in chapter 3. The sign on the coefficient is positive, as predicted, but its lack of statistical significance suggests either a different relationship between democracy on the one hand and peace treaties on the other, or the relatively complicated nature of the joint—versus monadic—analysis of this relationship.

The time-related variables are perhaps most surprising in this analysis. Duration of a war is never statistically significant. Moreover, the substantive effect of this variable is consistently at or very close to 0. The positive coefficient on the year in which a war ends suggests that that, if anything, peace treaties are *more* likely to be concluded in later than in earlier wars. This result should be particularly reassuring to readers concerned about the possible role of a secular time trend driving these results.

The final set of variables refers to the role of the United Nations in predicting peace treaties, which is the main rival to my own argument. Model 6 in table 5.1 amends the dependent variable to include UN Security Council resolutions that could serve in place of peace treaties. In other words, this model predicts a result of peace treaties or UNSC resolutions. Amending the dependent variable in this way does not, however, change the results. The growth of codified IHL continues, I argue, to exert significant downward pressure on the likelihood of peace treaty conclusion. The results of the regression analysis also do not suggest that UNSC resolutions serve in lieu of peace treaties. Indeed, there are only two instances of UNSC resolutions (both of which called for ceasefires) that could serve as peace treaties: Resolution 598 following the Iran-Iraq War of 1980–88, and Resolution 687 following the First Gulf War of 1990–91.

Models 3 and 4 include an indicator variable assessing whether one, both, or neither member of the dyad is a member of the UN at the time of the conflict. Here, the results for different time periods are inconsistent. For the analysis that includes the nineteenth and twentieth centuries, UN membership is significantly and negatively correlated with the conclusion of peace treaties. But when we exclude the nineteenth century and restrict the analysis to the twentieth century—the century when UN membership is most relevant—the sign of the coefficient flips, and it is no longer statistically significant. At best, we can say that the relationship between UN membership and the conclusion of peace treaties is indeterminate according to these results.

Table 5.2 explores this relationship further. While since 1945 most states have been members of the UN, not all states are. Several states—including

TABLE 5.2 Peace treaties and United Nations membership

	1816–2007		UN era only		
	Pre-1945	Post-1945	UN member (both)	UN member (one)	Non-UN member (neither)
Peace treaty	75% (123)	7% (7)	12% (7)	0% (0)	0% (0)
No peace treaty	25% (40)	93% (91)	88% (53)	100% (31)	100% (7)
Column total	100% (163)	100% (98)	100% (60)	100% (31)	100% (7)

China, North Korea, North Vietnam, and Israel—joined the UN after fighting major wars as recognized states in the UN era.[47] None of these non-UN members concluded peace treaties. Instead, *only* dyads where both parties are UN members use this war formality during the UN era. Dyads in which two UN members concluded formal peace treaties include: Spain and Morocco (Ifni War), El Salvador and Honduras (Football War), and India and Pakistan (Bangladesh War). Given that UN members appear to be more likely to conclude peace treaties than non-UN members in the UN era, it is difficult to sustain the argument that the existence of the UN accounts for the decline of peace treaties.

Tests for robustness, such as exclusion of the world wars, using the log of duration, or including the highest (rather than the average) level of ratification for a dyad, yielded stable results with respect to the coefficients on the *jus in bello* and *ratifications* variables; the great power and state death coefficients sometimes lose statistical significance in these specifications, while the coefficients on territorial exchange and military victory tend to become more statistically significant.

Qualitative Analysis

I use the same set of cases discussed in previous chapters in the analysis of declarations of war and compliance with IHL. The analysis of the Spanish-American War presented below shows that, as with declarations of war, the use of peace treaties was considered to be customary in warfare in the late nineteenth century. But as the laws of war began to proliferate in number and change in character, belligerents—especially those most obliged to comply—became hesitant to conclude peace treaties. This hesitance was particularly evident when they had violated IHL during the course of the conflict, as in the Boxer Rebellion. The case of the Simla Agreement that concluded the 1971 Bangladesh War between India and Pakistan is particularly interesting because it provides an opportunity to observe behavior my theory would not predict: the Indians declared war, but then violated IHL regarding repatriation of prisoners of war. The Pakistanis called their bluff, and forced them back to the equilibrium path of compliance, enabling the conclusion of the Simla Agreement that officially ended the war. The Falklands/Malvinas case is more typical of the post-Geneva era in its informality; here, the lack of a peace treaty is likely due at least in part to the absence of resolution on the key territorial issue at stake.

Custom, *Jus in bello*, and the Treaty of Paris   Similarly to the issuance of declarations of war at the start, the desirability and conclusion of a formal peace treaty at the end appears to have been taken for granted by the parties to the Spanish-American war. A formal peace was important to both sides because, without a peace treaty, a return to war was assumed. Spain had suffered enough hurt that it greatly feared an attack on its homeland, and the United States saw no honor in further beating a defeated enemy. Secretary of State John Hay described the US government's preferences: "A treaty of peace is of the highest importance to the United States if it can be had without the sacrifice of plain duty. The President would regret deeply the resumption of hostilities against a prostrate foe."[48]

The conclusion of a formal peace treaty was also important because it served as a public representation of Spain's cession of sovereignty over Cuba, which was soon to become independent, as well as Spain's agreement to cede Puerto Rico, Guam, and the Philippines to the United States. The first three articles of the treaty were devoted to these territorial dispositions, which had dominated the peace conference. Puerto Rico and Guam's futures were not particularly controversial. But Spain was both loath to surrender sovereignty over Cuba unless to transfer it to the United States, and extremely reluctant to give up its Philippine colony. Indeed, this last issue nearly terminated the peace conference prematurely.

After over a month of negotiations with very little progress, the US delegation gave an ultimatum to the Spanish peace commissioners. The key demand was for Spain to concede the Philippines (in addition to Puerto Rico, Cuba, and Guam, which had already been conceded) in exchange for $20 million. The cession of this final Spanish colony would be the death knell of Spain as a great power.

Upon receipt of the US ultimatum, the president of the Spanish Peace Commission, Eugenio Montero Ríos, sent a telegram to the Spanish minister of state Duque de Almodóvar del Río outlining the terms of the ultimatum. Montero Ríos added his own assessment:

> I believe that the American proposition is much more prejudicial than beneficial, and that it would be best for Spain as an ultimate proposition to offer to the U.S. gratuitously the Antilles and Philippines, with the provision that the colonial obligations shall pass with them; or the U.S. insure to Spain the necessary sum, so that she may cover these obligations if they remain at her charge. If the U.S. does not accept this proposition it is preferable to leave the Antilles and Philippines to them, because of lack of resources to defend them, and to terminate the negotiations without a treaty of peace.[49]

The Spanish government's response to the US demand was fearful and humbled. Almodóvar reported that "further resistance will be useless and the rupture of the negotiations which is threatened will be dangerous."[50] The danger of which Almodóvar spoke was twofold: Spain feared an American attack on Spain itself, and also feared "restless" internal forces that were "stimulated" by the "alarming" duration of negotiations.[51] Spain thus returned to the negotiating table with all pretense stripped. It was a conquered nation and would accept, rather than dictate, terms.

How did the extent of US and Spanish compliance with *jus in bello* affect the conclusion of the Treaty of Paris? As discussed in chapter 4, US and Spanish treatment of each other's soldiers and sailors was exemplary. The mutual respect and civility underlying high levels of compliance with *jus in bello* during the war continued during the peace negotiations. While it would be difficult to make the argument that high levels of compliance actively helped the peace treaty process along, it is probably not too far a stretch to surmise that noncompliance—especially by the Spanish—might have changed the nature of the conference or the terms of the treaty.

Contention over Spanish treatment of Cuban insurgents did surface during key moments in the treaty negotiations. In rejecting the Spanish demand that the United States assume Spain's debt in Cuba, the US

delegation argued that the debt was created to finance the very counterinsurgency that prompted US involvement in the conflict; the United
States refused to subsidize Spain's "uncivilized warfare."[52] This particular point notwithstanding, Spanish noncompliance with customary
jus in bello in Cuba does not appear to have affected the prospects for
a peace treaty, probably because this behavior had not been directed
against the United States.

The Spanish-American War was, in many ways, an archetypical traditional, formal war. Both sides were very much focused on the nuance of
formality—of who declared war when, scrupulous observance of *jus in
bello* once hostilities commenced, and engagement with all the formal trappings of a peace conference even though the winning side was in a position
to dictate virtually all the postwar terms. But this conflict was also one of
the last of a dying breed. With the opening of the Hague Conference only
one year after the war, a new era of interstate conflict began. As exemplified
by the Boxer Rebellion and subsequent wars, the formalities of war would
become less attractive—and, in consequence, less frequently used—in the
wars to come.

The Final Protocol of the Boxer Rebellion   The "Final Protocol," the peace
agreement between the Allies and the Chinese that officially ended the Boxer
Rebellion, occupies an ambiguous position. It was clearly a formal agreement covering many of the issues over which the conflict was fought. But it is
not titled a "peace treaty," nor do the words "peace" or "war" appear any-
where in the protocol. Moreover, it was not formally ratified by the Allied
parties to the protocol.[53] Nonetheless, the negotiations surrounding the protocol were described as "peace negotiations" in informal correspondence.[54]
The Allies themselves were clear, however, that the Final Protocol was not
meant to be a peace treaty, and they were clear about the reasons why:

> The Congress of the United States, the French Chambers, and the Bundesrat
> had not been asked to consent to a declaration of war. It is significant that in
> the important Budget Commission of the Reichstag doubts could be heard as
> to the propriety of concluding with China under these circumstances a "treaty
> of peace." The caption "Final Protocol," it seems, was deliberately chosen
> in order to point at those provisions in American, French, and German con-
> stitutional law which reserved the decision as to a declaration of war to the
> legislature. *It served the purpose of denying the legal existence of war.*[55]

Of the possible drivers of formal peace treaties to emerge from the quantitative analysis, violation of *jus in bello* was certainly present in this case. Chinese violations were severely punished in the Final Protocol.[56] Allied violations may well have led to reluctance to conclude a formal peace treaty that would explicitly recognize that the members of the Relief Expedition had been in a state of war. Such recognition would have been legally consequential, especially in light of the fact that every member of the Relief Expedition had signed the Hague Conventions one year earlier. In particular, both inhumane treatment of prisoners of war and pillage were expressly prohibited by the second 1899 Convention. The Relief Expedition members were guilty of violating both laws of war. Seven years later, the intentionally ambiguous status of the Final Protocol to the Boxer Rebellion would inspire the Chinese delegate to the meetings that produced the 1907 Hague Conventions to request that a requirement for a formal definition of war be included in the newest codification of *jus in bello*. His request was unsuccessful.[57]

The Simla Agreement   The 1972 Simla Agreement, which concluded the 1971 Bangladesh War, achieved three aims. First, it explicitly affirmed Indian and Pakistani commitment to the principles of the UN Charter. Second, it allowed for the resumption of diplomatic and trade relations. And third, it required that the Indians and Pakistanis each retreat to their side of the international border.

What the Simla Agreement did not do is at least as important as what it did do. It did not resolve the conflict over Kashmir, although there is speculation that India's prime minister Indira Gandhi and Pakistan's prime minister Zulfikar Ali Bhutto agreed informally to withdraw to the 1971 ceasefire line, called the "line of control" in the Simla Agreement.[58] It also contained no formal Pakistani recognition of Bangladeshi independence.[59]

In requiring that Indian and Pakistani forces retreat to behind international borders, however, the treaty contains an implicit recognition of the new Bangladeshi state, thus resolving the main issue under dispute. Indeed, the agreement formalized facts on the ground at this point; the Indians had departed Bangladesh in January of 1972, and it had been operating as a sovereign state for months prior to the treaty.

One outstanding issue during the Simla negotiations was India's detention of Pakistani prisoners of war. Their detention was a clear breach of the Third 1949 Geneva Convention, which states, "Prisoners of war shall be released and repatriated without delay after the cessation of active hostilities" (Article 118). A critical argument of this chapter is that states that violate *jus in bello* should be particularly unlikely to want to conclude peace treaties. Here, the victorious state—the one in a position to dictate terms—was in clear violation of *jus in bello*. How can this fact be reconciled with the conclusion and signing of the Simla Agreement?

While India was holding the POWs as a negotiating tactic to get Pakistan to recognize Bangladesh, this strategy failed precisely because India had declared itself to be in a formal state of war. Moreover, as a leader of the nonaligned movement, India had repeatedly stated its support for international law. To flout it so openly would be hypocritical and embarrassing. Pakistan filed suit against India in the International Court of Justice, arguing that because only Pakistan (given its nonrecognition of Bangladesh) had jurisdiction to try its soldiers who had been accused of committing genocide and crimes against humanity, India was in violation of the third 1949 Geneva Convention and must return the prisoners.[60] The *Times of India* titled one article on the issue "Pak Bid to Divert War Opinion Seen."[61] India eventually relented, leading to a Pakistani request that the court dismiss the case before a decision over jurisdiction was rendered. Perhaps tellingly, India has not signed a peace treaty with Pakistan since the 1972 Simla Agreement, despite continued skirmishing—including one major war in 1999—over Kashmir.

Victory without a Peace Treaty   The politics that shaped the start of the Falklands/Malvinas War also colored its end. The British clearly won the fight, as evidenced by local surrenders by Argentines, including Argentina's General Menendez at Government House in Stanley, the seat of the Falkland Islands government.[62]

But high-level negotiations and agreement proved elusive. The British demanded some sort of formal recognition of surrender or ceasefire, while the Argentines insisted on the end of sanctions. Moreover, the political situation within Argentina made the conclusion of a formal ceasefire (let alone a formal peace treaty) difficult to achieve. Argentine public opinion strongly opposed a formal ceasefire; Argentine military opinion strongly opposed Galtieri.[63] And on June 17, Galtieri's junta collapsed. Although this is not a case of state death, it did raise the question: from whom could the British accept surrender? The subsequent domestic political reshuffling in Buenos Aires appeared to preclude a negotiated end to the war.

British sanctions against Argentina were mostly lifted by July 1982, but some remained in place, especially those regarding arms trading. Argentina was actually stricter than the UK, in that it retained more sanctions against the British, although the British sought to extend sanctions until a formal cessation of hostilities could be reached.[64] Diplomatic relations resumed in 1990,[65] but the issue of ownership of the Falklands/Malvinas remains unresolved in that the British and Argentines never did come to a formal agreement.[66]

In this case, the lack of an agreement on the main territorial issue at stake appears to have been the critical impediment to any kind of peace treaty. If, as suggested by the results of the quantitative analysis reported in table 5.1, peace treaties sometimes serve as a kind of deed for territorial transfers, both parties must agree to that transfer. As of mid-2015, sovereignty over the Falklands/Malvinas continues to be contested. The islands may be to the British-Argentine relationship what the Kurile Islands have been to the Japanese and Russians since at least the end of World War II: a critical sticking point that prevents the conclusion of a peace treaty.[67] In the case of the Falklands/Malvinas, even the formality of a ceasefire is lacking, but this is perhaps not surprising in that the Argentines retain their homeland; it was an archipelago off their coast that they were forced to evacuate, not part of the Argentine mainland. In other words, the Argentine government, such as it was, did not have a gun to its head; it therefore had few incentives to accept the national humiliation of surrender.

To what extent did violations of *jus in bello* impede the conclusion of a peace treaty in this case? Here, the role of *jus in bello* seems limited at best. General comportment during the interstate war was good, as discussed in chapter 4. Where the law of war was most violated—in the creation of the quasi-blockade by the British—legal culpability for violation was limited, perhaps nonexistent. This is due in part to the absence of a declaration of war. An ineffective blockade is not considered a war crime, and the British really only offended their Argentine opponent with this blockade, as no neutral vessels were taken. Had neutral vessels attempted to enter the exclusion zone, however, the international outcry over a British violation of *jus in bello* might have been much louder. The British had few incentives to risk liability by negotiating a peace treaty.

The lack of formality of the Falklands War was felt keenly among the British military. Admiral Sandy Woodward, Commander of the Falklands Battle Group, described morale as: "Quite a problem, aggravated by 'war' never being declared or over."[68] Thus, the increasing codification of *jus in bello* that, I argue, has produced the informalization of interstate war may hinder warfighting not only by placing restrictions on how militaries fight, but also on how well they do so.

A Formal Relationship: Do Declarations of War and Peace Treaties Go Together?

Declarations of war are significant predictors of peace treaties, suggesting that the formalities of war often go together. The quantitative results discussed above indicate that war-dyads in which at least one party has issued a declaration of war are approximately 40 percent more likely to conclude peace treaties than war-dyads in which neither party has declared war. At the same time, declarations of war are not a perfect predictor of peace treaties, raising the question of when and why the formalities of war do not go together. There are a number of cases of undeclared wars concluded by peace treaties where the same question holds. Table 5.3 summarizes the relationship between declarations of war and peace treaties.

There are at least three reasons that wars begun with a declaration of war might not end with a peace treaty. First, belligerents might declare war expecting to be compliant with *jus in bello*, but fail to comply during the course of a war. Having declared war, these belligerents were obliged to comply with IHL; cognizant of their noncompliance at the end of the war, they might opt out of concluding a peace treaty in order to avoid the additional exposure to accountability during treaty negotiations. A recent history of the laws of war in World War I by Isabel Hull notes that the Allies clearly linked Germany's responsibility for its conduct during

TABLE 5.3 Declarations of war and peace treaties

	Peace treaty	No peace treaty
Declaration of war	86	21
No declaration of war	41	108

the war to the peace treaty. She quotes from a letter from Clemenceau to Bulow: "Germany's responsibility, however, is not confined to having planned and started the war. She is no less responsible for the savage and inhuman manner in which it was conducted."[69]

Second, wars that begin with declarations of war may not conclude with peace treaties when one party to a dyad is eliminated during the course of a conflict. We know, from the results reported above, that wars where one side experiences state death are less than half as likely to be conducted by peace treaties compared to wars where both states survive. This result is especially visible in a series of World War II dyads, where Germany, in particular, did not conclude peace treaties with many of its adversaries in part because of partition into East and West.

Third, in cases where only one party to a dyad declared war, even if that party was compliant with *jus in bello*, the other state that was not compliant would be unlikely to agree to conclude a peace treaty. The case of the Boxer Rebellion, discussed above, fits this template. The Chinese declared war upon the members of the Relief Expedition, but the egregious violations by the Relief Expedition gave the Western powers little incentive to conclude a formal peace treaty with the Chinese, especially given that the members of the Relief Expedition had so recently signed the 1899 Hague Conventions.

It is more difficult to understand why wars not begun with a declaration of war might end with a peace treaty. As above, the correlation between declarations of war and peace treaties is large and statistically significant. In examining the cases where the formalities of war have not gone together I am, therefore, trying to understand the exceptions to the rule. One possible explanation for cases where war is not declared but a peace treaty is concluded is that belligerents might be unexpectedly compliant with the laws of war and thus feel safer concluding a peace treaty at the conclusion of the war because they have little to fear in terms of accountability for violations of *jus in bello*. For example, both Honduras and El Salvador were compliant with *jus in bello* during the 1969 Football War, which was an undeclared war that was concluded with the Treaty of Lima in 1980.

The change in use of peace treaties has gone mostly unremarked in what is now a robust literature on war termination. This gap in the literature is problematic because peace treaties are more than mere formalities of war. Recent scholarship suggests that formal peace agreements have an independent effect on the duration and even perhaps the quality of peace.[70] If this is the case, then the declining use of peace treaties in interstate war is a troubling trend.

The conventional wisdom among international lawyers is that the decline in peace treaty use, as with the decline in declarations of war, is explained by the emergence of the UN system. While there may be some truth to this claim, the empirical analysis in this chapter casts doubt on it. UN Security Council resolutions do not appear to substitute for peace treaties, and those states that concluded peace treaties in the UN era were all UN members. Non-UN members who participated in wars did not conclude peace treaties.

Instead, the evidence suggests that the decline in peace treaties is more closely correlated with the proliferation of international humanitarian law. I argue that this is because states seek to limit their legal liability under this developing body of international law, and so they avoid taking steps, such as making peace treaties, that clearly demarcate states of war. When states violate the laws of war during a conflict, they appear to be especially unlikely to conclude peace treaties; this is because they seek to avoid the window of accountability that negotiations for such a treaty would open.

While the declining use of peace treaties in interstate war is of concern, contrasting the rate of peace treaty use in interstate versus civil war reveals a different puzzle. At the same time that interstate wars decreasingly conclude with peace treaties, civil wars increasingly do so. In the next several chapters, I explore the effects of the development of the laws of war on rebel groups in civil wars, in contrast with its effects presented in chapters 3, 4, and 5 on states in interstate wars.

6

DECLARATIONS OF INDEPENDENCE IN CIVIL WARS

The laws of war were created by states principally to govern their wars with each other. The previous three chapters have covered the empirical terrain marked by the changing use of war formalities in interstate war. Beginning with interstate wars makes sense, both because they are the starting point for the laws of war themselves, and because interstate wars were the most frequent form of armed conflict when these laws were first being codified.

Today, however, most wars are civil wars. As such, any understanding of how the development of the laws of war has affected the politics and conduct of modern combat would be incomplete without a parallel examination of war formalities in civil wars. Not surprisingly, the analyses of war formalities in civil versus interstate war will not be precisely parallel. The many differences between the two types of conflict are why they are typically treated separately, and it is unusual to address both types of war in a single book. But if we are to understand the historical arc of the project of international humanitarian law, we cannot begin and end the story with interstate wars. Civil wars have informed international humanitarian lawmaking throughout its history, and today's humanitarians have focused much of their effort on civil wars. I similarly turn my attention to civil wars in the next three chapters.

I begin by focusing on trends in the use of declarations of independence in civil wars. This analysis does not precisely mirror the discussion of declarations of war in interstate war presented in chapter 3. In the civil war context, I focus on declarations of independence instead of declarations of war, for several reasons. First, rebels and governments in civil war occupy dramatically different positions with respect to their international recognition. A degree of equality of status is presumed of states declaring war against each other that is absent from rebels versus states in the civil war context. Second, and related, secessionists declaring independence seek to redress this gap in status. And third, while rebel groups have a variety of war aims in civil wars, focusing on just one type of civil war is a helpful starting point in assessing the relationship between the laws of war and rebel group behavior.

Many rebel groups fighting civil wars—but particularly secessionists— are highly attuned to the preferences of the international community and the demands of international law. This claim may be controversial because international law, met with skepticism during interstate wars, is often viewed as being virtually absent from the realm of civil war. By its very nature, civil war defies domestic legal structures. And secessionist civil wars—those in which the rebel group seeks a new, independent state— pose an additional challenge to the fundamental principle of sovereignty that underlies international law.

Nevertheless, secessionist rebel groups are often attentive to the laws of war. For groups seeking their own independent state, this attentiveness will encompass both the laws of war regarding the resort to force (*jus ad bellum*) and the laws of war regarding the conduct of war (*jus in bello*). While other types of rebel groups are also attentive to the laws of war, I argued in chapter 2 that the unintended consequences of the proliferation of the laws of war ought to be most visible in the actions of secessionists. This is because, unlike other types of rebel groups, secessionists require the support of the international community to achieve their political aims. I explore this argument here by asking: under what conditions do secessionist rebel groups issue formal declarations of independence?

Secessionists will seek to uncover the preferences of the international community to maximize their chances of achieving their political aims. In the UN era, these preferences have been "traditionally averse" to unilateral declarations of independence.[1] While there was support for decolonization in the early UN era, this support did not extend to secessionist movements in, for example, newly independent states or states that had been independent for some time. The history of the 1970 Declaration on Principles of International Law Concerning Friendly Relations and Co-operation among States in Accordance with the Charter of the UN underlines this point.[2] The Declaration on Friendly Relations reaffirms the principles of territorial integrity, peaceful resolution of disputes, and political independence of states originally laid out in the UN Charter. It also addressed the principle of self-determination, at a time when two historical trends converged: the end of decolonization was in sight, and the Cold War was in full play. This meant that states needed to find a way to address new claims of ethnic and political self-determination while avoiding world war. As renowned international legal scholar Antonio Cassese shows, a cursory interpretation of the declaration might give the impression that it makes space for secession and secessionism. But "the overwhelming majority of States participating in the drafting of the Declaration took strong exception to the notion that peoples might have a right of secession."[3] What is more, as another international legal scholar puts it, "For a secession claim to be considered legal, State practice tends to emphasize consent of the parties involved as a necessary condition. . . . State practice suggests that there is very little, if any, support for unilateral declarations of independence . . . , where the government of a particular state demonstrates opposition to secession."[4]

The Syrian Kurds have responded to this preference by adamantly stopping short of a formal declaration of independence, and instead declaring an autonomous federal region.[5] For a group—the Kurds—that has sought independent statehood for nearly a century, this move is somewhat surprising. Especially given that the Syrian Kurdish Democratic Union Party (PYD) arguably controls the most effectively governed territory within Syria at this writing, why stop at declaring autonomy and not issue a formal declaration of independence? According to reports, "In an interview with Al Jazeera, Alan Semo, representative of the Syrian Kurdish Democratic Union Party (PYD) in the UK, insisted their intention was not to declare independence."[6] Doing so preserves their goodwill with the international community; this requires postponing a conversation about independence, but does not foreclose the option. Secessionists know they must step carefully around the representatives of the international community who are empowered to grant them recognition. They also know that the international community has opposed formal declarations of independence in the UN era. Consequently, I argue, we observe a decline in the use of unilateral declarations of independence since 1945.

Previous scholarship has not examined trends over time in the use of declarations of independence in civil war. In the remainder of this chapter, I begin with a discussion of why we should care about declarations of independence. I define them and provide an overview of the rate at which declarations of independence have been used. I then argue that because secessionist rebel groups lack, value, and seek international recognition, they are especially sensitive and responsive to the preferences of the international community. Thus, when the international community expresses its opposition to the use of unilateral declarations of independence, secessionists stop issuing them, even as secessionism itself increases.

I analyze declarations of independence in civil wars using an original dataset: the Civil War Initiation and Termination Data Set (C-WIT),[7] which is a companion dataset to I-WIT (and which is described further below). I also discuss several case studies, based on secondary sources, archival evidence, and interviews. I find, once again, that belligerents—in this case, secessionist rebel groups—react very strategically to the laws of war. But the strategic behavior of these actors, unlike states, is more likely to produce engagement with, rather than evasion of, the laws of war.

Declarations of Independence: An Overview

It is important to pay attention to declarations of independence for several reasons. First, the number of secessionist groups is on the rise,[8] but our understanding of secessionists as a category of rebel groups, and variation amongst secessionists, is lacking. Examining when and whether secessionists declare independence in civil wars offers one entry point into these questions.

Second, the existence and content of declarations of independence can signal behavior to come. For example, the Zapatistas' 1993 declaration of independence from Mexico explicitly invited the ICRC to monitor their behavior, conveying the message that the Zapatistas had an understanding of international humanitarian law as well as an appreciation for the international community's concern about compliance with IHL: "We also ask that international organizations and the International Red Cross watch over and regulate our battles, so that our efforts are carried out while still protecting our civilian population. We declare now and always that we are subject to the Geneva Accord."[9]

Third, a greater understanding of variation in declarations of independence may also help correct a potential bias in existing scholarship on secessionism, which tends to use declarations of independence as a criterion for identifying secessionist groups.[10] As more attention is paid to secessionism, it is important to include those secessionists that do not declare independence in our understanding of the general phenomenon. This point is especially salient if there are time trends in the rate at which secessionists declare independence. It also suggests that previous scholarship may have systematically undercounted the number of secessionists. The data presented in this chapter will be helpful in identifying secessionist rebel groups in civil wars that may have been excluded from previous lists; however, it will not aid in identifying nonviolent secessionist movements that have not declared independence.

Finally, while declarations of independence have historically been very controversial in international law, the International Court of Justice's (ICJ) 2010 advisory opinion on the legality of Kosovo's declaration of independence may well open the door to more declarations.[11] The ICJ found that declarations of independence in general, and Kosovo's declaration in particular, are not illegal under international law.[12] This landmark decision was undoubtedly assessed and observed by secessionists—and the countries from which they seek to secede—around the globe. One reason for its importance is the court's narrow focus on the legality of the declaration itself; it explicitly sought to avoid pronouncing on whether Kosovo had a right to secession or on the validity of any existing states' diplomatic recognition of Kosovo. Despite the claim made by a number of international lawyers and the Kosovars themselves that the ICJ opinion did not set a precedent due to the narrowness of the opinion,[13] other groups, among them Transnistria, Nagorno-Karabakh, Republika Srpska, and Palestine, have indicated they would treat it as establishing a precedent, thus increasing the odds of further declarations of independence.[14]

Defining Declarations of Independence

At least three sources can be used to define declarations of independence. First, historical examples, especially of the earliest declarations of independence, provide an inductive foundation for definition. Declarations of independence have a long history, although not as long as that of declarations of war, in part because a state system must be in place before polities start issuing declarations of independence. The 1320 declaration of Arbroath—a declaration of independence issued by the Scots under British rule (popularized by the movie "Braveheart")—illustrates this problem. In attempting to free themselves from their English overlords, the Scots beseeched the Pope to "deign to admonish and exhort the king of the English, who ought to be satisfied with what he has, since England used to be enough for seven kings or more, to leave in peace us Scots."[15] As historian David Armitage notes, the declaration of Arbroath was an appeal for peace talks, and was only "retrospectively baptized as a declaration of independence."[16]

Another famous early declaration was issued by the Dutch in 1581, when the Netherlands was still part of Spain. It was part of a long conflict, the Eighty Years' War, which concluded with the Thirty Years War and the Peace of Westphalia. The language of the Dutch declaration is strikingly similar to contemporary declarations of war: "So, having no hope of reconciliation, and finding no other remedy, we have, agreeable to the law of nature in our own defense, and for maintaining the rights, privileges, and liberties of our countrymen, wives, and children, and latest posterity from being enslaved by the Spaniards, been constrained to renounce allegiance to the King of Spain, and pursue such methods as appear to us most likely to secure our ancient liberties and privileges."[17] The declaration, known as the Dutch Act of Abjuration, argues for replacing Spanish rule with that of another prince, specifically the Duke of Anjou. Like the Scots in 1320, the Dutch did not seek an independent state *per se* but, rather, a different and kinder rule. Similarly, Crimea's 2014 so-called declaration of independence is the result of a Crimean referendum on joining Russia or remaining with Ukraine; it is less a declaration of independence than a declaration of irredentism.[18]

As David Armitage notes, it is the US Declaration of Independence that has had the largest global appeal. In contrast to the Scottish and Dutch declarations, the US Declaration of Independence calls clearly for the establishment of a new and free state, rather than appealing to a higher power for a better ruler or to be left alone: "[T]hese United Colonies are, and of Right ought to be Free and Independent States; that they are Absolved from all Allegiance to the British Crown, and that all political connection between them and the State of Great Britain, is and ought to be totally dissolved; and that as Free and Independent States, they have full Power to levy War, conclude Peace, contract Alliances, establish Commerce, and to do all other Acts and Things which Independent States may of right do." Like the US declaration, South Sudan's 2011 declaration of independence contains a list of justifications for secession and then "declares South Sudan to be a free and independent sovereign state." While all of these declarations contain explanations for seeking a transfer of sovereignty, only the US and South Sudanese declarations also proclaim that sovereignty to be independent.

A second source of definitions of declarations of independence is found in declarations of war. Declarations of war are defined as a belligerent's public proclamation of intention to engage in hostilities with another state. Declarations of war must be issued according to the rules of the declaring state. Declarations of independence may overlap definitionally with declarations of war, but cannot be precisely the same. Unlike a declaration of war, a declaration of independence does not necessarily precede the use of force, or indicate intentions to engage in hostilities with another state.[19] Just as not all secessionists declare independence, not all secessionists that declare independence use violence to press their claims. Most of the former Soviet republics declared—and gained—independence nonviolently; more recently, in September 2014 Scots took to the voting booths to decide a referendum on independence from the UK.

Additionally, any criterion that a declaration of independence "be issued according to the rules of the declaring state" does not make sense in this context. Many groups considering issuing a declaration of independence will lack rules for issuing such a declaration; indeed, it would be unlikely that any group—however well-established—would have articulated procedures for declaring independence, as such declarations are typically issued only once.[20]

Insofar as declarations of independence are meant to have legal standing, it also makes sense to look to international law to supply a definition. International law, however, lacks a formal definition of a declaration of independence, most likely because providing such a definition might seem to lend legitimacy to the act of declaring independence. Lawyers would be hesitant to take this step because declaring independence is an act that contradicts the basic principle of state sovereignty that undergirds the state system. Standard legal dictionaries thus have no entry under "declaration of independence."[21] Recently, though, Kosovo's 2008 declaration of independence excited a great deal of interest among international lawyers.[22] While neither legal dictionaries nor courts have defined declarations of independence, the United States' official written statement to the International Court of Justice on the question of the legality of the Kosovo declaration defines a declaration of independence as "an expression of a will or desire by an entity to be accepted as a state by the members of the international community."[23]

I define a declaration of independence as a public proclamation by an entity seeking to be accepted as a state by members of the international community that contains the reasoning behind a secessionist claim, and is issued by the group's leadership.[24] This definition adds to the relatively thin description offered in the US statement, and highlights the overlap between declarations of independence and declarations of war; it also describes most of the cases that are typically discussed as declarations of independence.

My definition does leave out certain cases. During a mid-nineteenth-century civil war, several of Colombia's provincial governors stated that they did not recognize the authority of the central government and claimed autonomy for their regions. But this statement would not qualify as a declaration of independence; these regions sought a new central government, rather than independent statehood.[25] Similarly, the October 1947 Manifesto of the Chinese People's Liberation Army, although not issued by a secessionist group, would not qualify as a formal declaration of independence, as its focus was to make a case against Chiang Kai-shek's government rather than to carve out a new and different state.[26] As written in the manifesto, "The aim of our army in this war, as proclaimed time and time again to the nation and the world, is the liberation of the Chinese people and the Chinese nation . . . to overthrow the arch-criminal of the civil war, Chiang Kai-shek, and form a democratic coalition in order to attain the general goal of liberating the people and the nation."[27] In sum, my aim in coding declarations of independence is to, first, identify secessionist groups by their stated war aims (distinct from any declarations of independence) and, second, to identify formal declarations of independence themselves.

In the analysis of declarations of independence below, I restrict my universe of cases to secessionist conflicts as identified by C-WIT. The percent of civil wars that are secessionist (represented by the solid line in figure 6.1) has exhibited a U-shaped curve over the past two centuries, rising since about 1900. The dashed line in figure 6.1 tracks the proportion of secessionist groups over this period that declared independence, and adds an important wrinkle to this story. Instead of a U-shaped curve, we observe something closer to an upside-down U, with a steady use of declarations of independence until the advent of the UN era, followed by a visible dropoff. Even though more civil wars are secessionist since 1950 or so, fewer and fewer of these secessionists declare independence formally.

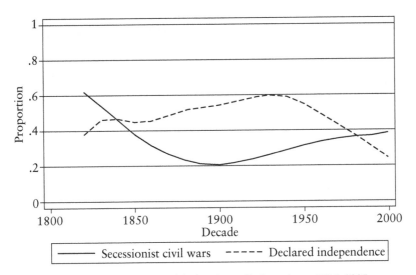

Figure 6.1 Secessionism and declarations of independence, 1816–2007

The combination of these trends raises at least two questions. First, given that secessionists have accounted for a rising proportion of civil wars, why have secessionist rebel groups been decreasingly likely to make formal declarations of independence? Second—and more generally—why and when do some groups declare independence, while others do not?

Theoretical Expectations

The receptivity of the international community to declarations of independence is a factor that any secessionist group must consider. To understand and identify the international community's preferences, it is first important to make a distinction between the international community's receptivity to secessionism and its receptivity to formal declarations of independence. The one refers to an end, while the other refers to a means to achieve that end.

The international community's attitude toward secessionism is multifaceted and has varied over time. Sovereignty norms have changed dramatically over the past hundred years or so. The principle of self-determination gained considerable favor after World War I.[28] Woodrow Wilson, for example, was very much affected by the plight of the Poles, who had been fighting to regain independent statehood since 1795. An international openness to self-determination was visible in the emergence of several new states, such as Ireland, in the immediate postwar period. The commitment to the principle of self-determination was further codified in Article 1(2) of the United Nations Charter, which states as one of the organization's purposes "To develop friendly relations among nations based on respect for the principle of equal rights and self-determination of peoples." Following World War II, the move away from the League's mandate system toward decolonization was further evidence of the salience of self-determination in world politics. Although a multitude of factors led to the creation of over 125 new states between 1945 and the present, the international community's receptivity to claims of self-determination was surely one of them.

As Robert Jackson and Mikulas Fabry have shown, the required governance capacity for acceptable secession has decreased over time. In previous eras, especially those when the international community was less sympathetic to claims of self-determination, would-be states had to demonstrate that they could defend their borders and govern their territory. This often entailed employing violence in order to achieve their political aims. Ironically, almost concurrent with the establishment of the 1934 Montevideo criteria for statehood, the international community stopped applying these criteria to some of the most successful secessionist movements. Instead, international recognition was granted to many groups that lacked state capacity,[29] often because a great power patron supported the group's claim to independence.[30]

Another wrinkle in the international community's support for self-determination, one that gets us closer to thinking about its changing attitudes toward declarations of independence, refers to the use of violence in secessionist conflicts. Increasingly, the international community has disapproved the use of violence to achieve statehood.[31] This attitude might be justified by the fact that states that secede violently are significantly more likely to engage in military confrontations with their neighbors—the states from which they seceded, or neighboring states that seceded around the same time—compared to states that seceded peacefully.[32] They are also more likely to experience civil war as new states. Secessionist groups have tended to heed the call to avoid violence; even though both the rate and the absolute number of secessionist movements have increased, the proportion of secessionists using major violence has declined since the turn of the twentieth century, and certainly since the creation of the UN in 1945. But this trend may not continue if, as recent scholarship has suggested, nonviolence is a less effective strategy for secessionists than it is for groups with other political aims.[33]

In addition to the trends of according recognition to groups lacking real governance capacity and disapproving of the use of violence, the international community has also expressed opposition to unilateral declarations of independence. This approach became apparent in the UN era: despite the stated support for self-determination, the principle of protecting state sovereignty and territorial integrity was elevated over the principle of self-determination. For example, the French, British, and US governments took the position during the conflicts that preceded the dissolution of Yugoslavia that "the attitude of unilateral recognition could be damaging for the international community," and, further, that "recognition . . . should only come as part of an overall peace agreement."[34] UN Security Council Resolution 787 on Bosnia and Herzegovina, issued in

1992, "strongly reaffirms its [the UN's] call on all parties and others concerned to respect strictly the territorial integrity of the Republic of Bosnia and Herzegovina and affirms that any entities unilaterally declared or arrangements imposed in contravention thereof will not be accepted."[35] The priority of the international community, in other words, has been to preserve the existing order. And while an exception was made for the decolonization of European empires, further secessions have not been as welcome.

The opposition to unilateral declarations of independence has been expressed clearly on several occasions. The EU requested that Croatia and Slovenia rescind their declarations of independence. South Sudan was advised not to issue a unilateral declaration, and heeded this advice, waiting until its admission to the international community was assured to declare independence. The declaration of independence issued in 2012 by the Tuareg in Northern Mali was rejected by both the African Union and the UN Security Council.[36] Until the very recent past, secessionist movements such as the one in Catalonia refrained from declaring independence because it seemed too antagonizing a step, both domestically and internationally.[37] The Scottish independence movement exercised similar restraint, holding a 2014 referendum as to whether such a declaration should be issued. When the referendum failed, the Scottish independence movement stepped back, consistent with the expectation that declarations of independence are issued with great care today. In contrast, when Crimea made a unilateral decision to secede from Ukraine (it was not approved by the Ukrainian government, nor is there a right to secede for Crimea included in the Ukrainian constitution), it received widespread condemnation internationally.

It is worth asking why groups are so careful about issuing declarations of independence. For secessionist rebel groups, the costs and benefits of declaring independence differ significantly from the costs and benefits states must weigh in deciding whether to declare war. For example, the bureaucratic and strategic compliance costs that accompany declarations of war do not apply in the case of declarations of independence. Declarations of independence are also principally useful as a signal to the international community. As such, secessionists—whose political success is dependent on the international community—must care about prevailing opinion regarding the legality of such instruments. If the international community is opposed to declarations of independence, then the costs of issuing such declarations may be prohibitively high.

My primary hypothesis is that, as the international community's opposition to unilateral declarations of independence has been clearly and repeatedly articulated in the UN era, the corresponding likelihood of groups to declare independence can be expected to decrease. But precisely because declarations of independence are a signal sent to the outside world, issuing these declarations may be beneficial when a group is so weak that it cannot survive without external support, and external support will not be forthcoming in the absence of some sort of announcement of the groups' aims. Thus, the cost-benefit analysis for secessionists considering declaring independence may be conditional on two factors: the attitude of the international community toward declarations of independence and the relative power of the secessionist group.

Like declarations of war in interstate war, declarations of independence in civil wars fall under the rubric of the laws of war governing resort to force. As the norms and laws of war have evolved, belligerents have responded strategically to better advance their political aims.

Empirical Analysis of Declarations of Independence

I draw on both qualitative and quantitative evidence to analyze when, and which, secessionist groups issue declarations of independence. As with prior analyses, I present a quantitative analysis first, to give a global perspective on declarations of independence. This chapter includes descriptions of key variables used in quantitative analyses of declarations of independence, civilian targeting by rebels in civil war, and peace treaties in civil war, laying the groundwork for the following two chapters. Because, however, my universe of cases—secessionist rebel groups—is relatively small, I do not conduct regression analysis in this chapter. Instead, I report bivariate correlations between various independent variables and declarations of independence as a first step in understanding these relationships.

This chapter also includes background information for the case studies used in my analysis of war formalities and compliance with international humanitarian law in civil war throughout the remainder of the book: the 1836 Texas Independence War; the 1950 South Moluccan Independence

War; and the war between North and South Sudan that led to South Sudan's independence in 2011.

Quantitative Analysis

The quantitative analysis for this chapter, as well as that for chapters 7 and 8, is based on data from the Civil War Initiation and Termination (C-WIT) dataset. C-WIT is the companion dataset to I-WIT (which was used in chapters 3–5) and is an original dataset that covers all civil wars, as identified by the Correlates of War list of civil wars, from 1816 to 2007. A detailed description of C-WIT is included in the online statistical appendix.

As a first cut in analyzing declarations of independence, I restrict my analysis to secessionist rebel groups, coded here as those rebel groups that seek their own independent states. Groups that seek to overthrow the central government, or seek only autonomy, are not coded as secessionist. For example, the FMLN in El Salvador is coded as aiming to overthrow the center; the Yemeni Young Faith Believers sought, among other things, autonomy (but not secession) for the northern Saada region; they are not coded as secessionist. However, the Acehnese, Chechens, and Poles have, at various times, fought for independent statehood, and are coded as secessionists.[38]

Description of Variables   Below, I describe coding of key variables included in the quantitative analysis of declarations of independence, and also in the analyses of civilian targeting and peace treaties (in chapters 7 and 8). Summary statistics for these variables can be found in the statistical appendix. In addition to variables used to test my own argument regarding the relationship between the international community's support for declarations of independence and the relative power of secessionist groups, I also include a number of variables meant to test for alternative explanations for the incidence of declarations of independence.

DECLARATION OF INDEPENDENCE

Declaration of independence codes for whether the rebels issued a formal declaration of independence from another state. To be counted as a declaration of independence, the statement must meet three criteria: it must be made publicly; it must state the reasoning behind the group's claim; and it must be issued by the group's leadership. That it be written is not a requirement.

PERIOD EFFECTS

UN era is a dummy variable for civil wars begun after 1945. This variable tests for the possibility that declarations of independence are less likely to be observed during the UN era than during earlier times. Figure 6.1 clearly demonstrates that there is a period effect in declarations of independence. My main argument in this chapter is that the decline of declarations of independence is driven by the international community's stated aversion to such declarations in the UN era.

BALANCE OF POWER

In addition to timing, we might also expect that military power affects a group's likelihood of declaring independence. It might seem that stronger groups would be more likely to declare independence than weaker groups because their probability of success is higher. But the reverse is also plausible: perhaps weaker groups are more likely to declare independence than stronger groups, especially in an era when the international community opposes unilateral declarations of independence. By this logic, weaker groups might use a declaration of independence as a means of shoring up their political campaign, while groups closer to the goal of achieving independence might be more likely to exercise restraint, trying to avoid costly missteps.

I measure rebel military strength in four ways. First, *rebel troops* is the absolute number of rebel troops. A relationship between rebel capability and declarations of independence may depend on exceeding a critical threshold of strength. Second, *force ratio (deployed)* is the size of rebel forces divided by the number of government troops deployed for a given conflict.[39] This variable captures the balance of power between the government and rebel forces, speaking to the basic principle that the stronger side is the more likely to win.[40] It is similar to Wood's measure of relative rebel capability, which is "a ratio of insurgent troops to a scaled number of government troops."[41] I use the number of government troops deployed for the specific conflict, rather than the total size of government's army, because some government troops are likely to be held back for international defense or other internal conflicts, while the totality of the rebel force is likely to be deployed against these government forces. For example, in a number of civil wars in China and Russia, in particular, the government has deployed only a small fraction of its forces to the conflict. By focusing on the ratio of troops actually fighting in a given conflict, the analysis remains somewhat more local. A third measure of rebel military strength, *force ratio (total)*, divides the number of rebel forces by the total number of government forces; although *force ratio (deployed)* is a better measure in many ways, there is a great deal of missing data in the denominator, and so using *force ratio (total)* could in theory allow for the inclusion of a greater number of observations. Given missing data in C-WIT, I also calculated *COW force ratio*, which uses the Correlates of War estimates of government military personnel to supplement the C-WIT measure.

PRIOR ADMINISTRATIVE BORDERS

As David Carter and Hein Goemans and, in another study, Ryan Griffiths have shown, states tend to be born along the lines of prior administrative units.[42] While there is no right to secession in international law,[43] the international community seems more willing to tolerate secessions of existing administrative units than attempts lacking such previously defined boundaries. Given their stronger ex ante prospects for independence, should we expect prior administrative units that seek secession to be more or less likely to declare independence, compared to secessionist groups lacking this status? As with the variable of rebel strength, either of two opposing logics could reign. The simpler logic suggests that administrative units will be especially likely to declare independence precisely because doing so will be more accepted by the international community. A more sophisticated logic, however, suggests the opposite: administrative units will be especially hesitant to declare independence precisely because their chances are relatively good, and they do not want to jeopardize those chances by antagonizing the international community.

I coded *internal administrative units* using a series of encyclopedias, including Daniel Elazar's *Federal Systems of the World* and Gwillim Law's *Administrative Subdivisions of Countries*, as well as Griffiths's dataset on protostates.[44] In addition to identifying which secessionist movements corresponded with existing internally administered political units, I coded for secessionist movements that had previously been independent, such as Tibet, and for those comprising several internally administered units, such as the southern US states in the Confederacy.

CONTROL VARIABLES AND ALTERNATIVE EXPLANATIONS

Number of factions. *Fragmentation* measures the number of factions in the rebel group, defined here as distinct but related groups fighting the same opponent and sharing the same political goals, but having separate military commands (and sometimes different names).[45] While most rebel groups in the dataset are not factionalized, some, such as the Kashmiri insurgents fighting India currently, contain dozens of factions.[46] I include this variable to control for the possibility, raised by a number of scholars, that more factionalized rebel groups will be especially likely to engage in outbidding—the competitive practice of trying to attract loyalty by taking increasingly extreme measures that can be contrasted with those of rival factions. The logic of outbidding has been used previously to explain why factionalized rebel groups are especially likely to engage in civilian targeting; here, I apply this same logic to explore the possibility that more fragmented rebel groups are especially likely to issue declarations of independence.[47] Note that this logic is an alternative to my own argument. I argue that declarations of independence are primarily meant for external consumption, while the outbidding logic would suggest that such declarations are meant primarily as signals to domestic constituents.

Ongoing secessionist movements. *Concurrent secessionist challenges* takes a value of 1 if the country from which the secessionist group seeks to secede is also fighting another secessionist movement at the same time. For example, the Indonesian government fought secessionists in Aceh and East Timor simultaneously. This variable is meant to test for the possibility that secessionists may be less likely to declare independence from a central government that is facing several simultaneous claims. Two alternative measures of this variable exist. Barbara Walter's measure of the number of potential future challenges counts how many such groups the central government might anticipate having to fight in coming years.[48] A critical limiting factor in employing Walter's version of this variable, however, is that it is based on the Minorities at Risk (MAR) dataset, which begins only at 1945. Another version of this variable is based on Ryan Griffiths's protostate dataset, which does go back to 1816.[49] Griffiths codes for the concurrence of secessionist movements in the same country. Griffiths's definition of protostate, however, has the effect of excluding many of the secessionist rebel groups in C-WIT; only one-third of secessionist rebel groups count as protostates for Griffiths.[50] Thus, analyses using Walter's and Griffiths's measures would be restricted to biased samples of the data. I therefore only use *concurrent secessionist challenges* based on C-WIT. Like the variable measuring group fragmentation, *concurrent secessionist challenges* helps test an alternative explanation, but this time where the central government is the key audience.

Analysis and Discussion   C-WIT identifies eighty-seven secessionist rebel groups from 1816 to 2007. The relatively small number of secessionist movements means that it is unlikely that regression analysis will yield significant results. I therefore approach the data more simply, with a list of bivariate correlations between secessionists that declare independence and the independent variables described above.

Among the correlations summarized in table 6.1, the UN era, military power, and internal administrative status of the secessionist group bear the strongest (although admittedly not very strong) relationships with declarations of independence. As we know from figure 6.1, secessionist groups are decreasingly likely to declare independence in the UN era; this is consistent with the negative—albeit not statistically significant—relationship

TABLE 6.1 Bivariate analysis of declarations of independence

Independent variable	Correlation	p-value
UN era	−.10	.39
Fragmentation	−.04	.70
Concurrent secessionist challenges	.02	.86
Rebel troops	.21	.11
Force ratio (deployed)	.15	.33
Force ratio (total)	.07	.66
COW force ratio	.19	.14
Internal administrative unit	−.12	.29

between declaring independence and the UN era. More intriguing are the relationships between military strength (captured here by *rebel troops, force ratio*, and *COW force ratio*) and the internal administrative status of secessionist rebel groups on the one hand, and declaring independence on the other. In part because the results are weak, one interesting hypothesis to explore is that the relationship between rebel strength and declarations of independence may be both fluid and conditional. The strongest secessionist rebels—those who have the greatest chance for independence— may be the least likely to declare independence, especially in the UN era when they know the international community is averse to such declarations. Weaker secessionists, on the other hand, may declare independence as a way to attract publicity to their cause. This logic suggests, first, that secessionist groups that declare independence will tend to do so early in their fight, when they are typically weak. The Indonesian case (discussed in greater detail in terms of the South Moluccan case, below) provides some evidence in favor of this hypothesis. Of four secessionist conflicts in Indonesia—the South Moluccas, West Papua, East Timor, and Aceh—rebels in three (South Moluccas, East Timor, and Aceh) declared independence at the very start of their wars, while the West Papuans issued a declaration of independence midway through their war with Indonesia, at a point when the war was going particularly poorly for them.[51] More generally, approximately three-quarters of secessionist rebel groups declared independence before the start of their civil wars, with the average declaration of independence issued about a year and a half prior to the onset of war.

This logic is also consistent with the negative relationship between internal administrative status and declaring independence, as groups with internal administrative status are born with a stronger hand in terms of the likelihood of secessionist success. In addition, we might expect that any separation between weaker and stronger rebels is more extreme in the UN era, when the international community's preference against declarations of independence is more clearly articulated.

The correlation between the ratio of rebel and total government forces that combines C-WIT and COW data on government forces (and therefore has the least missing data) and groups that declare independence suggests that stronger rebels are generally more likely to declare independence than weak rebels. This relationship is more pronounced in the post-1945 era than in the pre-1945 era, contrary to expectations.[52]

This finding, however, could well be an artifact of the dearth of data on this variable in the post-1945 era when compared to the pre-1945 era. My expectation is that the missing data are for the weaker rebel groups; were these data available, I expect that this result would flip and we would in fact observe that stronger rebels are less likely to declare independence in the UN era than they were previously.

Variables meant to help test hypotheses where declarations of independence are intended for audiences other than the international community did not suggest much support for these alternatives. The correlations between group fragmentation and concurrent secessionist challenges on the one hand and declarations of independence on the other are both in the wrong direction. In addition, they are both far from being statistically significant.

Qualitative Analysis

Looking at secessionist rebel groups from the perch of quantitative analysis suggests that rebel military power and timing (pre or post–UN era) may have an effect on whether and which groups issue declarations of independence. These two factors—strength and timing—may also affect *when* in the lifetime of a secessionist movement groups declare independence. For example, it could be that groups' decisions to declare independence depend on their strength at a given moment, coupled with signals being sent by the international community. The cross-case structure of the C-WIT data does not allow for within-case time-series analysis. Case studies are needed to explore this topic further.

Croatia's decision to declare independence at the start of its secessionist war, but then to rescind that declaration, illustrates the complicated role that the international community can play in secessionist wars, and may shed some light on the nuances of the relationship among timing, strength, and declarations of independence. Croatia's position from the beginning of the conflict was strong, in terms of military strength, internal administrative status, and claims on the principle of self-determination. Even so, the international community was sending clear anti-secessionist signals to the Croats at the beginning of their conflict. However, once it became clear that the West was willing to invest in Croatian independence—that is to say, that it would intervene in support of Croatia—the international community's explicit request that Croatia's declaration of independence be rescinded and a referendum postponed until after hostilities had concluded became easier for the Croats to honor.[53] Croatia's mid-course reversal on the decision to declare independence was thus determined directly by the international community.

Below, I consider in greater detail three cases of secessionist movements from three different historical eras. Each had to decide whether and when to issue a formal declaration of independence. In each case, although to different effect, the secessionists' perception of the preferences of the international community conditioned the decision as to when and whether to declare independence. Each group's assessment of its own strength also played into these decisions.

As with the interstate cases examined in chapters 3 through 5, I selected civil war cases based on variation on the independent and dependent variables. Consistent with the quantitative analysis, I drew from the set of secessionist rebel groups as identified by C-WIT. I chose one secessionist group that preceded the UN era and issued a declaration of independence—Texas in nineteenth-century Mexico—as an example of typical secessionist behavior pre-1945: to preview questions discussed in chapters 7 and 8, note that the Texans also engaged in little civilian targeting and did not conclude a true peace treaty with Mexico. Moving to the UN era, when declarations of independence become rare, I examine one case in the early postwar period and another more recent case. The South Moluccas, a weak secessionist group delimited by clear internal administrative borders, declared independence from Indonesia in 1950. Like the Texans, they engaged in little civilian targeting, and did not conclude a peace treaty with the Indonesian government. Unlike the Texans, the South Moluccans lost their independence war. The more recent case of South Sudan is one where secessionists refrained from declaring independence at the implicit request of the international community. The South Sudanese did engage in significant civilian targeting, and they concluded a formal peace agreement with the government, unlike the Texans or the South Moluccans. Because I refer to these cases in the remainder of this chapter as well as in chapters 7 and 8, a brief background is provided for each below.

Texas   Soon after Mexico won a hard-fought war of independence from Spain in 1821, Texas and the Texans found themselves in an awkward position politically. Much of Texas, then part of Mexico, had been settled by anglophones emigrating from the United States. Although according to its 1824 constitution Mexico had a federal structure, the central government soon began to try to tighten control over its constituent units. According to historian William Binkley, Mexico was particularly concerned about Texas as "the authorities suspected that the influx of colonists was part of an organized scheme to despoil Mexico of territory."[54] While previously neither the Spanish language nor Catholicism had been imposed upon Texas, Mexico's formal requirement of a state language and state religion made many Texans uncomfortable. This discomfort increased visibly with the restrictions on immigration imposed by the law of April 6, 1830, that would prevent non-Catholics from settling in Texas.[55] The establishment of a military dictatorship following a failed invasion and attempt at reconquest by Spain was even more troubling to Texans: they were concerned about the impact of import duties on their economy as well as questions of self-governance, particularly the effects on slave-owning Texans.[56]

The anglophone leadership of Texas, particularly the well-respected Stephen F. Austin, at first hoped to remain part of a truly federal Mexico. In late 1833, Austin traveled to Mexico City to propose that Texas become its own state within the Mexican federation and that the immigration law of 1830 be reversed. Following a lukewarm reception, Austin was arrested for treason on his way back to Texas, charged with having "advised the councilmen of Béxar to get everything ready to form a government to enable Texas to rule itself."[57] His followers continued to adhere to his wish that Texas not declare independence, even as he was imprisoned.[58] Upon his release, Austin wrote to friends that he had changed his position and now fully supported Texan independence.[59] Mexico tried to appease the Texans by accepting English as an official language and repealing the law of 1830, but these concessions were too little and too late.[60] Austin's change of heart meant that the secessionist movement that had been simmering beneath the surface for months if not years had received its most important blessing.

Mexico was unwilling to let Texas go without a fight. The Mexican army clearly outnumbered what the Texans could muster; this asymmetry was reflected in early Mexican victories at Goliad and, most famously, the Alamo. But just as Mexican forces decided to rest on April 21, 1836, they were overwhelmed by Sam Houston's forces at San Jacinto. Antonio López de Santa Anna, Mexico's premier general, former president, and effective head of state, was captured; he negotiated peace terms—including Mexican recognition of an independent Texas—as a condition of his release. Thus, the Texan independence war represents a rare case of a successful secessionist conflict. Within a few years, Texas had been recognized as an independent country by the United States, France, and Britain. The Texans soon realized they preferred annexation by the United States to independence, and Texas entered the union on December 29, 1845.

EXTERNAL PATRONAGE AND TEXAS'S DECISION TO DECLARE

For the men in Texas debating secession from Mexico, a declaration of independence was viewed as demanded by custom, but to be timed strategically. Declarations of independence had been considered several times before one was issued by the Texans on March 3, 1836. In November 1835, a consultation—a local political convention constituted to help determine Texas's future—decided against declaring independence, instead determining that the war aim was a return to the federal constitution of 1824, which Santa Anna had abrogated. At the heart of the Texan leaders' political strategy lay the hope that the other Mexican states would join in a revolution to restore the 1824 constitution.[61] This early reluctance to declare independence hinged on two additional factors: Texas's military weakness with respect to Mexico and its desire for support from the United States. Not declaring independence would "enlist more sympathy in the United States for a Texas that seemed to be following a purely idealistic course."[62]

Central to these prior debates, however, was not so much whether to declare independence as whether independence was in fact the Texans' aim. This issue was resolved during the consultation of March 1836. Once Texans realized that other Mexican states would not join them or come to their aid, survival demanded secession.[63] And once Texas decision-makers had agreed on the goal of independence, the question was not whether to issue a formal declaration, but rather when to do so. The precedent of the US Declaration of Independence sixty years prior was still very much felt among the world's secessionists.[64] To declare independence was a standard of appropriate behavior for groups seeking their own independent state.

Signals from the United States were important to Texas, beyond the example of the 1776 Declaration of Independence. By January 1836, it was clear to key Texan decision-makers that US aid would be contingent on a formal declaration of independence. According to historian Andreas Reichstein,

> Even though originally avoidance of diplomatic entanglements between the U.S. and Mexico had been a reason for the discretion of the Texans in the matter of independence, the three agents—Austin, Wharton, and Archer—learned what had also been revealed in letters already cited from private parties in the United States to the leading men in Texas: diplomacy notwithstanding, if Texas wanted to get material support from individuals and private organizations or volunteers for the fight against Mexico, then it had to declare its independence as quickly as possible. The three emissaries expressed this clearly; without a declaration of independence, no loans, no money, no help.[65]

Texas's formal declaration of independence followed soon thereafter, on March 3, 1836. The United States determined not only the timing of the Texas declaration of independence, but also, by example, its content. George Childress, tasked by the consultation with writing the Texas declaration of independence, consciously modeled it on the US example. Doing so shortened not only the drafting process, but also the length of debate on the declaration, which was accepted immediately and unanimously.[66] The US influence on the Texas decision to declare independence was especially salient in an era without a robust international community. Instead, the signals to be most heeded were those sent by the neighbor most likely to aid the Texas cause.[67]

"The World's Forgotten War"[68]: *Secessionism in the South Moluccas*   Negotiations surrounding Indonesia's independence from The Netherlands in 1945 were divisive and complex. Among the many issues at stake was the federal nature of the new Indonesian state. According to the December 1949 Round Table Agreement negotiating Indonesia's independence and constitution, the South Moluccas—a group of islands also known as the "Spice Islands"—was one of the regions guaranteed the right to self-determination under what was to be a federal system.[69]

Very soon after independence, however, Indonesian President Sukar-
no's government foreclosed the option of peaceful secession by reneging
on its acceptance of the federal constitution. The new, more centralized
governance structure produced a great deal of anger in Ambon, the principal island and eponymous city in the South Moluccas. In response to
an effective blockade by the Indonesian navy and anticipated landing of
Indonesian troops, the Republik Maluku Selatan (RMS) officially declared
its independence on April 25, 1950.[70] The civil war that followed was
initially intense but, by December 1950, had devolved into a very low-
intensity jungle war of guerrilla attrition, based primarily in the island of
Ceram after the city of Ambon fell.[71]

THE REPUBLIK MALUKU SELATAN ON THE WORLD STAGE

The relative military weakness of the South Moluccans was an important driver of the decision to declare independence. Isolated and poor, the
South Moluccans lacked resources. Appealing to the international community was their main strategy to improve their prospects. The international community had not, by 1950, expressed explicit opposition to
unilateral declarations of independence (this opposition became clearer
with the Declaration on Friendly Relations of 1970, described above),
and its support was a necessary condition for political success, as for all
secessionist movements. Additionally, the South Moluccans felt they had
a strong legal case. The South Moluccas constituted a first-level administrative unit—a province—within the new Indonesian state.[72] The declaration began with a reference to self-determination: "In order to comply
with the positive will and demands of the people of the South Moluccas
we hereby do proclaim the independence de facto and de jure of the South
Moluccas."[73] It also argued on the basis of the Round Table Conference,
a direct appeal to international law.

The international community could lend neither material nor moral
support if it did not know about the South Moluccan cause; thus, publicity was central to the achievement of their political aims, and the issuance
of a formal declaration of independence was part of this publicity campaign. Appeals to the international community have been made from 1950
through the present day in a variety of forums. Letters to the editor in
major western periodicals such as the *New York Times* and the *Christian*

Science Monitor strenuously objected to any reporting that questioned the legitimacy of South Moluccan independence, frequently referencing the fact that a Dutch court had recognized the right to secession and deploring the international community's failure to live up to its promise to raise the issue at the UN Security Council.[74] The Moluccans repeatedly pressed the Dutch government to intervene on their behalf.[75] They pled their case to the Australian and the United States governments.[76] Since 1966, the RMS government-in-exile has maintained an active presence in the Netherlands; it has a website and is a member in INGOs such as the Unrecognized Nations and Peoples Organization (UNPO).[77]

The South Moluccans made three arguments that they hoped would encourage the international community to support them against the Indonesian government.[78] First, they frequently appealed to the principle of self-determination of peoples.[79] Second, they made a legal argument that Indonesia lacked the right to take over the South Moluccas, which they argued was properly an independent state whose rights as such had been acknowledged by the Dutch government.[80] And third, they made a strategic argument: that the South Moluccas served as a critical part of a bulwark against communist expansion, and failure of their independence bid would increase the odds of a communist takeover in the region. In general, the South Moluccans sought to send the signal that they would be good and valued citizens of the international community. They even offered troops to the UN for use in the Korean War, in contrast to Indonesia's "support for the Chinese aggressor against the American Resolution of January 21, 1951."[81]

Ultimately, the South Moluccan independence war was lost. But the declaration of independence was successful in that it attracted attention from the international community. Without the declaration of independence, it is not clear that the South Moluccans would have received this attention, given their relative military weakness. Although the military phase of this conflict is over, the RMS continues to pursue the aim of independence today.

South Sudan   The creation of the new state of South Sudan in July 2011 was preceded by decades of civil war that began as soon as Sudan gained independence from the British in 1956. The civil war between North and South in Sudan has been among the world's longest and bloodiest.

Several related factors could be counted as "causes" of the war between North and South Sudan. Ethnic and religious differences between them drove the conflict to a large extent, with the Islamist North's attempt to impose the Arabic language and Islam on the Christian and animist South. The South suffered from poor infrastructural development, particularly compared to the North; this disparity was not helped by Britain's failure to incorporate any concessions for the South during the decolonization process.[82] When oil was discovered in the South, southerners accused the North of exploiting southern oil fields for northern profit.[83]

The war between the North and South is generally considered to have been fought in two phases. In the first phase, from 1956 to 1972, a southern insurgency responded to the northern government's attempt to Islamize and Arabicize all of Sudan. A peace agreement in 1972 promised more autonomy for the South. Then, politics in the North—specifically, the resurgence of an Islamist government—led Khartoum to renege on this agreement.

The second phase of the conflict began when hostilities resumed in 1983: Colonel John Garang was sent to quell dissent in the South, but instead defected to become a leader of the southern rebellion. Garang founded the Sudan People's Liberation Movement/Army (SPLM/A), which became the main opposition group to the North for decades to come.

The civil war between North and South Sudan is notable for many reasons. The southerners were extremely factionalized, with divisions along ethnic lines between the Dinka and Nuer, who are fighting each other today in the newly independent South Sudan.[84] Beyond ethnic politics, part of the disagreement among the leaders of the southern rebellion centered around war aims. As in Texas 150 years earlier, some sought to democratize while remaining within the state of Sudan, while others sought independence. The war was extremely internationalized, expensive, and long. Khartoum is said to have spent "up to half" its annual budget on the war.[85] A host of countries aided one side, the other, or sometimes both.

Major fighting ended with the conclusion of the Comprehensive Peace Agreement (CPA) of 2005. A key provision of the CPA was that the South could hold a referendum on independence six years later. In addition to the proposed independence referendum and ceasefire, the CPA included a powersharing plan whereby John Garang became vice-president of Sudan.[86]

A DECLARATION DEFERRED

To say that the South Sudanese secessionists did not declare independence is not entirely correct. They did declare independence on July 9,
2011, the very same weekend they were welcomed into the United
Nations as a member state. The puzzle here is why the Sudan People's
Liberation Movement/Army (SPLM/A) waited years to declare independence, when independence appeared to be a foregone conclusion
long before.

One explanation for this delay is that the South Sudanese conflict did
not begin as a secessionist war. It is not surprising that this change in war
aims would affect the likelihood of declaring independence; almost by
definition, we are very unlikely to observe a declaration of independence
in a nonsecessionist conflict. That said, the puzzle remains: the SPLM/A
could have declared independence once its secessionist war aims had been
solidified, but it chose not to do so.

Another explanation could lie in the fact that the SPLM/A was
extremely factionalized, especially when compared to the Moluccan case.
The SPLM/A was itself a splinter group of the Anya Anya II movement,
and subsequently split into several additional groups, including the Torit,
Bahr-al-Gazal, and South Sudan Independence Movement factions.[87]
Although rebel factionalization is a prominent feature of this case, the
results reported in table 6.1 showed little correlation between factionalization and declaring independence. What is more, the logic of outbidding embedded in any possible relationship between factionalization and
declaring independence would suggest that more factions would *increase*
the likelihood of a declaration of independence, while the opposite
occurred in this case.

The timing of the South Sudanese declaration of independence was in
fact driven by the framework set out in the 2005 Comprehensive Peace
Agreement (CPA), which had been negotiated with significant international assistance. The South Sudanese adhered scrupulously to the CPA
as part of a concerted effort to increase the odds that South Sudan would
become an internationally recognized independent state. The CPA specified that a referendum on independence could be held six years following the conclusion of the peace agreement, that is, in 2011. The South
Sudanese waited, even though the preference for secession was apparent
as early as 2009 (when planned midterm elections were postponed, and

subsequently deemed undemocratic), and launched a referendum six years to the day after the conclusion of the CPA.

The referendum clearly favored secession, but even after the results the South continued to wait to declare independence, again as specified by the CPA. The southerners knew that they could not declare independence prior to a referendum, and that, according to the CPA, a positive vote meant that South Sudan could become independent six months following the referendum.

July 9, 2011, was therefore the date upon which South Sudan could declare its independence. The declaration itself was a highly orchestrated event. Salva Kiir, South Sudan's first president, formally declared independence during a celebration in Juba, and handed the declaration to UN Secretary-General Ban Ki-moon, along with an application for UN membership. Ban Ki-moon then sent the declaration and application electronically to New York, where both the UN Security Council and the General Assembly were scheduled to meet that weekend. The timing of these meetings was not coincidental: while the UN certainly had other business to attend to, the meetings were planned to accommodate an immediate vote on South Sudanese membership in the UN.

For any new member that is also a new state, the United Nations strongly prefers that the state attain membership in its relevant regional organization prior to joining the UN. The relevant regional organization for South Sudan was the African Union (AU). For administrative and logistical reasons, the AU was not able to admit South Sudan by the given deadline in early July 2011, even though it was generally accepted that South Sudan would have become an AU member had a vote been taken. It is also customary for the chair of the relevant regional organization to introduce the UN membership resolutions, to demonstrate regional support for the new state and its UN membership. As a signal that South Sudan would have been admitted to the AU already, had time permitted, Rwanda—then president of the AU—sponsored the UN General Assembly resolution to admit South Sudan to the UN, which was approved.

It is important to note that South Sudan's declaration of independence was not a unilateral declaration of independence. The Government of Sudan accepted the results of the independence referendum and, in fact, recognized South Sudan on July 8, 2011, one day prior to the declaration of independence. The South had previously considered issuing a unilateral declaration of independence, particularly in the face of stalling tactics on the referendum from Khartoum, but it was cautioned strongly against doing so for fear of backlash from the international community. Had they issued a unilateral declaration, it likely would not have been recognized by other African states, and South Sudan's prospects for recognition would have been damaged. Throughout all these machinations, South Sudan hewed closely to the internationally sanctioned CPA, making sure that every "i" was dotted and every "t" crossed, especially when it came to the timing of the declaration of independence. The international community sent clear signals to South Sudan, and the South Sudanese heeded them carefully, to their benefit. This case is one of the few where behaving according to the dictates of the international community led to a successful outcome for recent secessionists.

With the ICJ's 2010 advisory opinion on Kosovo's unilateral declaration of independence, declarations of independence have become a hot button issue in international law. The controversy over the Kosovo case highlights a main point of this chapter: decisions by secessionists whether and when to declare independence are made for strategic reasons. This strategy is governed largely by the signals sent by the international community, be that a powerful neighboring state as in the case of nineteenth-century Texas, or the United Nations today. Thus, until very recently, the Catalans, the Scots, and the Kurds have all hesitated to declare independence for fear of backlash from the international community whose support is essential to the realization of their political aims.

The evidence presented in this chapter also suggests a possible relationship between a rebel group's military strength and its likelihood of declaring independence. Especially of late, the strongest groups may be the least likely to issue declarations of independence because they are the closest to achieving their political aim and do not want to create any rancor with the international community. The weakest groups, on the other hand, may use declarations of independence as a way of announcing their presence to the world: they cannot receive any support from the international community if the international community is not aware of their existence, and their declarations of independence serve as a type of calling card. It may also be the case that internal support for declarations of independence varies depending on the group's strength at a particular time. Very new or weak groups might be especially inclined to declare independence, but might later walk that decision back as they gain in strength or change their strategies. Certainly, we observe both the Kurds and the Palestinians stepping very carefully today as they accumulate indicators of international recognition and inch toward recognized statehood.[88]

Secessionists are very aware of their appearance before the international community, perhaps more so than other types of rebel groups, because secessionists know that support from the international community is essential to international recognition of a new state. This attentiveness to the desires of the international community is not limited to declarations of independence. It is also visible in how secessionists conduct and conclude their wars, the subjects of chapters 7 and 8. Good behavior by secessionists is not always rewarded by the international community, however. This disconnect between what the international community says and does has not yet, it seems, filtered down to secessionists, who appear to have been poor updaters. Unlike scholars, secessionists are focused on the here and now of survival, and so lack the global perspective enjoyed by scholars. For the near term, secessionists' difficulty in updating serves the international community well, as these groups may be more attentive to direct signals than to the experiences of previous less successful secessionists. Insofar as updating occurs in the longer term, however, reliance on secessionists' inability to observe the conduct and consequences for similar groups may not be a viable strategy for an international community that seeks to govern the commencement, conduct, and conclusion of one of the most common types of civil wars today.

Secessionism and Civilian Targeting

As with declarations of independence, secessionists must balance their military and political aims when deciding whether to comply with the laws of war. In this chapter, I focus my analysis on civilian targeting,[1] both because it is the most important issue within international humanitarian law and also because the prohibition is likely to be better known than other laws such as those regarding treatment of cultural property. In other words, the rule rebel groups are most likely to consider is that they should not target civilians. This analysis also has the advantage of contributing to existing literature on civilian targeting in civil wars, which has focused on the funding structure of rebel groups or the balance of territorial control between rebels and governments, with little consideration of war aims as a critical independent variable.[2]

A major theme of this book is that the proliferation of IHL has had different effects on states fighting interstate wars and on rebel groups fighting civil wars. As discussed in chapter 1, the framers of IHL paid little attention to how the laws they created would influence rebel groups, focusing instead on creating legal barriers to recognizing such groups. One conclusion that rebels could draw is that it pays to be a state, as only states are protected under international law. As the benefits of statehood have increased, we have observed a concurrent increase in secessionism.[3] Secessionists want to make a good impression on the international community. When the international community expresses an aversion to unilateral declarations of independence, secessionists are less likely to issue such declarations, as discussed in chapter 6. This chapter shows that state-seeking rebels are significantly more likely than other types of rebels to refrain from civilian targeting. I argue that secessionist restraint is due to attention to the preferences of the international community alongside military strategic factors associated with secessionism.

Civilian Targeting

The literature on civilian targeting in interstate war and the literature on civilian targeting in civil war have been curiously separate. As discussed in chapter 4, the literature on civilian targeting in interstate war has focused on two main variables: the military strategy of the target state and the war aims of the challenger. Valentino, Huth, and Balch-Lindsay, in one study, and Downes, in another, both show that states fighting opponents that use guerrilla warfare are themselves more likely to target civilians, compared to states fighting opponents that use conventional warfare.[4] Counterinsurgency induces civilian targeting in part because of the difficulty of distinguishing combatants from civilians, but also as a last-resort measure. War aims result in civilian targeting via a different logic: if one of the parties to the war seeks to annex territory from the other, the annexationist belligerent would, all else equal, prefer to acquire territory "cleansed" of any adversary populations. This desire may lead to civilian targeting—"ethnic cleansing"—by the annexationist state.[5]

Previous scholarship on civilian targeting in civil war has focused much more on group-level characteristics than on the nature of the fighting or the war aims of the belligerents. Stathis Kalyvas presents a theory of civilian targeting that rests on the degree to which a given territory is controlled militarily by the government or by the opposition.[6] Jeremy Weinstein argues that the funding and recruitment structure of rebel groups influences their propensity for civilian targeting: those groups that are funded via a third party or by contraband are less reliant on the civilian population for food and support, and therefore more likely to target that population.[7] Kathleen Cunningham has focused on the degree of cohesion within a given group: those groups that are most factionalized, she argues, are especially likely to target civilians via a logic of outbidding, whereby groups compete with each other to intimidate the civilian population and gain their allegiance.[8]

War aims constitute a key missing ingredient in the literature on civilian targeting in civil wars. Political aims condition the behavior of all belligerents—in interstate and civil war—and rebel groups are no exception. Recent scholarship has begun to examine war aims—from "legitimacy-seeking" rebels to secessionists—in analyses of rebel conduct in civil war.[9] In this chapter, I seek to contribute to this literature.

Theoretical Expectations

I argue that both military and political considerations tend to lead secessionist rebel groups to conclude that civilian targeting would be against their interests. From a military perspective, secessionists are a vulnerable population with a limited reach. The civilian population to which they have the greatest access—the population they could most easily target—is the population meant to comprise their new, independent state. They have little incentive to target that population. While it is possible that secessionists could target civilians just over the "border" in the state from which they seek to secede, doing so would put that same population at risk of retaliation. As Monica Toft and others have shown, groups are most likely to press secessionist claims when they are concentrated within a particular geographical area.[10] That concentration confers the advantage of numbers, but also the disadvantage of an easy target.

Secessionists have political incentives not to target civilians for many of the same reasons that restrain them from issuing unilateral declarations of independence. Only the international community can give secessionists what they want—international recognition—and it has very clearly expressed opposition to civilian targeting. The UN Security Council has issued a series of resolutions condemning civilian targeting in, for example, Afghanistan, Cambodia, and Somalia.[11] The UN Secretary-General also issues annual lists of shame that name "parties that recruit or use children, kill or maim children, commit rape and other forms of sexual violence against children, or engage in attacks on schools and/or hospitals in situations of armed conflict." The 2014 list included fifty-six Armed Non-State Actors (ANSAs). Interestingly, only twelve of these groups (about 20 percent) were secessionist.[12] UN efforts to call attention to these conflicts have increasingly been followed by Action Plans, which are a sort of contract between the UN and rebel groups. For example, in the 2009 Action Plan with the Moro Islamic Liberation Front (MILF), a secessionist group in the Philippines, the MILF explicitly accepts to be bound by specific international humanitarian laws regarding child soldiering.[13]

As discussed in chapter 2, secessionists may be more likely than other types of rebel groups to know the preferences of the international community and the laws of war for three reasons. First, many hire Western consultants to advise them in their relations with the international community. Second, secessionists seem to be particularly receptive to engagement with NGOs whose mission is to inform and train them in IHL. As these consultants and NGOs become more widely known, rebel groups are increasingly reaching out to them for support. For example, the NGO Geneva Call, whose mission it is to reduce armed non-state actors' use of land mines, child soldiering, and sexual violence, was approached by the secessionist Tuareg in 2012, upon the advice of lawyers working with the Tuareg.[14] And third, compared to rebel groups fighting resource wars, secessionist military personnel will likely include some defectors from the state military who received training in IHL. Secessionists are likely, therefore, to realize that targeting civilians may harm their reputation with respect to the international community and thus damage their prospects for recognition.

A related advantage of restraint when it comes to secessionists and their relationship with civilians is that restraint signals capability. Restrained groups are disciplined groups, and disciplined groups are generally preferred by third parties as partners. Thus, by refraining from targeting civilians, secessionists serve their own military aims by not endangering their own population and also send signals to the international community of their willingness and capacity to be good citizens of that community.

There will be times, however, when secessionists do have incentives to target civilians.[15] One corollary of my argument is that civilian targeting by secessionists is most likely to occur when non-coethnics reside in the territorial area claimed by secessionists.[16] As in interstate war, here civilian targeting would be used for the purpose of ejecting an unwanted population from an area meant to be part of a new political entity. Thus, we should also expect to observe a relationship between civilian targeting and the degree to which secessionists are ethnically dominant within the region they claim. The most ethnically dominant secessionists would have fewer incentives to cleanse demographically unthreatening non-coethnics from the region they claim. Conversely, the least ethnically dominant secessionists may be most likely to target civilians—specifically, non-coethnics—for the purpose of ethnic cleansing.

Before turning to the results of the empirical analysis, it is important to note that the relationship between declarations of independence and civilian targeting by secessionists in civil war does not parallel the relationship between declarations of war and compliance with IHL discussed in chapter 4. In chapter 3, I argue that the proliferation of IHL led states to be reluctant to declare war because they would not want to step over the bright line of inarguable obligation to comply with IHL. By this logic, those states that did declare war might be those especially likely to comply: these are the states willing to engage IHL precisely because they have high expectations of compliance. But international law is much more ambiguous on secessionists' right to declare independence than it is on the right of states to declare war when fighting each other. Strategic secessionist behavior when it comes to *jus ad bellum* is not obviously linked to strategic secessionist behavior when it comes to *jus in bello*. If anything, we might expect that those secessionist groups declaring independence in the post-Geneva era would also be the most likely to target civilians, because they have already challenged the international community by issuing a formal declaration. This is another corollary of my argument. The overall correlation between declaring independence and civilian targeting is negative and statistically significant during 1816–2007. However, for UN-era, post-Geneva cases, when the international community's preferences against both declarations of independence and civilian targeting have been made very clear, the correlation is much weaker, and it is no longer statistically significant.[17]

When Do Rebel Groups Target Civilians?

As in the previous several chapters, I evaluate the expectations stated above against quantitative and qualitative evidence. The main finding of my analysis is that secessionists are significantly less likely to target civilians than are nonsecessionists. Additional findings illuminate differences in the types of civilians that secessionists target, time trends in violent secessionism and civilian targeting, and how rebel groups in general, and secessionists in particular, react when they are on the receiving end of civilian targeting by the governments they fight.

Quantitative Analysis

The universe of cases for this analysis is all civil war dyads as identified by C-WIT from 1816 to 2007. The universe of cases considered in this chapter is larger than that for the previous chapter because this chapter compares secessionists to other types of rebels, while chapter 6 focused exclusively on secessionists. Another difference is that I use two versions of the dataset in this chapter. In one version, the "original coding" version, considerable data is missing, particularly on the key dependent variable of rebel group civilian targeting. The other version, the "standardized coding" version, assumes that campaigns of civilian targeting are sufficiently noticeable that any missing data on this variable should be converted to a zero. Results based on both original and standardized codings are presented below, following discussion of coding of key variables.

Description of Variables   Below, I describe sources and coding used for variables employed in the quantitative analysis for this chapter. Unless otherwise noted, all variables are taken from C-WIT. Several variables are meant to test alternative explanations, as discussed below.

CIVILIAN TARGETING

I define civilian targeting as the intentional use of a strategy of inflicting violence against civilians, where violence includes the infliction of death or bodily harm (deportation or imprisonment are not counted unless accompanied by the infliction of death or bodily harm). This definition overlaps with those employed in analyses of civilian targeting in interstate war and civil war.[18] It is also similar to the definition used by the Uppsala Conflict Data Project's (UCDP) one-sided violence dataset, which is restricted to "the use of armed force by the government of a state or by a formally organized group against civilians which results in at least 25 deaths,"[19] and that used by the Global Terrorism Database, which codes for "threatened or actual uses of illegal force and violence by a non-state actor to attain a political, economic, religious, or social goal through fear, coercion, or intimidation."[20]

Recent events provide examples. Ukrainian rebels are believed to have shot down Malaysian Airlines Flight 17 on July 17, 2014. Although the rebels deny this accusation, many reports suggest that the missile was fired accidentally at a civilian plane; thus this incident would not be coded as one where civilians were targeted intentionally. By contrast, the Islamic State's siege and enslavement of the Yazidi in Iraq, begun in 2014, was clearly intentional, aimed at cleansing an area of a particular group. It fits the definition of civilian targeting.

SECESSIONISM

The coding for the key independent variable, *secessionist*, is the same used to delimit the universe of cases for the analysis of declarations of independence presented in chapter 6. Rebel groups that seek their own independent state are coded as secessionist.

THE ADDITIONAL PROTOCOLS

Another key independent variable is *post-AP*, a dummy variable for conflicts fought after 1977, when the two Additional Protocols intended to apply the 1949 Geneva Conventions to national liberation and civil wars were created. This variable allows testing of the possibility that rebel groups will be decreasingly likely to target civilians once there are laws of war explicitly applicable to civil wars. In some specifications, *post-AP* is interacted with *secessionist* to test for the possibility that secessionists became especially unlikely to target civilians in the post-AP era.

CONTROL VARIABLES AND ALTERNATIVE EXPLANATIONS

Balance of power. To capture the balance of power between the government and rebels, I again use *force ratio (deployed)*, based on the number of rebel forces divided by the number of government troops deployed for a given conflict. This variable helps tests for the possibility, advanced by scholars such as Reed Wood, that weaker groups may be more likely to target civilians than stronger groups because weaker groups lack the resources to win the allegiance of the civilian population nonviolently.[21]

Number of factions. I use *fragmentation* (described in the previous chapter) to measure the number of factions in the rebel group and to test for the possibility that the more fragmented the rebels are, the more likely they are to target civilians via a logic of outbidding.[22] As suggested by Cunningham, one alternative explanation is that fragmented rebels might be more likely than less fragmented rebels to target civilians as factions in the more fragmented group fight for power within the group.

Insurgency. *Insurgency* captures the overall military strategy employed by the group. Despite the fact that insurgency and civil war (or insurgents and rebels) are often equated, it is important to distinguish how wars are fought from the fact that they are fought, as well as from who is doing the fighting.[23] I adopt James Fearon and David Laitin's definition of insurgency as a means of guerrilla warfare, "characterized by small, lightly armed groups practicing hit-and-run tactics, usually from rural areas."[24] An example is the Chinese Civil War.[25] Insurgency is typically contrasted to conventional warfare, which is characterized by the use of heavy artillery and set-piece battles, such as in the American or Spanish Civil Wars.[26] I include this control to test for the possibility, suggested by scholars such as Mueller,[27] that guerrillas will be more likely than nonguerrillas to target civilians.[28]

Government civilian targeting. *Government civilian targeting* is defined exactly the same way as *rebels' civilian targeting*, except that the government is the perpetrator. It is included here to control for the possibility that rebels may target civilians in response to government targeting of civilians (or vice versa). Examples of government targeting of civilians include the Sierra Leone civil war against the Revolutionary United Front (RUF) in the 1990s, the Chechen civil war, the Bengali Independence War, and (albeit too recent to be included in these data) the ongoing Syrian civil war.[29]

Rebel group financing. *Contraband* captures one aspect of the financing structure of the rebel groups, and codes for whether the rebels finance their fighting at least partly through means such as the illegal mining, production, or sale of gems or drugs. It is meant to control for the possibility, advanced most strongly by Weinstein, that rebel groups that rely on contraband financing feel themselves more free to target civilians because they are less reliant on the support of the civilian population to prosecute their wars.[30] Weinstein's logic also captures the important possible role of lack of discipline in explaining variation in civilian targeting across rebel groups. As Morrow shows in the context of interstate wars, civilian targeting is an issue area within IHL that is particularly prone to violation because it can be committed, even against orders, by individual soldiers; in this respect, it differs from, for example, the use of chemical and biological weapons, which are typically centrally controlled.[31]

Democracy. *Polity* controls for the level of democracy of the government. Stanton and others suggest that rebels may be especially likely to target civilians when the rebels are fighting a democratic opponent because democratic publics will have little tolerance for their own civilian casualties.[32] Democracy may affect both rebel incentives to attack civilians and government incentives to attack civilians,[33] which may, in turn, provoke reciprocity that leads to rebel targeting of civilians.[34] *Polity* uses Polity2 from the Polity IV dataset as a measure of regime type, which ranges from -10 (most autocratic) to 10 (least autocratic). Using Polity2 rather than Polity allows the inclusion of more observations, which is especially helpful because a disproportionate number of missing observations in Polity are country-years with a civil war. While other measures of democracy are arguably superior to the Polity measure, none go back as far in time.[35]

Regression Analysis and Discussion   Given the dichotomous nature of the dependent variable, logistic regression is employed to analyze rebel use of civilian targeting as a military strategy. Consistent with the general argument of this chapter, I find that secessionists are significantly less likely than nonsecessionist rebel groups to target civilians. Tables 7.1 and 7.2 report these results based on standardized and original codings of the civilian targeting variables, and show this claim to be robust to multiple model specifications.[36] Based on results from models 2 and 3 in table 7.1, secessionists groups are 28–41 percent less likely to target civilians than are nonsecessionist rebels. This finding supports the main hypothesis of this chapter.

TABLE 7.1 Logistic regressions of civilian targeting by rebels (standardized coding)

	(1)	(2)	(3)	(4)
Secessionist	−.82 (.49) p = .09	−.89 (.53) p = .09	−1.27 (.67) p = .06	−1.68 (.81) p = .04
Insurgency	.79 (.44) p = .07	.59 (.48) p = .22	.51 (.55) p = .35	.63 (.56) p = .26
Civilian targeting by government (standardized)	2.66 (.44) p = .00	2.53 (.47) p = .00	2.37 (.56) p = .00	2.35 (.56) p = .00
Post-AP		2.32 (.65) p = .00	2.79 (.85) p = .00	2.17 (.95) p = .02
Secessionist * post-AP				1.86 (1.76) p = .29
Contraband financing			−.47 (.90) p = .60	−.29 (.89) p = .74
Fragmentation			.47 (.17) p = .01	.47 (.16) p = .00
Polity			−.06 (.05) p = .25	−.07 (.06) p = .19
Force ratio (deployed)	.00 (.09) p = .99	−.02 (.08) p = .80	−.05 (.12) p = .65	−.07 (.11) p = .52
Constant	−1.92 (.43) p = .00	−2.17 (.47) p = .00	−3.05 (.67) p = .00	−3.09 (.67) p = .00
N	148	148	130	130
Pseudo-R^2	.31	.40	.46	.46
Chi-2	0.0000	0.0000	0.0000	0.0000
% correctly predicted	79.05	81.76	82.31	82.31

Note: Standard errors in parentheses.

TABLE 7.2 Logistic regressions of civilian targeting by rebels (original coding)

	(1)	(2)	(3)	(4)
Secessionist	−.96 (.49) *p = .05*	−1.15 (.55) *p = .04*	−1.68 (.74) *p = .02*	−2.42 (1.03) *p = .02*
Insurgency	.80 (.44) *p = .07*	.62 (.49) *p = .21*	.51 (.56) *p = .37*	.67 (.58) *p = .25*
Civilian targeting by government (original)	2.30 (.45) *p = .00*	2.15 (.49) *p = .00*	2.03 (.58) *p = .00*	2.03 (.58) *p = .00*
Post-AP		2.54 (.70) *p = .00*	2.95 (.89) *p = .00*	2.13 (.95) *p = .03*
Secessionist * post-AP				2.58 (1.85) *p = .16*
Contraband financing			−.58 (.90) *p = .52*	−.37 (.88) *p = .67*
Fragmentation			.54 (.20) *p = .01*	.56 (.19) *p = .00*
Polity			−.07 (.06) *p = .20*	−.09 (.06) *p = .15*
Force ratio (deployed)	−.01 (.09) *p = .95*	−.03 (.08) *p = .73*	−.06 (.12) *p = .64*	−.08 (.11) *p = .48*
Constant	−1.60 (.43) *p = .00*	−1.85 (.46) *p = .00*	−2.90 (.71) *p = .00*	−2.97 (.71) *p = .00*
N	132	132	116	116
Pseudo-R^2	.27	.37	.45	.46
Chi-2	0.0000	0.0000	0.0000	0.0000
% correctly predicted	75.76	81.82	81.03	82.76

Note: Standard errors in parentheses.

Table 7.3 reports marginal effects for all significant variables. Figure 7.1 pulls out the marginal effects for secessionists. Perhaps because this analysis covers a much longer time period than most quantitative analyses of civil war, results on many of the control variables are inconsistent with previous scholarship. *Insurgency* is always positive, but only attains statistical significance at the .1 level in the most stripped-down model. This result is generally, although not strongly, consistent with the claim

TABLE 7.3 Marginal effects for significant variables (table 8.2, model 3)

Variable	Probability at zero	Probability at 1	Difference
Secessionism	0.68	0.39	–41%
Government targeting of civilians	0.18	0.68	260%
Post-1977	0.68	0.96	42%
Fragmentation (25th to 75th percentile)	0.59	0.69	17%

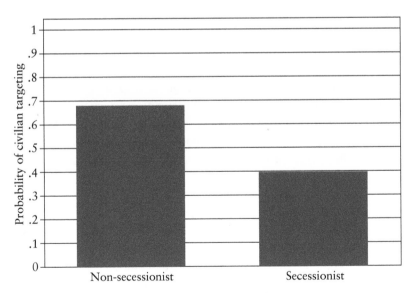

Figure 7.1 Secessionism and civilian targeting

that guerrillas are more likely to target civilians than are rebels who are not using guerrilla warfare, but it is inconsistent with the logic that guerrillas are less likely to target the civilian population because they depend upon civilians for support. Not surprisingly, rebels who are on the receiving end of civilian targeting by governments are approximately two and a half times more likely to engage in such targeting themselves, compared to rebels whose governments do not target civilians.[37] This result speaks to mixed findings regarding the role of reciprocity in previous scholarship on civilian targeting in interstate wars,[38] as well as more generally with compliance with international humanitarian law in interstate wars.[39] The results also reinforce existing claims about the relationship between group fragmentation and civilian targeting: more fragmented groups are 35–40 percent more likely to target civilians than are less fragmented groups.

Turning to additional alternative explanations, Jeremy Weinstein makes an influential argument that rebel groups financed via illegal sources (such as drugs or diamonds) are most likely to target civilians.[40] However, my results show that such contraband financing is never a significant predictor of civilian targeting. Indeed, in some specifications, the coefficient on this variable is negative. The coefficient on regime type also fails to attain statistical significance, in contrast to scholarship by Jessica Stanton.[41] Also in contrast with work by Stanton and, particularly, by Reed Wood, the indicator of the strength of the rebels relative to the government is consistently negative, but never at a statistically significant level.[42] When alternative measures of relative strength—using C-WIT's and COW's measures of total government forces—are substituted, this result is either consistent or the coefficient switches sign but remains statistically insignificant.

Whom Do Secessionists Target?   When secessionists engage in civilian targeting, we may expect this targeting to be directed at non-coethnics—those who would be a minority in a new state and are, perhaps, a majority in the existing state. Even though secessionists are significantly less likely than nonsecessionists to target civilians, about half of all secessionist groups do target civilians. In these cases, I suggest, belligerents target civilians as a means of cleansing territory of unwanted populations.

TABLE 7.4 Secessionist targets, 1816–2007

Target type	Distribution and illustration
Non-coethnics only	17 (47%) Moro Islamic Liberation Front (Philippines, 2000–2001; 2003)
Non-coethnics and coethnics	9 (25%) Liberation Tigers of Tamil Eelam (Sri Lanka, 1983–2001; 2006–2009)
Coethnics only	6 (17%) Kashmiri insurgents (India, 1989–present)
Neither/other[a]	4 (11%) Anti-monarchists (Two Sicilies, 1820)

Note: Some data are missing, due to insufficient information in a handful of cases to code these variables.

[a] These were typically cases where rebel troops engaged in indiscriminate targeting or rampaging.

Table 7.4 presents the distribution of targets among those secessionists that target civilians.[43] Note that this table explicitly selects on the dependent variable, to see what we can learn from examining variation among secessionists' targets. If secessionists more frequently targeted their own people rather than populations that they would prefer leave their area, my argument would be challenged. To some extent, however, finding that groups tend to target coethnics would be consistent with some relatively high-profile, and recent, cases: in Kurdish, Chechen, and Palestinian villages, central governments have successfully recruited locals to inform on their neighbors.[44] Likewise, Sri Lanka's Tamil Tigers are infamous for their extensive (although not exclusive) targeting of coethnics.[45]

These exceptional cases notwithstanding, the data tell another story. In the clear majority (70 percent) of instances of secessionists targeting civilians, secessionists target non-coethnics residing in territory claimed by the secessionists. The Acehnese, whose civilian targeting focused in part on the ethnic Javanese they wished to evict from the land they claimed, illustrate this phenomenon well.[46] Aceh expert Edward Aspinall describes an interview with a pro-Aceh independence fighter who argued that ethnic Javanese could destroy the ethnic integrity of Aceh.[47] Acehnese fighters posted notices of eviction aimed at Javanese in the area: "'Oh Javanese transmigrants on the land of Aceh-Sumatra, now take to your heels, do not stay in Aceh Sumatra.'"[48] Both this example and the more systematic data are consistent with the notion that such targeting is for the purpose of cleansing. Indeed, amongst the clear majority of secessionists that target non-coethnics, two-thirds of these groups appear to target non-coethnics exclusively.

A more robust test of this hypothesis employs regression analysis of the secessionist conflicts in C-WIT. To test the hypothesis that ethnically dominant secessionists less often target civilians in their own region, additional data was collected on each secessionist group's relative ethnic balance within the claimed secessionist region. Two measures of this variable are used for the analysis in table 7.5: *ethnic balance (1)* is coded in equal quintiles, ranging from the secessionists in question comprising a clear minority (0–20 percent) to an overwhelming majority (80–100 percent). *Ethnic balance (2)* is coded in unequal quintiles to account for the unsurprising fact that ethnic balance is not evenly distributed across quintiles. *Ethnic*

TABLE 7.5 Logistic regressions on civilian targeting by secessionist rebels (standardized coding)

	(1)	**(2)**
Ethnic balance (1)	−.51 (.30) *p = .09*	
Ethnic balance (2)		−.48 (.27) *p = .07*
Civilian targeting by government (standardized)	**2.99** (.71) *p = .00*	**2.98** (.71) *p = .00*
Fragmentation	.48 (.28) *p = .09*	.47 (.28) *p = .10*
Constant	−.62 (1.23) *p = .61*	−.87 (1.07) *p = .42*
N	67	67
Pseudo-R^2	.38	.38
Chi-2	0.0000	0.0000

Note: Standard errors in parentheses.

balance (2) is coded as follows: 1 (0–25 percent), clear minority; 2 (25–50 percent), minority; 3 (50–75 percent), clear majority; 4 (75–90 percent), predominant; and 5 (90–100 percent), overwhelming. As with the C-WIT data, this variable was coded using primarily secondary sources.

Those that are more dominant in their region should feel less need to cleanse non-coethnics. Thus, as *Ethnic balance* increases, the likelihood of civilian targeting should decrease. The results produce strong evidence in favor of this hypothesis. The most dominant secessionist groups in the regions they claim are approximately 25 percent less likely to target civilians when compared to the least dominant secessionist groups in the regions they claim. Robustness tests that collapse the ethnic balance variable to a binary value and consider the possibility that the effect is curvilinear (where ethnic groups with mid-level dominance would be most likely to target non-coethnics) do not yield particularly strong results; in this case, the effect of ethnic dominance on civilian targeting may in fact be linear.

The results of this analysis are also consistent with the claim of Kathleen Cunningham that factionalized self-determination groups (of which secessionists are one category) are particularly likely to target civilians.[49] Moving from the 25th to 75th percentile on this variable yields an approximately 10 percent increase in the likelihood of civilian targeting; the substantive effect of this variable is smaller than that of the degree of secessionist ethnic dominance in the region. The logic of reciprocity continues to exert the strongest influence on civilian targeting, with secessionists on the receiving end of government targeting more than two-and-a-half times more likely to engage in civilian targeting themselves, compared to secessionists not experiencing government targeting of civilians.

Does International Humanitarian Law Matter?   My argument suggests that all rebels, and particularly secessionists, will be less likely to target civilians as international humanitarian law develops and, especially, as it is extended to apply to civil wars. To test this hypothesis quantitatively, I included a variable for conflicts fought after 1977, when two Additional Protocols to the 1949 Geneva Conventions were created. The protocols—especially Protocol II—are meant to extend the 1949 Conventions explicitly to civil wars.[50] Per Article 1(4) of Additional Protocol II, "Protocol II Relating to the Protection of Victims of Non-International Armed Conflicts develops and supplements Article 3 common to the

Geneva Conventions of 12 August 1949 [and] shall apply to all armed conflicts . . . which take place in the territory of a High Contracting Party between its armed forces and dissident armed forces or other organized armed groups which, under responsible command, exercise such control over a part of its territory as to enable them to carry out sustained and concerted military operations." Protocol I is also relevant in that it extends the scope of existing international humanitarian law to include "armed conflicts in which people are fighting against colonial domination and alien occupation and against racist regimes in the exercise of their right of self-determination."[51]

On its own, this variable tests for whether rebels in general were less likely to target civilians after international humanitarian law was extended in this way. The 1977 Additional Protocols represent the culmination of the first stage of a movement to extend formal application of IHL to civil wars, or "internal armed conflicts."[52] By interacting war aims (secessionism) with the post-1977 period, I can further test for the possibility that secessionist rebel groups will be more likely than nonsecessionists to respond to this development in international law, and thus less likely to target civilians after 1977 than before. A consistently positive and significant coefficient on post-AP in tables 7.1 and 7.2 indicates that it is not, in fact, the case, that rebels in general after 1977 were less likely to target civilians. Indeed, the results suggest that rebels were up to 40 percent *more* likely to target civilians after 1977 compared to those before.[53]

Tests for robustness that include alternative specifications for the claim that civilian targeting by secessionists or rebels has decreased with the proliferation in IHL—particularly an indicator variable for the post-Geneva era[54] or a variable for the year in which the war began—yielded largely stable results. The coefficient on secessionism was always negative, although in some cases it dipped below the p=.1 level; if anything, this suggests that secessionists prior to the passage of these IHL treaties were more restrained than after. Similar results obtained when using an OLS instead of a logit model.[55]

One possible explanation for this unexpected finding is that the pressures of the international system on secessionist groups to conduct themselves in a certain manner are keenly felt even prior to the decision to engage in political violence. It is not just international humanitarian law that has proliferated over the time period discussed here, but also international law regarding the resort to force. As scholars such as Mikulas Fabry have shown, successful secessionists in the nineteenth century in particular earned statehood by literally fighting for their state.[56] With the rise of the principle of self-determination, however, statehood has become viewed more as a right in some quarters, perhaps especially for those movements that do not engage in violence. Thus, international recognition may well depend on secessionists' restraint not just *during* war, but even preceding a possible conflict; at least, this may be the perception by secessionists. If this is the case, we should expect that secessionists who have already made the decision to violate one set of international principles—those that oppose unilateral, violent secession—will perhaps be more determined to win and therefore less concerned about violating other principles of international law, such as those prohibiting the targeting of civilians.[57]

If, in fact, international community pressures are more keenly felt today than before, this suggests, as a first step, that secessionism may have become less violent over time. While most data on secessionism focuses on the post-1945 period, Ryan Griffiths's dataset identifies all secessionist movements from 1816 to 2011.[58] These data demonstrate a clear decline in the proportion of secessionist groups using violence to press their claims, even though secessionism itself is on the rise.[59] Figure 7.2 graphs the proportion of secessionist movements involved in wars that produced at least 1,000 battle fatalities.[60] It demonstrates a clear decline over the course of the past two centuries. After 1949, secessionist movements were half as likely to fight large-scale wars (defined as producing at least 1,000 deaths) compared to the pre-1949 period.[61]

Thus, it seems at least possible that a selection effect is driving the result on the *secessionist x post-AP* interaction term.[62] In other words, as the international community signals its aversion to secessionist violence, secessionists have listened, and are decreasingly likely to engage in large-scale war. Those secessionists least likely to take the cues of the international community have selected into war; it is perhaps not surprising that, if they ignore signals decrying the use of violence, they will further ignore signals regarding civilian targeting. The secessionist groups in the data analysis above, then, may represent particularly hard cases for the argument linking secessionism, civilian targeting, and the proliferation of IHL in that they have all selected themselves into conflict, and therefore are already arguably acting in ways contrary to the contemporary international legal landscape.

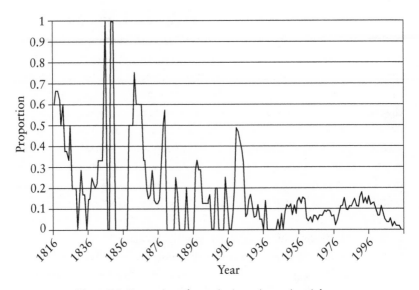

Figure 7.2 Proportion of secessionists using major violence

Two other factors could also account for this unexpected finding. First, it is possible that we simply have more information about civilian targeting in recent years compared to earlier years, and thus this apparent increase is an artifact of better reporting.[63] And second, any uptick in rebel civilian targeting could be a response to government civilian targeting. Here, future research on which governments signed the Additional Protocols when could be helpful in discerning whether the most civil war-prone states were the least likely signatories and, consequently, the least restrained in their warfighting. Related, Stanton examines the relationship between politically inclusive versus exclusive rebels fighting democratic versus autocratic regimes, and finds that this strategic interaction—not tested for here—helps account for significant variation in post-1989 civilian targeting in civil wars.[64]

Qualitative Analysis

The quantitative analysis provides important support for the claim that secessionists are less likely to target civilians compared to nonsecessionists. But it remains difficult to assess whether this distinction is due to military strategic needs or to a desire to please the international community, especially in more recent years. Another question is whether good behavior leads to good outcomes for secessionists. I investigate these questions further in the case studies below.

Texas   The Texas war of independence is largely consistent with the results of the quantitative analysis reported above, especially in tables 7.1 and 7.2. Neither side appears to have targeted civilians in this conflict. Notwithstanding the brutal slaughter of the Alamo defenders in late February and early March of 1836, Mexican attacks generally focused on combatants and not civilians. The civilian population of Texas certainly feared Mexican attacks, in part because of the savage fighting at the Alamo and Goliad.[65] Texans' fear of the advancing Mexican army produced the infamous "Runaway Scrape," in which a large segment of the Texan population fled east.[66] One of the Texas army's major challenges was in limiting desertions of soldiers wanting to protect their families and homes.

The Texans themselves had very limited military reach. Military engagements all occurred north of the Rio Grande, and within the territory claimed by Texas. Thus, the Texans lacked the capacity to target Mexican civilians, even if they had sought to engage in such behavior.

The Texan army did at times strike fear into the hearts of Texan civilians, although it would be difficult to argue that this behavior rose to the level of civilian targeting. Impressment to bolster military forces was zealous, and sometimes included property as well as people.[67] At times, the army engaged in plunder and maltreatment of the civilian population, but this behavior was due to indiscipline rather than a strategy of targeting civilians.[68] That said, such treatment was likely considered more acceptable when directed at the sizable Hispanic (Tejano) population, whose loyalty to the revolution was questioned by the ill-equipped soldiers of the Texas army in search of plunder.

As Paul Lack shows, Tejanos felt the brunt of ill treatment of civilians by the Texan army.[69] Maltreatment of the Tejano population is consistent with the claim that, when and if secessionists do target civilians, the civilians they target will be the ethnic minority in the secessionist region. But in the Texas case, this maltreatment was not directed from on high. On the contrary, leaders such as Sam Houston very much tried to avoid civilian targeting. Houston's position rested on two logics. First, he appears to have sought to minimize any conflict with the Tejano population. But he also saw an international dimension to restraint with respect to the civilian population: "The world would damn our cause if we shed blood at home."[70] Even if Houston's impression of the degree of global attention trained on the conflict in Texas was inflated, his reasoning is entirely consistent with the notion that secessionists recognize that they need international support and so will modify their behavior—including by avoiding the targeting of civilians—to increase the odds of receiving such support. This anecdote also suggests that secessionists' concern that key international supporters might disapprove of their civilian targeting well preceded the twentieth century; this could help account for the lack of a finding on the interaction term between the proliferation of IHL and secessionism in tables 7.1 and 7.2. In other words, it may be that secessionists were always sensitive to international concern about civilian targeting. If this is the case, then we would not expect to observe a strong effect of time—as represented by major IHL treaties—on secessionist compliance with international norms regarding civilian targeting.

Mexico's attitude toward the rest of the world was quite different. Knowing that a large proportion of Texas army volunteers were from the United States, Santa Anna declared a policy whereby foreigners fighting in Mexico were deemed "pirates" and would be shot rather than treated as prisoners of war. But rather than deterring volunteers, this policy backfired by inspiring more American sympathy for the Texan cause.[71]

South Moluccas   Knowing—or at least hoping—that the eyes of the world were upon them, the South Moluccans were an atypically restrained rebel group when it came to civilian targeting. Indeed, the Republik Maluku Selatan (RMS) army (the Angkatan Perang Republik Maluku Selatan, or APRMS) does not appear to have taken any offensive action against Indonesian troops, and may even have been willing to accept serious civilian casualties in order to increase their odds of recognition.[72]

By contrast, the Indonesian government was not restrained in its targeting of civilians when prosecuting this war. The South Moluccans understood that publicizing this type of behavior could attract supporters in the international community; thus, they were quick to level public accusations of civilian targeting at the Indonesian government. In outlets such as the *New York Times* and in petitions to the UN Security Council, they accused

the Indonesian government of "bombing and shelling unguilty population of the villages: Hutumuri, Aland, Amahusu, Latuhalat, Tulehu, Laha,
Haruku, Itawaka, Saparua";[73] imposing a "starvation blockade" upon
Ambon, even after a disastrous flood;[74] and using South Moluccan civilians as human shields.[75]

The South Moluccans did not respond in kind. Although their forces—
which had earned a reputation for military prowess during the Dutch
colonial period—engaged government troops, they did not target civilians. A major reason for South Moluccan "restraint" was certainly its lack
of capacity. The difficulty of reaching Jakarta in the 1950s from Ambon
was a constraining factor; contact with "the mainland" was minimal, and
typically via boat.[76] But their frequent outreach makes clear that the South
Moluccans were acutely conscious of their international profile. Given
that they were leveling accusations against the Indonesian government,
they appear to have been equally aware that bringing attention to themselves by attacking civilians in Jakarta would not bring them the international sympathy they so deeply desired.

South Sudan   In contrast to the South Moluccans, the conduct of the
Sudan People's Liberation Movement/Army (SPLM/A) during its civil war
with the North stands in clear contradiction to the claim that secessionist rebel groups are relatively unlikely to target civilians. The civil war in
Sudan was rife with civilian targeting by all sides. The Khartoum government targeted civilians in the South, typically via aerial bombing campaigns and by impeding humanitarian aid, throughout the conflict. The
North's attacks on southern civilians were so harsh as to invite serious
criticism from the international community, including a blanket UN Security Council Resolution that "strongly condemns the deliberate targeting of civilians and places protected under international law."[77] The US
secretary of state Madeline Albright and the Canadian foreign minister
Lloyd Axworthy each singled out the Sudanese government, calling for
an end to its "reprehensible" actions, which "clearly demonstrate to the
world that this administration is unconcerned with the human security of
its population."[78]

The civilian targeting engaged in by the South Sudanese rebels, however,
was not directed against the citizens of the North. At least in part, the
SPLM/A, which had primarily small arms unsuited to long-range attacks,

did not attack the North because it lacked the capability to do so.[79] However, even when the rebels obtained artillery and other heavy weaponry later in the war, they did not target the North.[80] Instead, the two main ethnic groups that comprised the SPLM/A—the Dinka and the Nuer—targeted each other's civilians during the course of the conflict.[81] This led to a civil war that continues in independent South Sudan as of late 2017.

The interethnic, intracoalition nature of the civilian targeting during this conflict fits best with the finding—although not necessarily the logic—that, among secessionist rebel groups, those that are most factionalized and most ethnically diverse will engage in the most civilian targeting. The logic behind the claim that factionalization leads to civilian targeting is one of outbidding: factions within a larger movement target civilians as a show of strength and to frighten ambivalent civilians into joining their side.[82] Here, the civilian targeting more closely resembled ethnic cleansing. But it was not for the purposes of eliminating ethnic northerners from the area. Instead, this case appears to be one where at least two enemies that had joined together to fight a third enemy never stopped seeing each other as threats.

One puzzling aspect of this case links the civilian targeting committed by the SPLM/A with subsequent support for South Sudanese independence from the international community. I have argued above that many rebel groups, and secessionist rebel groups in particular, seek to broadcast their compliance with IHL as a means to signal their willingness and capacity to be good citizens of the international community. The egregious human rights violations committed by the SPLM/A at first appear to stand in direct contradiction to this claim. To resolve this contradiction it is necessary to understand, first, the difference between what the international community says and what it does. For example, the international community has clearly stated a preference for nonviolent political change, including nonviolent secessionism.[83] As Erica Chenoweth and Maria Stephan have shown, however, while nonviolence is generally more politically effective than violence, this is not the case for secessionists.[84] Similarly, Bridget Coggins finds that it is "friends in high places"—and, not, for example, a demonstrated capacity to govern—that determines which secessionist movements gain international recognition.[85] If the community of states empowered to confer recognition on secessionist movements is willing to countenance the use of violence to press secessionist claims, it is perhaps not too far a stretch to believe that this same community is willing to overlook violations of IHL in the process.

Why, then, would secessionist groups believe—and, moreover, structure their actions based on this belief—that the international community would turn its back on groups that violate IHL? And to what extent did the SPLM/A share this belief? The international community walked a communications tightrope in this case, condemning civilian targeting by all sides to the conflict, but directing most of its ire at the North. More generally, it seems that secessionists may not be very attentive to precedent. Rather than surveying the history of similar conflicts to assess what did and did not work, they listen to the signals they are sent, particularly by the actors that can determine their specific fate.[86] A better test of how secessionist groups respond to condemnation by the international community might be one where the secessionist group, but not the government, is chastised for civilian targeting.[87]

The proliferation of laws regulating conduct during war has affected rebels engaged in civil war very differently from states engaged in interstate war. Compliance with this body of international law, and the norms that have developed alongside it, is often held up by the international community as one of the conditions for recognition of rebel groups. The prospect of recognition is especially important for one category of rebel groups—secessionists. The international community that has emerged in the UN era has had remarkable success in imposing its preferences on secessionist movements.

The finding that secessionists are less likely than nonsecessionists to target civilians is consistent with a growing literature that links the desire for international legitimacy with compliance with international humanitarian law, including treatment of prisoners of war and the use of child soldiers.[88] The UN has sent clear signals to rebel groups, in the form of action plans and shaming lists, of its disapprobation of violations of IHL. Rebels seem to have responded by sending signals of their own: publicizing their compliance with IHL via platforms such as Geneva Call,[89] and calling out governments for targeting civilians in rebel-held areas, as when the South Moluccans included these accusations in letters to the *New York Times* and petitions to the United Nations.

The growing influence of international law and the international community on the commencement and conduct of civil wars is clear. As discussed in chapter 6, secessionists refrain from declaring independence for fear of angering the international community. They exercise restraint when it comes to opportunities to violate IHL because they want to signal their capability and intent to be good citizens of that same community.

Does secessionists' sensitivity to the international community work? That is to say, are secessionists who exercise restraint in declaring independence and targeting civilians more likely to achieve their political aim of independent statehood than those who ignore the advice of the international community? The answer, at least to date, appears to be: no. Previous scholarship has shown that those secessionists most likely to obtain international recognition are those that have the support of a great power, the advantage of prior administrative boundaries, or both.[90] Conduct during conflict does not appear to affect secessionist success. One some level, what this suggests is that secessionists ought not necessarily heed the advice of the international community. On another level, it suggests that the international community would do better do maintain consistency in its principles, its advice, and its actions.

8

Peace Treaties in Civil War

It is harder to conclude peace treaties in civil wars than in interstate wars, for at least two reasons. First, there is always a legitimacy gap between the parties to civil war; such a gap does not necessarily exist between adversaries in an interstate war. The framers of the laws of war governing belligerent conduct during war tended to discuss civil wars almost exclusively in the context of ensuring that they were not granting recognition to rebel groups (as discussed in chapter 1). For the same reason, states fighting civil wars are often reluctant to come to the peace table: they do not want to concede the legitimacy of a rebel adversary. Second, in the great majority of civil wars (the exceptions being those that end with successful secessionism), at least one former belligerent must disarm in order for all to live together. This creates a commitment problem that is much more severe than for states, each of which typically maintains its military forces and retreats to internationally recognized borders after an interstate war.[1]

Despite the legitimacy gap and the commitment problem, peace treaties have followed civil wars for centuries. The history of peace treaties in interstate and civil war is entwined; prior to the emergence of the state system, it would be difficult to say whether a peace treaty fell into one or the other category. Systematic data suggest that peace treaties concluded around 10 percent of all civil wars during the nineteenth and early twentieth centuries. In the UN era, however, this number has risen steadily, if slowly. Today one-third of all civil wars are concluded via the use of a formal peace treaty. The rising use of peace treaties to conclude civil wars contrasts with the declining use of peace treaties to conclude interstate wars, discussed in chapter 5. This presents a puzzle: why, especially given the challenges of concluding peace treaties in civil wars, is the rate of peace treaty use in civil wars rising while the rate of peace treaty use in interstate wars is in decline?

To add to this puzzle, the relationship between peace treaties in civil wars and the duration of subsequent peace appears to differ from interstate wars. Among interstate wars that stop and resume at a later date, war-dyads ending in peace treaties see four more years of peace compared to wars ending without peace treaties (see chapter 5). Among civil wars that stop and later resume, war-dyads ending in peace treaties see, on average, three *fewer* years of peace compared to wars ending without peace treaties. When restricted to the post-1945 era—when the use of peace treaties in civil wars rose—this negative relationship is even more pronounced, becoming statistically significant.

I argued in chapter 5 that the decline of peace treaty usage in interstate war is attributable, in significant part, to the proliferation of international humanitarian law that creates incentives for states to refrain from stepping over bright lines that would oblige them to be accountable for violations of this body of law. While it might be aesthetically pleasing to argue the converse here—that both rebel groups and the governments they fight are increasingly inclined to conclude peace treaties as a consequence of the proliferation of the laws of war—this logic does not apply. Part of the reason for the lack of symmetry has to do with international humanitarian law itself, which is, by design, considerably weaker and more vague in the civil war context than in the interstate war context. Also, even if certain rebels—such as the secessionists who refrain from targeting civilians, described in chapter 7—would like to tout their compliance with IHL in the face of government noncompliance, it is much easier for the typically more powerful government to veto a peace treaty (for reasons of noncompliance) than it is for the typically less powerful rebels to force one (by virtue of compliance).

Instead, I argue, peace treaties in civil wars are on the rise because of the expressed preferences of the international community in favor of such agreements. This expression is visible via public statements made by representatives of organizations such as the United Nations, and also via the training and deployment of a corps of international mediators in the UN era. Even if belligerents in civil war are not as explicitly focused on the laws of war as are belligerents in interstate war, the governments and rebels fighting civil wars certainly pay attention to the preferences of the same international community that designed international humanitarian law. While the increased use of peace treaties in civil wars may appear to be a positive development, an unintended consequence of the international community's taste for peace treaties may be that too much focus has been trained on these agreements, at the expense of the peace that follows.

Peace Treaties in Civil War: An Overview

More civil wars today end via negotiated settlements than they did prior to 1945. According to C-WIT, civil wars are more than twice as likely to conclude with peace treaties—agreements that are significantly more comprehensive than ceasefires or truces—since 1945 compared to the pre-UN era. The difference is even starker when we compare the post–Cold War era to what came before. From 1989 to 2007, more than half of civil wars ended with peace treaties; from 1816 to 1989, not quite 11 percent of civil wars were concluded by peace treaties. While a number of scholars have noted this trend,[2] it has not been examined fully. International legal scholar Christine Bell is an exception: Bell notes the rising use of peace treaties in civil wars, and argues that these treaties constitute a new type of agreement in international law—a "lex pacificatoria" whose purpose tends as much to domestic regime change as it does to conflict resolution.[3]

Understanding when peace treaties are reached, what they contain, and whether they work is increasingly important as they have become a more common tool in the resolution of civil war. Prior research on civil war termination has focused on the causes and consequences of intervention, including peacekeeping and mediation, and on the relationship between the content of peace agreements and the durability of peace.[4] A smaller set of scholars has taken on the question of whether negotiated settlements to conclude civil wars are more effective at inducing peace compared to other options.[5]

Scholarship on why and when peace treaties conclude interstate war is more available.[6] Among those scholars who have examined peace treaties in interstate war as a dependent variable, Kyle Beardsley finds that mediation increases the likelihood of formal agreements—including treaties, armistices, and ceasefires—in the short term.[7] While drawing on Beardsley's research on mediation, I add to it by exploring the time trend in both mediation and peace agreements, focusing explicitly on one type of peace agreement (peace treaties), and also focusing on the civil war context by applying both quantitative and qualitative methods.

As others have noted, the existence of a peace treaty might be less consequential for peace than external support in the form of intervention, or the content of the treaty. In the civil war context, Isak Svensson has examined the relationship between various types of mediation and the conclusion of a peace agreement, but has not compared mediation to other possible pathways to war termination.[8] Page Fortna finds a positive effect of peacekeeping on the duration of peace after civil war.[9] Michaela Mattes and Burcu Savun argue that peace agreements after civil war that include information-providing and commitment-ensuring provisions are especially likely to be effective.[10] Caroline Hartzell and Matthew Hoddie examine the relationship between power-sharing provisions and the duration of peace.[11] Aila Matanock points to the importance of provisions that allow for rebel group participation in post-war elections for a durable peace;[12] similarly, Madhav Joshi, Eric Melander, and Jason Quinn argue that the sequencing of peace agreement provisions around elections is crucial to preventing the recurrence of violence.[13] Monica Toft focuses on security-sector reform, arguing that this is the essential explanation for the duration of peace after civil war.[14] Skepticism about the efficacy of peace treaties in civil war notwithstanding, the reasons for their increasing use demand attention. The remainder of this chapter therefore takes a broader view, examining why peace treaties have been on the rise after civil wars.

What is a Peace Treaty in the Civil War Context?

I use essentially the same definition for peace treaties in interstate wars and civil wars: a peace treaty is a written document that describes a contract between belligerents to cease hostilities and resolve issues under dispute. It must be signed by parties to a conflict.[15] As with interstate wars, I do not count ceasefires, armistices, or truces as peace treaties because these are meant to produce a temporary cessation of hostilities and not necessarily to resolve issues under dispute. Nor do I include UN Security Council resolutions, even though one could make a stronger argument for inclusion in the civil war context than in that of interstate war, treating them as equivalent to peace treaties.[16] Excluding UNSC resolutions biases the data against my argument regarding both the rising use of peace treaties in civil war and the international community's role in this trend.

My definition is very similar to that used by the well-known Uppsala Conflict Data Program's Conflict Termination Dataset: "A *peace agreement* is defined as an agreement concerned with the resolution of an incompatibility signed and/or publicly accepted by all, or the main, actors in a conflict."[17] Similarly, the Peace Accords Matrix project identifies comprehensive peace agreements as having two main features: "(a) the major parties to the conflict were involved in the negotiations that produced the agreement; and (b) the substantive issues underlying the dispute were included in the negotiations."[18]

Recent civil wars offer numerous examples of peace treaties. The 1995 Dayton Accords that helped end the war in Bosnia resolved issues under dispute for multiple dyads involved in the conflict. With secessionist demands from Bosnian Serbs, Bosnian Croats, and Bosniaks, the war was a particularly complicated one, leading to significant international intervention. This intervention played a critical role in the establishment of several ceasefires that preceded the design and adoption of the peace treaty. The accord divided Bosnian territory among Serbs, Croats, and Bosniaks; established conditions under which military forces would be withdrawn; noted the inclusion of the Republika Srpska and the Federation of Bosnia and Herzegovina as the country's two constituent units; and set out the distribution of members of parliament along ethnic lines.

The Dayton Accords serve as a baseline example of a modern peace treaty concluding a civil war.[19]

Similarly, the Lancaster House Accords that concluded the Rhodesia War of 1972–79 resolved major differences between Ian Smith's white-majority government and the Patriotic Front it was fighting. The Lancaster House Agreement was a comprehensive political settlement that resolved the issues of majority rule, black/white seat apportionment in the legislature, constitutional issues, the ceasefire, and elections to be held in the immediate future.[20]

By contrast, the Moro secessionists that began fighting the Philippines in 1972 have signed numerous agreements with the Philippine government, but none until recently qualified as a peace treaty. The 1977 Tripoli Agreement concluded between the Moro National Liberation Front (MNLF) and the Philippine government detailed an autonomy agreement, but failed to establish procedures for implementation, leading to its immediate collapse. A 1996 agreement was similarly comprehensive on paper, but did not include the main rebel group at the time—the Moro Independence Liberation Front (MILF)—thus failing to meet the criterion of being signed by the parties to the conflict.[21]

Similarly, even though a 1987 agreement between the Sri Lankan government and the Liberation Tigers of Tamil Eelam (LTTE) contained some political content beyond a commitment to a truce—mentioning that the North and East provinces should be allowed to hold a referendum on their integration as one political unit—it was not a comprehensive political settlement. Indeed, LTTE leader Velupillai Prabhakaran stated that he did not believe this part of the agreement was sustainable, and the agreement was never written down or signed. Thus, it was not a formal peace treaty.[22] It was not the failure of these agreements to prevent future conflict that prevents them from being peace treaties; if only successful peace treaties were coded as such, we would not be able to make believable claims about the effects of peace treaties on the duration of peace. Rather, these agreements do not qualify as peace treaties because they fail to meet the standards of comprehensive settlement of issues under dispute (either via content or participation), or of being written, formal documents.

Patterns of Peace Treaty Use in Civil Wars

Peace treaty use has increased in the UN era, and particularly in the post–Cold War era. Before 1950, the rate of peace treaty use in civil wars fluctuated, but never exceeded 25 percent; the mean is closer to 10 percent. After 1950, however, that rate steadily inclines. Figure 8.1, based on data from C-WIT, graphs this trend. This incline is especially notable after the end of the Cold War: fourteen of thirty-seven civil wars that ended in the 1990s and eight of twenty-four civil wars that ended in the 2000s were accompanied by peace treaties.

Other datasets reveal a similar story. Figure 8.2 is based on UCDP data on internal armed conflicts, which have a much lower battle-death threshold for inclusion (twenty-five) than the Correlates of War list of civil wars that forms the basis for C-WIT (1000 deaths). UCDP covers 1946 to 2008. Figure 8.2 shows that the rate of peace treaty usage for intrastate armed conflicts has risen over the past sixty years, particularly since the end of the Cold War. Toft also finds that the percent of civil wars ended via negotiated settlements since 1940 has risen from zero in the 1940s to 40 percent in the 1990s.[23]

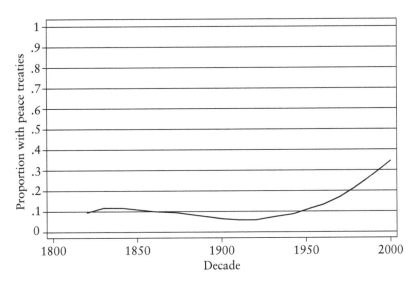

Figure 8.1 Proportion of civil wars ended with peace treaties

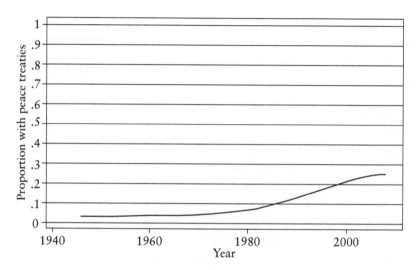

Figure 8.2 Proportion of internal armed conflicts ended with peace treaties. From UCDP conflict termination data.

Similarly, of 151 post-1945 civil wars identified by Michael Doyle and Nicholas Sambanis,[24] approximately one-third were accompanied by peace treaties. Doyle and Sambanis identify two 1950s peace treaties, one in the 1960s, six in the 1970s, four in the 1980s, and thirty in the 1990s. Their data exhibit a general upward trend over the entire period, with a dramatic increase in peace treaties concluding civil wars in the 1990s. While the number of civil wars begun in the 1990s is also much higher than in previous decades (and the number of wars ended in a given decade roughly tracks the number of wars begun in the decade), there is a fifteen-fold increase in the use of civil war peace treaties from 1950 to 2000, but only a three-fold increase in the outbreak of civil war in the 1990s as compared to the 1950s.

This change raises several questions: Why would governments be willing to lend legitimacy to rebel groups by concluding peace treaties with them? Why would this change occur beginning in the mid-twentieth century? To what extent is the increased use of peace treaties in civil wars related to the decreased use of peace treaties in interstate war?

Theoretical Expectations

The use of peace treaties has increased in civil wars because the international community has expressed a clear preference in favor of these treaties. There are both normative and strategic reasons why the international community prefers peace treaties in the UN era. A normative interpretation of this preference refers to key clauses of the UN Charter.[25] Article 1(1) of the UN Charter lists as the first of four purposes of the UN: "To maintain international peace and security, and to that end: to take effective collective measures for the prevention and removal of threats to the peace, and for the suppression of acts of aggression or other breaches of the peace, and to bring about by peaceful means, and in conformity with the principles of justice and international, adjustment or settlement of international disputes or situations might lead to a breach of the peace."

Chapter 6 of the charter covers the "Pacific Settlement of Disputes." It urges contentious or warring parties to resolve differences via mechanisms such as mediation, and also suggests that the Security Council might intervene for the purpose of conflict resolution. The nature of dispute resolution is discussed further in Chapter 7 (Articles 39–51). Those actors committed to the principles of the UN Charter will tend to view intervention for the purpose of conflict prevention and resolution as a public good.[26] Peace treaties punctuate these interventions, clearly establishing agreements made and conditions to be kept.

A strategic interpretation of the UN-era preference for peace treaties also begins with the UN Charter, but rests both on the principles embedded in the charter and on organizational politics. One way for the UN to create and establish its own relevance in global politics is to offer its services as a mediator and, at times, to authorize military interventions—that is, peacekeeping operations. Today, the office of the UN's Department of Field Support in New York, which comprises the administrative arm of the Department of Peacekeeping Operations, employs over 400 people and has a budget of $67 million.[27] In 2006, the UN's Department of Political Affairs created a Mediation Support Unit that includes a team of mediation experts available to deploy to conflicts around the world.[28] As Bell notes, the creation of such an office is likely to expand the corps of international mediators who will push for mediation for organizational as well as principled reasons.[29] Since 2006, the training and availability of mediators has increased via courses offered by the Swiss Ministry of Foreign Affairs, the Centre for Humanitarian Dialogue's annual Oslo Forum, and the United Nations Institute for Training and Research.[30] Beardsley points out that third party mediators typically prefer that negotiations end with a peace treaty, in part because "it is easier to take credit for being a promoter of peace if there is a resulting document with the third party listed as the peace broker."[31] Note that the possibility that key actors in the international community might act strategically in promoting interventions that could end in peace treaties because they seek to advance their organizational interests is not incompatible with a sincere belief in the principles stated in the UN Charter. Either way, the international community's interest is peace, defined at a minimum as the absence of conflict; and today such peace tends to be codified in peace treaties.

Even if the international community prefers civil wars to end with peace treaties, this preference on its own is insufficient to explain current practice. The argument that the international community prefers peace agreements over alternative forms of war termination is potentially problematic, in that this preference applies equally to interstate and civil wars. Yet the rate of peace treaty use in interstate wars has been in decline, while it appears to be on the rise in civil wars. Why?

To answer this question, we must begin by examining the incentives of the different parties to civil war separately. Consider first the preferences of a government. I argued in chapter 5 that the decline in peace treaties in interstate war is due to the rise in codified laws of war. As the laws of war have proliferated over time, states—the belligerents engaged in interstate war—try to avoid taking steps that would unequivocally oblige them to comply with international humanitarian law. Like peace treaties, international humanitarian law is preferred and supported by the international community. States that fight interstate wars typically possess more legitimacy than the governments and rebel groups fighting civil wars. The governments fighting civil wars are frequently politically and military weaker than those fighting interstate wars—because, for example, they tend to be poor or to have questionable human rights records. All else equal, then, governments that are the targets of rebellion might find themselves at a reputational disadvantage and therefore be more inclined to concede to the wishes of the international community than states fighting interstate wars. Indonesia's behavior during ceasefire negotiations over East Timor's independence struggle in the early 1980s exemplifies this dynamic. Indonesia agreed to negotiate in the midst of internal political turmoil, in part to make possible future negotiations with Australia over resource-sharing more credible.[32] States fighting interstate wars are better positioned to sidestep the preferences of the international community than are the parties to civil war. As Beardsley notes, governments also might accept mediation strategically as a stalling tactic during a civil war.[33]

The international humanitarian legal regime itself is much weaker in the civil war context than in the interstate war context. While the 1977 Additional Protocols to the 1949 Geneva Conventions theoretically extend the conventions to the realm of civil war, this extension only applies to recognized belligerents. But the bar for recognizing "belligerency" that would trigger the laws of war has been strategically set to be both vague and high. It is therefore unlikely that governments fighting civil wars perceive evading the obligations entailed under the laws of war as much of a challenge, or necessity, especially when compared to states fighting interstate wars. The tension between complying with the laws of war and concluding a peace treaty is therefore much less in the civil war context.

Now consider the preferences of the rebel groups fighting civil wars. For most rebel groups, a seat at the peace talks table is a desirable goal.[34] It lends legitimacy to these groups' claims to governance.[35] The GAM in Aceh, for example, entered into talks with the Indonesian government explicitly for the purposes of gaining recognition and legitimacy.[36] According to one scholar, "GAM saw the peace process as central to its strategy of internationalization and viewed internationalization as the only way to achieve independence."[37] There are two possible exceptions to this broad claim. First, there are some groups that might prefer continued fighting over peace. Rebels funded by lootable resources that can be traded on black or gray markets might rather continue to profit from war economies than give up those profits.[38] Second, as the likelihood of being prosecuted for any war crimes—the liability costs discussed in chapter 2—increase over time, particularly alongside the growth of transitional justice institutions such as the International Criminal Court, rebels guilty of having committed war crimes may be reluctant to approach a peace table where they might be subject to prosecution.[39] Nonetheless, and even if rebels would be suspicious of government promises made in a peace treaty, we should generally expect rebels to be willing to sit down for negotiations with their opponents.

Now consider jointly the preferences of governments and rebel groups fighting civil wars. Rebel groups will typically be eager to conclude peace treaties. Governments fighting civil wars might be less concerned with international humanitarian legal issues than states fighting interstate wars, but they may still be somewhat reluctant to join peace talks. Whereas rebels seek the legitimacy accorded by a seat at the table, governments strive to deny that legitimacy to rebels. This was certainly a concern for the Indonesian government in negotiating with the GAM, so much so that they explicitly avoided the label of "cease fire" in the early 2000s, which implied recognition of the GAM as a legitimate belligerent; instead, they adopted the term "Humanitarian Pause."[40] As Molly Melin and Isak Svensson suggest, the reluctance to accord legitimacy to rebels by agreeing to negotiate with them is sometimes justified; the Sri Lankan government that negotiated with the LTTE in 2003 fell quickly after the negotiations.[41] And insofar as rebels are less inclined to violate the laws of war than governments—perhaps especially in secessionist civil wars, as discussed in chapter 7—it would be much easier for governments to veto a peace treaty based on their past international humanitarian law noncompliance than it would be for rebels to push for a peace treaty given their own compliance and their desire to hold the government accountable. So even though the international community and rebel groups might prefer a peace treaty, the government will often resist. The "legitimacy gap" between governments and rebels thus helps account for the relatively modest rise in peace treaty use in civil wars, compared to its dramatic decline in interstate wars.

To get belligerents to the peace table, the international community typically must persuade governments and sometimes must persuade rebels. The carrots used by the international community to attract belligerents to the peace table include foreign and military aid as well as improved legitimacy and recognition.[42] The sticks include actual or threatened military intervention, as outlined in Chapters 6 and 7 of the UN Charter.

The international community's preference for negotiated settlements over letting belligerents fight to the end has been clearly stated on several occasions. The UN has publicly offered to mediate a number of recent conflicts, including in Ukraine,[43] Thailand,[44] and Syria.[45] Calls for "peaceful resolution of dispute" are commonly issued, as in Libya,[46] Burundi,[47] and even countries where the UN has already deployed peacekeepers, such as the Democratic Republic of Congo (DRC).[48] Regular calls for negotiated settlement have been made in the cases of the Western Sahara,[49] Syria,[50] and Yemen.[51] Returning to the Acehnese case, the end of the Cold War provided a potential opening when the international community's general interest in conflict resolution was on the upswing.[52]

This clear international preference in favor of peace treaties notwithstanding, the path to such treaties is neither quick nor direct. Two mechanisms are typically used by the international community to aid conflict resolution and secure a peace treaty. The first and most important mechanism is mediation, whereby a third party brings belligerents to the negotiating table. While a mediator's initial goal is often to achieve a ceasefire, mediation creates a precedent for non-violent conflict resolution, and for the negotiation of a formal and full peace treaty. The second mechanism is military intervention, typically in the form of peacekeeping operations. Such operations separate the two (or more) sides, and may effectively induce a draw or stalemate. If neither side believes it can win definitively on the battlefield, the peace table may become more attractive. But because peacekeeping follows peace treaties at least as often as it precedes them, my focus in this chapter is on mediation as the international community's preferred route to a peace treaty.

My expectation, therefore, is that mediation will be highly correlated with peace treaties in civil wars. More specifically, multilateral mediation ought to lead to peace treaties, as it signals the international community's commitment to resolve a particular conflict.

When Do Civil Wars End with Peace Treaties?

My argument suggests that civil wars with mediation by the international community are most likely to end with peace treaties because the international community tends to prefer negotiated to military conflict resolutions. While there have been instances of mediation since the early nineteenth century, it is much more frequently used today than in the past. Thus this preference can also explain the rise in peace treaties in the UN era, which marks the beginning of the modern international community.

Before delving into the empirical analysis, it is important to address two issues that are both theoretical and methodological. First, it could be that, while there is a statistically significant correlation between mediation on the one hand and peace treaties on the other, this correlation is endogenous. In other words, perhaps the peace treaty enables mediation in some way, rather than the other way around. This is certainly the case with peacekeeping, as peacekeepers are often deployed after peace treaties are signed.[53] One means of addressing this potential endogeneity problem is by paying attention to sequence. In none of the cases analyzed below does a peace treaty precede mediation. Note that this does not preclude the possibility that other types of agreements, such as ceasefires, are concluded prior to mediation.

Second, there could be a selection effect at work. Perhaps there is some independent factor about the cases that experience mediation that makes them also more likely to conclude with peace treaties. The likeliest candidate for such a factor is the relative tractability of the conflict. If it were the case, for example, that mediators selected the easiest cases to intervene in, then it would be difficult to argue for an independent effect of mediation. Previous research by Beardsley, however, has shown effectively that mediators tend to be sent to the most challenging cases.[54] What is more, typical government reluctance to negotiate with rebels should mean that the intervention of the international community (through, for example, mediators) is only accepted in very hard cases when all other options—including military options—have been exhausted.[55] And, as Kenneth Schultz argues, even if there is a selection effect that makes mediation more likely in some cases than others, this may attest to the effectiveness of mediation—it is selected *because* it works—thus underlining the general point made here.[56] A related selection effect may pertain to the type of mediation. Secessionist movements may be particularly eager to engage with international mediators, given their heightened value for international recognition; in response, governments might be unwilling to accept multilateral mediators such as those from the UN in secessionist conflicts. This was certainly the case in Aceh, where the Indonesian government had three requirements for a mediator: "No foreign state; no UN body; and no military institution."[57] The possibility of a selection effect in this type of case is folded into the theory in that I expect multilateral mediation to be more likely to produce a peace treaty than unilateral mediation.

As with previous chapters, I employ both qualitative and quantitative analysis to explore the conditions under which peace treaties are concluded in civil war. I focus on the role of the international community, via mediation, as a key predictor of peace treaties. I present the quantitative analysis first, followed by a final discussion of the three case studies discussed in the two previous civil war chapters.

Quantitative Analysis

The universe of cases for this analysis is all civil war dyads as identified by C-WIT, from 1816 to 2007—the same as for the analysis in chapter 7. One difference between the analysis below and the regressions presented in chapter 7 is that there is very little missing data on the variables of interest for this chapter. Thus, I did not need to resort to standardized coding as in chapter 7; no such adjustments have been made to the data analyzed below.

Description of Variables   I begin by describing key independent variables, with a focus on those not included in the earlier analyses of declarations of independence or civilian targeting in civil war. As with the analyses in chapters 6 and 7, variables are drawn from the C-WIT dataset unless otherwise noted.

Mediation. C-WIT defines mediation as the noncoercive involvement of a third party, where the third party communicates with the warring parties, and they with the mediator, about the issues that are at stake in the dispute, and where one of the third party's stated objectives in this communication is to help resolve the dispute. This excludes a third party advising one side only, or appeals by the parties to a third party, humanitarian intervention, or "talks about talks." It can include the provision of a neutral space to host peace talks.

The mediation variable is coded categorically for the purposes of the regression analysis described below. This variable takes a value of 0 when the case did not receive mediation. It takes a value of 1 when the case received mediation by a single state party. For example, in a 1989 war between Papua New Guinea and islanders from Bougainville, New Zealand, the Solomon Islands, and Australia attempted mediation separately and at different times (therefore *mediation* = 1 for all these observations).[58] The variable takes a value of 2 when multilateral mediation occurs—that is, when several countries band together to mediate, or when an IGO or INGO mediates. I take the participation of two or more countries working together, or INGOs or IGOs, to be representative of the international community. For example, the western allies (France,

Russia, and the United Kingdom) mediated the 1829 Treaty of Andrianople that ended the Russo-Turkish War and the Greek War of Independence. More recently, the Henri Dunant Center, an NGO based in Geneva, helped negotiate a 2000 ceasefire in Aceh; the Finnish-based NGO Crisis Management Initiative also mediated in Aceh five years later. Less successfully, the United Nations has designated at least three high-level special representatives or envoys for Syria since the start of the Syrian civil war in 2011.[59] Consistent with the consensus in the literature on the rising use of mediation over time,[60] both mediation and multilateral mediation are significantly and positively correlated with how recently a war occurred.

War Outcomes. C-WIT codes for the general military outcome of a war. This variable can take on one of five values: 0=tie or draw; 1=slight victory for one side, where the fighting was fairly even but one side had a bit of an edge; 2= clear victory for one side; 3=extreme victory for one side; and 7=military victory by a third party.[61] *Draw* is based on the first category of military outcome (0=tie or draw) and is collapsed to a binary variable. *Rebel victory* is a binary variable that is coded as 1 if the military outcome is 1, 2, or 3 and the rebels were the victorious side.[62] Government victory is the reference category, and is similarly coded as a binary variable that takes a value of 1 if the military outcome is 1, 2, or 3 and the government was the victorious side.[63]

Military outcomes and peace treaties may be linked in a few ways. In the civil war context, government victory in particular often translates to the elimination of the other side as a means to avoid the recurrence of conflict. In these cases, we are unlikely to observe a peace treaty. While the majority of civil wars result in military—usually government[64]—victory, this percentage has been changing over time.[65] Page Fortna and Monica Toft have each noted that the percentage of civil wars ending in draws has been on the rise.[66] When faced with a stalemate, governments may grudgingly accept peace negotiations—and a subsequent treaty—rather than the prospect of continued years of fighting. As William Zartman has argued, mutually hurting stalemates may make conflicts "ripe" for conflict resolution.[67]

Regression Analysis and Discussion   As with declarations of independence and rebel civilian targeting, I use logistic regression to analyze the conclusion of peace treaties, given the binary nature of the dependent variable. Table 8.1 reports results on the relationship between the use of mediation and the existence of peace treaties.

TABLE 8.1 Logistic regressions on peace treaties in civil war 1816–2007

	(1)	(2)	(3)	(4)	(5)	(6)	(7)	(8)
(Type of) mediation	1.32	1.34	1.27	1.29	1.32	1.26	1.47	1.32
	(.20)	(.21)	(.22)	(.23)	(.28)	(.32)	(.32)	(.26)
	$p = .00$	$p = .00$	$p = .00$	$p = .00$	$p = .00$	$p = .00$	$p = .00$	$p = .00$
Contraband		.82	.89	.85	1.55	–.20	.09	.79
		(.45)	(.45)	(.46)	(.54)	(.77)	(.62)	(.51)
		$p = .07$	$p = .05$	$p = .06$	$p = .00$	$p = .80$	$p = .89$	$p = .13$
Rebel victory			.22	.27	.85	.80	.30	.55
			(.45)	(.45)	(.54)	(.60)	(.61)	(.51)
			$p = .63$	$p = .56$	$p = .11$	$p = .18$	$p = .63$	$p = .28$
Draw			.72	.70	.39	–.29	–.42	.62
			(.60)	(.60)	(.78)	(.95)	(.87)	(.71)
			$p = .23$	$p = .25$	$p = .61$	$p = .76$	$p = .64$	$p = .38$
Secessionist				–.02	–.26	–.91	–.03	–.76
				(.43)	(.54)	(.72)	(.60)	(.53)
				$p = .96$	$p = .63$	$p = .21$	$p = .96$	$p = .15$
Polity score					–.03			
					(.04)			
					$p = .52$			
Force ratio (deployed)						.03		
						(.11)		
						$p = .76$		
Force ratio (total)							.13	
							(.32)	
							$p = .68$	
Rebel factions								–.11
								(.14)
								$p = .44$
Government factions								.00
								(.20)
								$p = .99$
Rebel civilian targeting								–.25
								(.55)
								$p = .64$
Government civilian targeting								.78
								(.58)
								$p = .18$
Constant	–2.61	–2.88	–3.00	–3.00	–3.37	–2.86	–2.85	–2.99
	(.27)	(.32)	(.36)	(.38)	(.50)	(.52)	(.53)	(.54)
	$p = .00$	$p = .00$	$p = .00$	$p = .00$	$p = .00$	$p = .00$	$p = .00$	$p = .00$
N	270	251	251	250	192	140	129	208
R^2	0.20	0.23	0.24	0.24	0.27	0.21	0.25	.26
LR Chi-squared	47.90	51.27	52.66	53.50	43.84	23.73	31.04	47.34
Prob > chi2	0.0000	0.0000	0.0000	0.0000	0.0000	0.0006	0.0000	0.0000
Log likelihood	–96.08	–84.46	–83.76	–83.17	–59.59	–43.73	–46.46	–68.97
% correctly predicted	84.44	84.46	84.46	84.40	87.50	86.43	86.05	84.13

Note: Results are based on summary dyads. Standard errors in parentheses.

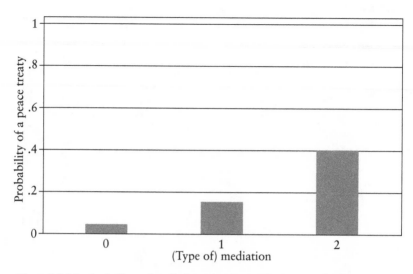

Figure 8.3 Marginal effects of mediation on peace treaties. 0=no mediation, 1=single party mediation, 2=multilateral mediation.

The empirical results strongly support a positive role for mediators as precursors to peace treaties in civil war. Civil wars with mediation are more than six times more likely to end in peace treaties than unmediated civil wars. Unpacking the mediation variable is even more telling. Multilateral mediations are more than twice as likely to end in peace treaties compared to unilateral mediations (see figure 8.3). What is more, the change in baseline probabilities—and not just the percentage change when changing the type/presence of mediation—is significant, moving from a 5 percent chance of a peace treaty with no mediation to 15 percent with unilateral mediation to 40 percent with multilateral mediation.

By contrast, other variables frequently mentioned in the literature as important alternative predictors of peace treaties do not generate statistically significant coefficients in models where mediation is included. Although the coefficient on contraband financing—which it is often argued prolongs civil war and therefore thwarts the possibility of a peace agreement—is statistically significant in some models, the sign on the coefficient is positive, suggesting that civil wars where rebels are financed via contraband may be more, not less, likely to end in peace treaties. The state's polity score, the balance of forces between the rebels and government, and the degree to which the government and rebels are factionalized do not appear to be related to the conclusion of a peace treaty, contrary to previous research.[68] The relationship between rebel victory and draws on the one hand and the conclusion of peace agreements in civil wars on the other is as unclear here as in prior scholarship;[69] on balance, there may be a weakly positive relationship between rebel victory and the conclusion of a peace treaty in civil war, but the coefficient on draws neither takes a consistent sign nor is statistically significant. Secessionism generates a consistently negative coefficient, suggesting that secessionist civil wars may be slightly less likely to conclude with peace treaties compared to nonsecessionist civil wars, but this relationship is not statistically significant.

The strongest positive result from table 8.1 is that civil wars that experience mediation are significantly more likely to end with peace treaties than civil wars without mediation. This finding raises the methodological question of which wars are the most likely to experience mediation. It is not the case that the peace treaty caused mediation in some way: in every instance of mediation in C-WIT, the mediation preceded any peace treaty.

It could, however, be a case of spuriousness insofar as there are features of certain civil wars that lend themselves to mediation *and* to peace treaties. While there is a robust literature on where peacekeepers go,[70] the literature on where mediators go is less developed. In an important foray into this topic, Bernd Beber has shown that even when mediator deployment is controlled for, the effect of mediation on civil war settlement remains positive and significant.[71] Kyle Beardsley similarly finds that mediators tend to be deployed to extremely difficult interstate conflicts, and that mediated conflicts are twice as likely to end in formal agreements as unmediated conflicts, even when controlling for the deployment of mediators.[72]

Qualitative Analysis

The quantitative analysis above demonstrates a clear correlation between the involvement of mediators and the conclusion of a peace treaty. The case studies presented below delve into the mechanism of influence of external actors more deeply, and also help clarify the role of other factors—such as the military outcome of a war—in the conclusion of peace treaties. I use the same cases that were used in chapters 6 and 7, in discussions of declarations of independence and civilian targeting by rebel groups in civil war.

Only one of the three cases discussed below—the civil war between North and South in Sudan—was accompanied by a peace treaty. Rebels were victorious in both the Sudanese and Texan cases, but the so-called Treaty of Velasco intended to end the Texan independence war was, in fact, not a treaty. Among these three cases, international mediation was only present in the South Sudan case. But the conclusion of a peace treaty in that case did not lead to peace: South Sudan and Sudan continue to have serious disagreements, and the treaty that ended this war enabled the independence of South Sudan, which is now mired in its own civil war.

Texas My prediction with respect to the formal conclusion of Texas's war of independence from Mexico is that, in the absence of mediation, a peace treaty would not have been concluded. This prediction is potentially belied by the Treaty of Velasco. Thus, this case represents a possible exception to my argument, and affords the opportunity to analyze off-the-equilibrium path behavior. As I describe below, however, the Treaty of Velasco does not, in the end, qualify as a formal peace treaty because it was concluded under considerable duress and never ratified by Mexico.

Two versions of the Treaty of Velasco of 1836, meant to end the Texas war of independence from Mexico, were signed—one public, one secret. Neither was ratified by Mexico. After the Mexican general Santa Anna had been taken prisoner at San Jacinto, the Texan leadership debated his fate. While many of the soldiers who had fought in the war argued for a public trial and execution, the Texas president David Burnet argued that "Santa Anna dead is no more than Tom, Dick or Harry dead, but, living, he may avail Texas much."[73]

The public version of the agreement led to a cessation of hostilities between the two armies, which were to retreat to their respective territories and exchange prisoners of war. The secret version included Santa Anna's promises to facilitate Mexico's recognition of Texas as an independent state, if Santa Anna were allowed to return home safely.[74]

The Treaty of Velasco was negotiated without international mediation.[75] But the history of the document undermines any argument for labeling it as a formality of war. Mexico never ratified the agreement.

Additionally, the Mexican government, arguing that Santa Anna lacked the power to negotiate, decided to renew its efforts to reconquer Texas.[76] One could make the case that the mob of Texans who took Santa Anna prisoner aboard a ship en route to Vera Cruz (where Santa Anna was to be released back to Mexican forces) violated the terms of the agreement. But a more convincing argument speaks to the point that central governments are often the unwilling parties to civil war peace treaties. Santa Anna negotiated under duress, and so it is not surprising that he went back on his word and his signature. Indeed, when Santa Anna was reelected president of Mexico in 1838, rather than recognizing Texas, he launched a new although brief invasion. Four years later, a second invasion was followed by a signed armistice that, like the Treaty of Velasco, was never ratified, "for it stated that Texas was part of Mexico."[77]

The Treaty of Velasco was also unpopular in Texas. To a certain extent, this opposition reflected dissatisfaction over infighting within the government rather than over the terms of the treaty.[78] It is interesting to consider the outcome had an international mediator been present at the negotiations. The likelihood is that a mediator would not have approved of negotiating with a prisoner, would have forced the Texans to make concessions, and would have sought domestic support on both sides before suggesting that an agreement be committed to paper. It may very well be that such efforts would not have been successful and a treaty could not have been concluded. Texans would probably have been no worse off, as the agreement, such as it was, was effectively dissolved fairly quickly. Conflict between Texas and Mexico recurred intermittently until after the Mexican-American War ten years later, which was concluded with the Treaty of Guadalupe Hidalgo in 1848. In that treaty, Mexico recognized it had lost Texas, which, by this time, was one of twenty-nine United States.

South Moluccas   The lack of international mediation in the South Moluccan case suggests the absence of a peace treaty. This case, however, is perhaps more helpful in understanding the role that government military victory can play in stymying a peace treaty. Indeed, swift government military victory and mediation may be related, as one can preclude the other.

The South Moluccans failed in their bid for independence. Their forces were routed by those of the government, and no peace terms were offered. Here, the reasons for the lack of a peace treaty may have had more to do with the government than with the South Moluccans. The rebels made multiple efforts, consistent with the outreach discussed in chapter 7, to arrange for UN mediation. International humanitarian lawyer Karen Parker notes seven such appeals from July through September 1950.[79] The United Nations Commission for Indonesia agreed to mediate, offering its "good offices" on several occasions.[80] In each instance, they were turned down by the Jakarta government. Internal notes from the UN Commission on Indonesia (UNCI) indicate concern about being prevented—by the Indonesian government—from entering Ambon and from being allowed to provide mediation services.[81] The stated objection from the Indonesian government was that the direct involvement of the UNCI would lead the Amboinese to believe that their cause had risen to "an international level."[82] The government's response illustrates two dynamics. First, the high prospects for victory made a treaty appear unnecessary: the government expected it could simply impose its will on the rebels. Second, the Indonesian government was concerned about according legitimacy to the rebels by negotiating with them.

By the time the South Moluccans had found a champion in the United States, which had agreed to raise the matter at the Security Council, the die was cast. The central government was canny regarding timing, and knew it must defeat the South Moluccans before their claims could be made on the UN stage. In the words of one historian of the conflict, "The international interest in the South Moluccan conflict, however slight it might be, was an incentive for the RI [Republic of Indonesia] to stamp out the RMS [Republik Maluku Selatan] as soon as possible."[83]

For the government, a peace treaty with the South Moluccans that would, presumably, amend Indonesia's latest constitution to offer them greater autonomy would set a dangerous precedent. Indonesia had been beset with civil war upon independence, including secessionist conflicts in Aceh and West Papua, along with the South Moluccas. The Acehnese had already been granted greater autonomy than other provinces within Indonesia: making the same concessions for the West Papuans, the South Moluccans, and the Sulawesi would weaken the government's tenuous grasp throughout the archipelago, and might encourage additional challenges.

South Sudan   The 2005 Comprehensive Peace Agreement (CPA) was the last in a string of decades-long attempts to end the war between North and South in Sudan. My main hypothesis regarding the conclusion of peace treaties in civil war is that international mediation will increase the likelihood of a peace treaty. Of the three cases discussed in this section, this one affords the most opportunity to observe the behavior of mediators. My expectation is that mediators would not only try to bring the parties to agreement, but also attempt to formalize any such agreement. Thus, we ought to observe a positive correlation between the number of mediation attempts and the number of possible formal peace treaties.

Over the last several decades in Sudan, there has been a multitude of attempts at mediation; mediators included Jimmy Carter, Olusegun Obasanjo, the OAU, Egypt, Libya and, most successfully, the Intergovernmental Authority on Development (IGAD), an African international governmental organization, part of whose mission is to promote and maintain peace on the continent. In this case, therefore, the question is not so much whether mediation helped the belligerents conclude a peace treaty, but rather why and how a peace treaty was concluded in 2005 and not at another time.

One variable that stymied the peace process for years was the highly factionalized nature of the rebels in the South.[84] Consistent with arguments from scholars such as David Cunningham (but contrary to the results of the statistical tests reported above), the multiple splits among the rebels allowed the government to weaken its opponents by signing individual agreements with specific factions at various times. For example, the government of Sudan signed a peace agreement with Riek Machar's South Sudan Independence Movement/Army (SSIM/A) and Kerubino Kwanyin Bol's Sudan People's Liberation Movement and Army, Bahr el Ghazal Group (SPLM/A-BGG), in 1997, but this agreement did not include John Garang and the main faction of the Sudan People's Liberation Movement (SPLM).[85] Even without government interference, the rebels did not agree among themselves on key issues such as whether the movement was truly democratic and, particularly important, who would lead it. But these divisions were at least temporarily overcome by 1999, with a unity agreement between the Garang and Machar factions.

Once the rebels presented a united front, but to a degree even before then, mediation by the international community was welcomed by those fighting in the South.[86] The rebels' warm reception of mediators was driven, at least in part, by the fact that the mediators were viewed as sympathetic. The mediators were appalled by what they viewed as government abuses in and of the South. Even with relatively neutral mediators, such as IGAD, the rebels were more likely to cooperate in negotiations than the government, which was itself so riven with factions that it could not come to an agreement,[87] and left IGAD-led negotiations in 1994 to protest a proposal for self-determination for the South.[88] That the rebels would welcome, even seek, international mediation is not surprising—having a seat at the table lent them legitimacy, and forcing Sudan's government to hear their proposals increased the odds of achieving their political aims.

What is more puzzling is why the government of Sudan finally agreed to a peace treaty in 2005. The government's previous strategy had been to thwart any efforts at peace that did not call for a unified and theocratic Sudan. However, the CPA included provisions for self-determination, a referendum on independence for the South, and strict limitation of Shari'a law to the North.

Khartoum agreed to the CPA because its circumstances had changed. By the early 2000s, Sudan faced a unified rebel movement that had brought the war to a military stalemate, as well as a deteriorating economy.[89] War-weariness across Sudan put domestic pressure on the government to negotiate. The timing of mediation in this case is also consistent with Melin and Svensson's argument that mediators often go to the hardest cases.[90]

According to the International Crisis Group, the timing of the CPA negotiations was driven by "the ruling party's desperate effort to survive."[91] In addition to the fight on the military front, the government was under siege diplomatically. The September 11, 2001, attacks against the United States put Sudan under Western scrutiny. At this point, writes Oynstein Rolandsen, "Engaging in talks became a matter of survival for NCP [National Congress Party] leaders."[92] Additionally, the crisis in Darfur produced tremendous pressure from the international community to come to an agreement with the South, and the window of opportunity to do so appeared to be closing. As one scholar of the country and its conflicts put it, "As the vision of a quick victory in Darfur evaporated, the insurgency became internationalized, heaping opprobrium and reprobation on Khartoum, which made it all the more essential to conclude a settlement with the SPLM/A at Navaisha before the Sudan government lost its remaining credibility with the international community as peacemakers."[93] Even as the Sudanese government's credibility at the peace table was eroding, the international community "conspicuously" refrained from condemning Khartoum during a special UN Security Council session in November 2004.[94] The government of Sudan took the opportunity to sign the memorandum of understanding that became the basis for the CPA concluded the following year.

External involvement was "a necessary ingredient" for the conclusion of a peace treaty between North and South.[95] While the CPA would face multiple implementation challenges between 2005 and the independence referendum in 2011, its conclusion in 2005 was a significant achievement.[96] It did lead to at least a temporary end of armed conflict between North and South. During the interim period from 2005 to 2011, it was the southerners who were the preferred allies of the international community, as the conflict in Darfur raged on. Of course, the great and sad irony of the CPA was that it set the South up for independence, and South Sudan is now in need of a new peace to halt the bloodshed that has marred its first years.

The modern international community has, since the end of World War II and certainly since the end of the Cold War, been more successful at engineering peace treaties to conclude civil wars than interstate wars for at least three reasons. First, the consensus in favor of peace treaties as the preferred mode of conflict resolution emerged in the UN era. The UN era is also when the dominant type of war shifted from interstate to civil. Thus, the international community has had more opportunities to urge peace treaties on belligerents in civil wars than belligerents in interstate wars. Second, the double legitimacy gap—between the governments fighting civil wars versus those fighting interstate wars, and between governments and their rebel opponents—increases the comparative likelihood of the conclusion of peace treaties in civil wars. Third, the tension between two sets of norms—modern international humanitarian law, which creates incentives against signing peace treaties, and the preference for negotiated settlements, which pushes belligerents toward treaties—is resolved differently in the civil war context because the international community tends to have more leverage over parties to civil war than over parties to interstate war.

The international community's preference for peace treaties has been clearly stated on numerous occasions.[97] In practical terms, this preference is expressed via the deployment of mediators. Not only has mediation become increasingly common, it is clearly tied to the conclusion of peace treaties: mediation leads to a sixfold increase in the likelihood of a peace treaty.

Peace treaties are on the rise in civil wars because of the international community's preference for them. But the norm in favor of negotiated settlements, like the norms embodied in international humanitarian law, may produce unintended, even perverse, consequences. Several scholars have noted that peace treaties, in civil war in particular, may not be very effective at creating lasting peace. In this vein, Beardsley finds that while the short-term effects of mediation are positive, the longer-term effects are not. This discrepancy is attributed in part to agreements that are unsustainable and even unreachable in the absence of a constant third-party presence.[98] Mehmet Gurses, Nicolas Rost, and Patrick McLeod show that while involvement in mediation increases the subsequent duration of peace, the existence of mediated *agreements*—for instance, peace treaties subsequent to mediation—significantly decreases the duration of peace.[99] Toft's comparison of different types of civil war termination suggest that negotiated settlements—particularly when they neglect to provide for security-sector reform—are much less likely to effect enduring peace than are military victories, particularly rebel victory. Although the rising use of peace treaties in civil wars has been driven by good intentions, it may mask significant longer-term negative effects. I discuss these and other unintended consequences of the development of the laws of war in the book's conclusion.

EVASION, ENGAGEMENT, AND THE LAWS OF WAR

War, both interstate and civil, has become highly regulated. Today's extensive laws regarding the conduct of war were conceived to govern how interstate wars are fought, but they have also unintentionally affected the manner in which these wars are begun and ended. The current preferences of the international community seek to determine how civil wars commence and conclude, but they also—again, unintentionally—have created incentives for secessionists in particular to shape their conduct in war to comply with international humanitarian law.

The unintended consequences of the proliferation of international humanitarian law, and the regulation of war more broadly, have thus had very different effects in the interstate versus civil war contexts. If states, in their wars with each other, avoid declaring war and concluding peace treaties in an attempt to create ambiguity as to whether IHL applies, we might consider rolling back the laws of war. But any such consideration must be backstopped by a parallel view of civil wars, which are much more common today, and where certain rebel groups are increasingly trying to engage positively with the laws of war.

International norms combine with the legitimacy and strategic needs of belligerents to tie together trends in war formalities and warfighting in interstate and civil war. In interstate wars, the proliferation of codified IHL—a body of law designed and embraced by the international community—has created disincentives for states to admit that they are in a state of war, where their obligation to comply with IHL would be unequivocal. The desire to evade legal liability has led states to stop declaring war and concluding peace treaties in their wars with other states. But in civil wars, an overlapping set of international norms has produced different, sometimes opposite, trends. Secessionists—rebel groups particularly sensitive to the preferences of the international community—have responded eagerly to UN-era international norms instead of stepping back from them, precisely because they seek the legitimacy that only the international community can bestow upon them. They tread very carefully when it comes to declaring independence formally, targeting civilians, and even the decision to use violence at all; they note the preferences of the international community every step of the way. Even governments involved in civil wars, whose legitimacy tends to be low both domestically and internationally, attend to the preferences of the international community, and this is in part why we observe a rise in the use of peace treaties to conclude civil war that contrasts with the decline in their use in interstate war.

How can we assess the value of these various regulations on war? Using the metric of mitigating the human costs of war, I argue that the benefits are mixed, but that the positive effects are by no means guaranteed in the future.

Even though states seek to maintain some ambiguity as to their obligations to comply with IHL by avoiding the formalities of interstate war, it is not clear that the absence of formalities has affected compliance adversely, as shown in chapter 4. More important, interstate war is rarer today than civil war. According to the Uppsala Conflict Data Program, of forty armed conflicts ongoing in 2016, only two (between India and Pakistan and Eritrea and Ethiopia) were purely interstate. The rest were either internal or internationalized internal armed conflicts, and over half of these were being fought over territorial issues, such as secessionism.[1] Thus, any improvement in the conduct of secessionists is helpful given the long-term trends in the nature of armed conflict. On the plus side, the responsiveness of secessionists to international norms about the use of violence is a win for the laws of war. On the minus side, the contrasting use of peace treaties in interstate versus civil wars may have exactly the opposite effect on the durability of peace than we would prefer. Lotta Themnér and Peter Wallensteen argue that "one positive development since 2011 is the increase in the number of peace agreements being signed."[2] Agreements, however, are not necessarily inherently positive, and successful design of agreements to end civil wars is particularly challenging because of the acute commitment problems inherent in these conflicts.

Given these mixed results, the task going forward should be to improve upon successes and remediate failures. I therefore turn next to three key policy takeaways, regarding: the process of making IHL; the tension between how the international community tells secessionists to behave and how the international community responds to secessionist behavior; and the differential rates and effects of peace treaty usage in interstate versus civil wars.

Who's in the Room?

How law is made has long-term effects on how it is received. As shown in chapter 1, the percent of attendees at major IHL conventions who are military personnel has declined markedly over the past two centuries. The growing gap between the "law-makers" and the "law-takers" reflects a misalignment of incentives that has led states to step back from engaging the formalities of war.

The military should be more involved in the process of making IHL. The NGOs and human rights advocates at the vanguard of many IHL movements are often wary of the military, and thus might be reluctant to include them in conversations. But military personnel in general prefer to fight in battlefields with rules, and their preferences often align with those of NGOs in interesting ways. New international humanitarian laws are likely to be most successful when there is genuine practical input from militaries.

Two ongoing efforts at IHL lawmaking provide an opportunity to observe the relationship between the NGO/humanitarian community and the military in real time. Recent efforts have been focused on specific weapons—land mines, cluster munitions, autonomous weapons systems, and cyber weapons—rather than on the principles of warfighting. This shift is worth noting, as weapons-focused lawmaking may be more likely to include the military compared to other types of lawmaking because the military can provide practical input on how particular weapons are or may be used.

Killer Robots

The Campaign to Stop Killer Robots seeks a ban on fully autonomous weapons (also known as lethal autonomous weapons systems, or LAWS). Specifically, the campaign seeks to ban "weapons that can select and engage targets without meaningful human control."[3] A unique feature of this campaign is that it seeks to ban a type of weapon that does not yet exist. A more usual feature is the central role played by NGOs in the campaign. Indeed, according to one key figure in the campaign, only NGOs may officially be members of the campaign.[4] The centrality of NGOs notwithstanding, the campaign has engaged with military personnel from the United States and other countries, particularly Canada. Part of this engagement occurs via the UN's Convention on Certain Conventional Weapons (CCW) process, as CCW hosted a series of meetings on killer robots/LAWS in 2014 and 2015. Working with the military on this issue has been fruitful, in part because many members of the military harbor significant reservations about autonomous weapons systems; they prefer to keep military decision making in human hands.[5] That the military are included in these conversations is promising. But given the definitional issues inherent in legislating a technology that is as yet notional,[6] there may be some risk in not making players from industry as well as from the military more central to this effort.

Cyber Weapons

The legal momentum around the use of cyber weapons in war has been both more and less formal than the Campaign to Stop Killer Robots. While there has been significant debate around what actions taken in cyberspace could constitute an act of war,[7] I focus here on the Tallinn Manual,[8] which is meant to interpret *jus in bello* for the cyber realm. While the Tallinn Manual does address the question of what might constitute an act of cyber war, or armed attack, its focus is on what type of cyber-conduct is permissible under existing international humanitarian law. The charge of the project was *lex lata*—the interpretation of existing law—rather than *lex ferenda*, the creation of new law.

While not law in itself, the Tallinn Manual has been extremely influential because it is the first major attempt to apply IHL to the cyber realm. The working group that was created to write the manual was hosted under the auspices of the NATO Cooperative Cyber Defence Center of Excellence, the group itself consisted of renowned legal scholars from NATO countries, and the manual has been published by a top academic press.[9] The Tallinn Manual is a model code meant to serve as a reference for governments around the world.[10]

The nascent stage of international law with regard to the cyber realm affords an important opportunity to examine the process of making IHL. While, as above, the Tallinn Manual is not law, it is likely to be used as an important source should states ever consider drafting a treaty on IHL and cyber weapons.[11] One of the striking features of the process of drafting the Tallinn Manual has been who was in the room, particularly compared to past IHL efforts. Of the forty members of the International Group of Experts, seven (17.5%) were uniformed military, and several more—including Michael Schmitt, the project director—were retired military. The group also included several NGO representatives. By contrast, there were few to no representatives from ministries of defense. According to Schmitt, states kept the group that drafted the Tallinn Manual at arm's length, despite the need for legal direction on cyber issues: "They desperately wanted an answer, but were equally desperately afraid of the answer they would get."[12] This interpretation suggests an interesting disconnect between efforts distanced from states (even if meant to govern their behavior), such as the Tallinn Manual, and those initiated by states. Insofar as military input into the Tallinn Manual trickles up to any future endeavors to produce a treaty governing the use of cyber weapons in war, the inclusion of the military at this critical first step may mitigate the "lawmaker" versus "law-taker" divide. But it also could be that the politics of treaty making overwhelm the decisions taken in the Tallinn process such that the original input of the military is rolled back. To some extent, this dynamic is already observable in the United Nations Group of Governmental Experts (UNGGE), an intergovernmental group on cyber weapons. The UNGGE has issued a series of brief reports calling for additional study and compliance with existing law, but focusing more on civil society as partners than the military.[13]

While both the Tallinn process and, to a lesser extent, the Campaign to Stop Killer Robots appear to include military personnel more than the efforts described in chapter 1, this difference may be due in part to the fact that both movements are focused on a particular type of weapon or technology. State militaries are already studying and using cyber weapons, and are also very concerned about and interested in autonomous weapons systems. Industry has played a much less central role in both of these efforts, even though industry cooperation will be required for any future regulation. With these new technologies, therefore, we may be observing a new type of divide between "law-makers" and "law-takers."

IHL Lawmaking and Rebel Groups

Even if state military personnel are in the room when major IHL provisions are being discussed and negotiated, non-state military personnel are typically not. For recent efforts, such as those on lethal autonomous weapons systems and cluster munitions, one reason for the absence of rebel groups from these discussions is that they do not have the resources to acquire or use such weapons. Cyber weapons, on the other hand, have been used in civil wars from Georgia to Syria, and are accessible to rebel groups such as the Islamic State. But the more important reason for the exclusion of rebel groups from these discussions has to do with their status. International law is founded on a system of state-to-state interaction. Rebel groups challenge this system by challenging the sovereignty of states. International law is therefore unlikely to be receptive to the inclusion of actors that chip away at its foundation; by recognizing rebel groups, the makers of international law would be undermining their own enterprise. According to its director, the Tallinn project's decision to focus on interstate war was a deliberate one, driven by the fact that there is more analysis, treaty law, and jurisprudence on interstate than civil war.[14] While the Tallinn Manual does discuss non-international armed conflicts, the discussion of international armed conflicts is much more developed.

Negotiations around issues like killer robots, while clearly important, are inherently focused on a few state militaries as targets. If such weapons were ever to be used, they would likely be used by major powers. But most wars today are not wars between states, nor are they wars within the boundaries of major powers. Most wars today are civil wars, fought in the developing world, where weapons like killer robots are extremely unlikely to be deployed, even if they were to be developed.

By focusing so much on issues pertinent primarily to states and state militaries, the framers of international humanitarian law risk marginalizing their project as a whole because of its inherent hostility toward engagement with rebel groups. This is not to condemn this hostility, but to note its important effects. We can therefore consider at least two gaps between the "law-makers" and the "law-takers": between the international lawyers/NGOs who provide the impetus for many of these efforts and the military; and, between the states who are signatories to IHL treaties and the non-state actors they fight. Excluding the military might make militaries less likely to look upon the law favorably; conversely, including rebel groups in some fashion might make them more likely to comply with IHL. One such effort toward inclusion has been made by the NGO Geneva Call, which has created Deeds of Commitment—an instrument parallel to a multilateral treaty—for rebel groups to pledge publicly not to use land mines or child soldiers, or to engage in sexual violence.[15] While it is difficult to judge the efficacy of the Deeds of Commitment, improvements in compliance may be worth the trade-off of according legitimacy to rebel groups.

The Secessionists' Dilemma

Secessionists require the support of the international community if they are to achieve their political aims. This is one reason why secessionists are particularly attentive to the stated preferences of the international community regarding the use of violence, civilian targeting, and declaring independence. A dilemma arises, however, when we consider the efficacy of responsiveness to the desires of the international community. For as it turns out, behaving well does not necessarily end well for secessionists.

For example, in their influential book on the relative efficacy of nonviolent political campaigns, Erica Chenoweth and Maria Stephan find that nonviolence—the international community's preferred mode of political contestation—is generally more effective than violence, except in the case of secessionists.[16] As discussed in chapter 7, secessionists are less likely than nonsecessionist rebels to target civilians, in part to send signals of compliance to the international community. But this compliance does not necessarily pay off. Few secessionists succeed. For example, the GAM in Aceh very much tailored their messaging to the international community, but, in the end, walked away without any international recognition.[17] And we certainly observe plenty of cases of the converse—like the SPLM/A in Sudan—where secessionist rebels engaged in brutal civilian targeting, and yet gained an independent state, while the more restrained secessionists did not.

To a limited extent, this dilemma might not be felt by secessionists, who are unlikely to conduct a global survey of what works and what does not work. But insofar as the international community cares about secessionists' use of violence, targeting of civilians, declarations of independence, and peace treaties, they should not count upon continued ignorance. Secessionism itself diffuses.[18] What is more, secessionists have taken advantage of informal opportunities to meet with each other, and these encounters may generate additional platforms and meetings.[19] Recent events underline this point, with Catalans present at the 2014 Scottish independence referendum; Catalans held their own vote three years later. At some point, secessionists will recognize the contradiction between what the international community prescribes and how it behaves. Indeed, we may have reached that point already. At this writing, Catalans and Iraqi Kurds have both recently held independence referendums and have seen significant pushback from the Spanish and Iraqi central governments as well as from the international community more generally. It remains to be seen how today's secessionists will respond: will they shelve their plans for independence, or will they push harder, frustrated by the lack of support from an international community whose advice they have been trying to heed?

Thus, the secessionists' dilemma is equally a dilemma for the international community. Secessionism challenges the foundational principle of international relations—state sovereignty. Much of the edifice of international law and norms has been built on this principle. And so even when secessionists bear many of the trappings of statehood—when they control territory, have a population, and are capable of engaging in international relations—the international community often withholds international recognition and its attendant benefits. This leaves many de facto states in limbo. And while some have continued to reach out to the international community, broadcasting their compliance with its norms, others, such as Eritrea during its independence war, have turned away from the international community because of its perceived failure to reward good behavior with recognition.

New strategies are needed to engage secessionists. To a certain extent, Palestine has been paving the way by seeking recognition from the UN General Assembly, after its application for membership was vetoed by the United States in the Security Council. In bypassing the Security Council, Palestine has been able to accede to a number of international organizations and enjoy some of the benefits of UN membership. Similarly, Kosovo, while not a member of the UN, has gained membership in the IMF and hosts offices from a number of additional international organizations; Kosovo is also recognized by nearly 100 countries.[20] On a much smaller scale, the Polisario Front of Western Sahara has fought somewhat successfully for one of the benefits of membership—the protection of sovereign coastal waters—by persuading the EU that a fishing rights agreement that would have given Morocco rights to fish waters claimed by Western Sahara was more trouble than it was worth.[21]

Decentralizing recognition could be one strategy—already used in a number of cases—to tie good behavior more explicitly to the benefits of statehood. Syria's Kurds are currently receiving military aid from the United States as well as from other countries because of their demonstrated capacity and compliance.[22] Here, key players in the international community that are legitimacy-rich might be at the vanguard, with other actors, for whom recognition is more strategically fraught, behind. For groups like the Syrian Kurds, however, this strategy is unlikely to work; certainly, the United States has been reluctant to convert aid to recognition, even while acknowledging the considerable assistance lent by the Kurds in the Syrian civil war.

Another strategy could be to create new categories of membership in key, but less politically sensitive, international institutions such as the Universal Postal Union and the International Telecommunications Union. Even limited membership in these organizations could translate into significant benefits for de facto states, and continued membership could again be tied explicitly to good behavior. For example, if Somaliland had an internationally recognized central bank, it would be better able to access international markets as well as obtain shipping insurance for trade.[23] Such a linkage would create an undeniable double standard, but one that might be preferable to the status quo for citizens of de facto states.

Today, when the international community says "jump," the secessionist response is often "how high?" But as the international community is not there to cushion their fall, secessionists will soon realize that the link between good behavior and rewards is mostly false. Given the twin forces of increasing civil war and increasing secessionism, the viability of this fiction may be eroding.

The Fall and Rise of Peace Treaties

The declining use of peace treaties in interstate war and the rising use of peace treaties in civil war is doubly puzzling. First, why would peace treaty usage decrease in one type of war but increase in another? Chapters 5 and 8 answer this question by contrasting the status and incentives of belligerents in interstate and civil war alongside the changing preferences of the international community. But this explanation generates a second puzzle: why are peace treaties correlated with longer peace spells in interstate war, but shorter peace spells in civil war? In other words, at least at a surface level, peace treaties appear to be effective in interstate war, but defective in civil war.

Understanding the answer to this question is critically important given that most wars today are civil wars, and a rising percentage of civil wars has been concluded with peace treaties mediated by the international community. As of this writing, thirty-six internal armed conflicts are ongoing, and at least twenty of these have received mediators at some point.[24] As shown in chapter 8, civil wars that receive mediators are six times more likely to conclude with peace treaties than civil wars without mediators. The convergence of these trends is cause for concern. But there is no simple solution. It would be foolish, for example, to completely stop making peace treaties in civil war because of an observed correlation between peace treaties and decreased peace years.

Peace treaties are correlated with longer peace spells in interstate war and shorter peace spells in civil war because the commitment problem is typically more severe in civil than in interstate wars. With the rare exception of successful secessionism, the parties to civil war must live together after the war has ended. Not only will the distrust that began the war probably still be present, it will have likely been exacerbated by warfighting. Getting the losing side to disarm is often the thorniest aspect of the commitment problem (and one that contrasts with interstate war, where the parties typically keep their militaries). The reluctance to disarm may prevent peace treaties from being fully realized in civil war. What is more, the commitment problem may be deepened by belligerents—particularly rebels, or whichever is the weaker side—using negotiation as a stalling tactic.[25] Peace treaties may buy time to rebuild forces and mount a new offensive.

Recent research has focused on how well-designed peace treaties may remediate the problem in civil war. This research is reflected in practice, as the typical number of civil war peace agreement provisions almost doubled from 1989 to 2006.[26] But a true commitment problem will require more than clever design to solve. Many of the provisions that are candidates for solving the commitment problem—such as monitoring of disarmament or elections—cannot be executed without outside intervention that requires sustained resources.

Juxtaposing the historical rates of victory and peace treaties in interstate versus civil wars helps illustrate this point. Over the past 200 years, both types of war tend to end in victory at similar rates. But peace treaties are much more correlated with draws in civil wars than in interstate wars, setting an even more challenging stage for an already difficult post-conflict transition.

The international community, therefore, must temper its taste for negotiated settlements.[27] Intervention should only occur when the international community has solved its own commitment problem in terms of the deployment of appropriate resources. Half-measures may do more long-term harm than good if they enable or exacerbate the commitment problem inherent in civil war, and thus compound the human costs of war. However appealing they might seem, peace treaties may not always be the answer.

Unanswered Questions

Exploring the consequences of the development of international norms regulating war over the past two centuries raises many questions. These unanswered questions afford opportunities for future research, beginning with the process of making international law and norms. The 1949 Geneva Conventions, for example, are overdue for serious historical treatment. While we are fortunate to have numerous histories of international humanitarian law, none take the conventions as a whole—and the fourth, critical, convention, on treatment of civilians, in particular—as their main focus. A traditional diplomatic history of the Geneva Conventions would be extremely useful, as would a social and cultural history of these agreements.

One feature that would surely be central to any history of the Geneva Conventions is the critical role played by the ICRC in their creation. The ICRC's place in the history of the Geneva Conventions is similar to the role that many NGOs and INGOs play in international humanitarian lawmaking today. The growth of NGOs has prompted a series of studies on the topic.[28] Many are focused on the NGOs as the chief actor of interest.[29] But NGOs often seek to influence governments, and we have a poor understanding of how governments react to NGOs in this context. For example, the United States kept the Cluster Munitions Coalition (which, like the Campaign to Stop Killer Robots, sought a ban on a specific weapon) at arm's length. The 2008 Cluster Munitions Convention includes many US allies as signatories, but the United States declined to sign on the grounds that cluster munitions retained military utility. Several years later, the United States spearheaded an effort for a ban on older cluster munitions, but this effort failed because many of the signatories to the 2008 convention argued that the US-sponsored agreement would produce only minimal change. Had the United States been more engaged with the Cluster Munitions Campaign, it might have been more successful in having a final agreement reflect a position closer to its own preferences. The United States is considerably more engaged with the Campaign to Stop Killer Robots. This difference may be accounted for by a learning process undergone by the United States in its relationship with the NGO community.

Moving from the creation of law to the conduct of war, there also remains a great deal of research to be done on secessionism. In chapter 7, I showed that secessionists are less likely to target civilians than are non-secessionists, and that since the mid-twentieth century secessionists have also been decreasingly likely to engage in major violence. While the data supporting these claims cover a large swath of history, they do not delve into the history of each secessionist movement. Given the increasing rate of secessionism, understanding secessionist violence requires analysis of the full life cycle of secessionism, and particularly of the beginning of that cycle. Under what conditions do secessionists decide to employ violence to advance their cause? Does their use of violence against civilians vary over the course of a conflict? The increasing rate of secessionism—and, particularly, the increasing rate at which secessionists are controlling territory—also demands more policy analysis of options to engage secessionists. Can there be new tracks for some secessionists, like Scotland or Somaliland, to enjoy some of the benefits of junior membership in the international community without upsetting the edifice of state sovereignty and international law?

Wars of law occur when wars are fought lawfully, but also when legal regimes are in tension with one another. Both phenomena are evident in the domain of the laws of war. Thanks to the efforts of humanitarians over the past two centuries, much armed conflict is successfully regulated today. Indeed, the marked decline in the percentage of states fighting wars with each other is a change for which international humanitarian lawmakers deserve at least some credit. But many wars are conducted contrary to the ideals of these humanitarians, sometimes because of the unanticipated and unintended effects of the attempt to regulate war.

War is a horror, and so the drive to limit its negative effects is a strong one. But as this drive accelerates, it may create its own array of collateral damage. My aim in this book has been to step back and reflect on the forward motion of the international humanitarian legal movement. Only by lending a critical eye and taking stock can we make the readjustments that could help maximize the possibility of the laws of war as a force for good.

NOTES

Declaring War and Peace

1. I use the term international humanitarian law interchangeably with *jus in bello* and the "law of armed conflict." According to the International Committee of the Red Cross, the nongovernmental organization most closely associated with IHL, "International humanitarian law is a set of rules which seek, for humanitarian reasons, to limit the effects of armed conflict. It protects persons who are not or are no longer participating in the hostilities and restricts the means and methods of warfare. International humanitarian law is also known as the law of war or the law of armed conflict." See International Committee of the Red Cross, "What Is International Humanitarian Law?," December 31, 2014, https://www.icrc.org/en/document/what-international-humanitarian-law. For an important argument regarding the differences amongst these terms, see Evangelista 2008, 6–7.

2. Panico 1994, xiii.

3. UNHCR 1995.

4. Goltz 1994, C4.

5. Cornwell 1999, 16.

6. Shermatova 1998.

7. Goldberg 1992.

8. Booth and DeYoung 2014.

9. Myers 2014.

10. Zucchino 2017.

11. "PKK Statement to the United Nations," from Newsdesk Amsterdam, January 24, 1995, archived on Hartford Web Publishing, http://www.hartford-hwp.com/archives/51/009. html.

12. Department of Foreign Relations, Kurdistan Regional Government, "Current Foreign Representation in the Kurdistan Region," accessed May 28, 2015, http://dfr.krg.org/p/p. aspx?p=37&l=12&s=020100&r=363.

13. "Deed Of Commitment Under Geneva Call For Adherence To A Total Ban On Anti-Personnel Mines And For Cooperation In Mine Action," August 11, 2002, http://theirwords. org/media/transfer/doc/sc_iq_kdp_2002_03-0c4c08afbc118366c3cec3e0be81b06f.pdf.

14. Kurdistan Democratic Party Constitution and By-laws, 13th Congress, December 11–18, 2010, Erbil, http://www.kdp.se/kdpprogram.pdf.

15. Roberts and Sivakumaran 2012, 148; Sivakumaran 2012b, 119.

16. Huang 2016, 98.

17. Poole 1998, 33.

18. Mearsheimer 1994.

19. Morrow 2014.

20. Downes 2008; Valentino, Huth, and Croco 2006.

21. Wallace 2015.

22. Morrow 2014.

23. See for example Simmons 2009; Stein 2005; Hathaway 2002.

24. Weinstein 2007; K. Cunningham 2014; Kalyvas 2006; Parkinson 2013; Daly 2016.

25. Fortna 2015; Stanton 2013.

26. For a recent exception, see Jo 2015.

27. Posner 2014, 104. Recent books by Stephen Hopgood and Martti Koskenniemi are also in this vein, although their claims are not as unequivocal as Posner's. Hopgood 2013; Koskenniemi 2006.

28. Ohlin 2015.

29. Cunningham and Lemke 2013.

30. The commentaries are detailed explanations and interpretations of the conventions written by legal experts (often tied to the ICRC), and include discussion of debates had and positions taken during their negotiation.

31. Please see the online statistical appendix for replication data and additional information regarding these datasets, available at http://www.tanishafazal.com/publications/.

1. The Proliferation and Codification of the Laws of War

1. Fazal and Greene 2015, 833; Rothenberg 1994, 87–88.

2. Whitman, for example, argues that the laws of war were focused on identifying and rewarding victors, and written to sustain monarchs. Whitman 2012, 17.

3. Data from International Committee of the Red Cross, "Treaties, State Parties and Commentaries," accessed May 14, 2014, http://www.icrc.org/applic/ihl/ihl.nsf/vwTreatiesByDate.xsp.

4. Ober 1994, 13.

5. Cicero 1913, III, §107–15.

6. Tzu 1910, II, §17 and III, §6.

7. Fazal and Greene 2015, 832.

8. Kinsella 2011, 57–59; Fazal and Greene 2015, 834.

9. Johnson 1997, 104.

10. Whitman 2012, 137.

11. For example, at the turn of the seventeenth century, Spain and the Netherlands agreed in the *cuartel general* that every captain would offer captured prisoners for ransom within

twenty-five days. Spain and France came to a similar agreement in 1639, as did the United States and the UK during the War of 1812. Parker 1994, 52. See also "British-American Diplomacy: Cartel for the Exchange of Prisoners of War between Great Britain and the United States Army," from *Treaties and Other International Acts of the United States of America*, edited by Hunter Miller, vol. 2, *Documents 1–40: 1776–1880* (Washington: Government Printing House, 1931), posted to Avalon Project 2008, http://avalon.law.yale.edu/19th_century/cart1812.asp.

12. On customary law, see Verdier and Voeten 2015.

13. Koskenniemi 2002.

14. O'Connell 2005, 16.

15. In World War I, for example, the Allies' definition of contraband was revised and expanded several times, and included wool, castor oil, and a variety of foodstuffs (for both humans and animals). Moreover, the expansion of this contraband list was clearly part of a conscious strategy of manipulating the laws of war of the day. Pyke 1915, chap. 14; Hull 2014, 152, 186–87.

16. Neff 2000, 121.

17. Dunant 1939 (1862), 90. The wounded might have remained on the battlefield for days or even weeks at the time.

18. International Committee of the Red Cross, "Mandate and Mission," accessed May 15, 2014, http://www.icrc.org/eng/who-we-are/mandate/index.jsp.

19. The 1864 Red Cross Convention was also known as the 1864 Geneva Convention.

20. The most prominent was Jean Larrey's invention of "flying ambulances," which were horse-drawn carriages that quickly entered and exited the battlefield (in contrast to handheld litters), during the Napoleonic Wars. Gabriel 2013, 144.

21. For example, gains in British, French, and Russian military medicine were lost by the time of the Crimean war. Gabriel 2013, 152–61.

22. Barnett 2011, 79–80.

23. Barnett 2011, 80.

24. Moorehead 1998, 21.

25. For a history of this conference, see C. Davis 1962.

26. Kershner 2014.

27. The first definition of "civilian" in positive law can be found in Article 50 of the first Protocol Additional to the Geneva Conventions of August 12, 1949: "A civilian is any person who does not belong to one of the categories of persons referred to in Article 4 A (1), (2), (3) and (6) of the Third Geneva Convention and in Article 43 of this protocol." The aforementioned articles all define combatants, underlining the point that the definition of civilian within international humanitarian law remains a negative one.

28. Sandholtz 2007, 206–7.

29. See Preamble, Hague 1899 Convention (II). Interestingly, delegates to the 1874 Brussels Conference, which was convened to discuss developing the laws of war regarding land warfare, were willing to include civil wars, such as the Swiss Sonderbund War, in any code. Holquist 2015, 39.

30. Additional Protocol II, Article 1.

31. Hull 2014, 59.

32. Interestingly, there were no major IHL conventions in the aftermath of World War I. This is because international legal efforts in the interwar period focused on issues of *jus ad bellum* rather than *jus in bello*, with documents like the Kellogg-Briand Pact and Covenant of the League of Nations seeking to limit war's outbreak, rather than govern its conduct.

33. For a history of human rights and human rights law, see Hunt 2007.

34. Article 38 of the Convention on the Rights of the Child prohibits the use of children as soldiers and states, "State Parties undertake to respect and to ensure respect for rules of international humanitarian law applicable to children in armed conflicts which are relevant to the child."

35. Roberts and Sivakumaran 2012, 123–25.

36. Barnett 2011, chap. 4.

37. Hopgood 2013.

38. Koskenniemi 2002.

39. Witt 2012.

40. Ibid., 187.

41. Holquist 2015, 18.

42. Davis 1975, 10.

43. Scott 1920, 506. Benvenisti and Cohen cite military participation in the making of the early laws of war as evidence of the desire of military leaders to use IHL to solve a principal-agent problem with respect to their subordinates—by their account, this body of law was meant to solidify command and control. Interestingly, Davis notes that the United States included military personnel in its delegation to the 1899 Hague Conventions only after "reports had come to the State Department that other governments were appointing such delegates, and this course seemed a necessity for the United States." Benvenisti and Cohen 2014; Davis 1962, 74–75.

44. Best 1980, 147.

45. Hull 2014, 60.

46. Data taken from Scott 1915, 1-31; Final Record of the Diplomatic Conference of Geneva of 1949 1949; 1977; United Nations Diplomatic Conference of Plenipotentiaries on the Establishment of an International Criminal Court, Official Records 1998.

47. Davis 1975, 23–24, 192–97.

48. Wechsler 2000, 87.

49. Nine of 131 delegates (not quite 7 percent) to the 1954 Hague Convention were military members. Although the number of NGO observers was relatively low, many delegates were "cultural experts," including ministers of culture, professors of archeology, ambassadors to UNESCO, and various directors of national museums and libraries. Records of the Conference Convened by the United Nations Educational, Scientific and Cultural Organization Held at the Hague from 21 April to 14 May 1954, 87–96; Sandholtz 2007, 180–86; O'Keefe 2006, 92–93.

50. According to the ICRC, "Military necessity permits measures which are actually necessary to accomplish a legitimate military purpose and are not otherwise prohibited by international humanitarian law. In the case of an armed conflict the only legitimate military purpose is to weaken the military capacity of the other parties to the conflict. Military necessity generally runs counter to humanitarian exigencies. Consequently the purpose of humanitarian law is to strike a balance between military necessity and humanitarian exigencies." International Committee of the Red Cross, "Military Necessity," accessed September 28, 2015, https://www.icrc.org/casebook/doc/glossary/military-necessity-glossary.htm.

51. Sandholtz 2007, 180–86.

52. Best 1994, 92–94; Mantilla 2013, 404. See for example "Abstract of Official Report of the XVIth International Red Cross Conference, London, June 1938," National Archives, College Park, MD, Records of the American National Red Cross, 1935–1946, RG 200/Stack 130/Row 77/Compartment 22/Shelf 3/Box 72/Folder 5; "International Red Cross Conferences—Delegates, 1967–1952" RG200/Stack 730/Row 78/Compartment 14/Shelf 5/Box 106/Folder 041.

53. The one exception was an Air Force Reserve Colonel from the US Naval Academy. Carpenter 2014, 94.

54. Chameau, Ballhaus, and Lin 2014, appendix A. This task force comprised eighteen committee members, one of whom was former military.

55. My own research on this topic suggests that these records do not exist. For example, neither the Red Cross Records nor the US State Department appointment files contained information on appointments to these conferences, even though they included a great deal of other information on these meetings. See (all from the National Archives, College Park, MD): RG 200/Stack Area B190/Row 38/Compartment 2/Entry #P108, Records Relating to the ICRC, 1900–2005/Container #67; RG 200/Stack Area B190/Row 38/Compartment 2/Entry #108, Records Relating to the ICRC, 1900–2005/Container #25; RG 200/Stack Area B190/Row 38/Compartment 2/Entry #128, History Files, 1863–1993/Containers #39, #30; RG 59/Stack Area 250/Row 48/ Entry #826, General Records of the Department of State, Miscellaneous Appointment Records, Records Relating to Appointments to International Conferences, Commissions, and Boards/Box #3.

56. Theodore Roosevelt Jr. followed his father, the twenty-sixth president and his namesake, in government service to become the assistant secretary of the navy in 1921.

57. "Appointment Records for 1921 Conference on the Limitation of Armament to be held in Washington." Also see "Appointment Records for London Naval Conference of 1930." RG 59/ Stack Area 250/Row 48/ Entry #826, General Records of the Department of State, Miscellaneous Appointment Records, Records Relating to Appointments to International Conferences, Commissions, and Boards/Box #3.

58. Davis 1975, 22.

59. Davis 1962, chap. 5.

60. Cheibub, Gandhi, and Vreeland 2010.

61. Commentaries to earlier conventions are not available electronically, nor is the commentary to the 1998 Rome Statute available electronically. Because this type of content analysis requires the use of software to be efficient, nonelectronic commentaries were not consulted. See p. 26 of Commentary to 1st GC for a reference to commentary to 1929 Convention (in French).

62. Pictet 1952, 26.

63. Ibid., 26–27.

64. Content analysis, sometimes referred to as text mining, involves both high-level and fine-grained examination of large bodies of text. Content analyses explore corpora such as newspaper articles that cover a long period of time, the British National Corpus, the Corpus of Historical American English, TIME Magazine Corpus of American English, or Google Books. The commentaries lend themselves to this method: taken together, they include thousands of pages; some commentaries, such as the commentary to the 1998 Rome Statute, are nearly 2,000 pages on their own. Triffterer 2008; Abulof 2013, 11; Grimmer and Stewart 2013.

65. Pictet 1952, 51.

66. Ibid., 52.

67. Pictet 1958, 42–43.

68. A final set of discussions of the term "non-international" refers to issues specific to Convention IV, such as who might count as an "alien" versus a "national" in the context of a civil war. Pictet 1958, 43.

69. For an analysis of the history of the 1974–77 conferences that produced the additional protocols, see Mantilla 2013.

70. Mantilla 2013, 46.

71. Ibid., 243.

72. Pictet 1987, 1388.

73. One exception is a state's obligation to disseminate the protocol to members of armed groups. Pictet 1987, 1488.

74. According to the law regarding state responsibility, the state is obliged to ensure that all parties within the state comply with treaty obligations made by the state—even if said party is fighting against the state.

2. International Recognition, Compliance Costs, and the Formalities of War

1. This definition of international recognition is related to, but distinct from, Weber's definition of legitimacy as the right to rule. Weber 1964, 124, 382.

2. Krasner 1999, 14. This conception of sovereignty differs from, for example, Weber's exposition of domestic legitimacy as the basis of authority and the right to rule. Instead, I conceive of international legitimacy as being conferred upon international actors by the international community; the main benefit of recognition is membership in good standing in the international community. For a useful presentation of arguments from political philosophy regarding legitimacy, see Peter 2017. For an analysis of legitimacy accorded to major international organizations such as the United Nations (specifically, the Security Council), see Hurd 2007.

3. Finnemore and Sikkink 1998, 891.

4. Fazal and Griffiths 2014.

5. Fazal 2007, 14–17. Also see Coggins 2014b, 8; Fabry 2010, esp. chaps. 1 and 4.

6. Weinstein 2007, 75–79.

7. Aspinall 2009, 223.

8. Coggins 2014b, 33; Fazal and Griffiths 2014, 93–94.

9. Roth 2010.

10. Tilly 1975; Bean 1973.

11. Montevideo Convention on the Rights and Duties of States.

12. European Commission, "European Neighbourhood Policy and Enlargement Negotiations: Conditions for Membership," last updated June 12, 2016, http://ec.europa.eu/enlargement/policy/conditions-membership/index_en.htm.

13. Talmon 1993, 239, quoting Morrison.

14. Ibid., 242.

15. In doing so, they joined an increasing number of states moving away from the approach of recognizing specific governments or regimes. Talmon 1993, 244–48; Warbrick 1992.

16. Talmon 1993, 251.

17. Oeter 2014, 198.

18. Jo 2015, 32.

19. Coggins 2015.

20. Vidmar 2012, 171.

21. Hazen 2013, 67.

22. Armitage 2017, 164, 172.

23. Ibid., 178, 179.

24. Ibid., 206.

25. For example, Morrow's analysis of compliance with international humanitarian law includes a theory that is extremely complex, and presumes an extremely high standard of rational calculation on the part of states.

26. Morrow 2014; Downes 2007.

27. Morrow 2014, 88. By contrast, Downes, as well as Valentino, Huth, and Croco, argues that civilian targeting is often a strategy of desperation, one that should (implicitly) be

expected to be used later in wars. Downes 2006; Valentino, Huth, and Balch-Lindsay 2004; Valentino, Huth, and Croco 2006.

28. Morrow 2014; Valentino, Huth, and Croco 2006.

29. Morrow 2014, chap. 6.

30. International Criminal Court, "Statement of the Prosecutor on the Agreement of the Creation of a Special Jurisdiction for Peace in Colombia," September 14, 2015, https://www.icc-cpi.int/legalAidConsultations?name=otp_stat_24-09-2015.

31. My emphasis. UN Security Council Resolution 1961 (1961), Resolution of 24 November 1961, accessed October 6, 2017, http://www.un.org/en/ga/search/view_doc.asp?symbol=S/RES/169(1961).

32. Brownlie 1971, 364.

33. Sahadevan 2013, 139.

34. Stanton 2015, 11.

35. This point has methodological implications in that it suggests that there is not a selection effect because the decision to fight is not conditioned on the proliferation of codified IHL. Several scholars have noted a decline in interstate war and have, to some extent, attributed this decline to increased humanitarianism and the norms and actions of the international community (such as peacekeeping). Pinker 2011; Goldstein 2011. These claims have been challenged on both theoretical and empirical grounds. Braumoeller 2013; Fazal 2014; Fortna 2013; Fry 2013.

36. Kahl 2007, 11.

37. *Legal Lessons Learned from Afghanistan and Iraq* 2004, 1, 310.

38. Woodward 2004, 277; Kahl 2007, 16. For an analysis of the role of JAGs in aerial targeting decisions in the 1991 Iraq War and the 1999 Kosovo War, see Lewis 2003 and Lohr and Gallotta 2003, 474–76.

39. Capt. Robert McLaughlin, Australian Army, email message to author, November 3, 2010.

40. Dobbs 2003.

41. Gen. Mark Martins, email message to author, October 22, 2010.

42. Calculations made using the Correlates of War National Material Capabilities Data Set. Singer 1987; Singer, Bremer, and Stuckey 1972.

43. O'Hanlon and Livingston 2010, 3.

44. Committee to Protect Journalists 2003.

45. Brody 2004; Jones and Fay 2004.

46. Sandholtz 2007, 241–43; Forrest 2010, 61–63.

47. Sandholtz 2007, 195.

48. Fisher and Wong 2004.

49. Greene 2009, 26–27; *Final Report to the Prosecutor by the Committee Established to Review the NATO Bombing Campaign Against the Federal Republic of Yugoslavia*, S56, accessed October 6, 2017, http://www.icty.org/en/press/final-report-prosecutor-committee-established-review-nato-bombing-campaign-against-federal.

50. Betts 2001, 130.

51. Capt. Robert McLaughlin, email message to author, November 3, 2010. Importantly, notions such as "courageous restraint"—the idea that in counterinsurgency operations, it is better for counterinsurgents to take significant risks upon themselves to protect civilians—may be gaining credence and run counter to this logic. Felter and Shapiro 2017.

52. The ICC indicted Sudanese President Omar Al-Bashir, even though Sudan is not a party to the Rome Statute.

53. The UK and France could be subject to investigation via one of the two other primary routes, as they are state parties to the Rome Statute. For example, French forces that

intervened in Mali in 2012 are being investigated by the prosecutor alongside the Tuareg and Islamist rebels. The other UNSC members—the United States, Russia, and China—are not members of the ICC. See International Criminal Court, "Statement by ICC Prosecutor Concerning Mali," January 28, 2013, http://www.icc-cpi.int/en_menus/icc/press%20and%20 media/press%20releases/Pages/OTPstatement280113.aspx.

54. Kippenberg 2004, 14–17.

55. "Uniform Code of Military Justice," available online at Cornell Law School, accessed October 6, 2017, https://www.law.cornell.edu/uscode/text/10/802. In *United States v. Averette*, a private military contractor deployed during the Vietnam War successfully appealed a conviction by court martial because the Vietnam War was not a declared war. Schwarz 2002, 33–34. The 2004 Amendments to the Military Extraterritorial Jurisdictions Act amended the UCMJ to hold private citizens traveling with the military accountable in times of "declared war and contingency operations."

56. Holsti 2004, esp. chap. 2.

57. Benvenisti and Cohen 2014, 1390–91.

58. Tomz 2008; Wallace 2013.

59. Wallace 2013, 125–28.

60. Tomz 2008, 18.

61. Aldrich et al. 2006; Bayram 2017; Wallace 2013, 110–12; Koch and Nicholson 2015.

62. This case is discussed in greater detail in chapter 3.

63. Burke 1973, 1042.

64. D. Fischer 1982, 262.

65. Benvenisti and Cohen 2014.

66. Morrow 2014, chap. 1.

67. Hersh 2004.

68. Balz and Morin 2004; Wertheimer 2004; Bierman 2015; Karon 2004.

69. Human Rights Watch 2013b; Human Rights Watch 2015.

70. Ross 2004, 53, table 5; Dougherty 2007, 130, 136; B. Walter 2014, 5.

71. Perry and Chang 1980.

72. Cunha 1964.

73. Clodfelter 2008, 605–6.

74. Kalyvas 1999.

75. Aspinall 2007.

76. On the increasing benefits of statehood, see Fazal and Griffiths 2014. On the distinction between legal and political recognition, see Talmon 2013.

77. Huang 2016; Jo and Simmons 2013.

78. Fabry 2010, chaps. 5 and 6; Coggins 2011, 436, 444.

79. Talmon 1993, 249–51.

80. On the relationship between command and control structures and compliance with IHL by rebel groups, see Sivakumaran 2012a.

81. Salehyan, Siroky, and Wood 2014, 635, 640–43.

82. Byman and Kreps 2010, 10.

83. Coggins 2014b.

84. Bridget Coggins and Morgan Kaplan have each noted extensive rebel diplomacy that has emerged to attract external sponsors. Coggins 2014a ; Kaplan 2014.

85. Derecho Internacional, Web, "Declaration on the 'Guidelines on the Recognition of New States in Eastern Europe and in the Soviet Union' (16 December 1991)," November 20, 2015, http://www.dipublico.org/100636/declaration-on-the-guidelines-on-the-recognition-of-new-states-in-eastern-europe-and-in-the-soviet-union-16-december-1991/.

86. Jo 2015, http://www.dipublico.org/100636/declaration-on-the-guidelines-on-the-recognition-of-new-states-in-eastern-europe-and-in-the-soviet-union-16-december-1991/; Huang 2016; Richters 2014.

87. Jo and Thomson 2013, 331.

88. Kahler 2011, 25–27.

89. Network of Researchers in International Affairs, "From the NMA to the NMLA: The Shift to Armed Struggle," June 10, 2014, http://www.noria-research.com/from-the-nma-to-the-nmla-the-shift-to-armed-struggle/.

90. The Diplomat Advisory Group, "Independent Diplomat," accessed May 27, 2014, http://www.independentdiplomat.org.

91. Carne Ross of Independent Diplomat, interview with author, July 7, 2011; Pierre Hegay and Jeroen Zandberg of UNPO, interview with author, February 4, 2013.

92. Geneva Call, "Mission," accessed May 23, 2014, http://www.genevacall.org/who-we-are/.

93. Pascal Bongard of Geneva Call, email message to author, November 30, 2015.

94. Pascal Bongard, interview with author, May 18, 2015, Geneva, Switzerland.

95. Fazal and Konaev 2017.

96. For discussions of defection and desertion, see Lyall 2014; McLauchlin 2010; Oppenheim et al. 2015.

97. Geneva Call, "Their Words: Directory of Armed Non-State Actor Humanitarian Commitments," accessed May 23, 2014, http://theirwords.org/?country=MLI&ansa=228&document_type=3.

98. General Staff, "General Order No. 1: Promulgating a Code of Conduct Regulating the Affairs of the Bangsamoro Islamic Armed Forces, Prescribing its Powers, Duties and Functions, and Other Related Purposes," May 23, 2014, available on Geneva Call, "Their Words," http://theirwords.org/media/transfer/doc/sc_ph_milf_biaf_2006_09-9dbc781bd3fc677c268ce003582f4f58.pdf.

99. Here, the denominator is based on Philip Roeder's data on segment states, "juridically separate communities of people who purportedly have special claim to that jurisdiction as a homeland." For each year, the number of secessionist movements we identify is divided by the number of segment states as identified by Roeder. Roeder 2007, 12; Fazal and Griffiths 2014, 85.

3. Declarations of War in Interstate War

1. Thucydides 1954, 87 (section 88). This section is commonly referred to as "The Debate at Sparta and the Declaration of War." Note: Crawley's translation uses the same language regarding war being declared. Thucydides 1934, 50 (book 1, chap. 3, section 88).

2. Russell 1975, 6; Ober 1994, 13.

3. Ward 1805, 61-62; Lauterpacht 1947, 378.

4. Diamond 2015.

5. Obama to Seek Authority from Congress for Islamic State Fight 2014; Sargent 2015; Somin 2015; Senate Democrats Oppose "Blank Check" for Islamic State Fight 2015; Obama Faces Tough Sell to Get New War Powers to Fight IS 2015. In fact, there is currently a lawsuit pending on this issue. Epps 2016.

6. Leatherby 2015; Arkin 2015.

7. Livy as quoted in Hallett 1998, 68; Ward 1805, 56. The Romans were so dedicated to following this form of declaring war that when they intended to engage in war against a region too far from their boundaries, they would find a captured soldier from that far-off land, have him purchase a plot of land in Rome, and hurl said spear into that plot of land. Whitman 2012, 110.

8. Also see Neff 2005, 119.

9. Grotius 1738, book 3, chap. 3.

10. Vattel 1758, book 3, chap. 4, sections 51, 55–56.

11. Ward 1805, 47–51. Indeed, undermining state sovereignty has been considered a legitimate cause of war. Ward argues that the French conclusion of a treaty with the US colonies following their declaration of independence was tantamount to a declaration of war against Britain, and justified the British actions and declaration of war against France that followed it.

12. Thomas 1996, 80.

13. Ackerman and Grimmett 2002, 22–27; Brownlie 1963, 392–98.

14. Bill and Marsh 2010, 13; Martins 1994, 23.

15. Brownlie 1963, 402–4.

16. Garner 2004, 437.

17. Sarkees and Wayman 2010. I deleted two wars from the Correlates of War list of interstate wars. The Sino-Russian War of 1900 is excluded because it is virtually indistinguishable from the Boxer Rebellion; the Second Spanish Moroccan War of 1909 is excluded because it represents a case where the Spanish were essentially allied with the Moroccan government in fighting Moroccan irregulars.

18. Qualitative Data Repository, https://qdr.syr.edu.

19. Fazal et al. 2012. See the statistical appendix for a brief description of I-WIT.

20. Russian Declaration of War against Turkey 1828.

21. Hozier 1877–79, 122.

22. Four Days Later from Europe 1853.

23. The Turkish Manifesto 1877.

24. Elsea and Weed 2014, 48–75.

25. Indeed, constitutional clauses on declarations of war are increasingly likely to have such declarations take the form of declaring states of emergency. See recent constitutions of Tuvalu (2008), Kiribati (1980), Eritrea (1997), and Lithuania (1992).

26. Jones, Bremer, and Singer 1996, 171–72.

27. Morrow and Jo 2006, 105.

28. In a brief analysis of declarations of war, Morrow finds that democracies that have ratified the 1907 Hague Convention are especially unlikely to engage in surprise attacks. Morrow 2014, 167–68.

29. Text of the War Statement by Foreign Minister von Ribbentrop 1941.

30. The delay in the Japanese declaration of war appears to have been the impetus for the Third 1907 Hague Convention. See "Imperial Proclamation of War," accessed June 2, 2009, http://www.russojapanesewar.com/imp-proc-04.html. On Pakistan, see Browne 1971.

31. Grotius 1738, section 8.

32. Vattel 1758, section 60.

33. Maurice 1883, 4.

34. Nimmo 2001, 201.

35. Ward 1805, 17–34.

36. C. Davis 1975, 208–11.

37. Oddly, at the same time that declarations of war are used less frequently in interstate war, national constitutions increasingly include a "declare war" clause. My own survey of the ninety-six constitutions enacted between January 1, 1990, and March 1, 2015, shows that sixty-six contain explicit clauses that outline the procedures for issuing a formal declaration of war.

38. C. Davis 1975, 211.

39. Hull 2014, 59.

40. Minutes of Legal Commission Meeting of 27 August 1948, 9:45 am, Third Plenary Meeting, XVIIème Conference International de la Croix-Rouge, Stockholm, Box 107, Legal Commission, 1948 Conference, 3rd folder, National Archives, RG 200, stack area 730, row 78, compartment 14, shelf 5, 3.

41. O'Connell 2010, 2.

42. Even observers after the fact have concluded that IHL does not apply in the absence of a declaration of war. In his analysis of the 1999 Kosovo War, Richard Betts writes, "The laws of war did not fully apply because NATO had not formally declared war." Betts 2001, 130.

43. An alternative measure that I considered, but rejected, would be to include only treaties but not conventions. Here, for example, the four 1949 Geneva Conventions would be collapsed into one treaty. Measuring the extent to which a state is obliged to comply with IHL in this manner, however, is highly problematic because, in any given year, a state may have signed onto some, but not all, of the 1949 Geneva Conventions.

44. International Committee of the Red Cross, "Treaties, State Parties and Commentaries," accessed January 12, 2014, https://www.icrc.org/ihl.

45. Wallace argues that a main determinant of ratification of *jus in bello* treaties is recent wartime experience. His analysis, though, is limited to the 1949 Geneva Conventions and the 1977 Additional Protocols to the Conventions. Analysis of additional treaties would likely reveal that anticipation of war, a rival state's ratification behavior, and the newness of a particular state as a member of the international system also condition ratification behavior with respect to jus in bello treaties. Wallace 2012.

46. The correlation between *jus in bello* and the year in which a war ends is .94. The correlation between *mean ratifications* and the year in which a war ends is .59.

47. Katzenbach 2008, 228.

48. Lauterpacht 1968.

49. Freeman 1999, 573–615.

50. Rawls 1993, 212–54.

51. Hallett 1998, chaps. 2, 5; Hallett 2013.

52. Gurr, Marshall, and Jaggers 2014.

53. Freedom in the World 2015; Cheibub, Gandhi, and Vreeland 2010; Coppedge et al. 2015.

54. The argument that a divided government makes it more difficult for a leader to go to war was put forth by William Howell and Jon Pevehouse (2007).

55. Schlesinger 1973; R. Hendrickson 2015.

56. Tsebelis 1995, 289.

57. Heinisz 2002.

58. Coppedge et al. 2015.

59. Gurr, Marshall, and Jaggers 2014; Marshall, Jaggers, and Gurr 2011, 23.

60. J. Mueller 1989.

61. Correlates of War Project, "State System Membership List, v2011," 2011, http://correlatesofwar.org.

62. Cunningham and Lemke 2013.

63. Fazal and Greene 2015.

64. Ibid., 836.

65. Ibid., 837.

66. Marginal effects were calculated using *Clarify*. King, Tomz, and Wittenberg 2000.

67. These effects are based on coefficients based on model 5, which uses the systemic measure of the laws of war.

68. For an analysis of the development of these institutions and organizations, see Hathaway and Shapiro 2017.

69. Lauterpacht 1968, 63.

70. Ibid., 64–65.

71. Katzenbach 2008, 228. For a recent analysis of Katzenbach's position, see Griffin 2010.

72. Neff 2000, chap. 10. According to the *San Remo Manual on International Law Applicable to Armed Conflicts at Sea*, the rights and duties of neutrality extend to aircraft today. Another arena where neutrality may become increasingly salient is cyber-warfare, where cyberattacks may be routed through internet nodes in neutral states; if the neutral state failed to stop the attack from its "territory," it could be subject to reprisal.

73. Strachan 2014, 42.

74. Lok Sabha Debates 1962, vol. 9, 1257.

75. Note: there was limited authorization during the 1992 Bosnia war, but this pertained to postconflict stabilization operations and not the original use of force.

76. King, Keohane, and Verba 1994, 142–44. Goertz argues that, for multimethod research designs such as this one, scholars should focus on on-line cases. For the purposes of this chapter, on-line cases would be those predicted by the theory—cases of low ratification of IHL and declarations of war, and cases of high ratifications of IHL and no declarations of war. While I do not focus exclusively on those types of cases, they are included in my four-case set. Goertz 2017.

77. For discussions of the virtues of examining a typical case, see Herron and Quinn 2009; Gerring 2007, 91–97.

78. Smith 1994, 33; *Congressional Record*, March 17, 1898, 2916–19.

79. R. Hendrickson 2003, 9.

80. Spanish officer quoted in Hobson 1987, 86.

81. Brands 1995, 324. Roosevelt was stepping beyond his legal authority by issuing these and other orders, in the absence of approval by Secretary of the Navy Long.

82. Rosenfeld 2000, 16.

83. Quoted in Ofner 1992, 153. Trask 1981, 52, as told by Hobart's wife; Musicant 1990, 171.

84. Smith 1994, 43; Ofner 1992, 184.

85. Both Spain and the United States were signatories to the original 1864 convention, but not to the 1868 amendments, which pertained to treatment of the wounded in maritime conflicts.

86. Estado. 1905, 136, part 1, document 149, enclosure.

87. *Congressional Record*, April 25, 1898, 4244, 4252.

88. The secretary of war was legally constrained from calling up the militia and volunteers until a formal declaration of war was issued. Smith 1994, 62.

89. Smith 1994, 73; R. Hendrickson 2003, 23. NB: Musicant dates the ordering of the blockade to April 22. McKinley's request for a declaration of war also referenced April 22. *Congressional Record*, 55th Congress, April 25, 1898, 4229.

90. *Congressional Record*, 55th Congress, April 25th, 1898, 4252.

91. Estado. 1905, 164, document 8.

92. Three sources discuss a Chinese declaration of war. The first—*The Diary of Ching-shan*—has been widely denounced as a fabrication. Several additional sources rely on Ching's "diary"; their conclusions on this point can be disregarded. The second, more reputable source is Chester Tan's *The Boxer Catastrophe*. Tan is the first English-language historian to have relied on Chinese archival sources in his discussion of the conflict. Tan does mention an imperial edict declaring war that was issued on June 21, 1900; he cites a Chinese document—not Ching's diary—as a source. But it appears that this edict does not necessarily

meet the standard for a declaration of war. It was sent to the provincial governors (viceroys), but, according to Tan, they suppressed it from the public so as to limit the scope of the conflict (China was a largely decentralized state at the time). It was not sent to the Europeans and Japanese against whom the Chinese were fighting. More recently, Lanxin Xiang has documented the history of the Boxer Rebellion up to the Chinese declaration of war, providing a detailed history of court intrigue that suggests that such a decree actually did exist. Xiang's account accords with Tan's (and neither relies on the Ching-shan diary). The declaration was issued, by imperial decree, following an ultimatum to the foreign legations instructing them to depart Beijing under Chinese protection. Keown-Boyd 1991, 213, 308–10; Tan 1967, 75, 77, 83; Xiang 2003, 317.

93. Ward 1805, 62.

94. One possible objection to this explanation is the following: why would the other great powers be so inclined to follow the US lead? Also, it is somewhat difficult to reconcile a US anti-imperialist position with the US annexation just two years earlier of Puerto Rico and the Philippines as spoils of the Spanish-American War.

95. Not a State of War Yet 1900.

96. Sisson and Rose 1990, chap. 6.

97. United Nations High Commission on Refugees 2000, 60–61.

98. Sisson and Rose 1990, 150–51, 206.

99. Ganguly 2002, 51.

100. Nearly all the historiography on this conflict is biased toward one side or the other.

101. Sisson and Rose 1990, 143; Ganguly 2002, 62; Matinuddin 1994, 231.

102. Sisson and Rose 1990, 214.

103. Ibid. 1990, 230.

104. Indeed, the evidence suggests that neither India nor Pakistan possessed chemical or biological weapons. See Pakistan Country Profile 2015; India Country Profile 2015.

105. Compliance with the laws of war in this case is discussed in detail in chapter 4.

106. Sisson and Rose 1990, 217; Jackson and International Institute for Strategic Studies 1975, 82.

107. Zaheer 1994, 321, 357–58; Matinuddin 1994, 444–45.

108. Jack 1998, 503.

109. Freedman 2005, 1:4–8.

110. Freedman 1988, 28.

111. Eddy, Linklater, and Gillman 1982, 97; Freedman and Gamba-Stonehouse 1991, 84–89.

112. For a detailed account of Haig's mediation efforts, see Freedman and Gamba-Stonehouse 1991, Chs. 13–15.

113. Freedman and Gamba-Stonehouse 1991, 121–25.

114. M. Thatcher 1993, 208; Nott 2002, 304.

115. Sinclair 2002, 124–25.

116. Nott 2002, 272.

117. "Trading with the Enemy Act," Legislation.gov.uk, accessed January 23, 2011, http://www.legislation.gov.uk/ukpga/Geo6/2-3/89/introduction.

118. Freedman 2005, 2:90.

119. M. N. Schmitt 1991, 2–3.

120. Quoted in M. N. Schmitt 1991, 6.

121. Freedman and Gamba-Stonehouse 1991, 104.

122. Rock 1985, 116.

123. Freedman and Gamba-Stonehouse 1991, 148.

124. Rattenbach 1988, 244. Translated from the Spanish by the author.
125. Wieland 2015, 298.
126. Ibid., 299.
127. Freedman and Gamba-Stonehouse 1991, 134–35.
128. Dudziak 2012.

4. Compliance with the Laws of War in Interstate War

1. Valentino, Huth, and Croco 2006; Downes 2008; Wallace 2015.
2. Valentino, Huth, and Croco 2006, 355–56; Downes 2008, 4-5; Wallace 2015, 10
3. Morrow 2014, 112–17.
4. Morrow 2007.
5. Valentino, Huth, and Croco analyze the effect of having ratified the 1949 Geneva Conventions on civilian targeting, but do not include the reciprocal variables Morrow uses. Morrow discusses the difficulty of including the military strategic variables used by Valentino, Huth, and Croco, and also by Downes, but does not take the next step of recoding the data to surmount these difficulties Morrow 2014, 272–74.
6. If I were to include all twenty-four of the variables that Morrow uses in his primary quantitative analysis, I would be using close to thirty independent variables. I therefore drop some of his variables, add others, and end up with an analysis with twenty-two independent variables.
7. Morrow and Jo 2006.
8. Morrow 2007, 563.
9. Data collection can be a remarkably time-intensive effort—my colleagues and I found it to be so with I-WIT (and C-WIT—see chapters 6–8), and undoubtedly it was for the Morrow and Jo dataset. Morrow and Jo deserve congratulations for assembling such a useful tool.
10. Downes 2008, 59.
11. Ibid., 61.
12. Valentino, Huth, and Croco 2006, 362.
13. Ibid., 362–63.
14. Fazal and Greene 2015, 837–39.
15. These issues contrast with, for example, treatment of prisoners of war, which is often conducted at the unit level, and is thus more difficult for policymakers to monitor than, for instance, the use of chemical and biological weapons.
16. Senn 1959, 20–21.
17. Dasgupta 2002, 99, 223.
18. Simmons 1999, 12.
19. Spain acceded to the declaration in 1908. The United States never acceded to the Declaration of Paris.
20. Spain, however, rejected any restrictions on its right to issues letters of marque. "Privateers," GlobalSecurity.org, last modified May 7, 2011, http://www.globalsecurity.org/military/agency/navy/privateer.htm; International Committee of the Red Cross, Treaties, States Parties and Commentaries, "Declaration Respecting Maritime Law. Paris, 16 April 1856," accessed October 11, 2017, https://www.icrc.org/applic/ihl/ihl.nsf/Treaty.xsp?action=openDocument&documentId=10207465E7477D90C12563CD002D65A3. Trask 1981, 109.
21. Trask 1981, 109.
22. *Correspondence Relating to the War with Spain* 1902, 99, Shafter to AAG, July 6, 1898, 7:58 pm.
23. *Correspondence Relating to the War with Spain* 1902, 100, Cervera to Blanco, July 6, 1898.

24. Musicant 1990, 231.

25. Ibid., 473; Smith 1994, 152; *Correspondence Relating to the War with Spain* 1902, 79, Shafter to Toral, July 3, 1898.

26. *Correspondence Relating to the War with Spain* 1902, 92, Shafter to Alger, July 5, 1898.

27. Musicant 1990, 581.

28. Trask 1981, 365.

29. Musicant 1990, 345; Hobson 1987, 80–83.

30. Rosenfeld 2000, 157, 162.

31. Trask 1981, 8.

32. Ibid., 9.

33. Musicant 1990, 369; Trask 1981, 332.

34. Trask 1981, 366, 409, 416; Musicant 1990, 585, 590, 591.

35. Fazal and Greene 2015, 836.

36. The United States had signed the second Hague Convention on Land Warfare but did not ratify until 1902.

37. The 1856 Declaration of Paris did not apply, as the Boxer Rebellion was not a maritime war.

38. Duiker 1978, 201.

39. Tan 1967, 86.

40. China signed the final act in 1899, but did not accede to the second Hague Convention on Land Warfare (which is the relevant convention here) until 1907.

41. Keown-Boyd 1991, 115.

42. Duiker 1978, 160–61, 186. The Germans were highly motivated by their outrage over the Boxers' murder of Baron von Ketteler, the German consul to the Chinese court, while the Russians were especially interested in making inroads in Manchuria.

43. Keown-Boyd 1991, 205.

44. Duiker 1978, 114; Keown-Boyd 1991, 115.

45. Duiker 1978, 185.

46. Keown-Boyd 1991, 142.

47. Ibid.

48. Keown-Boyd 1991, 121, 142, 167, 243.

49. Wilkins 2008, chap. 6.

50. Ganguly 2002, 68; Jackson and International Institute for Strategic Studies 1975, 122, 136; Jahan 1972, 204; Matinuddin 1994, 470–71. Had the USS *Enterprise*, which was deployed to the Bay of Bengal on December 10th as a show of support to Pakistan, arrived a few days earlier, however, the efficacy of the Indian blockade could theoretically have been challenged. But most historians of and participants in the war saw the deployment of the *Enterprise* as little more than an empty US gesture. Matinuddin 1994, 313; Sisson and Rose 1990, 262–63.

51. Zaheer 1994, 370.

52. The Indians also engaged in limited ground offensives in Kashmir and Sind but, by all accounts, these do not appear to have led to maltreatment of civilians. Sisson and Rose 1990, 215.

53. Indeed, the United States considered challenging India's right to blockade precisely on the grounds that war had not been declared, but ultimately refrained from doing so when the undersecretary of state for political affairs U. Alexis Johnson pointed out that a state of war did, in fact, exist between India and Pakistan. Jackson and International Institute for Strategic Studies 1975, 222n27, 228n31.

54. Ganguly 2002, 60–61.

55. Sisson and Rose 1990, 157–60; Jackson and International Institute for Strategic Studies 1975, 33–35; Jahan 1972, 199, 203.

56. Levie 1985, 64.

57. Argentina possessed neither chemical nor biological weapons; Britain possessed chemical weapons at the time, but had renounced the stockpiling of biological weapons by acceding to the 1972 Biological Weapons Convention. The Chemical Weapons Convention, passed in 1993, was ratified by both Argentina (in 1995) and Britain (in 1996).

58. Freedman and Gamba-Stonehouse 1991, 130.

59. Eddy, Linklater, and Gillman 1982, 227, 249.

60. Indeed, British medical personnel appear to have taken extreme measures to rescue Argentine wounded by, for example, running into a burning building to rescue two Argentine soldiers. Eddy, Linklater, and Gillman 1982, 229; Jolly 2002, 75.

61. Eddy, Linklater, and Gillman 1982, 147.

62. Thompson 1992, 143; Levie 1985, 73. One prisoner of war, Captain Alfredo Astiz, raised an unexpected set of problems for the British. Astiz was deeply implicated in Argentina's "dirty war" and was wanted for trial by the Swedish and the French, who were pressuring the British to send him to Stockholm or Paris, rather than repatriate him as the Geneva Conventions demanded. According to Margaret Thatcher, the Astiz decision was not an easy one; ultimately, the British did repatriate him, but only after he was asked if he would be willing to meet with the Swedish and the French, a step to which the ICRC objected strenuously as being in violation of the Third Geneva Convention. The remainder of the Argentine prisoners of war were repatriated fairly quickly. M. Thatcher 1993, 208; Levie 1985, 72–74.

63. Freedman 2005, 2:658–60. The Indians had taken a similar route with respect to Pakistani POWs after the 1971 Bangladesh War.

64. Levie 1985, 65–66.

65. Freedman and Gamba-Stonehouse 1991, Order of Battle, 418–22.

66. Cardoso, Kirschbaum, and Van der Kooy 1987, 207.

67. M. Thatcher 1993, 190.

68. Quoted in Dillon 1989, 222.

69. Ibid., 223–24.

70. Levie 1985, 65–66.

71. Rattenbach 1988, 267. Translated by the author.

72. Ibid., 267–68.

73. Ibid., 273.

74. Eddy, Linklater, and Gillman 1982, 157.

75. Levie 1985, 66.

76. M. N. Schmitt 1991, 7.

77. Dillon 1989, 194–95.

78. Freedman 2005, 85–86.

79. Freedman and Gamba-Stonehouse 1991, 248.

5. Peace Treaties in Interstate War

1. Walsh and Ahmed 2014.

2. Bruno 2008.

3. Rugman 1995.

4. Russell 1975, 4.

5. Bryce 2006, 10.

6. Thucydides 1954, 358–60.

7. Vollrath 2004, 177–81.

8. Neff 2004, 365.

9. Fortna 2004, 196, 199–205. For challenges to this claim, see Lo, Hashimoto, and Reiter 2008; Werner and Yuen 2005.

10. Fortna 2004, chap. 3.

11. Human Security Report Project 2012, 150.

12. Grob 1949, 205.

13. Rozman 2000, 1.

14. Garner 2004, 1540.

15. Grewe 1992, 942–43; Steiger 2004, 79–96.

16. Coox 1985, 907.

17. The Kashmir issue resurfaced in the Bangladesh War and again remained unresolved by the resulting Simla Agreement.

18. Bell 2008, 53.

19. Fortna 2004, 45.

20. The vast majority of the peace agreements in the UDCP Peace Agreement Dataset conclude civil, and not interstate, wars, a subject addressed in greater detail in chapter 8. UCDP Downloads, accessed October 12, 2017, http://ucdp.uu.se/downloads/.

21. Rahman 1997, 315–18.

22. Additional post–Geneva era treaties include those following the Ifni War, the Cenepa Valley War, and the Badme Border War.

23. Georges Clemenceau, as quoted in Hull 2014, 10.

24. Sandholtz 2007, chap. 4.

25. For an excellent summary of the history of the laws of war regarding protection of cultural property, see Sandholtz 2007.

26. Ibid., 125, 177.

27. Ibid., 206–7.

28. Sandholtz 2010, 161–62.

29. As states tend not to ratify laws of war during the course of a conflict, using this number from the start or from the end of the war does not change the results. Wallace finds that conflict decreases the probability that a state will later ratify future international humanitarian laws. Wallace 2012.

30. Morrow and Jo 2006.

31. Morrow 2007, 563.

32. For instance, during the negotiations in Portsmouth, NH, to draft a treaty to conclude the Russo-Japanese War, Tsar Nicholas is reported to have written, "I am ready to terminate by peace a war which I did not start, provided the conditions offered us befit the dignity of Russia. I do not consider that we are beaten; our army is still intact, and I have faith in it." Etsthus 1988, 50. Also see Kecskemeti 1964, chap. 2.

33. Toft 2003b; Fortna 2009.

34. Grewe 1992, 939.

35. Employing a different cutoff—where military victory=0 in the case of draws, but 1 otherwise—does not alter the results.

36. Vasquez 1993; Gibler 2012.

37. Korman 1996; Wendt 1999; Zacher 2001.

38. Downes and Monten 2013.

39. Fazal 2007. Given that state death as a result of war has declined dramatically since 1945, this hypothesis would not predict a decrease in the number of peace treaties concluded following wars. It could, however, predict variation in the conclusion of peace treaties in the pre-1945 era.

40. Ibid., 1.

41. Bell 2008, 93–95. However, as I discuss in chapter 8, the UN system strongly supports the use of peace treaties to conclude civil wars.

42. D. Cunningham 2006.

43. A joint political constraint variable produces data for only twenty-three dyads. As discussed in chapter 3, two other alternatives, one from the Polity dataset and one from the V-Dem dataset, are not viable because xconst from Polity is highly correlated with (and indeed one of the variables used to index) the polity variable, and V-Dem only begins at the 20th century.

44. Fazal and Greene 2015.

45. This number (eighteen) counts major sets of conventions—such as the 1899 and 1907 Hague Conventions—as one law of war each.

46. This relationship is discussed in greater detail later in this chapter.

47. The People's Republic of China took China's seat at the UN in 1971, while the Democratic People's Republic of Korea joined in 1991, both well after the armistice following the Korean War. Israel joined in 1949 after its war of independence, and Vietnam became a member in 1977, after the Vietnam War.

48. US Department of State 1899, 48, Hay to Day, Washington, November 13, 1898.

49. Estado. 1905, 325, part 3, document 77, Montero Ríos to Almodóvar, Paris, November 21, 1898.

50. Estado. 1905, 333, part 3, document 90, Almodóvar to Montero Ríos, Madrid, November 25, 1898.

51. Estado. 1905, 333, part 3, document 90, Almodóvar to Montero Ríos, Madrid, November 25, 1898.

52. Reid 1965, 72.

53. Grob 1949, 208.

54. United States Department of State 1900, Mr. Conger to Prince Ching, September 10, 1900, p. 201.

55. Grob 1949, 208. Emphasis added.

56. Tan 1967, 216–23; Kelly 1963, 103. Also see Final Protocol, especially Articles 2 and 10.

57. C. Davis 1975, 211.

58. Ganguly 2002, 71.

59. Sattar 1998, 481.

60. Ibid., 482; International Court of Justice, ed. 1976.

61. Pak Bid to Divert World Opinion Seen 1973.

62. Eddy, Linklater, and Gillman 1982, 227, 259; Freedman and Gamba-Stonehouse 1991, 375–76.

63. Freedman and Gamba-Stonehouse 1991, 411.

64. Freedman 2005, 2:660–62.

65. Bell 2008, 51.

66. The former president of Argentina, Cristina Kirchner, pressed Argentina's claim to the islands as recently as 2010. Falklands, Iran, Palestine, Issues of Mrs. Kirchner Address to UN Assembly 2010.

67. Japan Rejects Putin's Claim It Is to Blame for Stalled Islands Talks 2015.

68. Council, Command of the Defence 2004, 9.

69. Hull 2014, 10.

70. Wallensteen 2015, 31.

6. Declarations of Independence in Civil Wars

1. Fierstein 2008, 419.

2. GA Resolution 2625(XXV), October 24, 1970.

3. Cassese 1995, 112.

4. Fierstein 2008, 430, 431.

5. Syria Civil War 2016.

6. Why Syria's Kurds Want Federalism 2016.

7. Please see the online statistical appendix for a description of C-WIT.

8. Fazal and Griffiths 2014, 84.

9. Bob 2005, chap. 4. See "First Declaration of the Lacandona Jungle," archived on Schools for Chiapas, accessed March 31, 2016, http://schoolsforchiapas.org/wp-content/uploads/2014/03/1st-Declaration-of-the-Lacandona-Jungle.pdf.

10. Coggins 2014b, 65; Griffiths 2016, 50; Regan and Wallensteen 2013, 274.

11. Bilefsky 2010; International Court of Justice 2010.

12. International Court of Justice 2010, Advisory Opinion, *ICJ Reports 2010*. See sections 79–84.

13. The sixth clause of Kosovo's declaration of independence states that "Kosovo is a special case arising from Yugoslavia's nonconsensual breakup and is not a precedent for any other situation." Kosovo Declaration of Independence, available on the Republic of Kosovo Assembly website, accessed May 14, 2015, http://www.assembly-kosova.org/common/docs/Dek_Pav_e.pdf. For evidence that the opinion was meant to be construed narrowly, and not set a precedent, see Peters 2015, 5, 6, 8, 9, 11; Thaci 2010; Security Council Meets in Emergency Session Following Kosovo's Declaration of Independence, With Members Sharply Divided on Issue 2008.

14. Peters 2015, 292; also see Wilde 2011, 152.

15. Cowan 2003, 144–47.

16. Armitage 2007, 42.

17. O. Thatcher 1907, 5:189–97.

18. The original language is available at http://pbs.twimg.com/media/BicHwbNIQ AAv49q.jpg, accessed October 13, 2017. Thanks to Svetlana Tsalik for translation assistance.

19. To be sure, not all declarations of war are accompanied by hostilities. A number of Latin American countries declared war against the Axis powers at the close of World War II in order to gain access to the peace conference. But these declarations are not included in the empirical analysis in chapter 3, because no troops were committed by these countries.

20. It should be noted, though, that some groups declare independence multiple times. Kosovo is an example.

21. Garner 2004; Fox 1997; Parry and Grant 1986.

22. Borgen 2008; Bothe 2010; Cirkovic 2010; Detrez 2011; Fierstein 2008; Milanovic and Wood 2015; Ryngaert 2010; Summers 2011; Szewczyk 2010; Vidmar 2009.

23. Written Statement of the United States of America regarding Accordance with International Law of the Unilateral Declaration of Independence with respect to Kosovo, Advisory Opinion of the International Court of Justice. April 2009. p. 51.

24. Interestingly, there is at least one instance of a declaration of independence in a non-secessionist civil war. During the Chinese Revolution of 1911 that brought Sun Yat-sen to power, provincial governors issued declarations of independence from the Qing central government, but did so with the goal of forming a new kind of national government rather than an independent state. Zarrow 2005, 34.

25. Ponce 2003, 170.

26. See "Manifesto of the Chinese People's Liberation Army," *Selected Works of Mao Tse-tung*, transcribed by the Maoist Documentation Project, 2004, http://www.marxists.org/reference/archive/mao/selected-works/volume-4/mswv4_22.htm.

27. Ibid.

28. The principle of self-determination first made global headlines during the French Revolution, and thus well precedes the twentieth century. But as it pertained to national groups seeking independent statehood, World War I appears to have been the turning point for its prominence on the world stage.

29. Finnemore 1996, 136.

30. Coggins 2014b.

31. Goertz, Diehl, and Balas 2016, 124–26.

32. Tir 2005, 731–32.

33. Chenoweth and Stephan 2011, 7.

34. Kinzer 1991.

35. Resolution 787 (1992), available on UN.org, accessed February 25, 2014, http://www.un.org/en/ga/search/view_doc.asp?symbol=S/RES/787(1992).

36. See UNSC Res 2056 (5 July 2012), cited in Tancredi 2014, 258.

37. Anna Arque of the Catalan group "Welcome, Mr. President . . . to the Independent State of Catalonia," interview with author, July 26, 2011. Catalan attempts to create a referendum on independence have been thwarted by the Spanish government. At the time of this writing, Catalan secessionists have conducted an independence referendum and declared independence and are now in a standoff with Madrid over their future.

38. I do not code groups such as the Islamic State, which seek to resurrect religiously based territorial sovereignties, as secessionist groups for two reasons. First, the territorial boundaries conceived by these groups are not clearly delimited. And second, these types of groups do not seek a state that would operate within the existing international community. Fazal 2018, 28–29.

39. The number of government troops deployed for a given conflict is taken from C-WIT in the first instance. When C-WIT does not contain this variable, it is taken from the Correlates of War number of military personnel.

40. Cunningham, Gleditsch, and Salehyan 2009, 574–75.

41. Wood 2010, 606.

42. Carter and Goemans 2011; Griffiths 2016, 8.

43. Cassese 1995, 123; Horowitz 2003, 72–73; Corten 2006, 232.

44. Elazar 1991; Law 1999; Griffiths 2016.

45. C-WIT distinguishes between groups and factions. A separate group is a rebel organization with distinct political aims as well as a separate military structure (e.g., ULIMO v. NPFL). Factions are subsets of groups; they share the same political goals, but may have distinct military commands. Thus, ULIMO v. Liberia and NPFL v. Liberia constitute two separate observations (war-dyads) in the dataset, but the multitude of Kashmiri factions are all part of one rebel group and hence constitute only one observation in the dataset.

46. Staniland 2012.

47. See for example Cunningham, Bakke, and Seymour 2012; Chenoweth 2010. On factionalization and peace treaties, see D. Cunningham 2006.

48. B. F. Walter 2009, 225.

49. Griffiths 2015.

50. Griffiths defines proto-states as "political jurisdictions with the following traits: (1) They have a minimum population of 1,000 people *and* a minimum size of 100 square kilometers and, (2) They *either* possess complete internal independence (indirect rule), (a) *Or* they are granted specific rights in accordance with a unit-wide ethnic group or nation, (b) *Or* they are the result of a territorial transfer in the last 10 years, (c) *Or* they are separated from the metropole by at least 100 miles." Griffiths 2015, 734–35.

51. The South Moluccan declaration of independence was issued on April 25, 1950, and launched the war for secession. The East Timorese declaration was issued on November 28, 1975; this declaration prompted the invasion by Indonesian forces that led to the secessionist war. The Acehnese declaration was issued on December 4, 1976, as the Free Aceh Movement (GAM) launched its rebellion against Jakarta. The West Papuan declaration of independence was issued in January 1967; the war began in July 1965. Full documentation of all cases is available via the C-WIT narrative reports.

52. For secessionists fighting civil wars in the pre-1945 era, the correlation between the COW force ratio and declaring independence is .16 (*p=.42*). For secessionists fighting civil wars from 1945 on, the correlation is .22 (*p=.22*).

53. Coggins 2006, 160.

54. Binkley 1952, 5.

55. Ibid.

56. Reichstein 1989, 62; Lack 1992, 3.

57. Reichstein 1989, 62.

58. Ibid., 75.

59. Lack 1992, 33.

60. Reichstein 1989, 75.

61. Binkley 1952, 78. In addition, garrisons at Goliad and Nacogdoches issued what were essentially renegade declarations of independence. These lacked legal standing, but were important as signals of public opinion Lack 1992, 70, 80.

62. Reichstein 1989, 136.

63. Binkley 1952, 97, 101, 128.

64. Armitage 2007.

65. Reichstein 1989, 139.

66. Ibid., 141.

67. This is consistent with the findings of an emerging literature on rebel diplomacy, which examines the outward-facing stance of rebel groups toward both specific patrons and the international community in general. Huang 2016; Kaplan 2014; Coggins 2014a.

68. Brackman 1952.

69. Prins 1960, 29–30; Christie 1996, 117–18; Higgins 2009, 170.

70. Chauvel 1990, chap. 18.

71. Brackman 1952.

72. Carter and Goemans 2011; Griffiths 2010.

73. Prins 1960, 36–37.

74. For example, C. Nikijuluw 1950; U.N. Seeks to Halt Amboina Fighting 1950; K. K. Nikijuluw 1952; 1,500 Ambonese March in Hague n.d.; K. J. Nikijuluw 1952.

75. Willem Sopacua, Vice-President of the Government-in-Exile of the Republik Maluku Seletan, correspondence with author, March 18, 2013.

76. Chauvel 1990, 366.

77. UNPO Representatives, interview with author, February 4, 2013.

78. Chauvel 1990, 376–77.

79. For example, see Resolution sent by South Moluccans to Chairman of UNCI, n.d. Series S-0681/Box 15/File 2/Acc. DAG13/2.00/UN Commission for Indonesia (UNCI): South Moluccas Affair (with Annexes).

80. Higgins 2009, 170.

81. Letter from South Moluccan Rep Dr. J. P. Nikjulow to the General Assembly of the United Nations, January 23, 1951. Also see Memorandum by P. W. Lokollo, Plenipotentiary representative and Minister of Food of the Republic Maluku Selatan, September 26, 1950.

UN Archives: Series S-0681/Box 15/File 2/Acc. DAG13/2.00/UN Commission for Indonesia (UNCI): South Moluccas Affair (with Annexes).

82. Thyne 2007, 736.

83. The link between resources and secession is one that has been discussed at length in the Acehnese case. See Aspinall 2007; Morelli and Rohner 2014, 3.

84. Jok and Hutchinson 1999.

85. Ibid., 136.

86. Garang's tenure as vice-president was very brief, as he was killed in a helicopter crash soon after taking office.

87. Thyne 2007, 738.

88. Approximately thirty countries have consular offices in Erbil. More than 130 countries—the majority of the current list of states—recognize Palestine, and national parliaments such as the British parliament as well as sovereign entities such as the Vatican have also recently extended recognition. Palestine is also currently a member of over twenty-five international organizations. Rudoren and Hadid 2015. Department of Foreign Relations, Kurdistan Regional Government, accessed October 13, 2017 http://dfr.gov.krd/p/p.aspx?p=37; Evan Bartlett, "Here are All the Countries that Recognize Palestinian Statehood," *Indy 100*, 2014, accessed May 14, 2015, http://i100.independent.co.uk/article/here-are-all-the-countries-that-recognise-palestinian-statehood--xkVle9I-8e. Iraqi Kurdistan held a referendum on independence in September 2017 but, at this writing, has not issued a formal declaration of independence. Fisher and Taub 2017.

7. Secessionism and Civilian Targeting

1. Civilian targeting is defined here as the conscious use of a strategy of inflicting violence—death or bodily harm—against civilians. This definition is discussed in greater detail below.

2. A recent exception is Fortna 2015.

3. Fazal and Griffiths 2014.

4. Valentino, Huth, and Balch-Lindsay 2004; Downes 2008, esp. 157–60.

5. One exception would be a case where the annexationist state seeks the territory because it is populated by coethnics. Here, we might expect civilian targeting of non-coethnics. Examples of this type of case include the Nagorno-Karabakh war and Russia's 2013 intervention in Crimea.

6. Kalyvas 2006.

7. Weinstein 2007, chap. 6; Salehyan, Siroky, and Wood 2014, 640.

8. K. Cunningham 2014, chap. 6.

9. Jo 2015; Huang 2016; Fortna 2015; Stanton 2015; Coggins 2015.

10. Toft 2003a, 21.

11. See UNSC Resolutions 1193, 1214 (on Afghanistan), 811, 864 (Angola), 771, 780, 1034 (Former Yugoslavia), 1009, 1019 (Croatia), 764, 819, 820 (Bosnia and Herzegovina), 880 (Cambodia), 1272 (East Timor), 993 (Georgia), 446 (Israel), 788, 1001 (Liberia), 812, 846, 918 (Rwanda), 1181, 1231, 1289 (Sierra Leone), 733, and 794 (Somalia). As listed in Samuels 2007, 131n286.

12. List posted on Human Rights Watch website, accessed October 16, 2017, http://www.hrw.org/sites/default/files/related_material/list%20of%20parties%20only.pdf.

13. "Action Plan between the Moro Islamic Liberation Front (MILF) and the United Nations in the Philippines regarding the issue of Recruitment and Use of Child Soldiers in the Armed Conflict in Mindanao," 2010, available on the Geneva Call website, http://theirwords.org/media/transfer/doc/1_ph_milf_biaf_2009_13-d74703efad5c37df5ab9842bc87e67a2.pdf.

14. Pascal Bongard, Policy Director for Geneva Call, interview with author, February 14, 2013.

15. For a similar argument to what follows, see Stanton 2016, 52.

16. Consistent with Wood, there may also be an element of timing, or sequencing, at work here, where secessionists may be most likely to target civilians at the start of a conflict when they are weak and lack other tools to attract supporters, and to cleanse the area they wish to claim in order to be able to make a stronger claim. Examining this logic requires fine-grained geo-referenced time-series data on emerging secessionists not available at present. Wood 2010, 605.

17. The correlation between secessionists that declare independence and those that target civilians is –.26 *(p=.01)* for the 1816–2007 time period. The correlation between secessionists that declare independence and those that target civilians is –.08 *(p=.59)* for the post-Geneva era.

18. For example, Downes, in his discussion of violence against civilians in interstate war, defines civilian victimization as "a military strategy chosen by political or military elites that targets and kills noncombatants intentionally or which fails to discriminate between combatants and noncombatants and thus kills large number of the latter" (Downes 2008, 13). In the case of civil war, Kalyvas defines violence as "the deliberate infliction of harm on people" and limits his analysis to violence against civilians, defined as "those who are not full-time members of an armed group" (Kalyvas 2006, 19).

19. Eck and Hultman 2007, 235.

20. Global Terrorism Database, "Codebook: Inclusion Criteria and Variables," p. 6, June 2017, National Consortium for the Study of Terrorism and Responses to Terrorism (START) website, http://www.start.umd.edu/gtd/downloads/Codebook.pdf.

21. Wood 2010, 604.

22. Cunningham, Bakke, and Seymour 2012.

23. Kalyvas and Balcells 2010; Fazal and Fortna 2013.

24. Fearon and Laitin 2003, 75.

25. The Chinese Civil War, following Mao's advice regarding insurgency, eventually became a conventional war.

26. Kalyvas and Balcells code for a third type of military strategy, "symmetric nonconventional" (SNC), which they say occurs "when the military technologies of the states and rebels are matched at a low level" Kalyvas and Balcells 2010, 418. C-WIT does not code for SNC wars. For the purposes of this book, this exclusion is not relevant, as SNC refers to government, not rebel, warfighting.

27. J. E. Mueller 2004, 19–20.

28. *Insurgency* and *secessionist* show a weak positive correlation, but this correlation is not statistically significant.

29. Human Rights Watch 2013a.

30. Weinstein 2007, chap. 6.

31. Morrow 2014, 116.

32. Eubank and Weinberg 1994; Stanton 2013, 1013; Chenoweth 2013.

33. Downes 2007.

34. Note, however, that there is an inverse relationship between democracy and civil wars. The democracies that are involved in civil wars are already outliers and may defy expectations in this respect as well.

35. For example, the Freedom House "Freedom in the World" dataset contains the second most commonly used measure (after the Polity score); it covers from 1972 to the present. Pzeworski et al.'s measure of democracy covers the post-1950 period; Bernhard et al. cover from 1991 to 1995; the Economist Intelligence Unit Democracy Index project begins with 2007. It is important to note that the practice of using Polity in analyses of civil war has been

criticized because Polity includes measures of civil war in some of its coding. But this issue is more salient for analyses of the onset of war rather than its conduct, as here. Vreeland 2008.

36. Results using an ordinary least squares model instead of logistic regression are stable.

37. A useful extension of this analysis would be to examine the sequencing of civilian targeting. Given the large substantive effect of reciprocity, it would be interesting to know which side tends to target civilians first.

38. Downes 2008, 71, 74–75; Valentino, Huth, and Balch-Lindsay 2004, 395.

39. Morrow 2007, 565.

40. Weinstein 2007, chap. 6.

41. Stanton 2013, 1016; Stanton 2016, 94–95.

42. Wood 2010, 608.

43. Data on targets were taken from coder's reports on wars in C-WIT.

44. Hawramy 2013; Chivers 2008; Blagov 2008; Omer 2014.

45. Lilja and Hultman 2011.

46. Ibid., 5.

47. Aspinall 2009, 73.

48. Ibid., 172–73, 191.

49. K. Cunningham 2011, chap. 6.

50. Earlier attempts to include civil wars, or "non-international armed conflicts," under IHL include Common Article 3 of the 1949 Geneva Conventions as well as Article 19 of the 1954 Hague Convention for the Protection of Cultural Property.

51. International Committee of the Red Cross, Article 1(4) of Protocol I, accessed June 28, 2013, http://www.icrc.org/applic/ihl/ihl.nsf/Article.xsp?action=openDocument&documentId=6C86520D7EFAD527C12563CD0051D63C.

52. Sivakumaran 2011, 222–24.

53. It is possible that there is a reporting bias in the dataset that is driving this result. As these violations become less acceptable to the international community, they may be more likely to be written about, and thus more likely to be noted by the coders for later wars. A related logic has been used to show that terrorism is systematically overreported in democracies or underreported in other regime types; human rights violations may be subject to a similar reporting bias. Drakos and Gofas 2006; Fariss 2014.

54. International legal scholars tend to give less weight to the 1977 Additional Protocols than to the 1949 Geneva Conventions because fewer states have ratified the Additional Protocols. As discussed above, however, and also in chapter 1, the Additional Protocols are critical because they are the major laws of war that explicitly apply to civil conflict.

55. Splitting the data into pre- and post-1977 samples yields insignificant findings for all coefficients, largely because the post-1977 sample is quite small. Rotating the base category also yields indeterminate findings; the most consistent result is that pre-1977 secessionists are especially unlikely to engage in civilian targeting (compared to all other base categories). That said, previous scholarship that focused primarily on post-1989 cases (and used a lower threshold for armed conflict, based on UCDP data) has found secessionism to have a negative and significant impact on civilian targeting. See for example Jo 2015, chap. 5.

56. Fabry 2010, chap. 3.

57. For a similar logic, see Fearon 1994, 239–44.

58. Griffiths 2016.

59. Fazal and Griffiths 2014, 86, 99.

60. That is, secessionist movements coded as having reached the Correlates of War threshold of 1,000 battle deaths.

61. These findings are consistent with Cunningham's analysis of self-determination movements, although she only examines the post-1960 era. K. Cunningham 2011, 279, 282.

62. Another interesting extension would entail modeling the possible selection effect here. Doing so would require extensive data on all—violent and nonviolent—secessionist groups, as well as an instrument that could be used to predict the first stage (selection into violent secessionism) but not the second stage (civilian targeting by secessionists). Such a model would necessarily limit the researcher's ability to compare secessionists to nonsecessionists.

63. For a similar claim regarding human rights violations, see Fariss 2014.

64. Stanton 2016, 98.

65. Binkley 1952, 107.

66. Lack 1992, 101, 222.

67. Ibid., 102.

68. Ibid., chaps. 7, 8.

69. Ibid., 187–89.

70. Ibid., 200.

71. Binkley 1952, 97; Reichstein 1989, 144.

72. Chauvel 1990, 389. If true, this strategy would be consistent with Kuperman's argument about moral hazard and intervention. 2008.

73. Petition to UNSC from "South Moluccan Youth," 17 October, 1950. UN Archives: Series S-0681/Box 15/File 2/Acc. DAG13/2.00/UN Commission for Indonesia (UNCI): South Moluccas Affair (with Annexes).

74. Nikijuluw letter to UNCI Chairman, 9 October 1950 UN Archives: SeriesS-0681/Box 15/File 2/Acc. DAG13/2.00/UN Commission for Indonesia (UNCI): South Moluccas Affair (with Annexes).

75. Telegram, Nikiljuluw to UNCI Secretariat, 1 August 1950. UN Archives: Series S-0681/Box 15/File 2/Acc. DAG13/2.00/UN Commission for Indonesia (UNCI): South Moluccas Affair (with Annexes).

76. While there were occasional flights, most South Moluccans did not have the funds to pay for airfare. As no large commercial boats traveled from Ambon to Jakarta in the 1950s, travel to Jakarta would have meant a risky 1,500-mile trip in a small boat. Willem Sopacua, vice president, RMS government-in-exile, interview with author, February 4, 2013.

77. World: Analysis Sudan 1999; Sudan's Cruel War 1986.Also see United Nations Security Council Resolution 1265.

78. Aid Group Says Sudan Bombed Its Hospital 2000; Axworthy Criticizes Sudan for Attacks 2000.

79. York 1993.

80. O'Loughlin 1997.

81. Berkeley 1996.

82. Cunningham, Bakke, and Seymour 2012, 73.

83. Goertz, Diehl, and Balas 2016, 15.

84. Chenoweth and Stephan do not make much of this important exception to their main finding, but it is easily explained by their argument. They argue that nonviolence trumps violence because it tends to attract a larger base of participants; it is easier to convince people to participate in a nonviolent protest than it is to persuade them to take up arms and risk their lives. Secessionists have an inherently limited participation base—they are geographically and, typically, ethnically circumscribed. Given that secessionists are unlikely to recruit national support for their cause, it is not surprising that broad-based nonviolence will be relatively unsuccessful for them.

85. Coggins 2011.

86. It is possible that secessionists look to nearby cases. Some scholars' arguments suggest that adjacent secessionists are relatively scarce, for reasons explained in B. F. Walter 2009. More recent scholarship suggests that secessionism may, in fact, be contagious. See Cunningham and Sawyer 2017.

87. We are unlikely to observe such cases, as government civilian targeting is typically more frequent and severe than that conducted by rebels, particularly in secessionist conflicts. There are only a handful of cases in C-WIT where secessionists targeted civilians, but governments did not. Several of those cases, such as that of the Two Sicilies, are idiosyncratic. One case that is more on point is that of the Moros in the Philippines in the early 2000s. While not singled out by groups such as the ICRC, the Moro Islamic Liberation Front (MILF) has appeared on the UN Secretary-General's "list of shame" for its use of child soldiers. The MILF's response was extremely positive. Not only did they conclude an Action Plan with the UN agreeing not to use child soldiers, they also signed Geneva Call's Deeds of Commitment on Child Soldiering and Anti-Personnel Land Mines.

88. Jo 2015, chaps. 3, 6, 7; Lasley and Thyne 2014, 290.

89. Geneva Call website, accessed October 17, 2017, www.genevacall.org. Geneva Call offers a platform for rebel groups to commit to comply with IHL. For analyses of which groups tend to make these commitments, see Fazal and Konaev 2016; Richters 2014; Gleditsch, Hug, Schubiger, and Wucherpfennig 2016.

90. Coggins 2014b, 9; Griffiths 2016, 8.

8. Peace Treaties in Civil War

1. B. Walter 2001, chap. 2.
2. Toft 2009, 51–52; Matanock 2017, 79; Walter 2001, 5-6; Howard 2003, 1.
3. Bell 2008, chaps. 6–9.
4. Regan 2000; Fortna 2008; Howard 2008; Beardsley 2011; Beber 2010; Bercovitch 1995; Mattes and Savun 2009; Matanock n.d.; Hartzell and Hoddie 2007; Joshi, Melander, and Quinn 2015; Akebo 2013.
5. Toft 2009, esp. 24, 150; De Rouen et al. 2010; Stedman, Rothchild, and Cousens 2002; B. Walter 2014. Fearon and Laitin make the interesting point that some peace treaties effectively mask military (usually government) victory. 2008, 12. C-WIT allows for this possibility. In other words, peace treaties and military victory are not treated as mutually exclusive categories. C-WIT shows 19 cases of rebel victory and peace treaties, 23 cases of government victory and peace treaties, and 14 cases of neither side being victorious and peace treaties from 1816–2007.
6. Fazal 2013.
7. Beardsley 2011, 201.
8. Svensson 2007a; Svensson 2007b.
9. Fortna 2008, 173.
10. Mattes and Savun 2009.
11. Hartzell and Hoddie 2007.
12. Matanock 2017.
13. Joshi, Melander, and Quinn 2015.
14. Toft 2009.
15. One difference is that in civil war I relax the requirement of ratification, as rebel groups typically lack formal ratification mechanisms.
16. Bell 2008, 95–96.
17. Kreutrz 2010, 245.
18. Joshi, Quinn, and Regan 2015, 552.
19. Belloni 2007, chap. 1; Ramet 2006, chap. 16.
20. Davidow and Harvard University Center for International Affairs 1984, chap. 8.
21. Rodil 2000, chap. 6.
22. Balasingham 2004, 110–13, annexure 1; Peiris 2009, 35–36.

23. Toft 2009, 7, fig. 1.1.

24. Doyle and Sambanis 2006.

25. Toft 2009, 52.

26. Beardsley 2011, 22, 23–24. The support for the pacific settlement of disputes is replicated in the Charter of the Organization of American States, the 2004 Rome Treaty of the European Union, and the NATO Charter. Interestingly, it is not replicated in the Charter of the African Union, which focuses more explicitly on respect of sovereignty of members.

27. United Nations | Field Support, "Field Support Facts," April 16, 2015, http://www.un.org/en/peacekeeping/operations/financing.shtml.

28. United Nations Peacemaker: Mediation Support Overview, accessed October 17, 2017, http://peacemaker.un.org/mediation-support.

29. Bell 2008, 44.

30. Katia Papagianni, Center for Humanitarian Dialogue, email message to author, May 19, 2016.

31. Beardsley 2011, 74.

32. Keller 2017, 138.

33. Beardsley 2011, 20.

34. Mitchell 1992, 277.

35. Guelke 2008, 68; Beardsley 2011, 20.

36. Akebo 2013, 110.

37. Kirsten Shutze, as quoted in Aspinall 2009, 227.

38. King 2001, 525.

39. Indeed, this is one of the major critiques of the ICC. Allan 2010, 243; Vinjamuri 2010, 196.

40. Akebo 2013, 200.

41. As part of these negotiations, the Sri Lankan prime minister Ranil Wickremesinghe "announced the renunciation of the classification of the LTTE as a terrorist organization. . . . This extended recognition to the LTTE and allowed it to enter into negotiations with the government as an equal partner" (Akebo 2013, 176). After a ceasefire agreement was reached, however, LTTE attacks restarted after a brief hiatus, and the prime minister's party fell from power. For a rich summary of this process, see Akebo 2013, chap. 5.

42. Beardsley 2011, 20, 32. Girod finds that the efficacy of aid depends on a combination of the resource wealth of the state experiencing civil war and the strategic importance of that state to a donor. Somewhat similarly, Donno argues that IGOs are particularly likely to require reforms of governments when there is a combination of good monitoring (e.g., election monitors) and geopolitical interest. It is possible that similar factors could influence the nature of the international community's leverage over states, as well as a government's decision to join peace talks. Girod 2012; Donno 2010.

43. Maigua 2014.

44. UN Calls for an End to Violence 2014.

45. UN-Arab League Mediation Process for Syria Crisis "On Track" 2012.

46. Libya: UN Calls for Peaceful Resolution 2013.

47. Harf 2015.

48. Unanimously Adopting Resolution 2211 (2015) 2015.

49. UN Annual Resolution on Western Sahara 2015.

50. Laub 2015.

51. UN Chief Calls for Negotiations 2015.

52. Aspinall 2009, 224–25.

53. Indeed, scholars such as Michael Doyle and Nicholas Sambanis suggest that peacekeeping operations may be especially likely to be deployed to cases where peace treaties have

been signed. Doyle and Sambanis 2006, 103–4. Data from C-WIT verify this claim; of the twenty-one cases involving both peacekeeping and peace treaties from 1816–2007, about half of the peacekeeping missions were deployed after the conclusion of the peace treaty, and provision for peacekeeping was sometimes included as one of the terms of the peace treaty.

54. Beardsley 2011, 47.

55. Melin and Svensson 2009. Separately, Svensson argues that mediators biased in favor of the government can help balance the scales between government opposition to, and rebel support for, mediation. Svensson 2007a.

56. Schultz 2010, 306.

57. Hasballah Saad, as quoted in Akebo 2013, 101.

58. *Partnering for Peace* 2012, 20.

59. These special representatives include Kofi Annan, Lakdar Brahimi, and Staffan de Mistura.

60. See Beber 2010, 1, for a useful review of the literature on this point.

61. Cases of rebel victory are fairly evenly distributed across the slight, clear, and extreme victory categories, with an additional four cases in the category of military victory by a third party.

62. If the war ended in a tie or draw, this variable is coded as zero, even though one could argue that a draw is often considered a victory for rebels.

63. C-WIT's military outcome codes for one other possibility—military victory by a third party. This is a very rare occurrence, with only four cases.

64. Toft 2010, 13-14.

65. Toft 2009, figure 1.1, p. 7.

66. Fortna 2009, 1; Toft 2010, 14.

67. Zartman 1985, 220. Conversely, however, it could also be that mediation or stronger forms of intervention could create a mutually hurting stalemate. Beardsley 2011, 34, citing Chester Crocker.

68. D. Cunningham 2006; Nilsson 2008; Hultquist 2013; Clayton 2013; Findley 2012; Gent 2011; Cunningham, Gleditsch, and Salehyan 2009.

69. Toft 2010, 5-9.

70. Fortna 2008; Gilligan and Stedman 2003; Doyle and Sambanis 2006.

71. Beber 2010, 140.

72. Beardsley 2011, chap. 3, 72–76, 205. Note that one difference between my analysis and Beardsley's is that he includes a broad range of peace agreements—such as ceasefires and truces—while my focus is exclusively on peace treaties. That said, we end up with very similar results, which should lend greater strength to the claim that mediation is strongly related to peace agreements.

73. Quoted in Lack 1992, 104.

74. W. Davis 2004, 282–83.

75. The British did attempt mediation after the treaty failed, but without success. Reichstein 1989, 170.

76. W. Davis 2004, 285.

77. Reichstein 1989, 170.

78. W. Davis 2004, 282.

79. Karen Parker, "Republik Maluku: The Case for Self-Determination," Briefing Paper of the Humanitarian Law Project, International Education Development, Association of Humanitarian Lawyers, accessed June 30, 2014 http://www.humanlaw.org/KPmaluku.html#33.

80. Prins 1960, 39.

81. The UNCI chairman expressed concern about extremist anti-Amboinese elements in Indonesia. Translation of a post-card received by Team Co-ordinator 2A, BANDOENG through ordinary postal channels, and dictated by Team Co-ordinator to Lt. Col. E. F. Aitken at 1130 hrs. 11 October 1950. UN Archives: SeriesS-0681/Box 15/File 2/Acc. DAG13/2.00/ UN Commission for Indonesia (UNCI): South Moluccas Affair (with Annexes).

82. UNCI Telegram to UN, n.d. UN Archives: SeriesS-0681/Box 15/File 2/Acc. DAG13/ 2.00/UN Commission for Indonesia (UNCI): South Moluccas Affair (with Annexes).

83. Prins 1960, 41–42.

84. Khalid 2003, 332–33, 335.

85. Ibid., 337; Sudan: Towards an Incomplete Peace 2003, 14, 16, 24.

86. Rolandsen 2013, 78–79.

87. Khalid 2003, 372.

88. Thyne 2007, 748.

89. Rolandsen 2013, 76.

90. Melin and Svensson 2009, 255.

91. Sudan: Towards an Incomplete Peace 2003, 11.

92. Rolandsen 2013, 79.

93. Collins 2008, 268. Rebels in Darfur were opposed to the CPA on the grounds that it would free up the government to prosecute its war against them in the west, and that a comprehensive agreement should cover the entire country, not just the South. Sudan: Towards an Incomplete Peace 2003, 19.

94. Collins 2008, 268.

95. Rolandsen 2013, 76–77.

96. Implementing Sudan's Comprehensive Peace Agreement 2008.

97. Related, Tir and Karreth find that membership in "highly structured international governmental organizations"—such as the UN or IMF—tends to produce enough pressure on members experiencing low-level conflict that membership itself ends up acting as a restraint on the likelihood of escalation to civil war. In such cases, states experiencing low-level conflict that are members of these IGOS are especially likely to sign peace agreements. Tir and Karreth 2018.

98. Beardsley 2011, 111.

99. Gurses, Rost, and McLeod 2008.

Evasion, Engagement, and the Laws of War

1. Allansson, Melander, and Themnér 2017.

2. Themnér and Wallensteen 2015, 536.

3. Bonnie Docherty, email message to author, July 7, 2016.

4. Bonnie Docherty, telephone interview with author, July 14, 2015.

5. Ibid.

6. Scharre and Horowitz 2015.

7. Gartzke 2013; Rid 2013; Waxman 2011.

8. Tallinn is the capital of Estonia, which suffered a massive distributed denial-of-service attack, allegedly from Russia, in 2007.

9. M. Schmitt 2013, x–xii.

10. In this respect, it is similar to the San Remo Manual on International Law Applicable to Armed Conflicts at Sea.

11. The creation of such a treaty is unlikely given the speed of technological development in this realm, which only heightens the importance of the Tallinn Manual.

12. Michael Schmitt, telephone interview with author, July 16, 2015.

13. See for example document A/68/98*, "Group of Governmental Experts on Developments in the Field of Information and Telecommunications in the Context of International Security," June 24, 2013, http://www.un.org/ga/search/view_doc.asp?symbol=A/68/98.

14. Michael Schmitt, telephone interview with author, July 16, 2015.

15. Fazal and Konaev 2016; Gleditsch et al. 2016.

16. Chenoweth and Stephan 2011, 7.

17. Aspinall 2009, 228.

18. Cunningham and Sawyer 2017.

19. For example, there is a version of the football World Cup for secessionist movements that has counted Kurdistan and South Ossetia as participants. M. Fischer 2014.

20. "Countries That Have Recognized Kosovo as an Independent State," accessed October 18, 2017, http://www.beinkosovo.com/countries-that-have-recognized-kosovo-as-an-independent-state/.

21. Dean Bialek of Independent Diplomat, interview with author, July 7, 2011. Contested sovereignty over Western Sahara has also stalled Morocco's plans for solar plants in the region. El Yaakoubi 2014.

22. Nissenbaum and Parkinson 2014.

23. Fazal and Griffiths 2014, 94.

24. IISS 2017.

25. Beardsley 2011, 153.

26. This statistic is based on an analysis of the number of provisions in comprehensive peace agreements. Data drawn from the Peace Accords Matrix.

27. Toft 2009, esp. chap 9.

28. A seminal work is Cooley and Ron 2002.

29. Prominent examples include Carpenter 2014; Barnett 2011; Avant, Finnemore, and Sell 2010.

References

1,500 Ambonese March in Hague; Seek Home Rule. n.d. *New York Times*. November 7.

Abulof, Uriel. 2013. Normative Concepts Analysis: Unpacking the Language of Legitimation. *International Journal of Social Research Methodology* 18 (1): 73–89.

Ackerman, David A., and Richard F. Grimmett. 2002. Declarations of War and Authorizations for the Use of Military Force: Background and Legal Implications. In *Declarations of War*, edited by Ernest V. Klun, 1–118. New York: Novinka Books.

Aid Group Says Sudan Bombed Its Hospital. 2000. *New York Times*, March 4.

Akebo, Malin. 2013. The Politics of Ceasefires: On Ceasefire Agreements and Peace Processes in Aceh and Sri Lanka. PhD diss., Umea University.

Aldrich, John H., Christopher Gelpi, Peter D. Feaver, Jason Reifler, and Kristin Thompson Sharp. 2006. Foreign Policy and the Electoral Connection. *Annual Review of Political Science* 9: 477–502.

Allan, Kate. 2010. Prosecution and Peace: A Role for Amnesty before the ICC. *Denver Journal of International Law* 39: 239–302.

Allansson, Marie, Erik Melander, and Lotta Themnér. 2017. Organized Violence, 1989–2017. *Journal of Peace Research* 54 (4): 574–89.

Arkin, James. 2015. After One Year of War on ISIS, No AUMF in Sight. *RealClearPolitics*, August 5.

Armitage, David. 2007. *The Declaration of Independence: A Global History*. Cambridge, MA: Harvard University Press.

——. 2017. *Civil Wars: A History in Ideas*. New York: Alfred A. Knopf.

Aspinall, Edward. 2007. The Construction of Grievance: Natural Resources and Identity in a Separatist Conflict. *Journal of Conflict Resolution* 51 (6): 950–72.

——. 2009. *Islam and Nation: Separatist Rebellion in Aceh, Indonesia*. Stanford: Stanford University Press.

Associated Press. 2016. Senate Will Not Take Up Obama's War Powers Request to Fight ISIS. *PBS News Hour*, January 10. http://www.pbs.org/newshour/rundown/senate-will-not-take-up-obamas-new-war-powers-request-to-fight-isis/.

Avant, Deborah D., Martha Finnemore, and Susan K. Sell, eds. 2010. *Who Governs the Globe?* Cambridge: Cambridge University Press.

Axworthy Criticizes Sudan for Attacks. 2000. *Globe and Mail*, March 8.

Balasingham, Anton. 2004. *War and Peace: Armed Struggle and Peace Efforts of the Liberation Tigers*. Mitcham, England: Fairmax Publishing.

Balz, Dan, and Richard Morin. 2004. Bush Poll Numbers on Iraq at New Low. *Washington Post*, May 25, A01.

Barnett, Michael. 2011. *Empire of Humanity: A History of Humanitarianism*. Ithaca, NY: Cornell University Press.

Bayram, Burcu. 2017. Due Deference: Cosmopolitan Social Identity and the Psychology of Legal Obligation in International Politics. *International Organization* 71 (S1): S137–63.

Bean, Richard. 1973. War and the Birth of the Nation-State. *Journal of Economic History* 33 (1): 203–21.

Beardsley, Kyle. 2011. *The Mediation Dilemma*. Ithaca, NY: Cornell University Press.

Beber, Bernd. 2010. International Mediation of Military Conflicts: Causes and Consequences. PhD diss, Columbia University.

Bell, Christine. 2008. *On the Law of Peace: Peace Agreements and the Lex Pacificatoria*. Oxford: Oxford University Press.

Belloni, Roberto. 2007. *State Building and International Intervention in Bosnia*. Security and Governance Series. London: Routledge.

Benvenisti, Eyal, and Amichai Cohen. 2014. War is Governance: Explaining the Logic of the Laws of War From a Principal-Agent Perspective. *Michigan Law Review* 112 (8): 1363–1416.

Bercovitch, Jacob. 1995. *Resolving International Conflicts: The Theory and Practice of Mediation*. Boulder: Lynne Rienner Publishers.

Berkeley, Bill. 1996. The Longest War in the World. *New York Times Magazine*, March 3.

Best, Geoffrey. 1980. *Humanity in Warfare*. New York: Columbia University Press.

——. 1994. *War and Law since 1945*. Oxford: Clarendon Press.

Betts, Richard K. 2001. Compromised Command. *Foreign Affairs*, July/August.

Bierman, Noah. 2015. Few Have Faced Consequences for Abuses at Abu Ghraib Prison in Iraq. *Los Angeles Times*, March 17.

Bilefsky, Dan. 2010. World Court Rules Kosovo Declaration Was Legal. *New York Times*, July 22, A4.

Bill, Brian, and Jeremy Marsh. 2010. *Operational Law Handbook*. Edited by Center for Law and Military Operations. Charlottesville, VA.

Binkley, William C. 1952. *The Texas Revolution*. Baton Rouge: Louisiana State University Press.

Blagov, Sergei. 2008. Russia Pays Millions in Rewards After Killing of Chechen Leader. *cnsnews.com*, July 7.

Bob, Clifford. 2005. *The Marketing of Rebellion: Insurgents, Media, and International Activism*. Cambridge Studies in Contentious Politics. New York: Cambridge University Press.

Booth, William, and Karen DeYoung. 2014. "Deeply Concerned" Obama sends warning on Crimea. *Washington Post*, March 1.

Borgen, Christopher. 2008. Kosovo's Declaration of Independence: Self-Determination, Secession and Recognition. *ASIL Insights* 12 (2), February 29. https://www.asil.org/insights/volume/12/issue/2/kosovos-declaration-independence-self-determination-secession-and.

Bothe, Michael. 2010. Kosovo—So What? The Holding of the International Court of Justice is Not the Last Word on Kosovo's Independence. *German Law Journal* 11 (7/8): 837–40.

Brackman, Arnold C. 1952. World's Forgotten War Ending in Spice Islands. *Christian Science Monitor*, July 29.

Brands, H. W. 1995. *The Reckless Decade: America in the 1890s*. New York: St. Martin's Press.

Braumoeller, Bear. 2013. Is War Disappearing? Paper presented at the Annual Meeting of the American Political Science Association, Chicago, IL.

Brody, Reed. 2004. *The Road to Abu Ghraib*. New York: Human Rights Watch.

Browne, Malcome W. 1971. Emergency Is Set. *New York Times*, November 24, p. A1.

Brownlie, Ian. 1963. *International Law and the Use of Force by States*. Oxford: Oxford University Press.

———. 1971. *Basic Documents on African Affairs*. Oxford: Oxford University Press.

Bruno, Greg. 2008. U.S. Security Agreements and Iraq. In *Backgrounder*, New York: Council on Foreign Relations. Last updated December 23. https://www.cfr.org/backgrounder/us-security-agreements-and-iraq.

Bryce, Trevor. 2006. The "Eternal Treaty" from the Hittite Perspective. *British Museum Studies in Ancient Egypt and Sudan* 6: 1–11.

Burke, S. M. 1973. The Postwar Diplomacy of the Indo-Pakistani War of 1971. *Asian Survey* 13 (11): 1036–49.

Byman, Daniel, and Sarah Kreps. 2010. Agents of Destruction? Applying Principal-Agent Analysis to State-Sponsored Terrorism. *International Studies Perspectives* 11: 1–18.

Cardoso, Oscar R., Ricardo Kirschbaum, and Eduardo Van Der Kooy. 1987. *Falklands—The Secret Plot*. Translated by Bernard Estell. East Molesy, UK: Preston Editions.

Carpenter, R. Charli. 2014. *"Lost" Causes: Agenda Vetting in Global Issue Networks and the Shaping of Human Security*. Ithaca, NY: Cornell University Press.

Carter, David, and Hein Goemans. 2011. The Making of the Territorial Order: New Borders and the Emergence of Interstate Conflict. *International Organization* 65 (2): 275–309.

Cassese, Antonio. 1995. *Self-Determination of Peoples: A Legal Reappraisal*. New York: Cambridge University Press.

Catalonia's Leaders Plan Secession from Spain. 2015. In *The Takeaway*, Public Radio International, April 16. https://www.pri.org/stories/2015-04-16/catalonias-leaders-plan-secession-spain.

Chameau, Jean-Lou, William F. Ballhaus, and Herbert S. Lin. 2014. *Emerging and Readily Available Technologies and National Security—A Framework for Addressing Ethical, Legal and Societal Issues.* Washington, DC: National Research Council and National Academy of Engineering of The National Academies.

Chauvel, Richard. 1990. *Nationalists, Soldiers and Separatists: The Ambonese Islands from Colonialism to Revolt, 1880–1950, Verhandelingen van het Koninklijk Instituut voor Taal-, Land- en Volkenkunde.* Leiden: KITLV Press.

Cheibub, José Antonio, Jennifer Gandhi, and James Raymond Vreeland. 2010. Democracy and Dictatorship Revisited. *Public Choice* 143: 67–101.

Chenoweth, Erica. 2010. Democratic Competititon and Terrorist Activity. *Journal of Politics* 72 (1): 16–30.

———. 2013. Terrorism and Democracy. *Annual Review of Political Science* 16: 355–78.

Chenoweth, Erica, and Maria Stephan. 2011. *Why Civil Resistance Works: The Strategic Logic of Nonviolent Conflict.* New York: Columbia University Press.

Chivers, C. J. 2008. Chechen Government Intensifies Scare Tactics, Rebels' Families Say. *New York Times,* September 29.

Christie, Clive J. 1996. *A Modern History of Southeast Asia: Decolonization, Nationalism and Separatism.* London New York: Tauris Academic Studies.

Cicero. 1913. *De Officiis.* Translated by Walter Miller. Loeb Classical Library. Cambridge, MA: Harvard University Press.

Cirkovic, Elena. 2010. An Analysis of the ICJ Advisory Opinion on Kosovo's Unilateral Declaration of Independence. *German Law Journal* 11 (7/8): 895–912.

Clayton, Govinda. 2013. Relative Rebel Strength and the Onset and Outcome of Civil War Mediation. *Journal of Peace Research* 50 (5): 609–22.

Clodfelter, Micheal. 2008. *Warfare and Armed Conflicts: A Statistical Encyclopedia of Casualty and Other Figures, 1494–2007.* Third ed. Jefferson, NC: McFarland & Company, Inc.

Coggins, Bridget. 2006. Secession, Recognition, and the International Politics of Statehood. PhD diss., Ohio State University.

———. 2011. Friends in High Places: International Politics and the Emergence of States from Secessonism. *International Organization* 65: 433–67.

———. 2014a. Petitioning Power: Rebel Diplomats and the Search for Independence. Working paper, University of California, Santa Barbara.

———. 2014b. *Power Politics and State Formation in the Twentieth Century: The Dynamics of Recognition.* Cambridge: Cambridge University Press.

———. 2014c. Secession and Rebel Diplomacy: Evidence from the Former Yugoslavia. Paper presented at the Annual Meeting of the American Political Science Association. Washington, DC.

———. 2015. Terrorism, Substitution, and Unintended Consequences: Do International Incentives Change the Intensity of Civil Wars? Working paper, University of California–Santa Barbara.

Collins, Robert O. 2008. *A History of Modern Sudan.* Cambridge: Cambridge University Press.

Committee to Protect Journalists. 2003. CPJ Releases Investigative Report on Palestine Hotel Attack. Press release, May 27.

Cooley, Alexander, and James Ron. 2002. The NGO Scramble: Organizational Insecurity and the Political Economy of Transnational Action. *International Security* 27 (1): 5–39.

Coox, Alvin D. 1985. *Nomonhan: Japan against Russia, 1939.* Stanford, CA: Stanford University Press.

Coppedge, Michael, Staffan Lindberg, Svend-Erik Skaaning, and Jan Teorell. 2015. Measuring High Level Democratic Principles using the V-Dem Data. *International Political Science Review* 37 (5): 580–93.

Cornwell, Rupert. 1999. Bitter Armenian Dispute Edges towards Accord. *Independent,* November 17.

Correspondence Relating to the War with Spain, Including the Insurrection in the Philippine Islands and the China Relief Expedition, between the Adjutant-General of the Army and Military Commanders in the United States, Cuba, Porto Rico, and the Philippine Islands from April 15, 1898 to July 30, 1902. 1902. Washington: Government Printing Office.

Corten, Olivier. 2006. Are There Gaps in the International Law of Secession? In *Secession: International Law Perspectives,* edited by Marcelo Kohen, 231–54. Cambridge: Cambridge University Press.

Council, Command of the Defence. 2004. British Maritime Document, edited by Ministry of Defence. Norwich, UK: Crown.

Cowan, Edward J. 2003. *'For Freedom Alone': The Declaration of Arbroath, 1320,* Scottish History Matters Series. East Linton: Tuckwell Press.

Cunha, Euclides da. 1964. *Rebellion in the Backlands (Os sertões).* Translated by Samuel Putnam. Chicago: University of Chicago Press.

Cunningham, David. 2006. Veto Players and Civil War Duration. *American Journal of Political Science* 50 (4): 875–92.

Cunningham, David, Kristian Skrede Gleditsch, and Idean Salehyan. 2009. It Takes Two: A Dyadic Analysis of Civil War Duration and Outcome. *Journal of Conflict Resolution* 53 (4): 570–97.

Cunningham, David, and Douglas Lemke. 2013. Combining Civil and Interstate Wars. *International Organization* 67 (3): 609–27.

Cunningham, Kathleen Gallagher. 2011. Divide and Conquer or Divide and Concede: How Do States Respond to Internally Divided Separatists? *American Political Science Review* 105 (2): 275–97.

——. 2014. *Inside the Politics of Self-Determination.* Oxford: Oxford University Press.

Cunningham, Kathleen Gallagher, Kristen Bakke, and Lee J. M. Seymour. 2012. Shirts Today, Skins Tomorrow: Dual Contests and the Effects of Fragmentation in Self-Determination Disputes. *Journal of Conflict Resolution* 56 (1): 67–93.

Cunningham, Kathleen Gallagher, and Katherine Sawyer. 2017. Is Self-Determination Contagious? A Spatial Analysis of the Spread of Self-Determination Claims. *International Organization* 71 (3): 585–604.

Daly, Sarah Zukerman. 2016. *Organized Violence After Civil War: The Geography of Recruitment in Latin America.* New York: Cambridge University Press.

Dasgupta, C. 2002. *War and Diplomacy in Kashmir, 1947–48.* New Delhi: Sage.

Davidow, Jeffrey, and Harvard University Center for International Affairs. 1984. *A Peace in Southern Africa: The Lancaster House Conference on Rhodesia, 1979*. Westview Special Studies on Africa. Boulder: Westview Press.

Davis, Calvin DeArmond. 1962. *The United States and the First Hague Peace Conference*. Ithaca, NY: Cornell University Press.

——. 1975. *The United States and the Second Hague Peace Conference: American Diplomacy and International Organization, 1899–1914*. Durham, NC: Duke University Press.

Davis, William C. 2004. *Lone Star Rising: The Revolutionary Birth of the Texas Republic*. New York: Free Press.

De Rouen, Karl, Mark J. Ferguson, Samuel Norton, Young Hwan Park, Jenna Lea, and Ashley Streat-Bartlett. 2010. Civil War Peace Agreement Implementation and State Capacity. *Journal of Peace Research* 47 (3): 333–46.

Detrez, Raymond. 2011. Recent International Advisory Opinion. *Harvard Law Review* 124 (4): 1098–1105.

Diamond, Jeremy. 2015. War Debate Looms for Congress. *CNN*, February 15.

Dillon, G. M. 1989. *The Falklands, Politics and War*. Houndmills: Macmillan Press.

Dixon, William J. 1994. Democracy and the Peaceful Settlement of International Conflict. *American Political Science Review* 88 (1): 14–32.

Dobbs, Michael. 2003. Halliburton's Deals Greater than Thought. *Washington Post*, August 28.

Donno, Daniela. 2010. Who is Punished? Regional Intergovernmental Organizations and the Enforcement of Democratic Norms. *International Organization* 64 (4): 593–625.

Dougherty, Beth K. 2007. Colombia. In *Civil Wars of the World: Major Conflicts Since World War II*, edited by Karl De Rouen and Uk Heo, 125–42. Santa Barbara: ABC-CLIO.

Downes, Alexander B. 2006. Desperate Times, Desperate Measures: The Causes of Civilian Victimization in War. *International Security* 30 (4): 152–95.

——. 2007. Restraint or Propelland? Democracy and Civilian Fatalities in Interstate Wars. *Journal of Conflict Resolution* 51 (6): 872–904.

——. 2008. *Targeting Civilians in War*. Ithaca: Cornell University Press.

Downes, Alexander B., and Jonathan Monten. 2013. Forced to be Free?: Why Foreign-Imposed Regime Change Rarely Leads to Democratization. *International Security* 37 (4): 90–131.

Doyle, Michael W., and Nicholas Sambanis. 2006. *Making War and Building Peace: United Nations Peace Operations*. Princeton, NJ: Princeton University Press.

Drakos, Konstantinos, and Andreas Gofas. 2006. The Devil You Know but Are Afraid to Face: Underreporting Bias and its Distorting Effects on the Study of Terrorism. *Journal of Conflict Resolution* 50 (5): 714–35.

Dudziak, Mary L. 2012. *War Time: An Idea, Its History, Its Consequences*. New York: Oxford University Press.

Duiker, William J. 1978. *Cultures in Collision: The Boxer Rebellion*. San Rafael, CA: Presidio Press.

Dunant, J. Henry. 1939 (1862). *A Memory of Solferino (Un Souvenir de Solferino)*. Washington, DC: The American National Red Cross.

Eck, Kristine, and Lisa Hultman. 2007. One-Sided Violence against Civilians in War: Insights from New Fatality Data. *Journal of Peace Research* 44 (2): 233–46.

Eddy, Paul, Magnus Linklater, and Peter Gillman. 1982. *The Falklands War*. London: Deutsch.

El Yaakoubi, Aziz. 2014. Western Sahara Dispute Dims Morocco's Solar Dreams. *Reuters*, January 2.

Elazar, Daniel. 1991. *Federal Systems of the World: A Handbook of Federal, Confederal, and Autonomy Arrangements*. Essex, UK: Longman Current Affairs.

Elsea, Jennifer K., and Matthew C. Weed. 2014. *Declarations of War and Authorizations for the Use of Military Force: Historical Background and Legal Implications*. Washington, DC: Congressional Research Service.

Epps, Garrett. 2016. Can the Courts Make Congress Declare War? *Atlantic*, June 1.

Estado., Spain. Ministerio del. 1905. *Spanish Diplomatic Correspondence and Documents, 1896–1900. Presented to the Cortes by the Minister of State [Translation]*. Washington, DC: Government Printing Office.

Etsthus, Raymond A. 1988. *Double Eagle and Rising Sun: The Russians and Japanese at Portsmouth in 1905*. Durham: Duke University Press.

Eubank, William, and Leonard Weinberg. 1994. Does Democracy Encourage Terrorism? *Terrorism and Political Violence* 6 (4): 417–43.

Evangelista, Matthew. 2008. *Law, Ethics, and the War on Terror*. Cambridge: Polity.

Fabry, Mikulas. 2010. *Recognizing States: International Society and the Establishment of New States since 1776*. Oxford: Oxford University Press.

Falklands, Iran, Palestine, Issues of Mrs. Kirchner Address to UN Assembly. 2010. *MercoPress*, September 24. http://en.mercopress.com/2010/09/24/falklands-iran-palestine-issues-of-mrs-kirchner-address-to-un-assembly.

Fariss, Christopher J. 2014. Respect for Human Rights has Improved Over Time: Modeling the Changing Standard of Accountability. *American Political Science Review* 108 (2): 297–318.

Fazal, Tanisha M. 2007. *State Death: The Politics and Geography of Conquest, Occupation, and Annexation*. Princeton, NJ: Princeton University Press.

———. 2013. The Demise of Peace Treaties in Interstate War. *International Organization* 67 (4): 695–724.

———. 2014. Dead Wrong? Battle Deaths, Military Medicine, and the Exaggerated Reports of War's Demise. *International Security* 39 (1): 95–125.

———. 2015. Is the Islamic State a Secessionist Movement? Blog post for the International Relations and Security Network, Zurich. http://www.css.ethz.ch/content/specialinterest/gess/cis/center-for-securities-studies/en/services/digital-library/articles/article.html/188149.

———. 2018. Religionist Rebels and the Sovereignty of the Divine. *Daedalus* 147 (1): 25–35.

Fazal, Tanisha M., and Virginia Page Fortna. 2013. Guerrillas in the Mist: Civil War and Insurgency, 1816–2007. Paper presented at the Annual Meeting of the International Studies Association, San Francisco, CA.

Fazal, Tanisha M., Virginia Page Fortna, Jessica Stanton, and Alex Weisiger. 2012. War Initiation and Termination (WIT) Coding Instrument and Data Set. Working paper, Columbia University.

Fazal, Tanisha M., and Brooke C. Greene. 2015. A Particular Difference: European Identity and Civilian Targeting. *British Journal of Political Science* 45 (4): 829–51.

Fazal, Tanisha M., and Ryan D. Griffiths. 2014. Membership Has its Privileges: The Changing Benefits of Statehood. *International Studies Review* 16 (1): 79–106.

Fazal, Tanisha M., and Margarita Konaev. 2016. Homelands Versus Minelands: When and Why do Rebel Groups Commit to Adhere to the Laws of War? Paper presented at the Annual Meeting of the International Studies Association, Atlanta, GA.

Fearon, James D. 1994. Signaling Versus the Balance of Power and Interests: An Empirical Test of a Crisis Bargaining Model. *Journal of Conflict Resolution* 38 (2): 236–69.

Fearon, James D., and David D. Laitin. 2003. Ethnicity, Insurgency, and Civil War. *American Political Science Review* 97 (1): 75–90.

——. 2008. Civil War Termination. Working paper, Stanford University.

Felter, Joseph, and Jacob Shapiro. 2017. Limiting Civilian Casualties as Part of a Winning Strategy: The Case of Courageous Restraint. *Daedalus*. 146 (1): 44–58

Fierstein, Daniel. 2008. Kosovo's Declaration of Independence: An Incident Analysis of Legality, Policy and Future Implications. *Boston University International Law Journal* 26 (2): 417.

Final Record of the Diplomatic Conference of Geneva of 1949. 1949. Berne: Federal Political Department.

Final Report to the Prosecutor by the Committee Established to Review the NATO Bombing Campaign Against the Federal Republic of Yugoslavia. N.d The Hague: ICTY.

Findley, Michael G. 2012. Bargaining and the Interdependent Stages of Civil War Resolution. *Journal of Conflict Resolution* 57 (5): 905–32.

Finnemore, Martha. 1996. *National Interests in International Society.* Ithaca, NY: Cornell University Press.

Finnemore, Martha, and Kathryn Sikkink. 1998. International Norm Dynamics and Political Change. *International Organization* 52 (4): 887–917.

Fischer, Dana. 1982. Decisions to Use the International Court of Justice: Four Recent Cases. *International Studies Quarterly* 26 (2): 251–77.

Fischer, Martha. 2014. Forget Brazil 2014: The Alternative World Cup. *French Football Weekly*, June 11.

Fisher, Ian, and Edward Wong. 2004. Battles in Najaf and Karbala Near Shiite's Religious Sites. *New York Times*, May 15, 9.

Fisher, Max, and Amanda Taub. 2017. A Will to Secede Doesn't Always Mean There's a Way. *New York Times*, September 29, A10.

Forrest, Craig. 2010. *International Law and the Protection of Cultural Heritage.* London: Routledge Press.

Fortna, Virginia Page. 2004. *Peace Time: Cease-Fire Agreements and the Durability of Peace.* Princeton, NJ: Princeton University Press.

——. 2008. *Does Peacekeeping Work? Shaping Belligerents' Choices after Civil War.* Princeton, NJ: Princeton University Press.

——. 2009. Where Have all the Victories Gone? Peacekeeping and War Outcomes. Paper presented at the Annual Meeting of the American Political Science Association, Toronto, Canada.

———. 2013. Has Violence Declined in World Politics? A Discussion of Joshua S. Goldstein's *Winning the War on War: The Decline of Armed Conflict Worldwide*. *Perspectives on Politics* 11 (2): 566–70.

———. 2015. Do Terrorists Win? Rebels' Use of Terrorism and Civil War Outcomes. *International Organization* 69 (3): 519–56.

Four Days Later from Europe: Official Declaration of War Between Turkey and Russia. 1853. *New York Times*, October 31, 2.

Fox, James. 1997. *Dictionary of International and Comparative Law*. 2nd ed. Dobbs Ferry, NY: Oceana Publications.

Freedman, Lawrence. 1988. *Britain and the Falklands War*. Making Contemporary Britain. Oxford: Basil Blackwell.

———. 2005. *The Official History of the Falklands Campaign*. 2 vols. Whitehall Histories, Government Official History Series. London: Routledge.

Freedman, Lawrence, and Virginia Gamba-Stonehouse. 1991. *Signals of War: The Falklands Conflict of 1982*. Princeton, N.J.: Princeton University Press.

Freedom in the World: Discarding Democracy: Return to the Iron Fist. 2015. Freedom House. https://freedomhouse.org/report/freedom-world/freedom-world-2015#. WejQWEyZNBw.

Freeman, Samuel, ed. 1999. *John Rawls: Collected Papers*. Cambridge, MA: Harvard University Press.

Fry, Dougls P., ed. 2013. *War, Peace, and Human Nature: The Convergence of Evolutionary and Cultural Views*. Oxford: Oxford University Press.

Gabriel, Richard A. 2013. *Between Flesh and Steel: A History of Military Medicine from the Middle Ages to the War in Afghanistan*. 1st ed. Washington, DC: Potomac Books.

Ganguly, Sumit. 2002. *Conflict Unending: India-Pakistan Tensions since 1947*. New York: Columbia University Press; Washington, DC: Woodrow Wilson Center Press.

Garner, Bryan, ed. 2004. *Black's Law Dictionary*. 8th ed. St. Paul, MN: Thomson West.

Gartzke, Erik. 2013. The Myth of Cyberwar: Bringing War in Cyberspace Back Down to Earth. *International Security* 38 (2): 41–73.

Gent, Stephen. 2011. Relative Rebel Strength and Power Sharing in Intrastate Conflicts. *International Interactions* 37: 215–28.

Gerring, John. 2007. *Case Study Research: Principles and Practices*. Cambridge: Cambridge University Press.

Gibler, Douglas M. 2012. *The Territorial Peace: Borders, State Development, and International Conflict*. Cambridge: Cambridge University Press.

Gilligan, Michael J., and Stephen John Stedman. 2003. Where Do the Peacekeepers Go? *International Studies Review* 5 (4): 37–54.

Girod, Desha M. 2012. Effective Foreign Aid Following Civil War: The Nonstrategic-Desperation Hypothesis. *American Journal of Political Science* 56 (1): 188–201.

Gleditsch, Kristian Skrede, Simon Hug, Livia Isabella Schubiger, and Julian Wucherpfennig. 2016. International Conventions and Non-State Actors: Selection, Signaling, and Reputation Effects. *Journal of Conflict Resolution*. 62 (2): 346–80.

Goertz, Gary. 2017. *Multimethod Research, Causal Mechanism, and Case Studies: The Research Triad*. Princeton: Princeton University Press.

Goertz, Gary, Paul Diehl, and Alexandru Balas. 2016. *The Puzzle of Peace: The Evolution of Peace in the International System*. New York: Oxford University Press.

Goldberg, Carey. 1992. Armenia Choking as Economic Stranglehold Tightens. *Los Angeles Times*, September 20.

Goldstein, Joshua S. 2011. *Winning the War on War: The Decline of Armed Conflict Worldwide*. New York: Dutton.

Goltz, Thomas. 1994. Severed Ears, Slavery and the Azeri: A Forgotten, Brutal War. *Washington Post*, August 7.

Greene, Brooke C. 2009. Normative Ambiguity and the Limits of Compliance: Noncombatant Immunity in America's (Not Too) Recent Wars. Working paper, Columbia University.

Grewe, Wilhelm G. 1992. Peace Treaties. In *Encyclopedia of Public International Law*, edited by Rudolf Bernhardt, 3:938–46. Amsterdam: Max Planck Institute for Comparative Public Law and International Law.

Griffin, Stephen M. 2010. The Legal Justification for the Vietnam War: Backwards and Forwards with Nicholas deB. Katzenbach. Paper presented at The American Experience in Southeast Asia, 1946–1975, US Department of State.

Griffiths, Ryan D. 2010. Catch and Release: Expansion, Contraction, and the Downsizing of States. PhD diss., Columbia University.

——. 2015. Between Dissolution and Blood: How Administrative Lines and Categories Shape Outcomes. *International Organization* 69 (3): 731–51.

——. 2016. *Age of Secession: The International and Domestic Determinants of State Birth*. Cambridge: Cambridge University Press.

Grimmer, Justin, and Brandon Stewart. 2013. Text as Data: The Promise and Pitfalls of Automatic Content Analysis Methods for Political Texts. *Political Analysis* 21 (3): 267–97.

Grob, Fritz. 1949. *The Relativity of War and Peace: A Study in Law, History, and Politics*. New Haven, CT: Yale University Press.

Grotius, Hugo. 1738. *The Rights of War and Peace*. Translated by J. Barbeyrac. 3 vols. London: Innis & Manby.

Guelke, Adrian. 2008. Negotiations and Peace Processes. In *Contemporary Peacemaking: Conflict, Peace Processes and Post-War Reconstruction*, edited by John Darby and Roger MacGinty, 63–77. New York: Palgrave MacMillan.

Gurr, Ted Robert, Monty Marshall, and Keith Jaggers. 2014. Polity IV Project: Political Regime Characteristics and Transitions, 1800–2013. Polity IV Individual Country Regime Trends, 1946–2013. Last updated June 6. http://www.systemicpeace.org/polity/polity4.htm.

Gurses, Mehmet, Nicolas Rost, and Patrick McLeod. 2008. Mediating Civil War Settlements and the Duration of Peace. *International Interactions* 34: 129–55.

Hallett, Brien. 1998. *The Lost Art of Declaring War*. Urbana: University of Illinois Press.

——. 2013. *Declaring War: Congress, the President, and What the Constitution Does Not Say*. Cambridge: Cambridge University Press.

Harf, Marie. 2015. United States Calls for Peaceful Resolution to Crisis in Burundi. Edited by Department of State. Washington, DC.

Hartzell, Caroline, and Matthew Hoddie. 2007. *Crafting Peace: Power-Sharing Institutions and the Negotiated Settlement of Civil Wars.* University Park: Pennsylvania State University Press.

Hathaway, Oona. 2002. Do Human Rights Treaties Make a Difference? *Yale Law Journal* 111 (8): 1935–2042.

Hathaway, Oona A., and Scott J. Shapiro. 2017. *The Internationalists: How a Radical Plan to Outlaw War Remade the World.* New York: Simon & Schuster.

Hawramy, Fazel. 2013. Kurdish Security Forces Shield Region from Iraq Security Woes. *Al Monitor*, July 24.

Hazen, Jennifer. 2013. *What Rebels Want: Resources and Supply Networks in Wartime.* Ithaca, NY: Cornell University Press.

Heinisz, Witold J. 2002. The Institutional Environment for Infrastructure Investment. *Industrial and Corporate Change* 11 (2): 355–89.

Hendrickson, Kenneth E. 2003. *The Spanish-American War.* Westport, CT: Greenwood Press.

Hendrickson, Ryan C. 2015. *Obama at War: Congress and the Imperial Presidency.* Lexington: University Press of Kentucky.

Herron, Michael, and Kevin Quinn. 2009. A Careful Look at Modern Qualitative Case Selection Methods: Dartmouth University. *Sociological Methods and Research* 45 (3): 458–92.

Hersh, Seymour M. 2004. Torture at Abu Ghraib. *New Yorker*, May 10.

Higgins, Noelle. 2009. *Regulating the Use of Force in Wars of National Liberation. A Study of the South Moluccas and Aceh.* Leiden: Brill.

Hobson, Richmond Pearson. 1987. *The Sinking of the "Merrimac."* Annapolis: Naval Institute Press.

Holquist, Peter. 2015. Codifying the "Laws and Customs of War." Paper presented at The Laws of War as an International Regime: History, Theory, and Prospects, Princeton University.

Holsti, Ole. 2004. *Public Opinion and American Foreign Policy.* Ann Arbor: University of Michigan Press.

Hopgood, Stephen. 2013. *The Endtimes of Human Rights.* Ithaca, NY: Cornell University Press.

Horowitz, Donald L. 2003. A Right to Secede? In *Secession and Self-Determination*, edited by Stephen Macedo and Allen Buchanan, 50–76. New York: New York University Press.

Howard, Lise Morjé. 2003. The Rise and Decline of the Norm of Negotiated Settlement. Paper presented at Georgetown Junior Faculty Workshop on Intervention, Washington, DC.

——. 2008. *UN Peacekeeping in Civil Wars.* Cambridge: Cambridge University Press.

Howell, William, and Jon Pevehouse. 2007. *While Dangers Gather: Congressional Checks on Presidential War Powers.* Princeton, NJ: Princeton University Press.

Hozier, Henry Montague. 1877–79. *The Russo-Turkish War.* London: William MacKenzie.

Huang, Reyko. 2016. Rebel Diplomacy in Civil Wars. *International Security* 40 (4): 89–126.

Hull, Isabel. 2014. *A Scrap of Paper: Breaking and Making International Law during the Great War*. Ithaca, NY: Cornell University Press.

Hultquist, Philip. 2013. Power Parity and Peace? The Role of Relative Power in Civil War Settlement. *Journal of Peace Research* 50 (5): 623–34.

Human Rights Watch. 2013a. *Death from the Skies: Deliberate and Indiscriminate Air Strikes on Civilians*. April 10. https://www.hrw.org/report/2013/04/10/death-skies/deliberate-and-indiscriminate-air-strikes-civilians.

——. 2013b. *La Plaine des Morts*. December 3. https://www.hrw.org/fr/news/2013/12/03/tchad-le-regime-de-hissene-habre-commis-des-atrocites-systematiques.

——. 2015. Hissene Habré. Available from https://www.hrw.org/tag/hissene-habre.

Human Security Report Project. 2012. *Human Security Report 2012: Sexual Violence, Education, and War: Beyond the Mainstream Narrative*. Vancouver: Human Security Press.

Hunt, Lynn. 2007. *Inventing Human Rights: A History*. New York: W. W. Norton.

Hurd, Ian. 2007. *After Anarchy: Legitimacy & Power in the United Nations Security Council*. Princeton, NJ: Princeton University Press.

ICRC. 1977. Official Records of the Diplomatic Conference on the Reaffirmation and Development of International Humanitarian Law Applicable in Armed Conflicts, Geneva (1974–1977). Berne: Federal Political Department.

IISS. 2017. Armed Conflict Database, edited by IISS. Accessed October 18, 2017. https://acd.iiss.org.

Implementing Sudan's Comprehensive Peace Agreement: Prospects and Challenges. 2008. Washington, DC: Woodrow Wilson International Center for Scholars.

India Country Profile. 2015. In *NTI*. Last updated June. http://www.nti.org/learn/countries/india/biological/.

International Court of Justice, ed. 1976. Case Concerning Trial of Pakistani Prisoners of War. The Hague.

——, ed. 2010. Accordance with International Law of the Unilateral Declaration of Independence in Respect of Kosovo. The Hague.

Jack, Homer A. 1998. The India-Pakistan Crisis at the United Nations. In *50 Years of Indo-Pak Relations, Vol. I*, edited by Verinder Grover and Ranjana Arora, 499–518. New Delhi: Deep & Deep.

Jackson, Robert Victor, and International Institute for Strategic Studies. 1975. *South Asian Crisis: India, Pakistan, and Bangla Desh; A Political and Historical Analysis of the 1971 War*. Praeger Special Studies in International Politics and Government. New York: Praeger.

Jahan, Rounaq. 1972. *Pakistan: Failure in National Integration*. New York: Columbia University Press.

Japan Rejects Putin's Claim It is to Blame for Stalled Islands Talks. 2015. *Japan Times*, April 18.

Jo, Hyeran. 2015. *Compliant Rebels*. Cambridge: Cambridge University Press.

Jo, Hyeran, and Beth A. Simmons. Forthcoming. Can the International Criminal Court Deter Atrocity? *International Organization*.

Jo, Hyeran, and Catarina Thomson. 2013. Legitimacy and Compliance with International Law: Access to Detainees in Civil Conflicts, 1991–2006. *British Journal of Political Science* 44 (2): 323–55.

Johnson, James Turner. 1997. *The Holy War Idea in Western and Islamic Traditions.* University Park: Pennsylvania State University Press.

Jok, Jok Madut, and John F. Hutchinson. 1999. Sudan's Prolonged Second Civil War and the Militarization of Nuer and Dinka Ethnic Identities. *African Studies Review* 42 (2):125–45.

Jolly, Rick. 2002. Surgeon Commander, Falklands Field Hospital. In *Memories of the Falklands*, edited by Iain Dale, 73–75. London: Politico Publishing.

Jones, Daniel M., Stuart A. Bremer, and J. David Singer. 1996. Militarized Interstate Disputes, 1816–1992: Rationale, Coding Rules, and Empirical Patterns. *Conflict Management and Peace Science* 15 (2): 163–213.

Jones, Anthony R., and George R. Fay. 2004. *Executive Summary: Investigation of Intelligence Activities at Abu Ghraib.* Combined Joint Task Force Seven, United States Army.

Joshi, Madhav, Eric Melander, and Jason Michael Quinn. 2015. Sequencing the Peace: How the Order of Peace Agreement Implementation Can Reduce the Destabilizing Effects of Post-accord Elections. *Journal of Conflict Resolution* 61 (1): 4–28.

Joshi, Madhav, Jason Michael Quinn, and Patrick Regan. 2015. Annualized Implementation Data on Comprehensive Intrastate Peace Accords, 1989–2012. *Journal of Peace Research* 52 (4): 551–62.

Kahl, Colin. 2007. In the Crossfire or the Crosshairs? Norms, Civilian Casualties, and US Conduct in Iraq. *International Security* 32 (1): 7–46.

Kahler, Miles. 2011. State Building and State Survival: Polynesia in the 19th Century. Paper presented at the Annual Meeting of the American Political Science Association, Seattle, WA.

Kalyvas, Stathis N. 1999. Wanton and Senseless?: The Logic of Massacres in Algeria. *Rationality and Society* 11 (3): 243–85.

———. 2006. *The Logic of Violence in Civil War.* Cambridge: Cambridge University Press.

Kalyvas, Stathis N., and Laia Balcells. 2010. International System and Technologies of Rebellion: How the End of the Cold War Shaped Internal Conflict. *American Political Science Review* 104 (3): 415–29.

Kaplan, Morgan. 2014. Strategies of Insurgent Diplomacy: Evidence from the Middle East and North Africa. Paper presented at the Annual Meeting of the International Studies Association, Toronto, Canada.

Karon, Tony. 2004. How the Prison Scandal Sabotages the US in Iraq. *Time*, May 4.

Katzenbach, Nicholas deB. 2008. *Some of It Was Fun: Working with RFK and LBJ.* 1st ed. New York: W. W. Norton & Co.

Kecskemeti, Paul. 1964. *Strategic Surrender: The Politics of Victory and Defeat.* 1st Atheneum ed. New York: Atheneum.

Keller, Nora. 2017. From Guns to Roses: Explaining Rebel Use of Nonviolent Action. PhD diss., Columbia University.

Kelly, John. 1963. *A Forgotten Conference: The Negotiations at Peking, 1900–1901.* Geneva: Librairie E. Droz, 1963.

Keown-Boyd, Henry. 1991. *The Fists of Righteous Harmony: A History of the Boxer Uprising in the Year 1900.* London: Leo Cooper.

Kershner, Isabel. 2014. After Failed Peace Talks, Pushing to Label Israel as Occupier of Palestine. *New York Times*, May 4.

Khalid, Mansour. 2003. *War and Peace in Sudan: A Tale of Two Countries.* London: Kegan Paul.

King, Charles. 2001. The Benefits of Ethnic War: Understanding Eurasia's Unrecognized States. *World Politics* 53 (4): 524–52.

King, Gary, Robert O. Keohane, and Sidney Verba. 1994. *Designing Social Inquiry: Scientific Inference in Qualitative Research.* Princeton, NJ: Princeton University Press.

King, Gary, Michael Tomz, and Jason Wittenberg. 2000. Making the Most of Statistical Analyses: Improving Interpretation and Presentation. *American Journal of Political Science* 44 (2): 341–55.

Kinsella, Helen M. 2011. *The Image Before the Weapon: Critical History of the Distinction between Combatant and Civilian.* Ithaca, NY: Cornell University Press.

Kinzer, Stephen. 1991. Germans Follow Own Line on Yugoslav Republics. *New York Times,* December 8.

Kippenberg, Juliane. 2004. *The International Criminal Court: How Nongovernmental Organizations Can Contribute to the Prosecution of War Criminals.* Human Rights Watch. September 10. https://www.hrw.org/report/2004/09/10/international-criminal-court/how-nongovernmental-organizations-can-contribute.

Koch, Michael T., and Stephen P. Nicholson. 2015. Death and Turnout: The Human Costs of War and Voter Participation in Democracies. *American Journal of Political Science* 60 (4): 932–46.

Korman, Sharon. 1996. *The Right of Conquest: The Acquisition of Territory by Force in International Law and Practice.* Oxford: Clarendon Press.

Koskenniemi, Martti. 2002. *The Gentle Civilizer of Nations: The Rise and Fall of International Law 1870–1960.* Cambridge: Cambridge University Press.

——. 2006. *From Apology to Utopia: The Structure of International Legal Argument.* Cambridge: Cambridge University Press.

Krasner, Stephen D. 1999. *Sovereignty: Organized Hypocrisy.* Princeton, NJ: Princeton University Press.

Kreutz, Joakim. 2010. How and When Armed Conflicts End: Introducing the UCDP Conflict Termination Dataset. *Journal of Peace Research* 47 (2): 243–50.

Kuperman, Alan J. 2008. The Moral Hazard of Humanitarian Intervention: Lessons from the Balkans. *International Studies Quarterly* 52 (1): 49–80.

Lack, Paul D. 1992. *The Texas Revolutionary Experience: A Political and Social History, 1835–1836.* College Station: Texas A&M University Press.

Lasley, Trace, and Clayton Thyne. 2014. Secession, Legitimacy and the Use of Child Soldiers. *Conflict Management and Peace Science* 32 (3): 289–308.

Laub, Zachary. 2015. Low Expectations for UN Syria Talks. *Council on Foreign Relations,* May 6. https://www.cfr.org/interview/low-expectations-un-syria-talks.

Lauterpacht, Elihu. 1968. The Legal Irrelevance of the "State of War." Paper presented at the Annual Meeting of the American Society of International Law, Washington, DC.

Lauterpacht, Hersh. 1947. *Recognition in International Law.* Cambridge: Cambridge University Press.

Law, Gwillim. 1999. *Administrative Subdivisions of Countries: A Comprehensive World Reference, 1900 through 1998.* Jefferson, NC: McFarland.

Leatherby, Lauren. 2015. Whatever Happened to the Debate over Use of Force against ISIS? *National Public Radio*, June 17.

Legal Lessons Learned from Afghanistan and Iraq. 2004. Vol. 1. *Major Combat Operations (11 September 2001 to 1 May 2003)*. Charlottesville, VA: Center for Law and Military Operations.

Levie, Howard S. 1985. The Falklands Crisis and the Laws of War. In *The Falklands War: Lessons for Strategy, Diplomacy, and International Law*, edited by Alberto R. Coll and Anthony C. Arend, 64–77. Boston: George Allen & Unwin.

Lewis, Michael W. 2003. The Law of Aerial Bombardment in the 1991 Gulf War. *American Journal of International Law* 97 (3): 481–509.

Libya: UN Calls for Peaceful Resolution of Disputes after Attack on Government Official. 2013. UN News Centre. http://www.un.org/apps/news/story.asp?NewsID=44312#. WejxhkyZNBw.

Lilja, Jannie, and Lisa Hultman. 2011. Intraethnic Dominance and Control: Violence Against Co-Ethnics in the Early Sri Lankan Civil War. *Security Studies* 20 (2): 171–97.

Lo, Nigel, Barry Hashimoto, and Dan Reiter. 2008. Ensuring Peace: Foreign-Imposed Regime Change and Postwar Peace Duration, 1914–2001. *International Organization* 62: 717–36.

Lohr, Michael F., and Steve Gallotta. 2003. Legal Support in War: The Role of Military Lawyers. *Chicago Journal of International Law* 4 (2): 465–78.

Lok Sabha Debates 1962. Vol. 9. Third Congress. New Delhi, India: Lok Sabha Secretariat, 1962.

Lyall, Jason. 2014. Why Armies Break: Explaining Mass Desertion in Conventional War. Unpublished manuscript.

Maigua, Patrick. 2014. UN Offers to Mediate over the Ukrainian Political Crisis. United Nations Radio. March 3. http://www.unmultimedia.org/radio/english/2014/03/un-offers-to-mediate-over-the-ukrainian-political-crisis/#.Wejy5EyZNBw.

Mantilla, Giovanni. 2013. Under (Social) Pressure: The Historical Regulation of Internal Armed Conflicts through International Law. PhD diss., University of Minnesota.

Marshall, Monty, Keith Jaggers, and Ted Robert Gurr. 2011. Polity IV Project: Political Regime Characteristics and Transitions, Dataset Users' Manual: Center for Systemic Peace.

Martins, Mark S. 1994. Rules of Engagement for Land Forces: A Matter of Training, Not Lawyering. *Military Law Review* 143: 4–160.

Matanock, Aila. 2017. *Electing Peace: From Civil Conflict to Political Participation.* Cambridge: Cambridge University Press.

Matinuddin, Kamal. 1994. *Tragedy of Errors: East Pakistan Crisis, 1968–1971.* 1st ed. Lahore, Pakistan: Wajidalis.

Mattes, Michaela, and Burcu Savun. 2009. Fostering Peace after Civil War: Commitment Problems and Agreement Design. *International Studies Quarterly* 53 (3): 737–60.

Maurice, Sir John Frederick. 1883. *Hostilities without Declaration of War: An Historical Abstract of the Cases in which Hostilities Have Occurred between Civilized Powers Prior to Declaration or Warning, from 1700 to 1870.* London: H. M. Stationery Office.

McLauchlin, Theodore. 2010. Loyalty Strategies and Military Defection in Rebellion. *Comparative Politics* 42 (3): 333–50.

Mearsheimer, John J. 1994. The False Promise of International Institutions. *International Security* 19 (3): 5–49.

Melin, Molly M., and Isak Svensson. 2009. Incentives for Talking: Accepting Mediation in International and Civil Wars. *International Interactions* 35: 249–71.

Milanovic, Marko, and Michael Wood, eds. 2015. *The Law and Politics of the Kosovo Advisory Opinion*. Oxford: Oxford University Press.

Mitchell, C. R. 1992. External Peace-Making Initiatives and Intranational Conflict. In *The Internationalization of Communal Strife*, edited by Manus I. Midlarsky, 274–96. New York: Routledge.

Moorehead, Caroline. 1998. *Dunant's Dream: War, Switzerland and the History of the Red Cross*. New York: Carroll & Graf.

Morelli, Massimo, and Dominic Rohner. 2014. Resource Concentration and Civil Wars. NBER Working Paper 20129. Accessed October 13, 2017. http://www.nber.org/papers/w20129.pdf.

Morrow, James D. 2007. When Do States Follow the Laws of War? *American Political Science Review* 101 (3): 559–72.

——. 2014. *Order within Anarchy: The Laws of War as an International Institution*. Cambridge: Cambridge University Press.

Morrow, James D., and Hyeran Jo. 2006. Compliance with the Laws of War: Data Set and Coding Rules. *Conflict Management and Peace Science* 23 (1): 91–113.

Mueller, John. 1989. *Retreat from Doomsday: The Obsolescence of Major War*. New York: Basic Books.

Mueller, John E. 2004. *The Remnants of War*. Ithaca: Cornell University Press.

Musicant, Ivant. 1990. *Empire by Default: The Spanish-American War and the Dawn of the American Century* New York: Henry Holt & Co.

Myers, Stephen Lee. 2014. Putin, Flashing Disdain, Defends Action in Crimea. *New York Times*, March 5.

Neff, Stephen. 2000. *The Rights and Duties of Neutrals: A General History*. Manchester: Juris Publishing.

——. 2004. Peace and Prosperity: Commercial Aspects of Peacemaking. In *Peace Treaties and International Law in European History From the Late Middle Ages to World War One*, edited by Randall Lesaffer, 365–81. Cambridge: Cambridge University Press.

——. 2005. *War and the Law of Nations: A General History*. Cambridge: Cambridge University Press.

Nilsson, Desirée. 2008. Partial Peace: Rebel Groups Inside and Outside of Civil War Settlements. *Journal of Peace Research* 45 (4): 479–95.

Nikijuluw, Charles L. 1950. Stand of South Moluccas: Struggle for Independence is Said to be No Revolt. Letter to the editor. *New York Times*. November 11.

Nikijuluw, Karel K. 1952. Stand of South Molucca: Creation of the Public is Declared Expression of the People's Will. Letter to the editor. *New York Times*. September 22.

Nikijuluw, Karl J. 1952. The War in the Moluccas. *Christian Science Monitor*, 1952

Nimmo, William. 2001. *Stars and Stripes Across the Pacific: The United States, Japan, and Asia/Pacific Region, 1895–1945*. Westport, CT: Praeger.

Nissenbaum, Dion, and Joe Parkinson. 2014. U.S. Giving Military Aid to Kurds in Fight Against Insurgents. *Wall Street Journal*, August 11.

Not a State of War Yet: Policy of the United States is to Prevent a Formal Recognition of War—Other Powers Join It. 1900. *New York Times*, June 22, 2.

Nott, John. 2002. *Here Today, Gone Tomorrow: Recollections of an Errant Politician*. London: Politico's.

O'Connell, Mary Ellen. 2005. *International Law and the Use of Force: Documentary Supplement*. New York: Foundation Press.

——. 2010. *Final Report on the Meaning of Armed Conflict in International Law*. The Hague: International Law Association.

O'Hanlon, Michael, and Ian Livingston. 2010. *Iraq Index: Tracking Variables of Reconstruction & Security in Post-Saddam Iraq*. Washington, DC: Brookings Institution.

O'Keefe, Roger. 2006. *The Protection of Cultural Property in Armed Conflict*. New York: Cambridge University Press.

O'Loughlin, Ed. 1997. Sudan's Southern Rebels Ready for Final Push. *Sydney Morning Herald*, August 30, 25.

Obama to Seek Authority from Congress for Islamic State Fight. 2014. *New York Times*, November 5.

Ober, Joshiah. 1994. Classical Greek Times. In *The Laws of War: Constraints on Warfare in the Western World*, edited by Michael Howard, George J. Andreopoulos and Mark R. Shulman, 12–26. New Haven, CT: Yale University Press.

Oeter, Stefan. 2014. The Role of Recognition and Non-Recognition with Regard to Secession. In *Self-Determination and Secession in International Law*, edited by Christian Walter, Antje von Ungern-Sternberg and Kavus Abushov, 45–67. Oxford: Oxford University Press.

Ofner, John L. 1992. *An Unwanted War: The Diplomacy of the United States and Spain over Cuba, 1895–1898*. Chapel Hill: University of North Carolina Press.

Ohlin, Jens David. 2015. *The Assault on International Law*. Oxford: Oxford University Press.

Omer, Mohammed. 2014. Who Are Israel's Palestinian Informants? *AlJazeera*, September 6.

Oppenheim, Ben, Abbey Steele, Juan F. Vargas, and Michael Weintraub. 2015. True Believers, Deserters, and Traitors: Who Leaves Insurgent Groups and Why. *Journal of Conflict Resolution* 59 (5): 794–823.

Pak Bid to Divert World Opinion Seen. 1973. *Times of India*, May 14, 1.

Pakistan Country Profile. 2015. In *NTI*. Last updated December. http://www.nti.org/learn/countries/pakistan/biological/.

Panico, Christopher. 1994. *Azerbaijan: Seven Years of Conflict in Nagorno-Karabakh*. New York: Human Rights Watch.

Parker, Geoffrey. 1994. Early Modern Europe. In *Laws of War: Constraints on Warfighting in the Western World*, edited by Michael Howard, George J. Andreopoulos and Mark R. Shulman, 40–58. New Haven, CT: Yale University Press.

Parkinson, Sarah. 2013. Organizing Rebellion: Rethinking High-Risk Mobilization and Social Networks in War. *American Political Science Review* 107 (3): 418–32.

Parry, Clive, and John P. Grant. 1986. *Parry and Grant Encyclopaedic Dictionary of International Law*. Dobbs Ferry, NY: Oceana Publications.

Partnering for Peace: Australia's Peacekeeping and Peacebuilding Experiences in the Autonomous Region of Bougainville in Papua New Guinea, and in Solomon Islands and Timor-Leste. 2012. Queanbeyan, NSW: Australian Civil-Military Centre.

Peiris, G. H. 2009. *Twilight of the Tigers: Peace Efforts and Power Struggles in Sri Lanka*. New Delhi: Oxford University Press.

Perry, Elizabeth, and Tom Chang. 1980. The Mystery of Yellow Cliff: A Controversial "Rebellion" in Late Qing. *Modern China* 6 (2): 123–60.

Peter, Fabienne. 2017. Political Legitimacy. In *The Stanford Encyclopedia of Philosophy*, edited by Edward N. Zalta. Summer 2017 Edition. https://plato.stanford.edu/entries/legitimacy/.

Peters, Anne. 2015. Has the AO's Finding that Kosovo's DoI was not Contrary to International Law Set an Unfortunate Precedent? In *The Law and Politics of the Kosovo Advisory Opinion*, edited by Marko Milanovic and Michael Wood, 291–313. Oxford: Oxford University Press.

Peters, Jeremy. Obama Is to Seek War Power Bill From Congress. 2015. *New York Times*. February 11.

Pictet, Jean. 1952. *Commentary to First 1949 Geneva Convention, For the Amelioration of the Condition of the Wounded and Sick in Armed Forces in the Field*. Geneva: International Committee of the Red Cross.

——. 1958. *Commentary to 4th 1949 Geneva Convention, Relative to the Protection of Civilian Persons in Time of War*. Geneva: International Committee of the Red Cross.

——. 1987. *Commentary on the Additional Protocols of 8 June 1977 to the Geneva Conventions of 12 August 1949*. Geneva: International Committee of the Red Cross.

Pinker, Steven. 2011. *The Better Angels of Our Nature: Why Violence Has Declined*. New York: Viking.

Ponce, Alvaro. 2003. *La Rebelion de las Provincias: Relatos Sobre la Revolucion de los conventillos y la guerra de los supremos*. Bogota: Intermedio.

Poole, David. 1998. The Eritrean People's Liberation Front. In *African Guerrillas*, edited by Christopher Clapham, 19–35. Oxford: James Currey.

Posner, Eric. 2014. *The Twilight of Human Rights Law*, Inalienable Rights series. Oxford: Oxford University Press.

Prins, J. 1960. Location, History, Forgotten Struggle. In *The South Moluccas: Rebellious Province or Occupied State*, edited by J. C. Bouman, 9–47 Netherlands: AW Sythoff-Leyden.

Pyke, H. Reason. 1915. *The Law of Contraband of War*. Oxford: Clarendon Press.

Rahman, H. 1997. *The Making of the Gulf War: Origins of Kuwait's Long-Standing Territorial Dispute with Iraq*. Reading, UK: Ithaca Press.

Ramet, Sabrina P. 2006. *The Three Yugoslavias: State-Building and Legitimation, 1918–2005*. Washington, DC: Woodrow Wilson Center Press; Bloomington, IN; Indiana University Press.

Rattenbach. 1988. *Informe Rattenbach: El drama de Malvinas*. Buenos Aires: Ediciones Espartaco.

Rawls, John. 1993. *Political Liberalism*. New York: Columbia University Press.

Records of the Conference Convened by the United Nations Educational, Scientific and Cultural Organization Held at the Hague from 21 April to 14 May 1954. 1954. Paper read at Conference Convened by the United Nations Educational, Scientific and Cultural Organization Held at the Hague from 21 April to 14 May 1954.

Regan, Patrick M. 2000. *Civil Wars and Foreign Powers: Interventions and Intrastate Conflict*. Ann Arbor: University of Michigan Press.

Regan, Patrick M., and Peter Wallensteen. 2013. Federal Institutions, Declarations of Independence and Civil War. *Civil Wars* 15 (3): 261–80.

Reichstein, Andreas V. 1989. *Rise of the Lone Star: The Making of Texas*. Translated by Jeanne R. Willson. College Station: Texas A&M University Press.

Reid, Whitelas. 1965. *Making Peace with Spain: The Diary of Whitelaw Reid*. Austin: University of Texas Press.

Richters, Sven. 2014. Norm Diffusion Beyond the State: Legitimacy and Non-State Actor Commitment to Humanitarian Norms. MA thesis, Graduate Institute of Geneva.

Rid, Thomas. 2013. *Cyberwar Will Not Take Place*. London: C. Hurst & Co.

Roberts, Anthea, and Sandesh Sivakumaran. 2012. Lawmaking by Nonstate Actors: Engaging Armed Groups in the Creation of International Humanitarian Law. *Yale Journal of International Law* 37 (1): 107–52.

Rock, Grey. 1985. Planning and Preparing for a Disaster—Argentina and the Falklands. *Naval Review* 73: 115–21.

Rodil, B. R. 2000. *Kalinaw Mindanaw: The Story of the GRP-MNLF Peace Process, 1975–1996*. Davao City, Philippines: Alternate Forum for Research in Mindanao.

Roeder, Philip G. 2007. *Where Nation-States Come From: Institutional Change in the Age of Nationalism*. Princeton, NJ: Princeton University Press.

Rolandsen, Oystein H. 2013. Sudan: The Role of Foreign Involvement in the Shaping and Implementation of the Sudan Comprehensive Peace Agreement. In *Mediation and Liberal Peacebuilding: Peace from the Ashes of War?*, edited by Mikael Eriksson and Roland Kostic, 76–91. London: Routledge.

Rosenfeld, Harvey. 2000. *Diary of a Dirty Little War: The Spanish-American War of 1898*. Westport, CT: Praeger.

Ross, Michael L. 2004. How Do Natural Resources Influence Civil War? Evidence from Thirteen Cases. *International Organization* 58: 35–67.

Roth, Brad R. 2010. Secessions, Coups and the International Rule of Law: Assessing the Decline of the Effective Control Doctrine. *Melbourne Journal of International Law* 11 (2): 1–48.

Rothenberg, Gunther. 1994. The Age of Napoleon. In *The Laws of War: Constraints on Warfare in the Western World*, edited by Michael Howard, George J. Andreopoulos and Mark R. Shulman, 86–97. New Haven, CT: Yale University Press.

Rozman, Gilbert. 2000. Introduction. In *Japan and Russia: The Tortuous Path to Normalization, 1949–1999*, edited by Gilbert Rozman, 1–14. New York: St. Martin's Press.

Rudoren, Jodi, and Diaa Hadid. 2015. Vatican to Recognize Palestinian State in New Treaty. *New York Times*, May 13.

Rugman, Jonathan. 1995. Armenia Pays Dearly for Karabakh Victory. *Guardian*, September 16, 14.

Russell, Frederick. 1975. *The Just War in the Middle Ages*. Cambridge: Cambridge University Press.

Russian Declaration of War against Turkey. 1828. *London Times*, May 4.

Ryngaert, Cedric. 2010. The ICJ's Advisory Opinion on Kosovo's Declaration of Independence: A Missed Opportunity? *Netherlands International Law Review* 57 (3): 481–94.

Sahadevan, P. 2013. Managing Internal Conflicts in India, Nepal, Sri Lanka and Myanmar: Strategies and Outcomes. In *Policy Choices in Internal Conflicts: Governing Systems and Outcomes*, 77–189. New Delhi: Vij Books India Pvt Limited.

Salehyan, Idean, David Siroky, and Reed Wood. 2014. External Rebel Sponsorship and Civilian Abuse: A Principal-Agent Analysis of Wartime Atrocities. *International Organization* 68 (3): 633–61.

Samuels, Kirsti. 2007. *Political Violence and the International Community: Developments in Law and Policy*. The Hague: Martinus Nijhoff Publishers.

Sandholtz, Wayne. 2007. *Prohibiting Plunder: How Norms Change*. New York: Oxford University Press.

——. 2010. Plunder, Restitution, and International Law. *International Journal of Cultural Property* 17: 147–76.

Sargent, Greg. 2015. Obama's War Authorization Request Is Way Too Broad. And the Damage Has Already Been Done. *Washington Post*, February 11.

Sarkees, Meredith Reid, and Frank Whelon Wayman. 2010. *Resort to War: 1816–2007*. Washington, DC: CQ Press.

Sattar, Abdul. 1998. Simla Pact: Negotiation Under Duress. In *50 Years of Indo-Pak Relations, Vol. I*, edited by Verinder Grover and Ranjana Arora, 472–96. New Delhi: Deep & Deep Publications.

Scharre, Paul, and Michael Horowitz. 2015. Should "Killer Robots" Be Banned. *National Interest*, June 26. http://nationalinterest.org/feature/should-killer-robots-be-banned-13196.

Schlesinger, Arthur. 1973. *The Imperial Presidency*. Boston: Houghton Mifflin.

Schmitt, Michael, ed. 2013. *Tallinn Manual on the International Law Applicable to Cyber Warfare*. Cambridge: Cambridge University Press.

Schmitt, Michael N. 1991. *Blockade Law: Research Design and Sources*. Buffalo: William S. Hein & Co.

Schultz, Kenneth A. 2010. The Enforcement Problem in Coercive Bargaining: Interstate Conflict over Rebel Support in Civil Wars. *International Organization* 64 (2): 281–312.

Schwarz, Lawrence J. 2002. The Case for Court-Martial Jurisdiction Over Civilians Under Article 2(a)(10) of the Uniform Code of Military Justice. *The Army Lawyer*, Department of the Army Pamphlet 27-50-357 (October/November): 31–37.

Scott, James Brown, ed. 1915. *The Hague Conventions and Declarations of 1899 and 1907, Accompanied by Tables of Signatures, Ratifications and Adhesions of the Various Powers and Texts of Reservations*. New York: Oxford University Press.

——, ed. 1920. *Proceedings of the Hague Peace Conferences*. New York: Oxford University Press.

Security Council Meets in Emergency Session Following Kosovo's Declaration of Independence, With Members Sharply Divided on Issue. 2008. *United Nations*, February 18.

Senate Democrats Oppose "Blank Check" for Islamic State Fight. 2015. *New York Times*, March 11.

Senn, Alfred Erich. 1959. *The Emergence of Modern Lithuania*. New York: Columbia University Press.

Shermatova, Sanobar. 1998. The Silk Way for Oil. *Moscow News*, September 10.

Simmons, Beth A. 1999. *Territorial Disputes and Their Resolution: The Case of Ecuador and Peru*. Washington, DC: United States Institute of Peace.

——. 2009. *Mobilizing for Human Rights: International Law in Domestic Politics*. Cambridge: Cambridge University Press.

Sinclair, Ian. 2002. Sir Ian Sinclair: Legal Adviser to the FCO, 1976–84. In *Memories of the Falklands*, edited by Ian Dale, 124–26. London: Politico's Publishing.

Singer, J. David. 1987. Reconstructing the Correlates of War Data Set on Major Capabilities of States, 1816–1985. *International Interactions* 14: 115–32.

Singer, J. David, Stuart Bremer, and John Stuckey. 1972. Capability Distribution, Uncertainty, and Major Power War, 1820–1965. In *Peace, War, and Numbers*, edited by Bruce M. Russett, 19–48. Beverly Hills: Sage Publications.

Sisson, Richard, and Leo E. Rose. 1990. *War and Secession: Pakistan, India, and the Creation of Bangladesh*. Berkeley: University of California Press.

Sivakumaran, Sandesh. 2011. Re-envisaging the International Law of Internal Armed Conflict. *European Journal of International Law* 22 (1): 219–64.

——. 2012a. Command Responsibility in Irregular Groups. *Journal of International Criminal Justice* 10: 1129–50.

——. 2012b. *The Law of Non-International Armed Conflict*. Oxford: Oxford University Press.

Smith, Joseph. 1994. *The Spanish-American War: Conflict in the Caribbean and the Pacific, 1895–1902*. New York: Longman.

Somin, Ilya. 2015. Reactions to the Obama Administration's proposed ISIS AUMF. *Washington Post*, February 15.

Staniland, Paul. 2012. Organizing Insurgency: Networks, Resources, and Rebellion in South Asia. *International Security* 37 (1): 142–77.

Stanton, Jessica. 2013. Terrorism in the Context of Civil War. *Journal of Politics* 75 (4): 1009–22.

——. 2015. The Impact of Civilian Targeting on Civil War Outcomes in the Post-Cold War Era. Working paper, University of Pennsylvania.

——. 2016. *Violence and Restraint in Civil War: Civilian Targeting in the Shadow of International Law*. New York: Cambridge University Press.

Stedman, Stephen John, Donald Rothchild, and Elizabeth M. Cousens, eds. 2002. *Ending Civil Wars: The Implementation of Peace Agreements*. Boulder: Lynne Rienner Publishers.

Steiger, Heinhard. 2004. Peace Treaties from Paris to Versailles. In *Peace Treaties and International Law in European History from the Late Middle Ages to World War One*, edited by Randall Lesaffer, 59–102. Cambridge: Cambridge University Press.

Stein, Jana von. 2005. Do Treaties Constrain or Screen? Selection Bias and Treaty Compliance. *American Political Science Review* 99 (4): 611–22.

Strachan, Hew. 2014. *The Direction of War: Contemporary Strategy in Historical Perspective*. Cambridge: Cambridge University Press.

Sudan: Towards an Incomplete Peace. 2003. Nairobi and Brussels: International Crisis Group.

Sudan's Cruel War. 1986. *Washington Post*, September 24.

Summers, James, ed. 2011. *Kosovo: A Precedent? The Declaration of Independence, the Advisory Opinion and Implications for Statehood, Self-Determination and Minority Rights*. Leiden: Brill.

Svensson, Isak. 2007a. Bargaining, Bias and Peace Brokers: How Rebels Commit to Peace. *Journal of Peace Research* 44 (2): 177–94.

——. 2007b. Mediation with Muscles or Minds? Exploring Power Mediators and Pure Mediators in Civil Wars. *International Negotiation* 12: 229–48.

Syria Civil War: Kurds Declare Federal Region in North. 2016. *Al Jazeera*, March 17.

Szewczyk, Bart. 2010. Lawfulness of Kosovo's Declaration of Independence. *ASIL Insights* 14 (27). August 17. https://www.asil.org/insights/volume/14/issue/27/lawfulness-kosovos-declaration-independence.

Talmon, Stefan. 1993. Recognition of Governments: An Analysis of the New British Policy and Practice. *British Yearbook of International Law*: 231–97.

——. 2013. Recognition of Opposition Groups as the Legitimate Representative of a People. *Chinese Journal of International Law* 12 (2): 219–53.

Tan, Chester C. 1967. *The Boxer Catastrophe*. New York: Octagon Books.

Tancredi, Antonello. 2014. Secession and the Use of Force. In *Self-Determination and Secession in International Law*, edited by Christian Walter, Antje von Ungern-Sternberg and Kavus Abushov, 219–302. Oxford: Oxford University Press.

Text of the War Statement by Foreign Minister von Ribbentrop. 1941. *New York Times*, 6.

Thaci, Hashim. 2010. To Kosovans, Blair Is a True Hero. *Guardian*, September 2.

Thatcher, Margaret. 1993. *The Downing Street Years*. 1st ed. New York: HarperCollins.

Thatcher, Oliver J. 1907. *The Library of Original Sources*. Editors ed. 10 vols. New York: University Research Extension.

Themnér, Lotta, and Peter Wallensteen. 2015. Armed Conflict, 1946–2014. *Journal of Peace Research* 52 (4): 536–50.

Thomas, Raju G. C. 1996. *Democracy, Security, and Development in India*. New York: St. Martin's Press.

Thompson, Julian. 1992. *No Picnic: 3 Commando Brigade in the South Atlantic, 1982*. 2nd ed. London: L. Cooper.

Thucydides. 1934. *The Peloponnesian War*. Translated by Richard Crawley. New York: Modern Library.

——. 1954. *History of the Peloponnesian War*. Translated by Rex Warner. London: Penguin Books.

Thyne, Clayton. 2007. Sudan (1983–2005). In *Civil Wars of the World: Major Conflicts Since World War II*, edited by Karl DeRouen and Uk Heo, 2:735–51. Santa Barbara: ABC/CLIO.

Tilly, Charles, ed. 1975. *The Formation of National States in Western Europe*. Princeton, New Jersey: Princeton University Press.

Tir, Jaroslav. 2005. Keeping the Peace After Secession: Territorial Conflicts between Rump and Secessionist States. *Journal of Conflict Resolution* 49 (5): 713–74.

Tir, Jaroslav, and Johannes Karreth. 2018. *Incentivizing Peace: How International Organizations Can Help Prevent Civil Wars in Member Countries.* Oxford: Oxford University Press.

Toft, Monica Duffy. 2003a. *The Geography of Ethnic Violence: Identity, Interests, and the Indivisibility of Territory.* Princeton, NJ: Princeton University Press.

——. 2003b. Peace Through Victory? Paper presented at the Annual Meeting of the American Political Science Association.

——. 2009. *Securing the Peace: The Durable Settlement of Civil Wars.* Princeton, NJ: Princeton University Press.

——. 2010. Ending Civil Wars: A Case for Rebel Victory? *International Security* 34 (4): 7–36.

Tomz, Michael. 2008. Reputation and the Effect of International Law on Preferences and Beliefs: Stanford University. Working paper, last modified February. https://web.stanford.edu/~tomz/working/Tomz-IntlLaw-2008-02-11a.pdf.

Trask, David F. 1981. *The War with Spain in 1898.* New York: MacMillan.

Triffterer, Otto, ed. 2008. *Commentary on the Rome Statute of the International Criminal Court: Observers' Notes, Article by Article.* 2nd ed. Oxford: Hart Publishing.

Tsebelis, George. 1995. Decision Making in Political Systems: Veto Players in Presidentialism, Parliamentarism, Multicameralism and Multipartyism. *British Journal of Political Science* 25 (3): 289–325.

The Turkish Manifesto. 1877. *London Times,* April 28, 7.

Tzu, Sun. 1910. *Sun-tzu on the Art of War: The Oldest Military Treatise in the World.* Translated by Lionel Giles. London: Luzac and Co. In the public domain.

Unanimously Adopting Resolution 2211 (2015), Security Council Extends Mission, Intervention Brigade in Democratic Republic of Congo. 2015. In *United Nations: Meetings Coverage and Press Releases.* New York: United Nations.

UN Annual Resolution on Western Sahara Renews Call for Negotiated Political Solution to the Conflict. 2015. *Reuters,* April 28.

UN-Arab League Mediation Process for Syria Crisis "On Track," Says Official. 2012. UN News Centre, May 4. http://www.un.org/apps/news/story.asp?NewsID=41928#.Wej9FEyZNBw.

UN Calls for an End to Violence, Offers to Mediate. 2014. *Nation,* February 24.

UN Chief Calls for Negotiations to Resolve Yemen Crisis. 2015. PressTV, March 28. http://www.presstv.com/Detail/2015/03/28/403704/Ban-urges-talks-to-settle-Yemen-crisis.

U.N. Seeks to Halt Amboina Fighting: Unit for Indonesia Considers Steps Following Appeals by both Rebels and Dutch. 1950. *New York Times.* October 6.

United Nations High Commission on Refugees, ed. 2000. *State of the World's Refugees 2000.* Oxford: Oxford University Press.

UN High Commissioner for Refugees (UNHCR). 1995. *UNHCR CDR Background Paper on Refugees and Asylum Seekers from Armenia.* August 1. http://www.refworld.org/docid/3ae6a6560.html.

United Nations Diplomatic Conference of Plenipotentiaries on the Establishment of an International Criminal Court, Official Records. 1998. New York: United Nations.

United States Department of State. 1899. Papers Relating to the Treaty with Spain. Washington, DC.

———. 1900. *Papers Relating to the Foreign Relations of the United States, with the Annual Message of the President Transmitted to Congress December 3, 1900.* Washington, DC: US Government Printing Office. http://digicoll.library.wisc.edu/cgi-bin/FRUS/FRUS-idx?id=FRUS.FRUS1900.

Valentino, Benjamin A., Paul Huth, and Dylan Balch-Lindsay. 2004. Draining the Sea: Mass Killing and Guerrilla Warfare. *International Organization* 58 (2): 375–407.

Valentino, Benjamin A., Paul K. Huth, and Sarah Croco. 2006. Covenants without the Sword: International Law and the Protection of Civilians in Times of War. *World Politics* 58 (3), 339–77.

Vasquez, John A. 1993. *The War Puzzle*: Cambridge University Press.

Vattel, Emmerich de. 1758. *The Law of Nations or the Principles of International Law.* London: G. G. and J. Robinson.

Verdier, Pierre-Hughes, and Erik Voeten. 2015. How Does Customary International Law Change? The Case of State Immunity. *International Studies Quarterly* 59 (2): 209–22.

Vidmar, Jure. 2009. International Legal Responses to Kosovo's Declaration of Independence. *Vanderbilt Journal of Transnational Law* 42: 779–852.

———. 2012. Conceptualizing Declarations of Independence in International Law. *Oxford Journal of Legal Studies* 32 (1): 153–77.

Vinjamuri, Leslie. 2010. Deterrence, Democracy, and the Pursuit of International Justice. *Ethics and International Affairs* 24: 191–211.

Vollrath, Hanna. 2004. The Kiss of Peace. In *Peace Treaties and International Law in European History: From the Late Middle Ages to World War One*, edited by Randall Lesaffer, 162–83. New York: Cambridge University Press.

Vreeland, James A. 2008. The Effect of Political Regime on Civil War. *Journal of Conflict Resolution* 52 (3): 401–25.

Wallace, Geoffrey. 2012. Regulating Conflict: Historical Legacies and State Commitment to the Laws of War. *Foreign Policy Analysis* 8 (2): 151–72.

———. 2013. International Law and Public Attitudes toward Torture: An Experimental Study. *International Organization* 67 (1): 105–40.

———. 2015. *Life and Death in Captivity: The Abuse of Prisoners During War.* Ithaca, NY: Cornell University Press.

Wallensteen, Peter. 2015. *Quality Peace: Peacebuilding, Victory and World Order.* Studies in Strategic Peacebuilding. Oxford: Oxford University Press.

Walsh, Declan, and Azam Ahmed. 2014. Mending Alliance, U.S. and Afghanistan Sign Long-Term Security Agreement. *New York Times*, September 30.

Walter, Barbara. 2001. *Committing to Peace: The Successful Settlement of Civil Wars.* Princeton, NJ: Princeton University Press.

———. 2014. Why Bad Governance Leads to Repeat Civil War. *Journal of Conflict Resolution* 59 (7): 1242–72.

Walter, Barbara F. 2009. *Reputation and Civil War: Why Separatist Conflicts Are So Violent.* Cambridge: Cambridge University Press.

Warbrick, Colin. 1992. Recognition of States. *International and Comparative Law Quarterly*: 473–82.

Ward, R. Plumer. 1805. *An Enquiry into the Manner in which the Different Wars in Europe Have Commenced, during the Last Two Centuries, To Which are added the Authorities upon the Nature of a Modern Declaration.* London: J. Butterworth.

Waxman, Matthew C. 2011. Cyber-Attacks and the Use of Force: Back to the Future of Article 2(4). *Yale Journal of International Law* 36 (2): 421–59.

Weber, Max. 1964. *The Theory of Social and Economic Organization.* Edited by Talcott Parsons. New York: Free Press.

Wechsler, Lawrence. 2000. Exceptional Cases in Rome: The United States and the Struggle for an ICC. In *The United States and the International Criminal Court,* edited by Sarah B. Sewall and Carl Kaysen, 85–111. New York: Rowman & Littlefield.

Weinstein, Jeremy M. 2007. *Inside Rebellion: The Politics of Insurgent Violence.* Cambridge: Cambridge University Press.

Wendt, Alexander. 1999. *Social Theory of International Politics.* Cambridge: Cambridge University Press.

Werner, Suzanne, and Amy Yuen. 2005. Making and Keeping Peace. *International Organization* 59 (2): 261–92.

Wertheimer, Linda. 2004. Political Fallout of Abu Ghraib Scandal. *All Things Considered,* May 30.

Whitman, James Q. 2012. *The Verdict of Battle: The Law of Victory and the Making of Modern War.* Cambridge, MA: Harvard University Press.

Why Syria's Kurds Want Federalism, and Who Opposes It. 2016. *Al Jazeera,* March 17.

Wieland, Alexander R. 2015. *Foreign Relations of the United States, 1981–1988: Conflict in the South Atlantic, 1981–1984.* Department of State. Washington, DC: United States Government Publishing Office.

Wilde, Ralph. 2011. Self-Determination, Secession, and Dispute Settlement after the Kosovo Advisory Opinion. *Leiden Journal of International Law* 24: 149–54.

Wilkins, Jesse. 2008. The Making and Unmaking of Great Powers: The Role of Third Party Observers. PhD diss., Columbia University.

Witt, John Fabian. 2012. *Lincoln's Code: The Laws of War in American History.* New York: Free Press.

Wood, Reed. 2010. Rebel Capability and Strategic Violence against Civilians. *Journal of Peace Research* 47 (5): 601–14.

Woodward, Bob. 2004. *Plan of Attack.* New York: Simon & Schuster.

World: Analysis Sudan: A Political and Military History. 1999. *BBC News,* February 21. http://news.bbc.co.uk/2/hi/world/analysis/84927.stm.

Xiang, Lanxin. 2003. *The Origins of the Boxer War: A Multinational Study.* London: Routledge.

York, Geoffrey. 1993. Rebel Soldiers of Misfortune: Sudan. *Globe and Mail,* February 1.

Zacher, Mark W. 2001. The Territorial Integrity Norm: International Boundaries and the Use of Force. *International Organization* 55 (2): 215–50.

Zaheer, Hasan. 1994. *The Separation of East Pakistan: The Rise and Realization of Bengali Muslim Nationalism.* Karachi: Oxford University Press.

Zarrow, Peter Gue. 2005. *China in War and Revolution, 1895–1949.* Asia's Transformations. London: Routledge.

Zartman, I. William 1985. *Ripe for Resolution: Conflict and Intervention in Africa.* New York: Oxford University Press.

Ziegler, Karl-Heinz. 2004. The Influence of Medieval Roman Law on Peace Treaties. In *Peace Treaties and International Law in European History: From the Late Middle Ages to World War One,* edited by Randall Lesaffer, 147–61. New York: Cambridge University Press.

Zucchino, David. 2017. As Kurds Celebrate Independence Vote, Neighbors Threaten Military Action. *New York Times,* Sept. 25, 2017. https://www.nytimes.com/2017/09/25/world/middleeast/kurds-referendum.html.

INDEX